Third Edition

D1061590

Essentials of

Industrial

&

Organizational

Psychology

William Howell   *Robert Dipboye*

This publication has been provided by the

GULF LIBRARY ACQUISITION ENDOWMENT

Established through a generous gift from
The Gulf Oil Foundation
to promote
scholarly research and academic excellence
among the faculty and students
of Duquesne University

Essentials of Industrial and Organizational Psychology

Advising Editor in Psychology   Salvatore R. Maddi
The University of Chicago

Essentials of Industrial and Organizational Psychology

William C. Howell

Robert L. Dipboye

*Both of the
Jesse H. Jones Graduate School
of Administration and the
Department of Psychology,
Rice University*

Third Edition

The Dorsey Press
Chicago, Illinois 60604

HF5548.8
H66
1982

© THE DORSEY PRESS, 1976, 1982, and 1986

All rights reserved. No part of this publication may be reproduced, stored in a retrieval system, or transmitted, in any form or by any means, electronic, mechanical, photocopying, recording, or otherwise, without the prior written permission of the publisher.

ISBN 0-256-03396-X

Library of Congress Catalog Card No. 85–73007

Printed in the United States of America

1 2 3 4 5 6 7 8 9 0 ML 3 2 1 0 9 8 7 6

Preface

This edition, like its two predecessors, is addressed to the management student, the psychology student, and anyone else who is interested in what modern psychology has to say about organizations. It assumes no particular background—psychological or otherwise—and should be readily comprehended by anyone who is willing to read it thoughtfully. Its prime objective is to bring the really important ideas and developments from the field of industrial-organizational psychology to the attention of people who have not specialized in the area. These are, for the most part, the people with the greatest need to know. If the book does its job, some may become sufficiently interested to delve more deeply into the abundant literature which now exists in this field.

Two principles guided both the selection and exposition of material included in the manuscript. The first was to keep it simple; the second, to keep it relevant and nontrivial. It is the authors' belief that few of the important concepts in this field are inherently difficult to grasp if presented with the relatively nontechnical audience in mind. One need not sacrifice substance for comprehensibility. It is possible to tell the story without resorting to triviality simply by keeping technical jargon, methodological detail, and specific research data to a minimum. Every effort was made to do this throughout the following pages. The book does not pretend, therefore, to be a comprehensive review or account of the research literature. It does try to summarize where things stand on the important issues, taking into account the most recent research findings.

No attempt is made to sell the reader on any particular point of view although, like anyone else, the authors have their biases. One of these is the firm belief that there are few simple answers to organizational people problems. Human behavior is itself not simply determined; it could scarcely be otherwise within the complex setting of an organization. Thus

v

JUL 2 1 1986

the emphasis is on *understanding* such problems rather than presenting "cookbook" solutions to them. Often our understanding is at a fairly rudimentary level. Hence it is necessary to rely heavily on *theories*. For this reason the book is more theoretically oriented than is typical of elementary texts (especially in the industrial-organizational field). It is our contention that what often passes for sound practical advice can, without an adequate understanding of its theoretical basis, be worse than no advice at all. The reader may be amazed to discover how shaky the foundation is upon which some of today's most widely accepted management practices are based.

One final objective is to alert those who may have occasion to seek psychological goods and services to the potential dangers associated with their use. There are many incompetent, marginally ethical, and downright fraudulent purveyors of psychology in practice today. They thrive because managers are rarely in a position to judge their competence, and because they offer the kind of quick fix managers always seem to be seeking. Hopefully this book will make the reader a more discriminating consumer. It will also show him that even the best tests, training programs, evaluation systems, and organizational plans can be misapplied. Industrial-organizational psychology has much to offer managers, but only after they have reached at least a minimum level of sophistication. This book attempts to provide the essentials.

As the third edition, this version is in part a product of feedback from users and reviewers of the original. Among the suggestions so incorporated are a substantial reorganization and updating of the material on "organizational behavior" topics (especially *motivation and satisfaction, leadership,* and *organizational development*); expansion of the sections devoted to such timely "personnel" issues as *validity generalization, compensation and comparable worth,* and the *interview process*; addition of material on *stress* and *communication*; and an entirely new chapter on domains of I/O psychology that are somewhat removed from the personnel/OB mainstream (*consumer psychology, engineering psychology,* and *labor relations*). We have also tried to include more examples and illustrations of how theories and research data might be applied.

The two previous editions had an entire, and rather lengthy, chapter devoted to the *consumer* topic: in the first because it seemed to be an emerging branch of the field, and in the second, because it had received some favorable comment in the first edition! It is now rather clear that the consumer field has grown, but away from rather than closer to the rest of I/O psychology in much the same fashion as engineering psychology and union-management relations. Thus we saw no real justification for continuing to feature consumer behavior, and instead decided to give the reader a glimpse of *several* subspecialties that seem to occupy roughly similar status in the field today. Hence the *External Relations* chapter. In the process we hope simultaneously to satisfy the needs of those who commented favorably on our past inclusion of the consumer topic and those who criticized our omission of the other two topics. It is perhaps worth noting that in its most recent *Training Guidelines for I/O Psychology,* the Society for Industrial and Organizational Psychology saw fit to include these topics among the content areas that define the field.

We have, therefore, tried to respond both to the continuing evolution of the field and to "audience" reactions without compromising any of our original objectives. Everyone who has ever revised anything does that. But there were also criticisms that we did *not* heed, and it might be instructive to reflect briefly on a few of these as well. Some respondents complained that we still fail to include a lot of headings, pictures, cartoons, "slices of life," wide margins, and all the other "glitzy" features that supposedly heighten the reader's interest and the book's sales. One comment, for example, was that "every page looks exactly the same." And so it is in this edition as well. We are trying to convey important material to people who are at least minimally literate and who *care,* not provide entertainment or the illusion of simplicity to those who aren't and don't. Moreover, we are trying to present these "essentials" as economically as possible: remember, it is the reader who pays for all the "glitz." This is also the reason that we have resisted the temptation to go to a more impressive-looking (but costly) "hard-back" edition. We are fortunate to have a publisher who understands and supports our philosophy.

William C. Howell
Robert L. Dipboye

Acknowledgments

A number of our professional colleagues reviewed some or all of the material in the first two editions of this book, and their individual contributions were gratefully recognized in those volumes. Insofar as we have preserved the original contents, their contributions live on and we wish to reiterate our appreciation. We would also like to thank the many readers who took the trouble to write comments on the earlier editions. We considered all suggestions very carefully—even those that, for one reason or another, we elected not to incorporate into this version—and we feel that they had an important influence on our thinking. And last, but by no means least, we are grateful to Michael Hayes for his help in preparing large portions of the manuscript.

WCH
RLD

Contents

List of Figures

List of Tables

1

Definitions and Perspectives

The field that has recently become known as *industrial and organizational (I/O) psychology* represents the confluence of many streams of thought and activity. On the one hand, there is modern psychology, a discipline founded on the premise that human beings can understand themselves—and perhaps even improve upon their condition—by applying the methods of science to their own behavior. If scientific inquiry can help us understand the behavior of the solar system and subatomic particles, it is reasoned, why not the thoughts and acts of humans themselves? Our field then is very much a part of this broader endeavor to understand human behavior.

On the other hand, there are those in our field whose interests lie primarily in the *organization*—what it is, what it should be. Since before Adam Smith's time (the latter 1700s) economists, social philosophers, and ultimately management theorists have sought answers to basic questions about organizations and their management. How should organizations be designed to accomplish work? How should they be operated and managed? What is just compensation for various kinds of investment? What is the impact of organizations on other segments of society? These questions too have become the subject of scientific inquiry in recent years. Since organizations depend on people and people are becoming increasingly dependent on organizations, it is not surprising that the study of human and organizational behavior should merge. Organizations are formed and managed according to certain basic assumptions about people. Organizational psychology examines these assumptions.

Industrial and organizational psychology is more than just scientific inquiry; it is also practical application. Its scientific interest ranges from individual to interpersonal to organizational processes. Its practical concerns include everything from hiring practices to management principles to consumer reactions. Perhaps the best way to appreciate the scope of industrial and organizational psychology is to try to list all the possible ways *people* are involved in organizations. They are recruited, selected, placed, trained, evaluated, fired. They lead and are led. They form informal and formal groups. They communicate and all too often *fail* to communicate. They make decisions. They may become frustrated, develop ulcers, or start drinking heavily. They consume. They worry about pollution, accidents, and other undesirable by-products of our industrial society. The list is practically endless. Industrial-organizational psychology is directly interested in all of these things, both as objects for study and as practical problems to be solved. It seeks to *understand* people in the organizational context, particularly that of industry, and to *apply* what it learns in the interest of effecting some kind of improvement.

MAJOR EMPHASES PAST AND PRESENT

Industrial-organizational psychology has not always been the multifaceted field it is today. Its principal objectives, its ways of studying human beings, and its organizational focus have all changed a great deal over the years. Each change in emphasis has added new dimensions to the field. From modest beginnings as a practical adjunct to personnel management and marketing, it has branched out to touch virtually every aspect of organizational life, as we have just seen.

In the present section we shall trace this development from three different perspectives: (1) the *objectives* of the field, (2) its basic *methodological* orientation, and (3) its *content*. Our brief historical review will thus also serve to introduce several important distinctions that help define the field. That is, we will compare what it is like now with how it used to be in terms of objectives, methods, and content.

Objectives

The important distinction here is one we have already encountered: that between scientific and applied objectives. *Science* is concerned with explanation of events in nature irrespective of how such information might be used. It consists of a set of attitudes and some general rules for gathering information (the scientific method), all of which are aimed at maximizing the objectivity of reported findings. Scientific explanation is thus a matter of empirical fact rather than speculation, of objective data rather than opinion, faith, anecdote, or pure logic. Empirical data are usually gathered through carefully planned, systematic *research* efforts. The data-gathering process is typically guided by explicitly or implicitly stated *theoretical* notions. That is, rather than embarking on a haphazard search for explanatory data, the researcher develops a *theory*—an account of what he or she *thinks* is going on—and designs research to test it. To a great extent, therefore, scientific explanation involves the progressive refinement of theories on the basis of empirical evidence. We shall have more to say about research in a moment.

Application is the attempt to use scientific information for some utilitarian purpose. Often it involves translating theoretical notions into possible solutions to real-life problems. To the extent that the plausibility of a theory has been verified through empirical test and to the extent that its terms have been translated adequately, the solution may indeed prove to be a good one. The less evidence there is to support a theory—or the more ambiguous the evidence is—the less confidence we can place in a solution based on it. Industrial-organizational psychology is often forced to apply theoretical notions based on extremely sparse evidence. The alternative, however, is usually a solution based on no evidence at all!

As we have seen, industrial-organizational psychology carries on scientific research in an effort to answer basic questions about people in organizations (and, in fact, about organizations themselves). It develops theories and tests them. It also seeks to apply what it learns—sometimes, perhaps, before the principles are firmly established. That, in a nutshell, is the field *today*.

Until recently, the dominant emphasis was on applying rather than generating knowledge. Research, for the most part, was done to solve immediate, narrowly defined problems, not to produce generalizations or theories about behavior. The field was known simply as *industrial* psychology. As one writer suggests, its main function seemed to be "developing tools and techniques to help management do its job."[1]

Gradually the situation has changed in the direction of a better balance between scientific and applied goals. Systematic research, much of it directed toward issues of fundamental theoretical significance, has become a recognized part of the activity of the field. It would be difficult to pinpoint when this scientific trend began in earnest. The early 1960s is probably as good a reference point as any. About this time the modern organization theorists—people bent on explaining the behavior of organizations in scientific terms—began to attract serious attention. For the most part, these individuals were based in disciplines other than psychology, and as a result, the initial concepts were strongly influenced by thinking in sociology, political science, and the practice of management. These concepts introduced a much needed theoretical orientation into a branch of psychology that had never really managed to develop one on its own. Quite appropriately, those engaged in its work began referring to their field as *industrial-organizational* (I/O) psychology. This transition from strict application to application plus science marked a significant change in the self-image of the field. No longer did it feel that it had to depend exclusively on others for factual input; it could now generate its own explanatory data. It could develop and test its own theories of humans at work. While many feel industrial-organizational psychology is still deficient in theory and in the linkage between theory and research,[2] it has certainly made considerable progress in a very short time.[3]

Methodological Orientation

A second noteworthy distinction can be traced to the very beginnings of modern psychology. Historically, two major philosophies have governed the study of human behavior. One, which we shall call the *individual differences* approach, recognizes that people differ from each other in consistent ways and seeks to understand these consistent differences. A prime example of this approach is psychological testing. Testing applies a standard set of items (a test) to different people to find out who is strong and who is weak on various traits. If, in fact, what we measure are relatively stable differences, such information can help us make predictions about the individual's future behavior. We might use such data to help select employees.

The contrasting approach to the study of human thought and action looks for generalities rather than differences among individuals. It seeks to explain how people in *general* think or act as a function of various controlling conditions. We might call this the *general characteristics* approach. Here individual differences are seen as an unavoidable source of measurement error that serves only to limit what one can say about average or typical behavior. Much of what we call *experimental* psychology is based on the general characteristic philosophy. Many experiments have been done, for example, to discover how fast people can make some particular response under various circumstances. How long, for example, does it take a motorist to hit the brakes on an automobile in an emergency? The purpose, of course, is to make statements or predictions about *average* human reaction time (e.g., to prescribe following distances for highway driving). To the extent that people differ in their reaction time, which they do, we must consider our average predictions that much less trustworthy.

In the early 1900s, when both the science of psychology and its industrial branch were in their infancy, the predominant philosophy was that of general characteristics. Indeed, the two psychologists who are usually credited with founding the industrial branch, Walter Dill Scott and Hugo Munsterburg, were both trained in the classic experimental tradition. Later, prompted to a great extent by the success of military testing programs during World War I, industrial psychology shifted its emphasis toward individual differences. Subsequently, and in close parallel with the previously mentioned scientific trend, the interest in general characteristics has returned. Today there seems to be as much—if not more—activity devoted to the general characteristics of people and organizations as there is to differences among them.

It is important to note that the individual differences approach, although noted for its contribution to personnel selection, is not limited to applied objectives; neither do all general characteristics efforts have scientific aims. For example, we can use an intelligence test (which measures individual differences) to select clerical applicants (an applied goal) or to study intelligence (a scientific goal). We can design an industrial task on the basis of how rapidly people in general react in order to maximize productivity (an application) or to learn something about human sensory or response limitations (a scientific objective).

Content

Our final distinction involves classification of content areas of industrial-organizational psychology. How we divide up the field, of course, is somewhat arbitrary. Nevertheless, convention dictates the differentiation of at least the following major categories: *personnel, organizational, engineering,* and *consumer* psychology.[4] Each of these has its own unique mix of objectives and methodological emphases.

Personnel psychology has traditionally dealt with selection, placement, and training problems. It has also been deeply involved in the description and evaluation of jobs and in the appraisal of performance on those jobs. Much of the work done in this area has been (and still is) of an applied nature with a heavy individual difference orientation.

Organizational psychology, a major force behind the emergence of a true theoretical dimension within the field, is concerned chiefly with management functions and their implications for the organization and the people managed. Thus it includes scientific as well as applied questions, usually handled within the general characteristics framework. For example, it seeks to discover the effects of managerial style on job satisfaction and performance. Conversely, it seeks to understand human needs and the importance of various organizational factors in meeting these needs. What is the importance of pay? Recognition? Communication?

The last two areas each represent a rather small segment of the total industrial-organizational field. Both are chiefly concerned with general characteristics of people. Engineering psychology deals with the design of machines, jobs, and environments for the optimum functioning of human beings. One would scarcely think it necessary to create an entire specialty for so obvious a purpose. Such, however, has indeed been the case. There are many examples of poorly human-engineered tasks and systems in common use ranging from such simple devices as pliers to nuclear power plants. Since the World War II era, when engineering psychology first made its appearance, it has become much more common for human factors considerations to play a role in engineering decisions. Included among these are many of a "psychological" nature (hence *engineering psychology*).[5] Others, such as human anatomical and physiological considerations, are also incorporated into a broader field known as *human factors engineering* (or just plain *human factors*).[6]

Finally, *consumer* psychology, as the name implies, deals with the general characteristics of people as consumers—their attitudes toward buying as well as their actual purchasing behavior. Application of psychological principles to advertising and marketing represents one of the oldest interest areas in the entire industrial-organizational field. Fundamental research on consumer behavior also has a long history, although it has only recently begun to achieve recognition for its scientific potential.

In the following pages, the personnel and organizational topics receive the bulk of our attention. Consumer and engineering psychology are described briefly, together with another peripheral topic—*union-management relations*—in the final chapter. All three have a principal focus outside the physical or conceptual boundaries of the employing organization; hence Chapter 9 is called "External Relations."

Chronology

Piecing all three of the above distinctions together we arrive at somewhat the following chronological picture. Prior to World War I, industrial psychology was a struggling field, accepted enthusiastically by neither industry, which it sought to serve, nor by the new science of psychology, from whence it came. What little activity there was centered around application of general psychological principles to a variety of industrial problems. World War I ushered in the testing movement, and the field grew dramatically. Much of this growth involved application of the individual differences approach (via psychological tests) to personnel problems—notably selection and placement. In the period following the war, industrial psychology established itself as a personnel-oriented field.

World War II stimulated still further growth—this time in a number of new, but still largely applied, directions. Because of the vastly increased sophistication of warfare and the urgent need for rapid mobilization, training assumed a place alongside selection and placement as topics of focal interest. Experimental psychologists, drawn from the "purest" of scientific activities, were called upon to help design effective weapon systems, an activity that led ultimately to the twin specialties of human factors engineering and engineering psychology.

Finally, as a result of a number of converging pressures, the organizational and consumer areas began to develop. Although both had received some attention through the years, their emergence in the 1960s as full-fledged specialties gave the field an important theoretical boost, as we have just seen.

In the chapters to follow, the reader will have ample opportunity to sample the body of knowledge that comprises industrial-organizational psychology and to explore some of the ideas, techniques, and empirical facts that have given it definition. Before launching into this material, however, it is necessary to touch upon a few other facets of the field as it exists today.

APPLICATIONS AND RESEARCH

To this point we have been speaking of industrial-organizational psychology mainly as a body of knowledge. We add to this knowledge through scientific research and draw upon it in the interest of improving management. Naturally there is more to any field than a mere collection of facts. There are the *people* engaged in its work, the *research activities* through which scientific knowledge is acquired, and the *management functions* to which this knowledge may or may not be applied. Each of these other facets deserve brief introductory comment.

The Practitioner

The main practitioners of psychology in industry are people trained either to the masters or doctoral level in one of the specialties of psychology. Frequently, but not always, their training has been in the industrial-organizational areas. A substantial number have received training in clinical, counseling, social, or experimental branches of psychology. Some are in the direct employ of the organizations they serve—usually the larger corporations or government agencies—while many more are hired as consultants and are affiliated with consulting firms, universities, or are in private practice.

Not everyone who uses the information generated by industrial-organizational psychology is a trained psychologist. Many other individuals (we would hope, the reader included) can and should apply some of this material to the everyday functions of management. It is not necessary for a person to be a trained psychologist to conduct a good interview or to understand some of the things that contribute to effective leadership.

Frequently, however, management feels the need for professional help with such matters or with others (such as testing) for which only a professional is qualified. Even more frequently management fails to recognize the need for professional help until it is too late. Nowhere is the old ounce-of-prevention adage more appropriate than here. If management waits until there is a serious morale problem or until legal action is brought against the company for misuse of psychological tests before seeking professional help, the remedy may be long in coming and inordinately expensive. A far wiser course is to conduct periodic reviews of all major people-related activities with the aid of a qualified psychologist. A few rules of thumb for choosing reputable psychological services will be offered in a moment.

It is important to recognize that many who purport to offer help with people-related problems are neither capable nor ethical. Like the faith healer and the seller of snake oil, the psychological services quack thrives because the problems are serious, promotion is heavy, the market is gullible, and effective legal controls are virtually impossible to implement.

The field of psychology has made a sincere effort to help the public distinguish between qualified and unqualified practitioners. Through its national organization, the American Psychological Association[7] (and various affiliated regional, state, and local associations), it has set educational standards, formulated a code of ethics, and promoted certification and licensing laws in the states. While none of this guarantees an individual's competence or integrity, it is certainly a help. In any profession there are those who will push rules to or beyond the limit, especially—as is the case here—if there is a lot of money involved and the rules are hard to enforce. Nevertheless, some assurance is better than none. The businss executive should be wary indeed of the self-proclaimed psychologist who (1) is not a member of the APA or one of its affiliates, (2) is not licensed or certified to practice in the state, and (3) does not hold an advanced degree—usually the Ph.D.—in psychology from a reputable university. Naturally there are exceptions—responsible practitioners who, for one reason or another, do not subscribe to these criteria. Responsible or not, however, "outsiders" are subject to none of the APA safeguards: since they aren't members to begin with, they can't be expelled if they violate the code. Thus the only rules about which they must concern themselves are the hard-to-enforce legal ones.

More often than not, industry comes in contact with the psychologist and the field itself through a consulting organization. Many firms are engaged wholly or partially in the business of selling psychological services to industry, and they differ widely in the range and quality of services offered. Some of the very large ones, such as the Big Three (the Psychological Corporation, Science Research Associates, and Educational Testing Service), develop and market tests, carry on personnel and market research, implement training programs, and are very active in development of new tchniques. Others, such as Hay and Associates, ARRO, Essex Corporation, and Daniel Yankelovich, concentrate more on the areas of executive evaluation, skills research and training, human factors, and market research, respectively. The vast majority are smaller local concerns that administer test batteries, conduct interviews, evaluate executive candidates, run training programs, help with management problems, and handle any number of other day-to-day chores on a contract basis for the company.

It is as difficult to select a reputable consulting firm as it is to select a reputable psychologist. Here, however, are a few practical suggestions that could improve one's chances. First, never deal with a company that directly solicits business, especially if the pitch is accompanied by exaggerated claims. Second, pay no heed to the impressive list of "satisfied customers" supplied as references. Questionable consultants capitalize heavily on the willingness of naive clients to vouch for a service that they have decided to buy. Unless clients have some objective method for checking on the consultant's work, which is rarely the case, their satisfaction or dissatisfaction means nothing. Third, carefully check the background and credentials of the individual psychologists on the consultant's payroll (as noted earlier). Fourth, seek advice from large companies (such as Exxon Corporation, General Electric Corporation, AT&T, and many others) that employ their own psychologists. Company psychologists have no particular stake in which consultant gets the business of another firm but a considerable stake in the integrity of the profession. Similarly, the psychology department of a major university in the region may serve as a source of relatively impartial information. Finally, whatever consulting service is finally chosen, maintain records in such a way so as to evaluate its performance objectively. In most cases this is not as difficult or costly as it sounds, and it can add immeasurably to the value received. We shall return repeatedly in the following chapters to the business of evaluating psychological programs (testing, training, or whatever), whether supplied by consultants or implemented internally.

Research

As noted earlier, many psychologists are engaged wholly or partially in scientific *research* rather than direct *application* of knowledge. Even those who work chiefly in applications are obliged to have a good understanding of the scientific approach in order to make sensible use of research data. No introduction to the field would be complete, therefore, without at least a brief description of the research aspect of industrial-organizational psychology.

The basic purpose of most psychological research, of course, is to further our understanding of human thought and action. Knowledge is regarded as valid, from a scientific standpoint, to the extent that it is based upon direct observation. For observations to be considered trustworthy they must be objective, rather than private, and be replicable. That is, they must be made under conditions that any other scientist can duplicate, so that anyone who cares to can verify the observations to their own satisfaction. The so-called scientific method introduced earlier is really little more than a set of guidelines for making trustworthy observations and logical interpretations.

In the industrial-organizational area, research varies considerably along the dimension of specificity. At one extreme are studies designed to yield a solution to a specific problem without regard for how broadly the results might generalize to other problems. Such research is often called *applied* or *mission oriented.* At the other extreme is *basic* or *fundamental* research, the major objective of which is to understand basic processes that may underlie a lot of different problems. Basic studies usually focus on general principles or theories rather than on specific applications.

Of course, much research in the field falls somewhere between these extremes. We might, for example, wish to design a study to find out why morale is low in a particular plant. In doing so we would undoubtedly take cognizance of the considerable body of data and theory that has already been assembled on the general topic of job satisfaction. Our ultimate research design would probably reflect this body of knowledge, and whatever we discovered would add something to it.

This is not to suggest that research can—or should—always contribute significantly to both theory and immediate application or even that these goals are highly compatible. In most cases, one is achieved at least partially at the expense of the other, and we are forced to arrive at some compromise in designing our research. The reason is that the data of greatest *applicability* to a particular problem are those gathered under conditions identical to the ones characterizing the problem itself, i.e., the "real-world" situation with all its idiosyncrasies. Other things being equal, the most relevant setting for research on the morale problem in plant A is plant A itself. In contrast, the data of greatest *theoretical* importance are not tied to a particular situation and therefore reflect generalities to a greater extent than idiosyncrasies. The best setting for research with this aim would be either a well-chosen sample of *different* situations (e.g., plant A, B, C in company X, Y, Z), or an abstract version created to preserve *only* the general features of interest (e.g., a laboratory analog of the typical industrial situation).

Psychological research is carried out using a wide assortment of specific methods. Different as they may be, all are designed to promote the scientific goals of objectivity and replicability in the collection of observations (scientific data). They also serve to structure the conditions of observation such that investigators can make observations systematically and with minimal distortion from extraneous factors.

The matter of controlling extraneous influences is sufficiently important to warrant special comment. Most scientific observations are focused on the extent to which some presumed causal factor (usually referred to as the *independent variable*) is related consistently to some effect (the *dependent variable*). An example might be the relationship between alternative procedures for job training (the independent variable) and the rate at which trainees learn a particular job (the dependent variable). Now, the researcher who wishes to study this relationship must take every precaution to ensure that any observed changes in the dependent variable are indeed the result of the independent variable and not something else. One must control all factors other than job-training procedures—that is, negate their influence in some way. How does one do this? Usually through the research design itself. Suppose one designed a study to compare two different training methods (A and B) using two different groups of trainees. Suppose, further, that it turned out that the method A group learned the job consistently faster. Can one assume that method A is superior? Not unless one has controlled such factors as (1) the aptitude level of the trainees comprising the two groups and (2) the proficiency of the people administering the training. The researcher might have designed adequate controls into the study by (1) measuring the trainees' aptitudes in advance and assigning them to the groups on that basis (matching the groups insofar as possible in terms of aptitude) and (2) using the same training specialists for both groups. One of the main ways of evaluating research findings is to determine whether or not adequate controls were used in obtaining the observations.

Most scientific research designs fall within one of two broad categories: *naturalistic observation* and *experimentation*. The former involves observing the phenomenon of interest as it occurs in "real life" with minimum interference on the part of the investigator. Suppose we wished to find out whether dissatisfaction among workers is related to the size of work groups in which they function. We might approach this problem by selecting several roughly comparable work groups of different size in one or more companies and comparing them on the basis of turnover, absenteeism, or grievance rates (presumed indicants of of dissatisfaction). In the process we would have manipulated nothing directly; the employees would not even have been aware that they were being studied. By contrast, experimentation involves direct manipulation of independent variables. To do this, it is often necessary to carry out the research on people in places and under circumstances that differ considerably from anything found in the world of work. Sometimes the problem is removed completely to the laboratory for study. Returning to our size-satisfaction problem, we might seek an experimental solution by assembling several groups of college students, alike in all respects other than group size, and charging each with completion of an identical set of tasks. We might then compare the groups in terms of their average scores on a satisfaction questionnaire administered after all tasks were completed.

The advantages and disadvantages of both approaches should be fairly obvious. Experimentation offers control at the expense of realism. We can set up conditions for study exactly as we want them (for example, comparable people doing identical tasks under predetermined group circumstances). We can arrange to control extraneous factors directly. If the object of our study is some real-life problem, however, we may be forced to simplify it or otherwise alter it considerably in order to achieve a satisfactory level of control. College students, after all, are not factory workers; artificial groups are not real work groups; the tasks are probably contrived.

In the case of naturalistic observation, of course, the situation is exactly reversed. Since we are observing behavior in its natural setting, there is little problem with realism. Control, however, is another story entirely. In our hypothetical study of the relationship between size of work group and morale, for example, we are faced with the problem of finding *comparable* "real-world" work groups of different sizes to compare. For every characteristic we want to control (to make comparable), we have to find a group at each size level with and without that characteristic. Needless to say, the task of designing a well-controlled study rapidly becomes extremely cumbersome. Indeed, it becomes impossible if we are unable to find enough of the right kinds of groups.

Another common difficulty in naturalistic observation is the demand it places on the individual who must interpret and record what is happening. Since the events of interest take place within the context of a lot of ongoing activity, the observer must often decide what is and isn't relevant. Suppose our index of dissatisfaction was the incidence of hostility among group members. Someone would have to decide what acts were hostile. In experimentation the selection of what to measure is done in advance; the situation is usually structured so that only relevant events can occur, and these are clearly differentiated. Thus the researcher has merely to record their occurrence. One innovation that has greatly enhanced the potential reliability of naturalistic interpretations is the videotape system. With the observations preserved on tape, several judges can later review them, compare notes, and presumably arrive at a more objective description.

Our final point concerning naturalistic observation is that in the industrial-organizational area this is often the only feasible approach. One could hardly expect the management of an organization, for example, to reorganize itself completely six or eight different times just to permit an experimental investigation of organizational structures. On the other hand, one could naturalistically observe six or eight differently structured organizations.[8]

Management Functions

As noted earlier, many of the management functions to which psychology has directed its attention (e.g., selection, training, evaluation, etc.) are in practice assigned to people with little or no formal psychological training. For example, in one large company, the man who directs most of these functions was chosen for the position while serving as the company golf pro. In another, the personnel manager had a background in commerce; in another, public relations; in yet another, engineering. Training managers frequently have little formal—or even informal—background in training or learning principles. This does not mean, of course, that they are universally incompetent or unsuited for their positions. It simply points to the fact that if psychology is to have any significant impact on day-to-day industrial operations it must do so through people who are by and large unsophisticated in its language and concepts. A primary objective of the following chapters, therefore, is to bring the most essential terms and ideas within the grasp of anyone who wants them.

Fortunately, the basic ideas and philosophy underlying much of the formal material in this field is relatively easy to grasp, particularly if one has already come face to face with the problems inherent in industrial management. Only one thing is required: the reader must consider these ideas with an open mind. The seasoned manager—and even the skeptical student—often believes there is little that psychology could possibly reveal about people or management that he or she doesn't already know, and thus may reject potentially useful information prematurely simply because it looks either obvious or irrelevant. The material should be approached with a healthy degree of skepticism, but not prejudgment. While many of the conclusions may seem entirely consistent with common sense, there are also important exceptions. And one must remember that the manager is often obliged to choose among options, *all* of which appear sensible (at least to someone). Some understanding of the thinking and evidence behind these commonsense alternatives can thus be extremely useful.

CONCLUSION

We have covered a lot of ground in this chapter, much of it to be revisited later on. The main purpose was to emphasize the vast scope of modern industrial and organizational psychology. It encompasses a *body of knowledge* drawn from many branches of psychology and other sciences; a *research* enterprise that generates both basic and applied knowledge; an *applications* effort practiced by professionals, charlatans, and well-intentioned amateurs; and, finally a vast array of organizational *functions and problems* to which both the research and applications are directed. A secondary aim of the chapter was to draw a distinction between the legitimate and all-too-prevalent illegitimate practice of psychology in industry. In the final analysis, the only real safeguard against questionable practices is the informed and questioning manager.

NOTES

1. Korman, A. K. (1971). *Industrial and organizational psychology.* New York: Prentice-Hall.
2. Miner, J. B., & Dachler, H. P. (1973). Personnel attitudes and motivation. *Annual Review of Psychology,* 24, 379–402.
3. Dunnette, M. D. (Ed.). (1976). *Handbook of industrial and organizational psychology.* Skokie, Ill.: Rand McNally.
4. Bass, B. M., & Barrett, G. V. (1972). *Man, work, and organizations.* Boston: Allyn & Bacon.
5. Howell, W. C., & Goldstein, I. L. (1971). *Engineering psychology: Current perspectives in research.* New York: Appleton-Century-Crofts.

6. For the best available description and coverage, see the forthcoming book: Kantowitz, B. H., & Sorkin, R. D. *Human factors: Understanding people and system relationships*.

7. The address is 1200 17th Street N.W., Washington, D. C. 20036.

8. For practical solutions to many common design problems, see Campbell, D. T., & Stanley, J. C. (1963). *Experimental and quasi-experimental designs for research*. Skokie, Ill.: Rand McNally.

2

Major Philosophies of Organization
and Management

PSYCHOLOGY AND MANAGEMENT

As explained in Chapter 1, the organizational branch of I/O psychology is
of more recent origin than the industrial (personnel) branch and derives
from a quite different background. Today, the industrial part is closely
related to a broader field of practice known as *personnel and human resource management* (*PHRM* or just *HRM*) whereas the organizational
part is similarly related to the interdisciplinary *organizational behavior*
(*OB*) field. Courses, concentrations, and entire programs in OB and
PHRM have become commonplace in business schools. The training is often provided by psychologists and draws upon a content that overlaps
considerably with that of I/O psychology. The main differences are in the
level of specialization and orientation of the respective programs. The
business school programs tend to produce specialists in PHRM or OB for
careers in management; hence the curriculum context is of general business courses. By contrast, the typical product of an I/O psychology program will be trained intensively in both "I" and "O" content for a professional or scientific career; hence the curriculum context will be of general
psychology and research methodology rather than business and management.

The emphasis in the next three chapters is on topics shared by organizational psychology and OB. To appreciate how issues in *work motivation, satisfaction, leadership, group processes,* and the like came to dominate both specialties, and why particular viewpoints within each of these
problem areas developed as they did, the reader must first understand a
few basic philosophical distinctions. Unfortunately, distinctions usually

call for specialized terms, and terms, for definitions. So the purposes of this chapter are to explore the conceptual underpinnings on which modern theories of organization and management were built and to introduce the reader to a few essential labels.

ORGANIZATIONAL THEORY (OT) AND ORGANIZATIONAL BEHAVIOR (OB)

Much of the philosophical direction of modern organizational psychology and OB owes its existence to controversies about organization and management that predate by at least a quarter century the existence of either field. In the broadest usage of the term, *organization theory (OT)* refers to *all* fundamentally different viewpoints and emphases involved in such controversies—past and present. Thus competing theories on how one *should* organize and manage work, theories that describe what an organization *is,* theories that try to pinpoint what is *most important* about an organization, theories that focus on organizational *differences,* and theories that advocate particular ways to *study* organizations all would qualify as OT. Pugh[1] has captured as well as anyone the essence of this inclusive definition. For him, OT is "the study of the structure and functioning of organizations and the behavior of groups and individuals within them." By this definition, OT is more than just a collection of viewpoints on organizational management; it is also a field of *study.* Moreover, it is not just the study of entire *organizations* but of all the constituents of organizations as well: their structural, functional, individual, and group aspects.

Not everyone, however, subscribes to this inclusive definition. A fairly common distinction is made between the first and last portions, with the more *macro* "structure and functioning of organizations" part reserved for OT, and the more *micro* "behavior of groups and individuals within them" part called OB. Of these the OB focus, of course, is most directly related to I/O psychology.

Labels aside, the evolution of the basic philosophies underlying modern OB and OT follows a common thread. Macro, prescriptive theories came first; descriptive research at the micro (individual and group) level produced an alternative set of prescriptions; and eventually it became clear that neither macro nor micro considerations alone would suffice—that it would take an understanding of both, and then some, to either describe organizations adequately or to prescribe how they should be run. Let us now take a closer look at this sequence of events and ideas.

BACKGROUND

While the organization has been of interest to writers for thousands of years, it has only recently become the subject of intensive study. Systematic analysis of the organization goes back little beyond the present century, and scientific study only a few decades.

The reason, of course, is that emergence of the large organization as the primary instrumentality for accomplishment of work is a fairly recent development.[2] A hundred years ago we were a predominantly rural society. Much of what is now done by huge corporations was done in small shops. These were usually operated and managed by the owner, who often worked side by side with the employees. Naturally, in such an environment there was little need for formality. The entrepreneurs managed as they saw fit, intuitively and pragmatically, creating only what organization they needed as they went along.

Over the years, economic growth and technological innovation led to specialization, absentee ownership, and the emergence of the professional manager. Workers found themselves doing increasingly mundane tasks within an increasingly impersonal—even hostile—environment. As they saw it, managers were there for the sole purpose of getting the most out of the labor force, and the organization was designed chiefly to help them do it. Workers reacted to these developments by organizing themselves. The battle lines between labor and management thus became clearly drawn well before anybody really paid much attention to what an organization was or how it should be managed. It is little wonder that progress toward healing these wounds has been so painfully slow, even though a great deal has since been learned about both organizations and management.

Scientific Management

As one might expect, the first real studies of organization and management were aimed at increasing profitability. After all, large organizations had replaced small shops because they offered the potential for greater efficiency and vastly increased productivity. How, then, should one shape and manage an organization so as to realize this potential? What should be done to workers, their jobs, or both, to increase efficiency and reduce unit cost?

Around the turn of the century Fredrick W. Taylor, a mechanical engineer, attempted to deal with these problems through what has come to be called the *scientific management* approach.[3] Central to this approach was the time-and-motion study technique. The basic idea was to analyze work operations in minute detail to discover how each job could be done most efficiently. On the basis of these data, one could redesign and standardize jobs so that production would be less dependent upon the vagaries of the individual worker. Employees could be selected and trained in accordance with these new standards. The work force would thus become more highly specialized and more proficient. To ensure that these logically superior methods would actually result in greater productivity, Taylor proposed the adoption of monetary incentives. Thus the worker would reap some of the benefits of increased production. In theory, therefore, everyone should come out ahead. Workers would work more efficiently, produce more, and earn more; the company would grow and prosper.

Unfortunately for management, labor was highly suspicious of the whole scientific management approach from the very beginning. Feeling that they were entitled to a larger share of the increased profit than management was willing to give them, and believing (with some justification) that management would gradually reduce the incentive rate the more productive they became, workers fought scientific management vehemently. Even today the concept is anathema to many associated with the labor movement.

Scientific management represented the first reasonably comprehensive philosophy of management. By implication it also presented a rather pessimistic view of man's basic nature. The average worker was seen as lazy, stupid, inefficient, and undependable. The only possible way to make workers more productive was to make them more machinelike. Not only would this demand standardization of work activities but very tight management control as well. Since it was assumed that the worker's only reason for working was to earn money, monetary incentives were seen as the universal motivator.

Some of the basic ideas implicit in scientific management were developed more fully by Max Weber, a sociologist, and a number of managers-turned-writers during the next quarter century. In one form or another this sort of thinking became firmly entrenched in both the theory and practice of organizational management.

The Human Relations Movement

If we take Taylor's work as a point of departure for scientific management and the classical theory of organization, we should probably single out Elton Mayo's famous Hawthorne studies as having a comparable role in another, antagonistic trend, the so-called *human relations movement.* These studies were begun in 1927 at the Western Electric Company's Hawthorne works to find out how various working conditions influence employee productivity. It is not necessary here to recount all the important things this work revealed (after all, it continued for 15 years), except to say that it told us far more about how human motivation, attitudes, and social interactions can influence performance than it did about the effects of lighting, rest periods, and other *physical* aspects of the work situation.[4] At least, that's the way it was interpreted. The inescapable conclusion seemed to be that *human* considerations—friendships, sense of achievement, signs of recognition, social pressures and status, intrinsic job interest—are at least as powerful as the *structural* factors emphasized by the classical theorists in determining how hard people work and how happy they are doing it. This, of course, was in direct violation of all the major assumptions of scientific management. People do not work just for money; you cannot be sure that a more efficient organizational plan will yield higher production (people may conspire to defeat it); people are not interchangeable; and so on. Thus, where scientific management stressed organization of work to the exclusion of people, the human relations movement stressed people to the exclusion of structure and efficiency. An ironic postscript to this story is that subsequent reanalyses of the data suggest that the human relations interpretation is but one possible explanation for the findings.[5] Artifactual or not, however, the point was made, and it stuck.

Other Influences

Most of the theoretical viewpoints on organization and management that have appeared since are philosophic descendants of either the scientific management or the human relations movements (although in some cases they have departed considerably from the original ideas). Some contain elements of both. Pervasive though they were, however, these were not the only influences that shaped the emerging discipline of organization theory.[6] Political scientists recognized the important role of *power* and *influence* in the functioning of organizations. No matter how carefully designed or how responsive to human needs, an organization—like a state or a country—is a political entity; conflict among groups, individuals, and special interests is inevitable. Therefore, enlightened management requires the understanding of how such forces work so that instead of posing a threat to harmony and productivity, they can be put to constructive use.

Other contributions of more recent vintage have come from scientists in several discipiines who share an interest in *decision making*,[7] and from theorists who concern themselves with the properties of *general systems*.[8] Decision theory had its roots in classical economics, which held that both organizations and people operate rationally in making important choices. Since the late 1950s, however, the rationality assumption has come under fire both from within and outside the field of economics. Attention has shifted to the description of how decisions are made, and the results of these studies are beginning to show up in a variety of modern theoretical perspectives (e.g., motivation, leadership, group, and even structural theories).

The idea behind general systems theory was that in nature one finds complex, interactive, goal-oriented entities (systems) at levels ranging from single cells to entire ecosystems or societies. All, however, have some functional properties in common, and particular subsets share many characteristics. Organizations are classified as *social* systems, which belong to a broader category known as *open systems* (i.e., ones that interact meaningfully with an environment). The importance of this conceptualization was that it emphasized, first, that we can't learn much about organizations by studying one variable at a time (systems are *complex* and *interactive*), and second, that what we learn won't be very useful if we limit ourselves to internal workings and ignore interactions with the environment (organizations are *open* systems).

The Modern View

From these various influences has developed the broad and somewhat confusing array of theoretical concepts, research results, and practical advice that we call organization theory. Before proceeding further with our attempt to organize this material, a few general comments are in order.

First of all, modern theories represent the accumulation of ideas and methods from a number of formal disciplines. Engineers and industrial managers gave us the first practical rules for designing and managing organizations. A sociologist (Weber) provided the theoretical justification for this type of structure, while other sociologists, psychologists, political scientists, and even some economists criticized it for ignoring people. Some offered alternative organizing principles based on human relations considerations; others merely suggested modifications in the traditional approach (neoclassicism). All contributed empirical evidence of one sort or another in support of their views. Today, even though particular theorists may stress structure, power relationships, decision functions, group processes, leadership characteristics, or work design, most would admit that organizations are complex *systems* that encompass all these facets and more[9] (see Figure 2–1).

Second, a direct consequence of the first point is a lot of overlap among modern theories. Some deal with only a few variables that the theorist regards as fundamental to successful operation of the organization (for example, structure, or pay, or satisfaction of one's inner motives). Other more comprehensive theories try to incorporate a lot of variables and to show how they interact to produce various consequences for the organization. Such a theory, for example, might define a host of structural and human need considerations and predict how various combinations will affect production or morale. This is one reason why it is so hard to classify theories: Those that are alike on one dimension may be totally different on another.

A third general matter has to do with the orientation of the theories and theorists. Some are almost exclusively *descriptive* or *scientific*. That is, their primary goal is describing or explaining the behavior of organizations and the people in them. They want to unravel the complex interplay of factors that operate in such systems, and they have only a peripheral interest in how this information might be used. Others are chiefly *prescriptive*, concentrating on rules for "good" organization and manage-

FIGURE 2–1 Summary of Major Variables and Relationships Considered in the Study
of Organizations

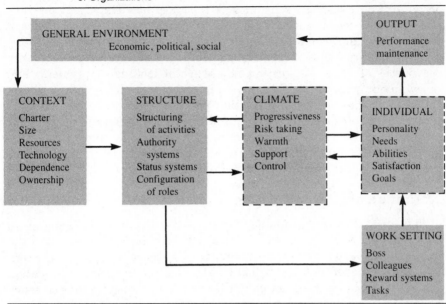

Note: Arrows denote principal directions of influence; many others of lesser presumed significance could be
drawn. Dashed boxes contain constructs that are largely subjective.

SOURCE: Adapted from Organizational structure and climate. Payne, R., & Pugh, D. S. (1976). In M. D.
Dunnette (Ed.), *Handbook of industrial and organizational psychology*, (p. 1127). Skokie, Ill.: Rand McNally.

ment. Some, of course, are both. Since prescriptive theorists are often in
the business of selling their ideas—literally as well as figura-
tively—through executive training programs and the like, one must
weigh very carefully the evidence on which their advice is based. In contrast, a purely descriptive theory may be supported by considerable evidence but its practical implications may be quite obscure. One often gets
the feeling that what it says is "All very nice, but what can I do about it?"
The last few years have seen the emergence of an increasing number of
theories that try to be both descriptive and prescriptive. We shall examine a few of them in the next three chapters.

A fourth point concerns interpretations. Many people, particularly
managers, tend to think in terms of absolutes: One theory must be right
and all the rest wrong. When the strengths and weaknesses of various positions are presented before a live audience, someone will invariably ask,
"Well, which one is *right?*" or "Which one do *you* think is right?" Prescriptive theorists, and indeed even some of the descriptive variety, reinforce
this attitude by contrasting their ("right") explanation with other
("wrong") ones. In the authors' opinion, nearly all the major kinds of theories have something of value to contribute. One cannot expect to solve all
problems or become the ideal manager merely by picking one theory and

sticking with it come hell or high water. A theory of how employees conceptualize fair treatment (*equity theory*) may give the manager some ideas for improving pay schedules. A theory of how employees perceive the consequences of their efforts (*expectancy theory*) may suggest ways of improving employee motivation. In short, the viewpoint advanced in this book is that organization and management theories are valuable mainly as sources of ideas, suggesting new ways of looking at problems and drawing our attention to things we might otherwise have missed. Often, rather than suggesting remedies, they point to areas in which more information is sorely needed: How equitable do the workers perceive their wages to be? Who does the work crew look upon as its real leader? This sort of help is a far cry from the ready-made answers the manager is always seeking, but it can be of far more lasting value.

Definition and Classification

It is ironic, but understandable in view of the diversity of the material, that everyone who organizes the OT or OB domain for the benefit of the student does so in a somewhat different way—thereby adding to the confusion. Some even feel compelled to organize the various classification schemes. While we shall not go to that extreme, we too find it necessary to impose some degree of order on our subject. Figure 2-1 summarizes that effort. What the reader should recognize, however, is that the key word is *impose:* This is just one of many possible ways to look at the material.

It represents a classification of what are considered today to be the main factors involved in organizational behavior and success shown roughly as they are believed to relate to one another. In essence it is a composite of all the theoretical orientations and research efforts introduced to this point and continued throughout the chapter (and indeed, the book). More than anything, it captures the philosophy of *modern systems theory* as described below.

Having established what OT is and, in general, how it evolved, we can now discuss specific theoretical emphases in more detail. We begin with those of a more *macro* nature: those emphasizing the organization as a whole rather than its human (individual and group) constituents. Since those of a more *micro* (humanistic or OB) nature constitute the focus of the next three chapters, we shall merely note their existence here for the sake of completeness.

MACRO ORGANIZATION THEORIES

Classical Theory

The main thrust of classical theory, as we have seen, is efficiency through design. In Haire's words, the aim is to "organize the work rather than the work group."[10] It is recognized, of course, that organizational goals must ultimately be achieved through people. However, people are seen as operating most effectively within the structure provided by a rational and unambiguous organizational plan. Therefore, one designs an organization by carefully subdividing the work, specifying clearly how each portion is to be done, and only then fitting people into the plan. An ideal *structure,* in other words, ensures an efficient operation. *Individuals* and *groups* need only be made to conform to this structure. In terms of Figure 2–1, the only boxes that matter are those of *structure* and *work setting.*

Bureaucracy

The typical form of structure that results from classical thinking is the bureaucratic model. Basic features of this model include division of labor, a well-defined hierarchy of authority and responsibility, an objective or impersonal handling of people, and heavy reliance on written procedures and records. All persons' relationship to their work, their co-workers, their supervisor and subordinates, and even their position within the hierarchy is clearly specified in a set of objectively determined rules. In theory, then, all persons should know what is expected of them. They should also recognize the penalties for failure to conform (reprimand, termination, etc.) as well as the rewards for competence (salary increase, promotion, etc.) and should be heartened in the knowledge that either condition is carefully documented. Since the whole scheme is based on impersonal logic, they should have no reason to complain of unfair treatment.

The reader should have little trouble recognizing the bureaucratic model in most familiar organizations. Government, military, industrial, church—in fact, virtually all organizations in our society were founded according to the bureaucratic philosophy. On paper they remain that way, although in practice few have actually realized the degree of rationality of efficiency envisioned. Most have had to admit that formal structure is but a part—perhaps even a relatively minor part—of what goes into an effective organization. Why, then, did bureaucracy become the model for 20th century organizations? Undoubtedly part of the answer lies in the scholarly arguments put forth by such influential writers of the period as Max Weber, the great German sociologist.[11] Part also is attributable to the sad state of affairs that characterized management in earlier times. Most organizations were run according to the personal whims of the individual or individuals in power—usually owner-managers—who were accountable to no one. Thus the bureaucratic model developed, as Bennis points out, "as a reaction against the personal subjugation, nepotism, cruelty, emotional vicissitudes, and subjective judgments which passed for managerial practices."[12] A highly structured, impersonal, rational sytem—even if imperfect—promised definite advantages over the existing arrangement. The early advocates of bureaucracy could scarcely have anticipated all the potential negative consequences of rigid structure and impersonality.

Management Theory

Classical theory is more than a commentary on human nature and a philosophy for organizational design. Primarily, it consists of compendia of practical management principles formulated by professional managers during the first third of this century. Foremost among these administrative or management theorists, as they are now called, were Henri Fayol, a successful chief executive officer of a French mining company; Lyndall Urwick, a British manager and consultant; James Mooney, a vice president of General Motors; and Luther Gulick, a manager and professor at Columbia University.

Whereas Taylor had stressed the organization of work itself, specialization, and economic incentives, Fayol's main theme was clarity in lines of authority and communication. His book *Administration Industrielle et Generale*[13] provided the first widely accepted set of rules for structuring an organization. Although conceptually very similar to Weber's views on the ideal (bureaucratic) model, Fayol's 14 principles were derived mainly from intuition and experience. So were the expanded lists provided by his successors: Urwick raised the number to 29; and Mooney, Sheldon (a British manager), and others increased the total to over 100. We shall spare the reader the full account of these rules and resort instead to a paraphrased version of a few main ones. Every manager has been exposed at one time or another to some of these prescriptions.[14]

1. Someone should be responsible for supervising each activity, and responsibilities should not overlap.
2. Each person should report to only one boss.
3. Authority should equal responsibility.
4. Activities (jobs) should be as uncomplicated, specialized, and clearly specified as possible.
5. A supervisor's span of control should not include more than five to seven subordinates.

Reasonable as they may seem, little solid evidence indicates that any of these principles leads to superior efficiency. In fact, a comprehensive study of such factors in a variety of firms led Woodward to conclude: "There can be no one best way of organizing a business."[15] What worked best seemed to depend very heavily on the kind of technology used and other idiosyncrasies of the particular firm. Another problem with classical prescriptions is that they are rarely as explicit as they seem. How far, for example, should specialization be carried? At the extreme it becomes ridiculous—thousands of people each doing one minute operation. Classical theory relies on rationality to dictate such limits. Unfortunately, people differ greatly in what they consider rational. Thus how far specialization should be carried boils down to a matter of human judgment, and our "objective" principle turns out to be highly subjective after all. The point is, management principles derived from classical theory are probably less valid and certainly far more difficult to implement than they seem.

Many other criticisms have been leveled against classical bureaucratic theory, particularly by human relations theorists. Most of these arguments center around three related difficulties: (1) lack of correspondence between the formal (planned) organization and the real one, (2) dehumanization, and (3) rigidity.

Few would question the fact that the organization as it exists on paper—the ideal plan represented in the organization chart—seldom bears much resemblance to the actual organization as it exists and functions in real life. We know, for example, that informal relationships have at least as much influence over a worker's behavior as do the formal ones. Social pressures from peers can make the worker limit his or her output, subvert formal rules, withhold information, or work harder, as the occasion demands. Informal communication systems (i.e., the grapevine) have become so widely accepted that at least one researcher has advised management to feed important information into the grapevine rather than to rely on formal channels.[16] What classical theory fails to recognize, then, is the fact that human beings will not necessarily conform to a rigid organizational structure, no matter how logical its design or clear its job descriptions or tight its management control. By pretending that the formally prescribed organization is the *only* organization, classical theory neglects at least half the story.

Classical theory completely ignores human values in the interest of efficiency. It would reduce humans to a simple machine—one that performs reliably the tasks assigned to it by the "divine plan," ignores all human distractions, and above all asks no questions. If an organization were successful in finding individuals to fit this mold or in shaping them to fit, one can easily imagine the ultimate intellectual level of its work force. The long-term consequences for both the organization and society could be serious indeed. Creative thinking and innovation would be stifled. Personalities would be blunted. Vast human resources would be wasted. Social critics have depicted quite vividly the spectre of a whole society composed of dull, unquestioning, organization men.

The fact is, of course, that bureaucracy has failed to subjugate humanity to its mechanistic design in any large sense. Where it has tried, man has somehow managed to serve human needs with or without the blessing of formal authority. Hence we see develop the informal organization referred to earlier. Still, the criticism is justified in reference to the *intent*—if not the *success*—of classical theory.

The third major charge against classical theory is that it emphasizes stability rather than change in a changing world. By structuring everything from the details of work operations to the flow of communication, little room is left for innovation. All the incentives are geared to conformity rather than creativity. The only way constructive change can occur is through modification of the structure, and that is possible only through the initiative of the system planners. In other words, classical theory assures that constructive ideas can only come from the top echelons of management and must be imposed upon the organization from the top down. Such notions, of course, fit in nicely with the portrayal of the average worker as stupid, lazy, and untrustworthy.

A rigidly structured organization would not only be resistant to change from within; it would be relatively insensitive to changes from without (i.e., it would ignore the *environment* and *context* boxes in Figure 2–1). Responsiveness to technological breakthroughs, changes in market conditions, and the like would be painfully slow. In a dynamic, changing society, therefore, an organization designed strictly along classical lines would find itself fighting a constant battle to keep pace—and losing.

The classical bureaucratic model, with its heavy emphasis on structure, can be attacked on many fronts. It seems neither an adequate description of existing organizations nor a particularly valid prescription to follow in seeking greater efficiency. Nevertheless, it is the model upon which most existing organizations were built and in which many present-day managers still believe. Even though it is an inadequate model, however, we should not completely discount structural variables. There is every reason to believe that the behavior of organizations and of the people in them can be influenced by some variables of the kind illustrated in Figure 2–1.

Neoclassical Theory

Criticisms of classical principles were heard, but not very loudly, even before Hawthorne and the human relations movement. Mary Parker Follett, a contemporary of both Weber and the management theorists and whose background was in philosophy and social science, argued convincingly the case for human and group considerations. Among the things she advocated was coordination of effort through mutual agreement—people working together to achieve common goals—in rather stark contrast to the prevailing emphasis on *hierarchical* control and interpersonal competition. Authority, in her view, belonged to the function or situation, not to the person occupying a supervisory role. Domination of one group or individual by another, she felt, was destructive. Mary Parker Follett was a woman well ahead of her times.[17]

As we have seen, however, not until the human relations movement was well under way did the shortcomings of classical theory begin to attract serious attention within the management community. The individual who did most to articulate the problems and to present some viable alternatives was Chester Barnard, whose book, *The Functions of the Executive*, appeared in 1938.[18] One reason that his views attracted more than casual interest may have been his considerable credibility as a manager: he held top executive positions in major public and private organizations over several decades and, like his classical predecessors, wrote largely from experience.

Barnard recognized the emptiness of formal authority in the absence of willing recipients: individuals can neither be coerced nor bribed to carry out an order that falls outside the range of what they consider reasonable. Barnard also recognized that, as individuals, people are ill suited to total conformity, and that opportunities for expression and communication are essential to effective organizational performance.

Most writers would classify Barnard as the epitome of neoclassicism. Follett seems to qualify also in terms of her ideas, if not her chronology, and many would include Herbert Simon, Ernest Dale, Joan Woodward, and a number of others in this category as well. Simon is perhaps best known for his objection to the rationality assumption in economic decision theory and his contributions to the systems view of organizations. Dale and Woodward both regarded the classical principles as hypotheses to be verified rather than assumptions to be taken on faith.[19]

What, then, is a neoclassicist? What is the position—if any—that ties such a heterogeneous lot together? Mainly, it seems to be a common reaction against the basic restrictiveness of classical theory without total rejection of the structural view. All tried to salvage something from the classical position (unlike the radical human relationists), but each did it in a slightly different way. Follett, Barnard, and Simon all recognized the need for structure in organizations but proposed that it could be achieved more satisfactorily through cooperation, participation, and voluntary inducement than through direct imposition and enforcement. Dale, Woodward, and a host of others sought to determine through empirical research which structural features are actually the most important.

Dessler[20] avoids the term *neoclassicism* altogether but captures rather nicely the distinctive and important niche that such individuals held in the evolution of organization theory. He sees them as "bridging the eras" between classicism and behavioral-systems theory. They represented the transition from the "one right way of organizing" dogma to the modern "complex, interactive, sociotechnical system" view. The latter, of course, includes structure, the individual, the environment, and many other factors as the legitimate concern of the theorist and the manager (as we saw in Figure 2–1).

Technology Theory

A number of theorists have focused their attention on the technology used by the organization to achieve its goals. By and large these theorists have been *descriptive* rather than *prescriptive*. They have sought to explain how organizations develop as a function of the techniques available to them and have generally suggested that material technology (modes of production or conversion process) has a profound influence on a variety of organizational phenomena.[21] Woodward, for example, surveyed 100 British manufacturing firms in an effort to find out what management practices contribute to business success.[22]

As we saw earlier, her findings on this score were rather disappointing. However, she made the interesting observation that "technical methods were the most important factor in determining organizational structure and in setting the tone of human relationships inside the firms." As illustrated in Figure 2–2, she was able to distinguish 10 different types of production systems, which she classified into three major groups: unit production, mass production, and process production. On virtually all the dimensions of organization—span of control, levels of authority, specialization, management style, and so on—firms *within* a category showed a considerable degree of similarity; however, the firms in any one category differed consistently from those in *other* categories. Within any category the most successful firms were the ones that conformed most closely to the typical or average pattern *for that group*. This finding led Woodward to conclude that the demands of different technologies tend to shape the kind of organization and style of management that develops. Further, an organization will be most successful if it patterns itself after the norm for its level of technology.

One can, of course, question the logic of Woodward's conclusions. Just because certain organizational patterns are more likely to be found in connection with certain technologies does not mean that one *causes* the other. Similarly, there could be many reasons other than inherent "appropriateness" for the apparent success of management and structural patterns geared to the norm for a particular technological group. It could be, for example, that they are successful because they conform to the expectations of the workers attracted into those industries.

Woodward's conclusions have also been questioned on empirical grounds. Another comprehensive study of the relationship between technology and structure in 46 firms produced findings that were not entirely consistent with Woodward's hypothesis. Hickson, Pugh, and Pheysey (1969) found that technology and structure are related only where the structural variables directly involve the work flow (the number of employees there are in various types of jobs on the work floor itself).[23] Such a situation is most commonly found in small organizations or at lower echelons of large ones. Since small firms were overrepresented in the Woodward study, it could well be that her interpretation, while a valid account of her data, was overgeneralized. In any case, the matter is far from settled.

Not all theorists who emphasize technology consider it the primary causal factor in organizational development. In fact, the modern view is that it, together with size and *dependence* (the nature of an organization's

FIGURE 2–2   Woodward's Classification of Production Systems

Production systems in South Essex industry

Group I Small batch and unit production	I Production of simple units to customers' orders	(5 firms)
	II Production of technically complex units	(10 firms)
	III Fabrication of large equipment in stages	(2 firms)
	IV Production of small batches	(7 firms)
Group II Large batch and mass production	V Production of components in large batches subsequently assembled diversely	(3 firms)
	VI Production of large batches, assembly- line type	(25 firms)
	VII Mass production	(6 firms)
Group III Process production	VIII Process production combined with the preparation of a product for sale by large-batch or mass-production methods	(9 firms)
	IX Process production of chemicals in batches	(13 firms)
	X Continuous flow production of liquids, gases, and solid shapes	(12 firms)
	(8 firms unclassified because too mixed or changing)	

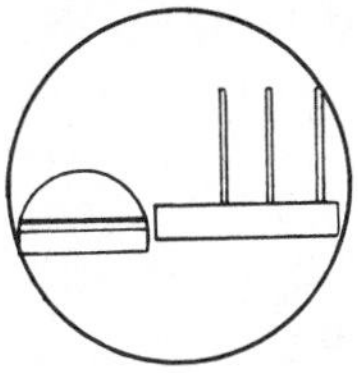

SOURCE: From Woodward, J. (1958). *Management and technology, problems of progress in industry.* London: Her Brittanic Majesty's Stationery Office.

reliance on other groups such as unions, government, etc.) represent the major constituents in the organization's *context* (see Figure 2–1). Context, in turn, is but one of several categories of variables—*climate* and the *general environment* being others—that determine an organization's structural features. This view, of course, is consistent with the position that the organization is a *sociotechnical system.*[24] Technology would be expected to have some influence on structure, and structure on performance, but only indirectly and in combination with a lot of other variables.

Modern Systems Theory

By now it should be clear that most modern theorists have abandoned the naive hope that one kind of structure or set of management principles would prove universally superior. Most recognize the complexity of organizational functions. However, this insight hasn't prevented widely different emphases from developing; on the contrary, it has encouraged such differences, as we said at the outset. Most of this book is spent examining very specific theoretical issues.

Some theorists, however, have maintained a molar perspective and, in that sense, have chosen the complexity itself as their point of emphasis. We refer to these as *modern systems theorists* since their common heritage was the general systems concept described earlier. Even within this group, however, one can find considerable differences in emphasis: some stress decision processes and are frequently classified as *decision theorists;* others concentrate on group processes (we have assigned them to a separate chapter); and still others focus on communication processes (they are sometimes called *information processing theorists*). Because their perspective is broader than most, systems theorists play a ubiquitous role in our story; the reader will find them, in James Bond fashion, popping up in all sorts of unexpected places.

Having said that, let us now consider a bit more specifically the underlying features of modern systems theory. The organization is viewed, as we said, as a *system* that operates upon certain inputs (raw materials, people, information) to produce certain outputs (products, services) within a certain kind of environment (political, competitive, social). Within this framework, one can develop (often with the aid of computers) hypothetical models describing how the system either does or might function. For either descriptive or prescriptive reasons, one can then run the models under various hypothetical conditions to see what designs would yield the most typical or the best performance. The reader may recognize similarities between this and the *operations research* approach so popular within the field of industrial engineering. Its greatest strength is that it takes cognizance of the complexity and dynamic character of the typical modern organization.

As might be expected, there are many kinds of systems theory. Trist's notion that the organization should be viewed as a sociotechnical system certainly qualifies for inclusion here as well as under technology theory. Perhaps a bit more representative, however, are the *open system* view developed by Katz and Kahn,[25] the *decision system* approach of March, Simon, Cyert, and their colleagues at Carnegie-Mellon University,[26] and the *information processing* view elaborated by Jay Galbraith.[27]

Open System Theory

According to Katz and Kahn, organizations have much in common with other "open systems" in nature (e.g., biological, physical). A system is viewed as any set of actively interrelated elements that operate as a bounded unit.[28] An open system is one in which there is a continuing cycle of energy exchange between the bounded unit and its external surroundings. Energy is brought in, transformed by the system, and returned to the environment in the form of a characteristic product that serves as the source of energy for the next cycle of activities. For example, raw materials, electric energy, and human effort might be inputs that are transformed by a manufacturing firm into a line of widgets (output), which the company sells to the public. Money from the sale of widgets is used to buy more raw materials, electric energy, and human effort (input) in order to repeat the process. To survive, the system must bring in more energy than it puts out, for it must constantly expend some energy combating the natural tendency of systems to disorganize. That is, in addition to producing a product the system must invest some of its resources in activities designed to maintain its integrity or structure. Thus, for example, money spent to improve working conditions, internal communications, or quality of supervision might help to reduce turnover or avoid grievances but not necessarily to produce more widgets.

All open systems are seen to have nine principal characteristics. The first five summarize everything said to this point: i.e., the system

1. Imports energy (input).
2. Transforms the inputs (throughput).
3. Turns out products (outputs).
4. Exhibits a cyclic pattern of activities.
5. Uses some of the imported energy to reduce "entropy" or disorganization.

The other four characteristics have to do with how the system carries out these functions and as such are elaborations upon the first four. The system

6. Operates on *information* as well as energy input, which allows it to recognize internal and external states and to adjust accordingly.
7. Moves toward a state of equilibrium in energy exchange (a consequence of entropy reduction).
8. Moves toward increased specialization (differentiation).
9. Has available a variety of ways to achieve any final state (equifinality).

Besides these general open system characteristics, organizations have some properties unique to *social* systems. Foremost among these is the definition of the boundaries and structure through which the system maintains an identity. Unlike physical and biological systems, with clearly identifiable *physical* structures, social systems are structured according to interrelated *events* or *activities*. Thus they are organized behaviorally rather than anatomically. For example, the relationship existing among members of a work group and their supervisor—role characteristics, communication patterns, influence relationships, and so on—constitutes the structure and definition of an organizational unit. It is not a matter of who the people are or where they are physically located.

The advocates of open system theory see this approach as a framework for analyzing and studying organizational behavior rather than as a theory in the strictest sense. They contrast their conception of the organization with the closed system model that characterizes traditional bureaucratic thinking. In the latter, as we saw earlier, emphasis is upon the internal organization exclusive of its interactions with the outside environment. It is assumed that the system has some self-defined purpose or set of goals and that through careful internal structuring, it can come progressively closer to achieving these goals.

By contrast, the open system model proposes that even the *objectives* of the system are developed through interaction with the outside world, and only through the process of information feedback can the system determine whether or not it is moving toward goal attainment (and if it is not, what corrective action is called for). In fact, open system theory plays down the importance of ultimate goal attainment in evaluating system effectiveness. Performance is not just a matter of how closely the organization comes to achieving its annual sales or profit objectives (i.e., its overall output criteria); rather, it is a function of how well the organization coordinates the activities of its units, how successful it is in acquiring inputs, how adequately it adapts to changing external conditions, and how well it does various other things *under specified conditions*. In short, open system theory recognizes that organizations are multifunctional entities and seeks both to describe and evaluate them on multiple bases.

Although it is easy to see that many organizational phenomena can be accounted for in terms of the general concepts of open system theory, it is not an easy matter to generate specific, unique, testable hypotheses on the basis of these concepts. Therefore, it is perhaps best to think of the open system approach as a general way of looking at organizations—a "big picture" perspective that may help to integrate a variety of more specific theoretical notions—rather than as a source of precise experimental predictions. In this sense open system theory is compatible with many other kinds of theories that we shall examine later. Cognitive theories that emphasize the motivational significance of human expectations, for example, focus on the system of information feedback. They make predictions about how feedback influences work performance and satisfaction through its effect on workers' expectations. For open system theory, however, this is but one part of a complex, interactive process.

Decision Theory

Like other systems theorists, the decision theorists stress the complex interactive nature of the organization and its role as a processor of information. Unlike the others, decision theorists are principally concerned with how organizations use the information in making decisions. Specifically, they seek to describe the mechanisms used by human organizations to resolve conflict and make choices.[29] An organization is thus viewed as an information-processing network with many decision points. If we understand how it makes decisions at each of these points, we understand the most critical behavior of the system.

Early decision models regarded organizational decision making as a rational, objective process based upon purely economic considerations. Being a rational entity, the organization should operate so as to maximize its expected profitability over some (usually long-term) time period. This would be accomplished by evaluating each decision alternative in terms of (1) the desirability of its possible outcomes and (2) the likelihood that each of these outcomes would actually occur. If an organization consistently selected options with the highest expected return at each decision level, it would perform optimally in the long run.

Economic models of this sort, like the bureaucratic scheme for organizing work, have been rather unsuccessful and for much the same basic reason: They are based on very questionable assumptions about human behavior. Individually or collectively, people simply do not operate according to this objective kind of "rationality." Maximizing the profits of the organization is not the only concern of those who make decisions—they have personal and group goals as well. Moreover, it may be difficult or impossible for people to estimate the relative desirability and likelihood of all possible decision outcomes. Without this capability maximization becomes a hopeless cause.

Recognizing these and other shortcomings in the classical economic model, modern decision theorists have proposed an alternative approach based on observed *behavior* rather than some rational idea. The Carnegie-Mellon group, for instance, suggests that organizations (and people generally) "satisfice" rather than optimize in making choices. That is, instead of carefully weighing the pros and cons of each possible course of action and choosing the one with the highest expected return, real decision makers set some *minimum acceptable level* of return and pick the first alternative that promises to exceed this level. They choose the first satisfactory solution rather than the very best one.

Behavioral theorists also argue that organizations operate in the *short term* rather than the long term in making decisions—usually, in fact, on a problem-by-problem basis. Likewise, they *evaluate* their decisions on the basis of short-term feedback. Thus, if the decision choice solves the immediate problem, it is likely to be judged a good one regardless of long-run consequences.

Finally, behavioral decision theorists contend that as a rule organizations strive to *avoid* rather than *predict* future uncertainties. Whereas the economic theorists believe decision makers make plans and choices based upon predictions of future labor costs, markets, competition, and the like, the behavioral variety feel that decision makers try to *control* these factors in order to make them as certain as possible.

In contrasting economic with behavioral decision theory, we can see that organization theories based on the systems concept range from those that virtually ignore people to some that regard man as the central component. Even in the case of the people-oriented versions, however, one would hardly call them *humanistic* in the same sense as the human relations theories. For the behavioral decision theorists, it is important to know how man operates in order to write better systems equations; for the human relations theorists, man is the primary object of study.

Information Processing Theory

The most completely developed and comprehensive theory of the organization as a system for handling information is attributable to Galbraith. To appreciate what it attempts to do, however, one must first consider a line of research carried out during the 1960s by investigators such as Burns and Stalker,[30] Emery and Trist,[31] and Lawrence and Lorsch.[32] The main issue addressed in these classic studies was how situational factors (such as those we have called *context* and *environment*) relate to structure, and peripherally, what significance situation and structure have together for organizational performance. The findings were rather consistent: the more predictable the situation or task facing an organization, the more appropriate becomes the *mechanistic* (classical) approach to organizing and managing; the less predictable the situation or task, the more appropriate becomes an *organic* (flexible, participative, even humanistic) approach. The more *differentiation* (or basic difference in attitude and perspective) there is among groups (such as production versus sales versus research) within an organization, the more necessary it becomes to invest resources in the *integration* function (e.g., to improve communications, provide liaison).[33]

Galbraith[34] concluded that the most sensible interpretation of these and other observations was in terms of the general concept of *uncertainty* and the organization's effort to reduce it—a model borrowed from the communication engineers. For them, *communication* is the process of reducing uncertainty; *information* is what one gets when uncertainty is reduced. As uncertainty from any source increases, the amount of communication required (or information to be processed) by the system in order to maintain its previous state goes up. Since all channels used in communication (human sensory systems; telephone wires, radio waves, etc.) have some limit on how much they can carry (i.e., a finite *capacity*), increased uncertainty will eventually exceed the capacity of the existing channels to reduce it (i.e., the system becomes *overloaded*). Then it becomes necessary either to increase capacity (e.g., add more channels) or to reduce the amount or quality of what is transmitted (e.g., tolerate incomplete or garbled messages).

The way in which Galbraith applied this conceptualization was by likening the organization to a large communication system composed of a variety of channels each with a different capacity to deal with uncertainty. The formal "chain-of-command" is one element; standard procedures manuals constitute another; elaborate computer systems for monitoring business activity might be another; problem-oriented "task forces" still another; and so on. The uncertainty with which these resources must deal comes from the environment (competition, markets, the general economy, government regulation, etc.) and a variety of internal sources (e.g., the technology and size of the organization; its diversity of products; its goals; its level of differentiation; and particularly, the complexity of the tasks it carries out). Now, the key idea is that any combination of organizational features has some total capacity; hence it is able to handle just so much uncertainty and no more. Similarly, any level of uncertainty requires a certain total capacity. Failing that, performance suffers in some way.

Assume that a company manufactures only one product, using a simple technology, in a stable environment. The capacity afforded by the classical mechanistic structure may be sufficient to handle the trivial amount of uncertainty generated by this highly predictable situation. Suppose now that a change in the market situation occurs that makes it unprofitable to continue producing just one product. Uncertainty has increased. The classical mechanisms, geared as they are merely to maintain the status quo, are overloaded (i.e., there is no capacity for doing market analysis, research and development on new products, planning). Hence management has two choices: it can *increase capacity* (e.g., hire market researchers, scientists, planners), or learn to live with *reduced performance* (e.g., try to stretch present resources to add new lines without the benefit of planning or research). If it hires research and development people, it sets up two distinct groups (R&D versus production), thereby increasing differentiation, adding more uncertainty, and taxing the classical management capacity even more. Now it again has two choices: add management capacity (e.g., a liaison person) to keep the two factions from each other's throats, or live with conflict (i.e., reduced performance and morale). Organic systems tend to have more capacity than mechanistic ones; therefore they work better in uncertain environments.

There is considerably more to Galbraith's theory than a cursory discussion can hope to reveal. For example, he distinguishes a number of strategies for both increasing capacity and decreasing uncertainty in the face of unavoidable increases in uncertainty. One of the more sophisticated is a structural arrangement known as the *matrix* organization in which capacity is increased by overlaying two distinct management systems: a *departmental* structure and a project or *product* structure. In the matrix form a person belongs to two hierarchies and answers to two bosses—a direct violation of classical rules. It has become an extremely popular form in many advanced engineering and research organizations because of its high information-processing capacity.

Viewed as a whole, the systems approach has proven quite useful not only as a means of understanding how organizations function but as a means of dealing with certain complex organization problems such as inventory control, cuing, and interdepartmental conflict. The problems with which it has been most successful are those whose basic dimensions are at least fairly well understood individually. It has been less successful where such imponderables as human nature or the general economic climate are part of the picture: Not enough is known yet in these areas to write sensible equations. Since it is obvious that such imponderables are a big part of any organization, systems theory presently falls far short of being able to produce the ideal organizational plan. It does, however, recognize the true complexity of organizations—the fact that one must consider many interacting variables in order to understand organizational behavior—and it has made at least some progress toward specifying what the important variables are. In contrast to the classic bureaucratic approach, it has given increasing attention to *human* variables. As the imponderables become less so, systems theory should become an increasingly powerful tool for organizational design and analysis. Research carried on within the framework of the humanistic theories may eventually provide the input necessary to flesh out the system theories.

MICRO THEORIES

We turn our attention next to those theories in which concern for the human being plays a central role (i.e., the *group process* and *individual* boxes in Figure 2–1). Though they disagree on which human qualities are most important, and some focus on the leader while others focus on the led (or the interaction of the two), such theories all take issue with the bureaucratic concept of man. They contend that human beings are basically responsible and creative; if they often fail to act accordingly, it is only because of the way they are treated in the typical bureaucratic scheme. Rigid control stifles their potential. Forced into the mold, they become just the sort of nonentities depicted by structural theory. This, humanists agree, is unfortunate not only for the humans but for the organization as well. One gets the most out of people not by making them conform but by arranging things so their inherent responsibility and creativity can express itself.

It might be worth noting in this regard that early human relationists based their appeal on practicality rather than altruism. From the very outset they tried to sell the idea that good human relations makes for happy workers, and happy workers are productive workers. In other words, organizations should be concerned about human well-being because it is profitable. Unfortunately the relationship between workers' *feelings of satisfaction* in their job and their *productivity* is not at all clear, as we shall see in the next chapter. Happy workers are not necessarily productive; making them happier does not guarantee greater productivity. Thus, if one buys the humanistic philosophy, one must do so because of a belief that there is some intrinsic value in having satisfied personnel. Miner calls this other goal *organizational maintenance*.[35] He feels that enlightened managers recognize that profitability and maintenance are *both* important goals and not necessarily interdependent. By *maintenance* he means the ability of an organization to withstand internal and external pressures that constantly threaten its integrity. If a company neglects cost control, it may look bad on the annual profit-and-loss statement. If it neglects human relations, it may ultimately come apart at the seams.

As noted earlier, the next three chapters are devoted completely to these humanistic theories and the research generated by them. We mention them here only in the interest of completing the picture.

CONCLUSION

Our purpose in this chapter was to introduce the reader to the full range of theoretical viewpoints on organizational behavior—philosophies and major points of emphasis. We saw that they tend to fall into two broad clusters: those having a relatively *macro* or *micro* orientation. The former cluster is sometimes referred to as *organization theory (OT)* in contrast to *organizational behavior (OB)*, which deals primarily with individual and group behavior (i.e., the micro cluster). However, the distinction is blurred by the fact that OT is sometimes used to denote the entire domain—the micro as well as the macro cluster. Viewed historically, one can see a transition from an *exclusively* theoretical orientation in which macro features (notably structural ones) dominated, to the modern era in which scientific research is considered vital to theorizing, both micro and macro variables are considered vital to an understanding of organizations, and understanding is considered a vital prerequisite to prescription. *Classical management theory* and *modern systems theory* best illustrate the endpoints on this historical and philosophical continuum. The *neoclassical* transition constituted a rather ill-defined set of intermediate positions.

Since micro (predominantly OB) topics occupy our full attention in subsequent chapters, the emphasis in the present one is on the more macro theories—past and present. Particular notice is given to *modern systems theory* in this regard both because of its currency and its inclusiveness.

It is perhaps useful to close this overview with a return visit to Figure 2–1. Here we see the principal groups of factors to which the various theories are addressed, assembled in a form consistent with the modern systems view. It is a greatly simplified version of what we know and probably even a simpler version of reality. Still, it illustrates several important points. First, if anything is to have an effect on organizational success, it will usually do so through people. The structural variables of the classicists, the context variables of the technology theorists, and even the forces of the general environment ultimately are filtered through individuals.

Second, the context and structure of the organization do play a role in both performance and satisfaction, but not necessarily by a direct route. In all likelihood, the combination operates through perceived *climate, task, reward,* and *group process* variables. For example, size alone does not produce poor morale or low motivation, although a large firm may have the potential to do so depending on how it is managed. If it is structured in the classical mode, it may convey the impression of stodginess, coldness, tight control, and lack of concern for the individual (*climate* factors). It may also provide workers with routine jobs and few intrinsic rewards (*work setting*). Both of these conditions would tend to create a "what the hell" attitude in the individual. However, the same firm might structure itself in small, task-oriented groups and use a management style that exuded warmth, trust, and support. The groups might be allowed considerable control over task structure, providing variety and a feeling of personal accomplishment. The individual might *care* about the work. Thus the tendency of size or technology to have an adverse effect might be mitigated by altering either climate or work environment through careful choice of management strategy.

Third, an organization's structure and context cannot be studied profitably without regard for the environment in which it functions. This situational view will be explored in depth in Chapters 3 & 5. We touched upon it here with reference to the appropriateness of *organic* versus *mechanistic* structures and Galbraith's concept of uncertainty reduction.

And finally, if there is a general lesson to be learned from this overview, it is that no one theory holds the key to organizational success. Each, however, may contribute something to our understanding of organizations—if only by pointing out areas in need of further research. Often what we can gain from such theories is not a direct solution to some pressing problem but guidance in asking intelligent questions. Classical theorists tried to devise a universal blueprint for organizational success and failed miserably because they ignored people. Human relationists have been accused of ignoring everything *but* people. It should be clear by now that many factors may contribute to organizational success, and we can ill afford to ignore any of them.

NOTES

1. Pugh, D. S. (1966). Modern organization theory. *Psychological Bulletin, 66,* 235–251.
2. Porter, L. W., Lawler, E, E., III, & Hackman, J. R. (1975). *Behavior in organizations.* New York: McGraw-Hill.

3. Taylor, F. W. (1911). *The principles of scientific management.* New York: Harper & Row.

4. Roethlisberger, F. J., & Dickson, W. J. (1934). *Management and the worker.* Cambridge, Mass.: Harvard University Press.

5. Parsons, H. M. (1974). What happened at Hawthorne? *Science, 183,* 922–931.

6. Perrow, C. (1972). *Complex organizations: A critical essay.* Glenview, Ill.: Scott, Foresman.

7. Cyert, R., & March, J. G. (1963). *A behavioral theory of the firm.* London: Prentice-Hall.

8. Boulding, K. E. (1956). General systems theory—A skeleton of a science. *Management Science, 2,* 197–208.

9. Bennis, W. G. (1966). Organizational developments and the fate of bureaucracy. *Industrial Management Review, 7,* 41–55.

10. Haire, M. (1964). *Psychology in management.* New York: McGraw-Hill.

11. Weber, Max (1946). *Essays in sociology* (H. H. Gerth & C. W. Mills, Ed. and trans.). New York: Oxford.

12. Bennis, Organizational developments, pp. 41–55.

13. Translated in English as H. Fayol (1949). *General and industrial administration.* London: Sir Isaac Pitman & Sons.

14. Pugh, Modern organization theory, 235–251.

15. Woodward, J. (1958). *Management and technology, problems of progress in industry.* London: H. M. Stationery Office.

16. Davis, K. (1963). Management communication and the grapevine. *Harvard Business Review, 31,* 43–49.

17. Follett, M. P. (1978). The giving of orders. In J. M. Shafritz and P. H. Whitbeck (Eds.), *Classics of organization theory* (pp. 43–51). Oak Park, Ill.: Moore.

18. Barnard, C. (1938). *The functions of the executive.* Cambridge, Mass.: Harvard University Press.

19. March, J. G. (Ed.) (1965). *Handbook of organizations.* Skokie, Ill.: Rand McNally.

20. Dessler, G. (1980). *Organization theory: Integrating structure and behavior* (pp. 38–43). Englewood Cliffs, N.J.: Prentice-Hall.

21. Hunt, R. G. (1970). Technology and organization. *Academy of Management Journal, 31,* 235–252.

22. Woodward. *Management and technology.*

23. Hickson, D. J., Pugh, D. S., Pheysey, D. C. (1969). Operations, technology, and organization structure: An empirical reappraisal. *Administrative Sciences Quarterly, 17,* 44–54.

24. Trist, E. L., & Bamforth, K. W. (1951). Some social and psychological consequences of the longwall method of coal-getting. *Human Relations, 4,* 1–38.

25. Katz, D., & Kahn, R. L. (1966). *The social psychology of organizations.* New York: John Wiley & Sons.

26. March, J. G., & Simon, H. A. (1958). *Organizations.* New York: John Wiley & Sons. Also Cyert and March. *A behavioral theory of the firm.*

27. Galbraith, J. R. (1977). *Organization design.* Reading, Mass.: Addison-Wesley Publishing.

28. Baker, F. (1973). *Organization systems.* Homewood, Ill.: Richard D. Irwin.

29. Cyert & March, *Behavioral theory.*

30. Burns, T., & Stalker, G. M. (1961). *The management of innovation.* London: Tavistock.

31. Emery, F. E., & Trist, E L. (1965). The causal texture of organizational environments. *Human Relations, 18,* 21–32.

32. Lawrence, P. R., & Lorsch, J. W. (1969). *Developing organizations: Diagnosis and action.* Reading, Mass.: Addison-Wesley Publishing.

33. Lawrence & Lorsch. *Developing organizations.*

34. Galbraith. *Organization design.*

35. Miner, J. B. (1969). *Personnel and industrial relations.* New York: Macmillan.

3

Motivation and Job Satisfaction

In any organization large differences can be observed among employees in the performance of their work roles. Some employees show enthusiasm and initiative in the exercise of their responsibilities. Others do what is required of them in a dependable and conscientious fashion but seldom go beyond requirements to show creativity or initiative. Still others act as if they were in suspended animation, exerting little effort on the job and failing to meet even the minimum performance standards. What factors account for these differences? Do the high-performance employees simply possess more ability? This explanation seems insufficient considering the fact that even the best selection techniques available are far from perfect. It seems much more plausible that a large part of the differences among workers in their performance is the result of motivational differences.

As we saw in the last chapter, each of the major theoretical approaches to organizations assumed somewhat different things about what people want out of their work and how management can tap these wants to obtain optimal performance. The scientific management theorists assumed that people are primarily economic. In return for good wages, employees are more than willing to submit to authority and work toward organizational goals. To motivate employees, management should simplify work so that it can be easily mastered and then provide economic incentives for achieving management standards. The early human relations theorists, as exemplified by the Hawthorne studies, assumed that people are primarily social. People want to be respected and loved by others and will seek membership in groups to fulfill these needs. To motivate employees to work toward organizational goals, management should treat them with consideration and sensitivity. The manager's tasks are to keep employees informed of decisions that affect them and to listen to their complaints and suggestions. Each subordinate should be made to feel important and useful. Later human relations theorists (sometimes called human resource theorists) claimed that the primary motive of workers is personal growth. People are motivated to achieve organizational goals if in doing so they can use and develop important abilities. Managers, according to this approach, should allow employees to participate in important decisions and should provide them with challenging jobs.

Several decades of research on motivation have made clear that the assumptions underlying these earlier theories were grossly oversimplified. Most contemporary theories of organizations tend to view humans as complex rather than primarily economic, social, or self-actualizing. In this chapter, we explore some of the leading contemporary notions concerning the role of human motivation in work settings. We consider such issues as what crucial needs determine why and how well people work, what process translates needs and preferences into work behavior, what factors in the work situation lead to feelings of satisfaction or dissatisfaction, what—if anything—feelings of satisfaction have to do with performance, and how effective some of the practical programs for improving work motivation have been.

ESSENTIAL CHARACTERISTICS OF MOTIVATIONAL THEORY

Although theories of motivation differ in many respects, most definitions of motivation have at least three common denominators. According to Porter and Steers, when "we discuss motivation, we are primarily concerned with: (1) what energizes human behavior, (2) what directs or channels such behavior, and (3) how this behavior is maintained or sustained."[1] Viewed from a broad perspective, it is senseless to say an employee is or isn't motivated. One employee, Ralph, may show unbounded enthusiasm in the performance of his job, while a second worker, Fred, emulates a mushroom from 9 to 5. Can we then conclude that Ralph is motivated and Fred is not? Fred might in fact be highly motivated to achieve recognition from his peers, and he may see a low level of performance as the means to achieve such recognition. Fred does not "lack motivation"; rather, he is motivated in the direction of different goals. Work motivation theorists who use the term *highly motivated employee* usually refer to an employee who tries to do a good job—who chooses goals that are compatible with those of the organization and who demonstrates a high degree of vigor and persistence in attempts to achieve these goals.

A second theme common to motivational theorists is that they look inside the person for causes of behavior. The direction, vigor, and persistence with which an employee performs a task is believed to result from internal motivating states such as needs, expectations, values, and attitudes. In this regard, motivational theorists can be contrasted with radical behavioral theorists (e.g., B. F. Skinner's views) who look only at directly observable environmental events when attempting to explain and predict behavior. If workers are working at a slow pace it is because conditions in the work environment (e.g., supervisor behavior, monetary incentives) reinforce them for doing so. To increase the pace, one manipulates environmental contingencies so that workers are reinforced for working faster. Radical behaviorists see little reason to consider the individual's needs, perceptions, or other such fuzzy concepts so dear to the heart of motivation theorists.

Much of the research supporting radical behavioristic notions has used animals (particularly rats and pigeons) as subjects. Although a radical behavior approach may be sufficient if one is concerned with the behavior of nonhuman subjects (even this is open to debate), the attempt to avoid all mention of motivational constructs runs into trouble when one extends the findings of animal research to humans in organizations.[2] Research with humans has made clear that behavior is affected not only by objective environmental events but also by the cognitions and feelings that persons hold with regard to these events.[3] Unlike mice, humans think about how they are being reinforced, so it is not surprising that the findings of behavioral research on animals are often hard to replicate with humans. A radical behavioral approach also leaves unanswered the crucial question of why one outcome is more positively reinforcing than another. Radical behaviorists define a positive reinforcer as a stimulus that, when it occurs contiguous to a behavior, increases the frequency of that behavior. If we ask why the stimulus increases the frequency of that behavior, the answer is likely to be, "Because it is positively reinforcing." There is then an obvious danger of circularity when reinforcement is defined in purely "objective" terms.

As we will discuss later in the chapter, the radical behavioral approach has inspired some very useful practical applications.[4] Modifying behavior by changing environmental contingencies is a more realistic approach than attempting to change behavior by modifying people's values or motives. On the other hand, to understand why people behave as they do in organizations, it seems that some use of motivational concepts is required.

THE RELATIONSHIPS AMONG WORK MOTIVATION, JOB PERFORMANCE, AND WORK-RELATED ATTITUDES

As will become apparent when we discuss some of the theories of work motivation, there are differing views on the relationships among work motivation, effective performance of the job, and work-related attitudes. Although many of the issues have yet to be resolved, two conclusions seem justified. First, the terms work motivation, performance, and attitudes refer to separate processes and should not be used interchangeably. Second, the relationships among these three variables are quite complex.

Work Motivation and Work-Related Attitudes

A common mistake is to equate work motivation with employees' work-related attitudes. For example, advocates of a human relations approach often use the terms *job satisfaction* and *motivation* interchangeably. It is important to clearly distinguish between these two constructs. We defined work motivation in terms of the direction, vigor, and persistence of an employee's work *behavior*. In contrast, work attitudes refer to an employee's subjective evaluations or feelings about persons, things, and events related to the job. Not only are these different constructs, but the relationship between attitudes and behavior is quite complex. The voluminous literature on work attitudes would require several books to completely discuss and analyze. We only attempt to summarize a small portion of three of the most frequently researched job attitudes: job satisfaction, job involvement, and organizational commitment.

Job Satisfaction

The degree to which an employee likes or dislikes aspects of the job is usually referred to as job satisfaction. Several intensively researched self-report (questionnaire) instruments have been developed to provide a standardized means of surveying the critical aspects of job satisfaction.[5] Table 3–1 illustrates the job descriptive index (JDI), one of the foremost of these instruments. Such devices yield separate measures for each *facet* of satisfaction: that is, satisfaction with *pay*, with *supervision*, and so on. To arrive at an *overall* satisfaction measure, the component scores must be combined in some way. Because there is a lot of variation among devices in terms of what facets are included and how the scores are combined, it is not surprising that different measures represent somewhat different definitions of satisfaction. Moreover, some instruments consider the situation only as it exists presently, whereas others include comparisons with ideal states (how things *should be*, or how the respondent would like them to be). Wanous and Lawler have summarized the major differences among these measures and have shown that they do, in fact, tap somewhat different kinds of feelings.[6] They suggest that there is no one best definition of satisfaction and that what one should measure depends primarily on what use one hopes to make of the measurements.

Job Involvement

Another job attitude frequently mentioned in the motivation literature is job involvement. Kanungo defined job involvement as the extent to which employees believe their jobs to be important to their self-concepts.[7] In his

TABLE 3–1 Sample Items from the Job Descriptive Index (Each Scale Is Presented on a Separate Page)

Think of your present work. What is it like most of the time? In the blank beside each word given below, write

___ Y ___ for Yes if it describes your work.

___ N ___ for No if it does NOT describe it.

___ ? ___ if you cannot decide it.

WORK ON PRESENT JOB

___ Routine
___ Satisfying
___ Good
___ On your feet

Think of the pay you get now. How well does each of the following words describe your present pay? In the blank beside each word, put

___ Y ___ if it describes your pay.

___ N ___ if it does NOT describe it.

___ ? ___ if you cannot decide.

PRESENT PAY

___ Income adequate for normal expenses
___ Insecure
___ Less than I deserve
___ Highly paid

Think of the kind of supervision that you get on your job. How well does each of the following words describe this supervision? In the blank beside each word below, put

___ Y ___ if it describes the supervision you get on your job.

___ N ___ if it does NOT describe it.

___ ? ___ if you cannot decide.

SUPERVISION ON PRESENT JOB

___ Impolite
___ Praises good work
___ Influential
___ Doesn't supervise enough

Think of the opportunities for promotion that you have now. How well does each of the following words describe these? In the blank beside each word put

___ Y ___ for Yes if it describes your opportunities for promotion.

___ N ___ for NO if it does NOT describe them.

___ ? ___ if you cannot decide.

OPPORTUNITIES FOR PROMOTION

___ Promotion on ability
___ Dead-end job
___ Unfair promotion policy
___ Regular promotions

Think of the majority of the people that you work with now or the people you meet in connection with your work. How well does each of the following words describe these people? In the blank beside each word below, put

___ Y ___ if it describes the people you work with.

___ N ___ if it does NOT describe them.

___ ? ___ if you cannot decide.

PEOPLE ON YOUR PRESENT JOB

___ Boring
___ Responsible
___ Intelligent
___ Talk too much

SOURCE: From Patricia C. Smith, Department of Psychology, Bowling Green State University, Bowling Green, Ohio 43403. Copyright 1969 by Bowling Green State University. Reproduced by permission. The complete forms, scoring key, instructions, and norms can be obtained from Dr. Smith.

job involvement questionnaire, an employee with high job involvement agrees with such items as "The most important things that happen to me involve my present job," "I live, eat, and breathe my job," "I like to be absorbed in my job most of the time," and "I consider my job to be very central to my existence." The highly involved employee disagrees with such items as "I usually feel detached from my job" and "To me, my job is only a small part of who I am." A related construct is *work involvement*, which can be defined as the extent to which persons value work, in general, and define themselves in their work activities. Other terms that have been used to express the same construct include *work ethic* and *central life interests*. A person who has high work involvement agrees with such items as "The most important things that happen in life involve work" and "Happiness comes mainly through work" and disagrees with such items as "Work should only be a small part of one's life" and "There are other activities that are more meaningful than work."

Organizational Commitment

Employees have attitudes concerning the organization in which they work as well the jobs they perform. Porter, Mowday, and Steers define organizational commitment as "the relative strength of an individual's identification with and involvement in a particular organization."[8] To measure this variable they developed a self-report instrument called the Organizational Commitment Questionnaire. High commitment is reflected in agreement with items such as "I talk up this organization to my friends as a great organization to work for" and "I really care about the fate of this organization" and disagreement with items such as "Deciding to work for this organization was a definite mistake on my part" and "I feel very little loyalty to this organization."

Do Attitudes Cause Performance?

Different theoretical approaches have proposed different relationships between attitudes and the motivation to perform effectively. One view, exemplified by the human relations theorists, is summarized in Model A of Figure 3–1. According to this model, work conditions influence the attitudes employees have toward their jobs and organization, and these attitudes, in turn, directly influence the amount of effort invested in the job. To have an effective work force, management should create work conditions that will instill favorable attitudes on the part of employees toward the organization. Employees with favorable attitudes will work hard, and those who work hard will tend to be effective. Another view, depicted in Model B of Figure 3–1, is that attitudes are the consequence, not the determinant, of motivation and performance.[9] Employees who work hard and succeed will feel pride in their accomplishments and will develop favorable attitudes toward their jobs and organization. This position implies that management need not be concerned directly with the

FIGURE 3-1   Alternative Views of the Causal Relationships among Work Motivation, Job Performance, and Work-Related Attitudes

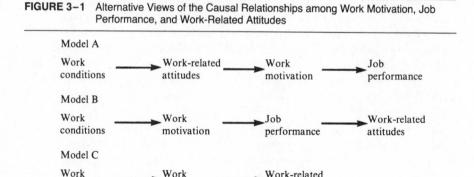

satisfaction of workers. The direct concern should be making sure that workers are motivated to work hard, that they have an opportunity to perform satisfactorily, and that they receive feedback sufficient to let them know about it. Still another position is that of Model C, Figure 3–1, which states that there is no direct causal link between work-related attitudes and job performance. Attitudes do not *cause* job performance, and job performance does not *cause* work-related attitudes. Rather, work-related attitudes and job performance are separate outcomes of different work conditions and motivational processes.[10] One implication of Model C is that management may have to do one set of things if it wishes to instill favorable attitudes and another set of things if it wishes to motivate employees to achieve higher levels of performance. This position is compatible with those who consider satisfaction as a legitimate end in and of itself, not a means to an end.[11]

From the vast number of studies examining the satisfaction-performance relationship, it appears that job satisfaction and performance are positively correlated to a small degree (i.e., increases in one tend to be associated with increases in the other).[12] The size of the relationship tends to be quite small, much smaller than one would expect from either Model A or Model B. A more substantial relationship has been found between job satisfaction and employee turnover. The findings indicate that employees who express satisfaction with their jobs are less likely to terminate employment than are employees who express dissatisfaction with their jobs.[13] Satisfaction appears to correlate negatively with absenteeism and tardiness as well, but these relationships have varied greatly from study to study.[14] Much less research has been conducted on job involvement and organizational commitment than on job satisfaction. The pattern of findings appear similar to those found with job satisfaction, however. The strongest relationships appear to be with turnover. The correlations with absenteeism and tardiness are much smaller and inconsistent. Employees who are committed to their organizations and in their jobs appear less likely to leave their organizations, less likely to be absent from work, and less likely to be tardy.[15] Similar findings have been reported between job involvement and both turnover and absenteeism.[16] The correlations with job performance are much smaller, however, indicating that one cannot accurately predict employee performance from their self-reported organizational commitment or their job involvement.

In summary, employee attitudes toward their jobs and the organization appear to be poor predictors of performance. The failure to find much of a correlation between job performance and work-related attitudes does not mean that all attempts to use attitudinal responses of employees to predict performance have ceased. Some hope still remains that different approaches to measuring attitudes may yet yield useful predictions. For example, Fisher has suggested that one may be able to do a better job in predicting job performance from employee attitudes if attitudinal measures more specific to what is being predicted are used.[17] Rather than using satisfaction with the job or commitment to the organization to predict whether a person will exert a lot of effort on the job, use attitudes of the person toward exerting effort. This is, in fact, very similar to what VIE theories of motivation have done, as we will discuss later in this chapter. Others have theorized that general attitudes predict performance only under certain conditions and for certain types of employees. These conditions and employee types are called *moderator* variables because they *moderate* or influence the strength of the attitude-performance relationship. Cherrington and his colleagues found that satisfaction and performance were positively related when persons were rewarded contingent on their quantity of performance but negatively related when they were rewarded for poor performance.[18] In another study, Steers found that employees with high achievement needs demonstrated a stronger performance-satisfaction relationship than did employees with low achievement needs.[19]

Although specific attitudinal measures and the use of moderator variables might allow somewhat better prediction, the fact remains that general attitudes toward the job and organization (such as satisfaction, involvement, and commitment) are weakly related to performance. These findings suggest that, contrary to Models A and B, there is no simple, direct causal link between general work-related attitudes and performance. In a review of the evidence relating to these models, Greene and Organ concluded that "both satisfaction and performance are caused by an additional variable(s), primarily rewards."[20] According to their analysis, a manager can increase the satisfaction of employees by providing them with rewards that they value. To increase performance as well, these rewards should be provided for good performance and employees should anticipate that they can achieve a high level of performance through their own efforts (see the discussion of VIE theory later in the chapter for a further discussion of similar ideas). In conclusion, Model C seems to have the most support, meaning that for all practical purposes, work-related attitudes and job performance are separate outcomes of similar but not identical processes.

This discussion should not be construed to mean that there are no important consequences of work-related attitudes or that management should ignore employee attitudes. As we have seen, improving employee attitudes toward the job and the organization can yield considerable benefits for many organizations in the form of lower turnover. Another argument is that increased employee job satisfaction is an objective worth pursuing on humanitarian and ethical grounds, regardless of any economic payoffs. Management should not expect, however, that enhancing employees' general attitudes toward their jobs or the organization will increase the motivation of these employees to perform their jobs more effectively.

Work Motivation and Job Performance

Although Model C in Figure 3–1 appears to fit the findings of past research better than the alternatives do, even this model is inaccurate insofar as motivation is presented as the *only* cause of performance. Motivation and performance are frequently discussed as if they are different terms for the same thing. These are distinct concepts, however, related in a very complex fashion. We defined *motivation* as the direction, vigor, and persistence of an employee's behavior. *Performance* refers to one of several outcomes of the employee's behavior and is the extent to which the employee achieves the standards that define "good" performance. For example, a salesperson might exert a large amount of effort in trying to make a sale (motivation) but may or may not actually make the sale (performance).

As important as motivation may be for understanding the effectiveness of a worker's performance, it is only one of several determinants.[21] Performance appears to be a function of at least four separate factors, as stated in the following formula:

$$P = f(M, A, K, E)$$

According to this formula, P, the level of performance, is a function of (i.e., f) M, the level of motivation; A, the level of the person's task ability; K, the level of knowledge the person has of the task requirements; and E, environmental factors hindering and facilitating performance. As is apparent from this formula, all the motivation in the world may not do much to improve performance if the workers do not have the ability to perform the job. On the other hand, a person with high ability may not need to exert much effort to succeed on a task. How accurately the employee comprehends the requirements of the task (K) also plays an important role. Motivated employees are only likely to exhibit high levels of performance if they invest their energies in those activities related to effective performance. For example, endless hours studying for a big exam isn't likely to yield good performance if all the time is spent studying the wrong things. An employee's performance level is often shaped to a large extent by environmental conditions. An employee could perform poorly on a task, not because of low motivation, incompetence, or incorrect knowledge of the task, but because of inadequate tools or a poorly functioning technology. Similarly, in circumstances where environmental factors operate in an employee's favor (easy tasks, assistance from co-workers), effective performance may come with little exertion of effort. Finally, we come to motivation. Other things being equal, organizations are better off the more motivated employees are to achieve organizational goals. There are some exceptions to this rule, however. On some types of tasks, particularly complex and poorly learned tasks, the relationship between motivation and task success has been shown to take the shape of an inverted U. Performance increases with increased motivation up to a point but decreases at high levels of motivation.

All four of the factors discussed so far (ability, motivation, knowledge, and environment) are usually involved to one degree or another in determining an employee's performance. An important part of a manager's job is diagnosing what the causes of employees' performance are and taking appropriate action (we'll have more to say about this in Chapter 6, which deals with performance appraisal). Employee motivation can be overemphasized, then, but most organizations could use a lot more of it. The theories that we are about to explore generally start with this premise and proceed to the point of suggesting ways for organizations to increase the motivation of employees to work toward organizational goals.

THEORIES OF WORK MOTIVATION

As we stated earlier, all motivational theorists are concerned with the direction, vigor, and persistence of work behavior, and they all, to some extent, look inside the employee for the causes of such behavior. There is considerable diversity, however, in the approaches taken by motivational theorists to understand and predict work motivation. We have already touched on some of the different views that exist regarding the relationship between work-related attitudes and performance. Now we will go into a bit more detail in comparing and contrasting some of the major theories of work motivation. One type of theory, need theory, has focused primarily on content and has asked "what" motivates employees. Other theories, such as the goal-setting and expectancy-valence models, have been much more process oriented and have focused more on the "how" than the "what" of motivation. Each of the approaches have contributed to what is known about work motivation. As we will now show, however, some theories appear to have contributed substantially more than others.

Need Theory

The most content-oriented of the motivational theories are the need theories. They hold that need states are essential for survival as well as maintenance of health and happiness. The idea is that when persons are deprived of (or deficient in) something that is important to their well-being, a need is created and corrective behavior is activated. To understand motivated behavior, one must therefore identify and classify needs.

This, it turns out, is no mean feat from a research standpoint. One problem, as noted before, is that our main access to need states is through the questionable avenue of self-reports. We generally try to measure needs by asking individuals through some sort of questionnaire or test what they value or want. What persons need, however, may not be the same as what they say they *want*. Addicts may not value or want heroin, but because they are physiologically and psychologically dependent on the drug, they need it. On the other hand, what persons say they *want* may not be what they *need*. A child screaming for an ice cream cone certainly wants ice cream but may not need it, either psychologically or physiologically.

If, rejecting self-reports, we try to infer needs from the direction and intensity of behavior, another problem arises: *circularity of definition*. Theoretically, we could postulate a different need for every identifiable object of a person's behavior. Noting, for example, that someone appears to be working for money, status, or a feeling of achievement, we might try to explain their behavior by postulating a money motive, a status motive, or an achievement motive. All we have done, however, is restate our suspicion in terms of internal states (motives). Unless we can find some independent way of verifying these states, we have explained nothing. We wind up with as many motives as there are potential objects of behavior (money, status, achievement, food, drink, shelter, variety of experience, *ad infinitum*).

There is no completely satisfactory solution to these or various other problems inherent in the classification of need states. Theorists generally looked for convergent evidence from a variety of measurements, observations, and experimental results and, after blending in a healthy portion of logic or supposition, arrived at what they consider a defensible position. Most postulate a relatively manageable list of basic needs to which other goal objects have become attached through learning.

Henry Murray's Theory of Manifest Needs

In the 1930s a personality theorist at Harvard by the name of Henry Murray presented a list of over 20 needs that he believed constituted basic personality traits.[22] Among these were the needs for achievement, affiliation, dominance, order, understanding, play, autonomy, aggression, and sex. Murray defined a need as a force, located somewhere in the brain, that creates tension when aroused. When a need is aroused, the person seeks goal objects that reduce the tension. Individuals learn to associate particular goal objects with the satisfaction of particular needs. Thus, one person might call friends to satisfy affiliation needs whereas another might go shopping.

According to Murray, all people have the same basic psychological needs but not to the same degree. Murray proposed that there is a hierarchy of needs, unique to each person, in which some of the needs are more important than others (are prepotent). When these prepotent needs are satisfied, the other needs become more important. He used a variety of methods to measure needs, including self-report questionnaires, interviews, observation of behavior, and projective techniques. The projective technique he developed is known as the Thematic Apperception Test (TAT), and it has been particularly influential in research on personality and motivation. People are shown a standard set of rather ambiguous pictures (e.g., a picture of an older man talking to a younger man who is gazing out a window) and asked to compose stories about them. Their needs purportedly influence the stories they compose (i.e., they will project themselves into the stories).

Murray's theory of needs is not one of the major psychological theories. Moreover, he had very little to say about work motivation. His ideas and methods of research are important, however, because of the influence they had on subsequent theorists and researchers. This influence will become apparent as we discuss the need theories of work motivation.

Maslow's Need Hierarchy

One of the most popular conceptualizations of work motivation was formulated by Maslow over 30 years ago.[23] Like many other theories, it holds that there are a few basic needs and people are motivated by the desire to achieve outcomes that satisfy these needs. Its distinctive feature concerns the organization of these basic needs. First, Maslow identified five need categories: *physiological* (basic survival) needs, *safety* needs, *social* (belongingness or love) needs, *ego* (self-esteem) needs, and *self-actualization* needs. Second, similar to Murray, he proposed that these categories are arranged in a hierarchy of importance and that behavior is controlled chiefly by the lowest one that is still unsatisfied. Unlike Murray, however, he proposed that there is hierarchical arrangement common to all humans, with the basic survival needs at the bottom of the hierarchy and the uniquely human ones (self-actualization or the need to realize one's potential) at the top. Thus, a person is motivated by food, drink, and the like only insofar as physiological needs are not being met. As these are satisfied, concern turns to safety needs (working conditions, job security); from there to social needs (personal friendships, group memberships); then to the ego needs (internal feelings of achievement, recognition for accomplishments); and finally, self-actualization needs (realizing potential, making creative contributions). In the case of only one category, self- actualization, is need gratification predicted to *not* reduce the potency of the need—indeed, the more chances people have to realize their potential, the greater their need to self-actualize is supposed to become. The achievement and self-actualization needs seem very similar. One can, however, achieve without necessarily realizing potential or realize full potential and still not achieve. A track star, for example, might satisfy all ego needs by winning a big race even at a relatively slow time, whereas it might take a record time to fulfill the need to self-actualize. Conversely, the track star might come in last in a very fast heat and feel that his or her full—if somewhat limited—potential has been realized.

Maslow's theory has two broad implications for organizational management.[24] First, it is important to find out where on the hierarchy employee need satisfaction has stopped so that an estimate can be made of what goal objects are likely to motivate the employees. If, for example, salary and fringe benefits were sufficient to take care of physiological and safety needs, but workers complained of social isolation, Maslow's theory suggests that the organization would be wasting money if it tried to use additional pay as a source of motivation. It would need to focus on the social atmosphere. The other implication is that the best interests of the organization are served by satisfying all the employees' lower needs so that they will be responsive to incentives more relevant to ego and self-actualization needs. These higher needs are more likely to motivate creative activities if the organization provides an environment conducive to the gratification of these needs.

Many of Maslow's ideas have gained wide acceptance among modern managers. Much of their popularity undoubtedly stems from their featured position in the writings of such influential theorists as Douglas McGregor.[25] In his book *The Human Side of Enterprise* McGregor contrasts the conventional, directive Theory X philosophy of management with the enlightened, humanistic Theory Y position. Central to Theory Y is the notion that organizations should recognize the employees' need hierarchy and try to arrange conditions such that in satisfying their own needs the employees can contribute maximally to the goals of the organization. Because in most instances their lower-order (physiological and safety) needs will already have been met, more attention should be given to social, ego, and self-actualization needs. People should be given the chance to interact, feel important, and be creative in a constructive way (through their work situation); otherwise, they will likely satisfy these needs in nonproductive—or even counterproductive—ways such as conspiring to limit production. Our interest at this point is not, however, with McGregor's theorizing but rather with the extent to which Maslow's hierarchy assumption has permeated managerial thinking.

Despite the rave reviews the Maslow theory was received from many managers, it is a conceptually flawed theory that research has failed to support. Several studies conducted in organizational settings have sought to determine whether the importance employees attach to each of the need categories is in any way related to how well they perceived these needs as being satisfied. Maslow's theory would predict, of course, that as a need becomes satisfied it should become less important and the next higher one should dominate. The appropriate way to test this hypothesis is to conduct longitudinal research in which one examines the relationship between satisfaction of needs and rated importance of the needs in the same individuals over time. Most of the studies of this type have provided little support for this hypothesis. "Satisfied" needs have not been found to be consistently less important than "unsatisfied" ones, and satisfaction of lower-level needs does not appear to affect the importance of those and higher-level ones in quite the way that Maslow predicted.[26] For example, Hall and Nougaim found that over a five-year period, as satisfaction of some needs increased, the importance of these needs increased rather than decreased.[27] Similarly, Rauschenberger, Schmitt, and Hunter found that as one need increased in importance all the others increased as well.[28] The few studies showing support for the "increased satisfaction—decreased importance" hypothesis have been cross-sectional studies, i.e., studies comparing different groups of people at the same time (e.g., Dachler and Hulin).[29] Moreover, the support appears limited to the lower-level needs. These few supportive results cannot easily offset the overwhelmingly negative results of the longitudinal studies.

It also seems clear from other research that the five-category system has little to justify it. Several researchers have used a statistical procedure known as factor analysis to determine just how many categories of needs can adequately account for the stated desires of employees.[30] We shall have more to say about this technique in connection with selection and placement in Chapter 7. Suffice it to say here that it is a procedure for estimating the number and structure of common dimensions that underlie (or define) any collection of multifaceted items. In the present application, the idea is that if indeed there are five need categories, a factor analysis of what people say they work for should yield five underlying dimensions. Statements regarding food, shelter, and the like should be heavily represented on a physiological need dimension; those involving insurance, retirement, and the like on a security need dimension; those involving friends and group memberships on a social needs dimension; and so on. Unfortunately, studies using factor analysis have not come up with groupings that agree with Maslow's classification.[31] Despite its intuitive appeal and popularity, the five-level need hierarchy, indeed *any* hierarchy at all, remains a highly speculative model of human motivation. Management theories derived from it must also be viewed with considerable skepticism.

Alderfer's ERG Theory

As originally formulated, then, Maslow's hierarchy is of dubious validity. Alderfer has attempted to improve on Maslow's theory by proposing only three categories of needs and somewhat different relationships among the needs.[32] The three categories are *existence* needs, which include both the physiological and safety needs from Maslow's theory; *relatedness* needs, which are Maslow's social needs; and *growth* needs, which include Maslow's self-esteem and self-actualization needs. Similar to Maslow, Alderfer predicts that as the existence needs of persons are satisfied, their relatedness needs become more important, and likewise, as the relatedness needs are gratified, the growth needs become more important. Alderfer places less emphasis, however, on the hierarchical ordering of needs and believes that a person may be motivated by more than one level at any one time. Also, Alderfer predicts that a person can move down the hierarchy (regress) as the result of frustration, as well as up the hierarchy as the result of fulfillment. In other words, an employee who fails to fulfill higher-order needs may place more importance on not only these needs but on lower-level needs as well. For example, employees who are continually frustrated in their attempts to self-actualize on dull and routine jobs might cope with this frustration by placing increasing importance on relatedness needs and channeling increasing amounts of energy into socializing and other behaviors that fulfill these needs. If their relatedness needs are also frustrated, they might move an additional step down on the hierarchy and place more importance on basic existence needs. A lonely employee, for example, might turn to eating, drinking, and other corporeal pleasures as substitutes for friends.

There have been only a few empirical tests of Alderfer's ERG model. A few studies have supported his predictions. Scherf, for instance, found that consumers who were frustrated in their relations with others valued consumer goods more than those whose affiliation needs were satisfied.[33] In claiming confirmation of ERG theory, Scherf made the questionable assumption that in valuing consumer goods, consumers were enhancing the importance of lower-level needs to compensate for the frustration of their higher needs. Alderfer has reported mixed support for his model in his own research.[34] The validity of the crucial aspect of the model, the systematic progression or regression of need importance along hierarchical lines, remains in doubt. Also, there is very little evidence to support Alderfer's classification of needs into the existence, relatedness, and growth categories.

Herzberg's Two-Factor Theory

Another viewpoint that has enjoyed immense popularity within organizational circles is Herzberg's two-factor theory of job satisfaction.[35] The

FIGURE 3-2   Factors Affecting Job Attitudes (As Reported in 12 of Herzberg's Investigations)

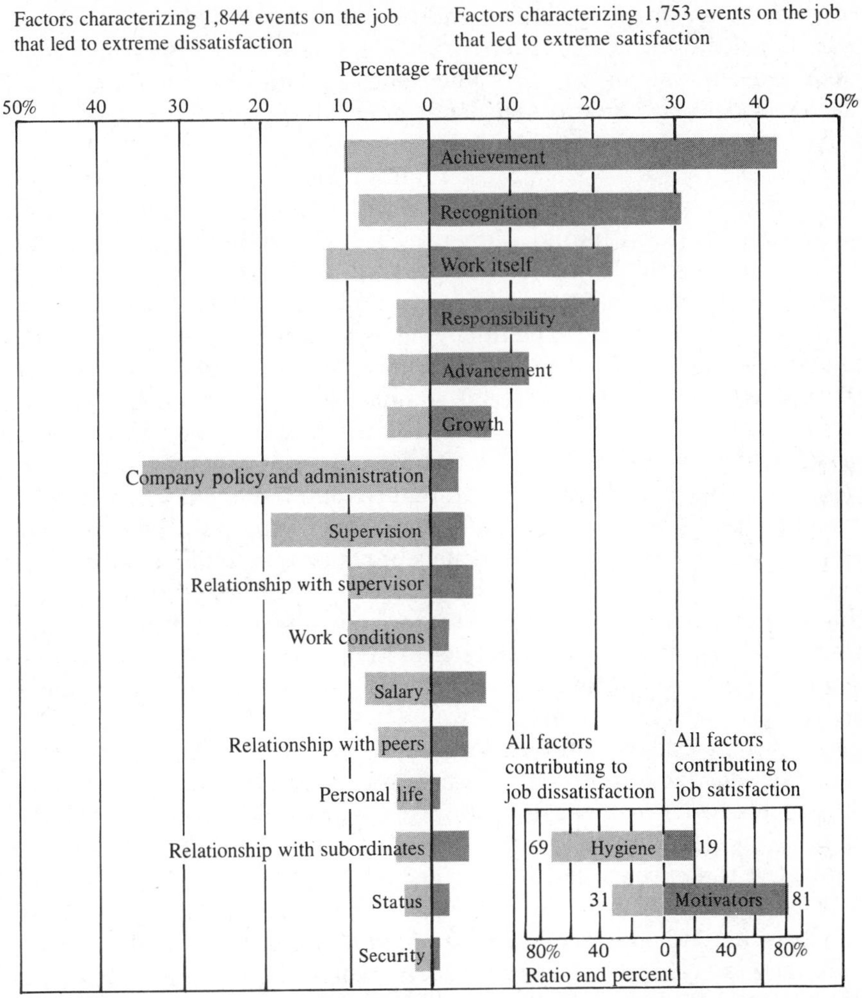

Factors characterizing 1,844 events on the job
that led to extreme dissatisfaction

Factors characterizing 1,753 events on the job
that led to extreme satisfaction

Percentage frequency

| 50% | 40 | 30 | 20 | 10 | 0 | 10 | 20 | 30 | 40 | 50% |

Achievement

Recognition

Work itself

Responsibility

Advancement

Growth

Company policy and administration

Supervision

Relationship with supervisor

Work conditions

Salary

Relationship with peers

Personal life

Relationship with subordinates

Status

Security

All factors
contributing to
job dissatisfaction

All factors
contributing to
job satisfaction

| 69 | Hygiene | 19 |
| 31 | Motivators | 81 |

| 80% | 40 | 0 | 40 | 80% |

Ratio and percent

SOURCE: Herzberg, F. (1968). One more time: How do you motivate employees? *Harvard Business Review, 46,* 53−62.

specific nature of Herzberg's theory is perhaps best illustrated in Figure 3–2, a summary of the results of 12 of his earlier investigations. In this research, workers were asked to describe specific events associated with their jobs that had made them extremely satisfied or dissatisfied. (This approach, variations of which we shall encounter in several other contexts, is known as the *critical incident* technique). The resulting stories, or critical events, were grouped into 16 categories, and the frequency of events falling under each category was tabulated. Looking at Figure 3–2, we see that few incidents mentioned involved status or security, while over half involved achievement in one way or another. Even more important from Herzberg's standpoint, stories falling under some of the categories were consistently positive, while those under other categories were typically negative. *Responsibility*, for example, was not only mentioned frequently, it was also usually mentioned in connection with *satisfying* incidents. *Supervision* was mentioned almost as frequently but nearly always with *dissatisfying* incidents.

Herzberg concluded from these findings that job satisfaction and dissatisfaction were two entirely different dimensions, not simply opposite ends of the same continuum. Moreover, he claimed that there are two different categories of job factors, one controlling satisfaction and the other dissatisfaction. These factors, in turn, serve two different sets of needs: first, the basic biological kind involving food, pain avoidance, and the like plus any others that have become associated with these basic drives through learning (notably money); second, the uniquely human needs for achievement and self-fulfillment. Factors serving the biologically based needs, which he termed *hygiene* factors, are responsible for dissatisfaction when they are absent and can reduce dissatisfaction when they are present. The others he called *motivators*. When provided, Herzberg theorizes, motivators can simultaneously increase job satisfaction and job motivation. A major distinguishing feature, according to Herzberg, is that hygiene factors are extrinsic to the job itself (company policy, supervision, salary, and so on), whereas motivators are intrinsic to the job (achievement, recognition of achievement, the nature of the work, and so on).

One way to understand Herzberg's notions is to think of how people react to hygiene factors outside the work setting. For instance, it is unlikely that people feel a rush of satisfaction at the sight or memory of their garbage being collected. It is more likely that they fail to even notice the event. Let the garbage fail to be collected, however, and dissatisfaction, outrage, anger, and a host of other negative feelings are likely to develop. Herzberg argued that management *should* provide good working conditions, pay raises, and considerate supervision. If these hygiene factors are not present, people will be dissatisfied. One should not expect, however, that providing these things will produce a general increase in employee motivation. All one can achieve with these extrinsic factors is a neutral state in which lower-level needs are no longer a problem. Unfortunately, the neutral point may escalate over time as employees become accustomed to their high pay, good supervision, and good working conditions. Consequently, it may take an increasing amount of the hygienes to keep them from being dissatisfied. Herzberg's only advice on this score is to "do the best you can." He admits knowing no answers.[36]

Herzberg argues that if managers want to motivate their employees they can do so only through the factors associated with the job itself that tap motivation needs. To motivate workers, managers should make the work more interesting and less routine; they should recognize work that is well done; they should allow employees autonomy in the performance of their tasks; and they should promote those who perform well. In other words, the job should be restructured so that it becomes more meaningful, more challenging, and more intrinsically rewarding to the workers—a process frequently referred to as *job enrichment.*

Two-factor theory has not been supported in the research. Much of the evidence is summarized by Dunnette, Campbell, and Hakel. When one tests two-factor theory as Herzberg did with the critical incidents method, the evidence generally supports his theory: Hygienes are mentioned more frequently as a source of dissatisfaction than satisfaction, and motivators are mentioned more frequently as a source of satisfaction than as a source of dissatisfaction. However, this clear differentiation between hygiene and motivators is found only when the critical incident approach is used. When other techniques are used to test the theory, nearly all the factors have substantial positive and negative effects on satisfaction.[37] When biases in the Herzberg critical incidents approach are controlled, even this approach fails to yield support for the two-factor theory. The major bias in the technique appears to be that it confuses events (what happened) with agents (what made it happen). Schneider and Locke have shown that the same classes of events produce both satisfaction and dissatisfaction, depending on how the person interprets them.[38] If workers judge an event to be satisfying, they attribute its occurrence to their own efforts; but if they see it as dissatisfying, they blame it mainly on others (as agents). Another criticism is that Herzberg has misinterpreted his own data. The grouping of factors is not as clear-cut as he claims. In Figure 3–2, for example, salary (which he labels a hygiene factor) is mentioned about as many times as a source of satisfaction as it is a source of dissatisfaction. Indeed, *all* the factors contribute somewhat to both satisfaction and dissatisfaction. Whatever else may be said about it, the two-factor theory presents an oversimplified picture of human motives and their relationship to satisfaction and performance. Whether or not need-satisfying factors sort themselves into two clusters has been shown to depend on a lot of other things: the organizational environment, the individual's personality and sex, and the method of gathering data. Considering all the above-mentioned limitations to the theory, the two-factor generalization seems to have little merit.

Needs as Traits

Although Maslow, Herzberg, and Alderfer gave little attention to the personality differences that exist among people, such differences do exist. For example, some individuals are likely to strive for belonging and acceptance across all kinds of situations because their social needs form a stable trait in their personality. Others appear to have personalities in which self-actualization and esteem are the more dominant needs. The findings of research and practical attempts to motivate employees have made increasingly clear that management must deal with individuals if it is to put to good use most of the theoretical notions regarding needs, motivation, job enrichment, and indeed many of the other concerns of the industrial-organizational field that we have yet to visit: selection, training, even consumer psychology. It is simply not sufficient to operate according to broad assumptions about large groups of employees: what motivates the blue-collar worker or the middle manager or the hard-core trainee, what is the best way to lead, what should middle managers be trained in. Two theories of work motivation that focus on individual differences in needs are McClelland's theory of achievement motivation and Hackman and Oldham's job characteristics model.

Achievement Motivation.   One of the principal kinds of need identified in both need hierarchy and two-factor theories is the need to achieve. In our society it is common for people to report that they derive pleasure from the mere accomplishment of some task. Some individuals seem driven to exceed recognized standards in everything they do—not too surprising in view of the heavy emphasis our society places on competition and success. Others, perhaps because they have experienced more than their share of failure, express little interest in achievement. Casual observations such as these, together with a lot of systematic research, suggest that the need to achieve may be an extremely important factor in the kind of task a person will undertake, the kind of job that will be done once it has been undertaken, and the degree of satisfaction the person will experience once it is done.

Some theorists, notably David McClelland and his co-workers, have concentrated exclusively on the achievement motive (usually designated nAch), attempting to find ways to measure it, to discover how and why people differ in terms of it, and to see how it influences their behavior.[39] McClelland's approach to measurement makes heavy use of the Thematic Apperception Test (TAT), which we discussed earlier as one of Henry Murray's contributions to need research. Persons are assigned a high nAch score to the extent that the stories they make up from the pictures of the TAT tell of striving to achieve some standard of excellence. Having used the TAT with a large number of people in a variety of different studies, McClelland has been able to construct nAch norms against which to gauge the responses of the individual subject.

Not only do people vary in their need for achievement but, according to Atkinson's extension of need achievement theory, they also differ in their desire to avoid failure.[40] The amount of achievement-oriented activity a person shows in a particular situation depends on the extent to which need for achievement outweighs fear of failure. The person with high nAch and low fear of failure prefers moderately difficult tasks because they present realistic chances to succeed but are sufficiently challenging so that the person can be proud of success. The high-fear-of-failure person avoids tasks of moderate difficulty and prefers ones that are either very easy or almost impossible. A very easy task allows this type of individual to escape failure altogether, whereas a very difficult one provides a ready excuse for the inevitable failure; after all, the person might say, no one could have succeeded on a task *that difficult.*

Consequently, an organization can motivate people whose need for achievement outweighs their fear of failure by assigning them moderately difficult tasks.[41] These persons also prefer, and are motivated by, tasks that provide concrete feedback concerning the results of their performance, that allow control over what happens, that permit innovative and unique solutions, and that require the person to think ahead and plan. Moreover, McClelland has presented evidence that the economic growth of firms and even whole societies bears a rough correspondence to characteristic nAch levels.[42] The results of nearly 20 years of research have led McClelland to conclude that people do differ reliably in nAch but that these levels are subject to change through training.

Probably the most obvious practical implication of the theory would be that a match should be effected between people's nAch and their job requirements. Either (1) they should be assigned work in accordance with their nAch (e.g., high-nAch workers should be placed in what to them is a moderately demanding job) or (2) they should be trained to whatever nAch level is demanded by their job. Low-nAch individuals would either be kept in routine jobs and motivated by other means or they would be trained to change their level of need for achievement. Considering individuals' nAchs might prove more effective in dealing with the so-called disadvantaged individuals, for example, than merely assuming that once lower-order needs are gratified they will automatically seek more challenging work (Maslow) or that once their jobs are enriched they will bring enthusiasm to their work (Herzberg).

The implications of achievement motivation theory for organizational management are once again less straightforward than they seem. First, a substantial amount of the research evidence does not support the main contentions of the theory.[43] Second, measures based on the interpretation of TAT stories are often unreliable (for a discussion of reliability in measurement, see the chapter on selection).[44] Third, even its foremost advocates would not suggest that nAch is the only important factor in either individual or organizational success. Little attention has been given to the way nAch interacts with characteristics of work environments or with other needs to influence performance and satisfaction (to do so obviously requires a more comprehensive process theory, which we encounter in the next section). The ethical implications of branding people as having low nAch or trying to change so basic an aspect of their personality also have been raised by some critics. Perhaps the biggest problem with a nAch-matching strategy is that it requires a measurement of both nAch and *perceived* job difficulty for each individual. It is not enough to merely establish some *objective* scale of difficulty, for what the person believes—not reality—governs behavior.

Hackman and Oldham's Job Characteristics Model.

Similar to McClelland, Hackman and Oldham proposed that persons possess stable needs that determine how they react to job characteristics.[45] Drawing from Alderfer's work, they distinguish between employees who are high in growth need strength (i.e., value self-actualization and achievement) and those who are low in these needs. Employees who are high in growth need strength are predicted to respond with more motivation to five core job characteristics. These job characteristics are presented in Figure 3–3. *Skill variety* is the degree to which the job involves activities that require a wide range of abilities and skills. *Task identity* is the degree to which the job requires a whole and identifiable piece of work to be completed as opposed to an isolated operation. *Task significance* is the degree to which the job has substantial impact on the lives or work of other people. A heart surgeon probably experiences more of this than, say, a clerical worker in a paper clip factory. *Autonomy* is the degree to which one is allowed to perform a job in the way one wishes.

These core job characteristics affect three critical psychological states that, in turn, control the motivation and satisfaction of employees: (1) the experienced *meaningfulness* of the work, that is, the extent to which a person believes the job is important, valuable, and worthwhile; (2) the experience of having *responsibility*, that is, the extent to which the employee feels responsible for results of the work; and (3) the *knowledge of results*, that is, the extent to which the employee has knowledge of how well she or he is doing. According to the model, employees who experience these psychological states are more satisfied with their jobs and show more internal motivation (i.e., they work hard because they want to, not because they are forced to), lower rates of absenteeism and turnover, and high-quality work (but not necessarily high quantity). Hackman and Oldham further predict that persons with high growth needs will respond in these ways to the core job characteristics to a much greater extent than will a person who places less importance on growth needs.

While the idea of distinguishing the motivational components of jobs seems quite reasonable, the evidence so far has failed to support several key elements of Hackman and Oldham's model. For one thing, some have found that fewer than five dimensions are needed to distinguish the motivational components of jobs.[46] Also, the growth needs have not been found to moderate the effects of task characteristics in the manner proposed. In fact, the most consistent support for the model is the finding that employees are more satisfied to the extent that they perceive the five key job characteristics to be present, regardless of the strength of their growth needs.[47] Even these findings are somewhat suspect, however,

FIGURE 3–3   Hackman and Oldham's Job Characteristics Model

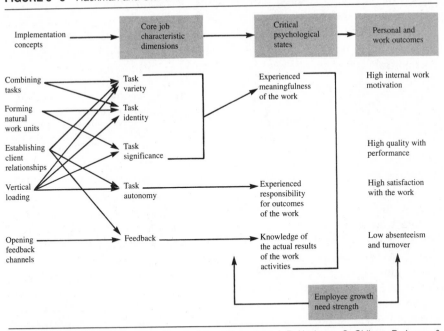

SOURCE: Adapted from "A new strategy for job enrichment" by J. R. Hackman, G. Oldham, R. Janson & K. Purdy. *California Management Review*, Summer 1975, 62. Copyright 1975 by the regents of the University of California. Reprinted from *California Management Review*, 27, no. 4, 62, by permission of the regents.

given that most researchers have measured the core job characteristics with employee self-reports rather than with more objective task measures. Because of the correlational nature of most of the past research, one cannot safely conclude that increases in the core characteristics *cause* increased satisfaction. It is just as likely that high satisfaction causes workers to describe their job core positively or that some third variable, such as successful performance, causes the person to report both high satisfaction and a high degree of the core characteristics.

Process Theories of Work Motivation

Whereas need theorists focused primarily on "what" motivates employees, process theorists are more concerned with "how" needs and wants are translated into action. The process theories that we will discuss are goal-setting theory, equity theory, expectancy-valence theory, and cognitive consistency theory.

Locke's Goal-Setting Theory

As we have shown, need theories of work motivation have not done well in predicting the behavior, performance, and attitudes of employees. Part of the reason may be that needs are too abstract to be useful. A person says that friends, marriage, social memberships, and receiving letters are all important, so the need theorist concludes that there is a social need underlying all these goals. The measured need is then used to predict all sorts of behavior. Unfortunately, as Hulin and Triandis recently concluded from a review of the need literature,

> Research suggests that more will be learned by asking why . . . decisions were made and what the goals were, than by invoking abstract motives or needs . . . the more abstract constructs are, and the further they are removed from the specific job outcomes verbalized by workers, the less their predictive power.[48]

Cherrington and England recently conducted a study that supports these observations. They found that simply asking workers how much they would like an enriched job allowed better prediction of their actual satisfaction with the job than did measures of needs or values.[49]

As the findings of Cherrington and England demonstrate, a preoccupation with finding needs and other predispositions buried in the psyche of the employee may lead researchers to overlook some obvious and faithful approaches to predicting work motivation. This brings us to Edwin Locke, who avoids abstract motives and needs and concentrates on conscious intentions. Locke's theory is presented in Figure 3–4 and in its essential form is quite simple: people behave, insofar as conditions permit, directly in accordance with their plans. External events, or existents, such as financial incentives or past performance, trigger a cognitive process in which individuals evaluate the event against their values.[50] Values are simply what the person wants or aspires to achieve. To the extent that external events fall short of their values, and to the extent that the values are important, they experience an emotional reaction in the form of dissatisfaction with the event. The consequence of this emotional reaction is a goal or intention for future action. The most direct determinant of behavior, according to Locke, is the person's conscious intention.

The ideal that we can predict to some extent what people will do on the basis of what they say they will do is so obvious that it has attracted little interest among industrial psychologists until recently. Some of the consequences of goal theory, however, are neither obvious nor trivial. Almost all of the research testing Locke's theory has focused on the relationship between goal and task performance. Numerous field and laboratory experiments have provided substantial support for two of Locke's predictions.[51] In a recent review of this research, Locke and his colleagues concluded that 99 of 110 experiments support the prediction that people perform better the harder the goal, as long as they accept the goal.[52] Another prediction that has been consistently supported is that specific goals produce higher levels of performance than no goals or admonitions to do your best.

FIGURE 3-4   Locke's Goal Model of Work Motivation

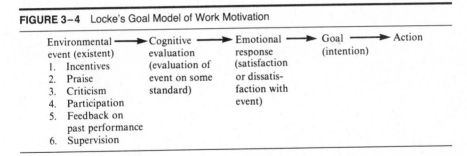

Environmental →	Cognitive →	Emotional →	Goal →	Action
event (existent)	evaluation	response	(intention)	
1. Incentives	(evaluation of	(satisfaction		
2. Praise	event on some	or dissatis-		
3. Criticism	standard)	faction with		
4. Participation		event)		
5. Feedback on				
past performance				
6. Supervision				

Other predictions of Locke have received less support. Perhaps the most interesting and the least obvious of Locke's predictions is that goals mediate the effects of money, feedback, and participation on performance. Locke argues that knowledge of results does not improve performance unless the knowledge leads the person to set higher performance goals. Similarly, monetary incentives and employee participation in decision making only improve performance if they encourage employees to accept and set more difficult task goals. Contrary to the theory, monetary incentives seem to induce higher performance independent of whether goal setting occurs or not.[53] Also, goal setting does not appear capable of increasing performance significantly unless there is also feedback of results. Intending to do well is not enough. One needs knowledge of results that will allow an assessment of progress toward achievement of goals.[54] There is insufficient evidence to strongly support or deny Locke's predictions regarding participation in decision making.[55] People who are assigned goals for their performance do appear to perform as well as people who set their own goals. In many of these studies, however, the subjects probably were anxious to cooperate with the experimenter and willing to accept whatever they were assigned to do. Whether or not participation facilitates the effects of goal setting when persons are not so cooperative remains an open question.

Although the amount of research supporting some of Locke's propositions is quite impressive, one wonders how many factors modify the importance of intentions. What, for example, about nAch? Supposedly high-need-for-achievement individuals prefer moderate goals. What about self-esteem? A person with low self-esteem might expect and even accept failure. Such people might be unlikely to set difficult goals for themselves and might even perform better with easy goals. Locke concludes that past research has not convincingly demonstrated the existence of any individual difference variable other than task ability. High-task-ability persons appear to increase their performance more in response to increases in goal difficulty than do low-task-ability persons.[56] Despite the lack of consistent findings, research on individual differences in the effects of goals appears to be a promising area for future research.

Another problem that remains largely unexplored is just what is responsible for the effects of goals on performance. Locke and his colleagues claim that

> Goals affect task performance by directing attention and action, mobilizing energy expenditure or effort, prolonging effort over time (persistence), and motivating the individual to develop relevant strategies for goal attainment.[57]

Only recently have attempts been made to assess some of these effects.

Perhaps the biggest deficiency in goal-setting research and theory at present is that they have not provided much insight into how goals are established in the first place. In this regard, the VIE theories that we will next discuss appear to complement our knowledge of the effects of goals.

Valence-Instrumentality-Expectancy (VIE) Theory

By far the most comprehensive cognitive process theories are based on behavioral decision theory and view individuals as attempting to maximize their own subjective expected utility.[58] Phrased in another way, these models view employees as deciding among alternative courses of action. They decide to do those things that they anticipate or expect will best further their interests. Work motivation is viewed as a decision to either exert a high amount of effort on the job or a low amount of effort. Employees are predicted to *choose* to exert a high amount of effort if they expect that high effort will benefit them more than will low effort. Expectations or perceptions of the likelihood of future events play an important part in these theories. Hence, these theories have been referred to collectively as *expectancy, valence-expectancy,* or *valence-instrumentality-expectancy (VIE)* theory. We will use the term *VIE theory.*

In the first major statement of the VIE theory of work motivation, Vroom proposed that the effort a person exhibits in the job is a function of three components: (1) *expectancy,* or how likely the employee perceives that effort will pay off in good performance, (2) *instrumentality,* or how likely the employee perceives that good performance will pay off in outcomes such as money, a sense of accomplishment, and so forth, and (3) *valence,* or how desirable or undesirable the employee anticipates each outcome will be. The valence component is not exactly the same as that of *value,* but it is close. A possible promotion, for example, might have a high positive valence for an individual, leading him or her to work hard in an effort to achieve it. Having received the promotion, however, the person might feel that its value was less than anticipated.

In predicting work behavior, then, Vroom and most other VIE theorists are concerned more with the person's anticipations of future events than with the actual experience of these events. Table 3–2 provides an example of the processes that Vroom proposed in his VIE theory. In the example, person A and person B are faced with a choice. Do they increase

TABLE 3–2   Illustration of Vroom's VIE Model

1. What is the valence (V) of meeting the production goal?

	Person A			Person B		
Alternative Outcomes	Valence of Outcome(v)	Instru-mentality(i)	v × i	Valence of Outcome (v)	Instru-mentality (i)	v × i
Monetary bonus	10 ×	.5	= 5	10 ×	.8	= 8
Supervisory praise	5 ×	.2	= 1	5 ×	.4	= 2
Feelings of pride	5 ×	.6	= 3	10 ×	.3	= 3
Peer recognition	4 ×	.5	= 2	10 ×	.5	= 5

Valence (V) of meeting production goal = Sum of products of v's and i's
Valence for A = 5 + 1 + 3 + 2 = 11
Valence for B = 8 + 2 + 3 + 5 = 18

2. What is the expectancy (E) of meeting production goal when person chooses each behavior option?

Behavioral Option	Expectancy of Meeting Goal?	
	Person A	Person B
Exert a lot more effort	.8	.6
Continue with same level of effort	.2	.7

3. What is the motivational force (F) to choose each behavioral option?

Behavioral Option	Person A E × V = F	Person B E × V = F
Exert a lot more effort	.8 × 11 = 8.8	.6 × 18 = 10.8
Continue with same level	.2 × 11 = 2.2	.7 × 18 = 12.6

4. Which behavioral option is each person likely to choose?

a. Person A will choose to exert a lot more effort (8.8>2.2).
b. Person B will choose to continue with the same level of effort (12.6>10.8).

the amount of effort they are investing in the task to achieve production goals, or do they continue with their current level of effort on the task? According to Vroom's theory, these persons will first make a calculation of just how attractive or positively valent meeting the production goal is to them. In answering this question, they will, in turn, ask two additional questions: (1) How likely is it that achieving the production goal will result in outcomes such as getting a bonus, feeling better about oneself, gaining a promotion, and receiving supervisor praise? and (2) How attractive or valent is each of these outcomes? The instrumentality and the valence for each outcome is multiplied, and these products are summed to compute the valence of achieving the production goal. In our example, person A appears to have a lower valence for achieving the production goal than person B because A anticipates that achieving the goal is less likely to yield attractive outcomes. Just because the valence of meeting the production goal is higher does not mean, however, that the person will increase effort on the task. Before making their choice, persons A and B also estimate the expectancy that achieving the production goal will result from each behavioral option. Person A, in our example, believes that the odds are about 8 in 10 that he will meet the production goal if he exerts a lot more effort but only about 2 in 10 if he doesn't invest more effort. In contrast, person B believes that the odds are slightly better if she doesn't invest more effort on the task. Now that we have calculated the valence of achieving the production goal and the expectancy of achieving it through each behavioral option, we can make predictions as to what the person will choose to do by multiplying the *valence* of the production goal by the *expectancy* that the behavioral option will result in achievement of the production goal. This product gives us the motivational tendency to choose each option, which we refer to as F. The option with the highest product or F is the one the person is predicted to choose. In our example, person A is more likely to choose the option of exerting more effort, whereas person B is more likely to continue with the same level of effort. Another prediction that could be made, which isn't strictly in accordance with Vroom's original model, is that person A is less motivated to choose either option than is person B. We will have more to say about the *within-subjects* and *between-subjects* use of the model.

VIE theory in one form or another has been the focal point for much—if not most—of the research on job motivation and satisfaction over the last two decades. Some studies have sought to determine which version is best; others have tried to verify or refute some of the major underlying assumptions. Results so far offer at least moderate support for some of the broader aspects of the theory.[59] Expectancies, valences, and instrumentalities have all been shown in one study or another to influence performance or satisfaction. Some evidence even suggests that the components interact more or less as they are supposed to in predicting performance and satisfaction.[60]

Unfortunately, the more specific aspects of the theory often run into trouble. It is becoming apparent that most people do not combine cognitive elements (expectancies, valences, etc.) in a multiplicative fashion. Also, their expectancies and valences often do not combine multiplicatively to influence performance. Doubts also exist as to whether people very often go through the elaborate and complex cognitive evaluations assumed to occur in the model.[61] Frequently, it is found that either valences or expectancies account for practically all the observed effects.[62]

The mixed results of past research may be, in part, the result of misapplication of the theory. The theory was originally presented to predict choices made by individual workers among discrete alternative courses of action, such as in our example in Table 3–2. An employee decides whether to "exert more effort" or "continue the same level of effort." To predict which action will be taken, one would measure expectancy of meeting performance standards by exerting more effort and expectancy of meeting these standards by continuing at the same level. These expectancies would then be multiplied by the valence of meeting performance standards. Which course of action the person chooses depends on which action is associated with the largest product of expectancy and valence. In contrast to this *within-person* use of the model, most research tests have used the model to predict differences *between people*. Each person is asked to judge the probability that working hard will lead to achieving job standards and the valence of meeting these standards. The persons for whom the product of expectancy and valence is higher are predicted to show more effort in their work than persons for whom the product is lower. In the example presented in Table 3–2, one might look only at expectancy and valence associated with exerting "a lot more effort" rather than approaching it as a choice between options. Taking this approach, the prediction is that person B will exert more effort in the job than will person A. As indicated earlier, this approach is not entirely consistent with the original version of VIE theory, which attempted to predict the individual choices made by a person between discrete options. Moreover, several studies have shown better prediction of behavior is obtained with the within-subject version than with the between-subjects version.[63]

Another common practice that appears to violate the original intent of VIE theory is to measure valences by presenting subjects with a list of standard outcomes (salary increases, sense of achievement, etc.) and having them rate the desirability of each. A criticism of this practice is that a standard list of outcomes does not tap the outcomes really important to individual workers, thereby violating another aspect of Vroom's original model. VIE theory has been shown to yield better predictions when each person generates their own outcomes rather than when a common list is used for everyone.[64] Other research suggests that using only desirable outcomes allows for better prediction than using both desirable and undesirable outcomes.[65]

Many industrial and organizational psychologists believe that VIE theory is the best available theory of work motivation and that once expectancy, valence, and instrumentality are properly measured, much better results will be obtained. Recent research showing significant improvements in prediction obtained through improved measurement and the within-subjects approach supports this view.

Cognitive Consistency Theory

VIE theory predicts that people making decisions are guided by the outcomes that they anticipate will result from these decisions. Humans are rational, according to this view, in that they seek to maximize their outcomes. But what happens once a decision is made? Some theorists predict that once persons are committed to a course of action, they often become more *rationalizing* than rational in their actions. Staw and his associates have conducted a series of studies showing that when persons suffer losses as the result of past decisions, their subsequent decisions are often guided by attempts to justify these past losses.[66] Thus, an executive who suffers large losses in profit as the result of bad investments might continue to pour money into these investments in the hope of rectifying the past losses.

Cognitive consistency theorists attribute such behavior to a need for cognitive consistency. That is, people prefer that their attitudes, beliefs, and perceptions about something be compatible with one another (in cognitive consonance) rather than contradictory. The latter condition, when it exists, sets up an aversive motivational state (called *cognitive dissonance*), which the individual strives to overcome either cognitively (by changing the situation responsible for the cognitions) or behaviorally. Consider this example. After long deliberation, you choose from among several jobs one that appears to have the greatest likelihood of yielding benefits in the form of such positively valent outcomes as challenge, compensation, and status. After a few months on the job, however, you find that it is not as challenging, profitable, or prestigious as you thought it would be. As a result, you experience dissonance, a motive state that prods you into doing something to restore order to your troubled cognitions. You might come to the conclusion that you were misled and that this poor decision is not your responsibility. Consequently, you might very well search for another job. What if you cannot easily deny responsibility or find another job? Under these circumstances, cognitive consistency theorists predict that you might attempt to justify your unfortunate choice of jobs by praising it and investing more time and energy in the performance of your duties.

Cognitive dissonance theory has stimulated a large amount of research, probably because so many of its predictions seem to conflict with common sense. One study actually found that persons who were induced to perform a boring, repetitive task for very little money rated the task as more interesting than those who were paid a large amount to perform the same task.[67] Supposedly, the low-paid persons were in a state of cognitive dissonance, and to resolve it they mentally enhanced the task. It is doubtful that these findings have many practical implications. We would not suggest that management can get workers to like and work hard on their dull, routine tasks by inducing them to work on these tasks for little pay! Even if this strategy worked (which seems doubtful), one would have to question seriously the ethics of such a scheme. Nevertheless, the findings highlight a phenomenon that managers should be aware of: People can find themselves—as a consequence of past commitments—acting in a rationalizing rather than rational manner.

More recent versions of consistency theory place more importance on the *self-esteem* and *self-concept* of the person. According to this approach, if the aversive effects of dissonance occur, they do not result from incongruence between just any two cognitions. Rather, a person is most likely to suffer from incongruity between a cognition involving the self and some other cognition. If a person experiences dissonance as the result of performing a dull task for little money, for example, it is because performing the task is inconsistent with the person's self-perception as an intelligent, rational human being who doesn't do dumb things such as that. Of course, if the person's self-perception was of a dumb individual to begin with, performing a dull task for little money might arouse no dissonance at all.

Along these lines, Korman posed a *self-consistency* theory of work motivation in which he proposed that people are motivated to maintain consistency with their self-evaluations.[68] For high-self-esteem persons, it is consistent to succeed and inconsistent to fail. Low-self-esteem persons, however, perceive themselves as incompetent and tend to reject success and accept failure. The most radical version of self-consistency theory would predict that low-self-esteem persons actually prefer to fail and are dissatisfied when they succeed. Korman's theory has been supported insofar as high-self-esteem persons tend to perform at higher levels than do low-self-esteem persons. As one might suspect, however, there is very little evidence for the radical self-consistency prediction that low-self-esteem persons actually try to fail.[69] Additionally, there are many explanations for why low- and high-self-esteem persons might differ in behavior besides the motive to maintain self-consistency. For instance, low-self-esteem persons might tend to do more poorly because they have less ability to perform the task. Another possibility is that low-self-esteem persons do not try hard so that they can later blame their failures on their lack of effort. Rather than representing an attempt to be consistent, their behavior may be an attempt to protect against further loss of self-esteem.

One serious problem still plagues consistency theory generally. It is hard to make specific predictions outside the pristine environment of the laboratory, when there are so many ways for the individual to resolve cognitive inconsistencies. Just because no change in a worker's output or attitude is observed after a state of dissonance is induced, for example, doesn't mean that there has been no dissonance or that the worker hasn't taken steps to resolve it. Perceptions of the situation simply may have been altered to reduce the dissonance. By the same token, it is almost impossible to disprove dissonance theory. If we fail to get an expected result, we can always claim there has been a change in some inaccessible cognitive process.

This is not the only criticism, incidentally, leveled against dissonance theory. Some argue that it is not necessary to postulate an aversive condition at all. In fact, an alternative approach, which relies more heavily on perceptual inference processes and less on motivational ones—social information theory—has become the more popular way of explaining dissonance phenomena.[70] In essence, it holds that people form attitudes on the basis of inferences that they draw from observation of behavior (including their own) and the external stimulus conditions under which it occurs. They attribute to themselves or others attitudes consistent with their inferences.

Equity Theory

Equity theorists try to account for differences in work behavior on the basis of the individual's perception of fair or equitable treatment. What, they ask, are the cognitive processes involved in one's conception of fairness? How does one deal cognitively and behaviorally with situations that one judges to be inequitable?

J. S. Adams, in his theory of equity, made use of these notions in several ways.[71] Perceived equity is viewed as a cognitive state in which the ratio of a person's work investment (inputs) to return on that investment (outcomes) is consonant with some norm (a hypothetical or real other person). Fairness is defined by other's input-outcome ratio. In lay terms, people compare what they are getting for their effort against what they think some reference person is getting for his or her effort. To the extent that people see their input-outcome ratio deviating from other's, a state of inequity is set up. Deviation could be in either direction; that is, people could see themselves as being *over- or undercompensated*. In either case, the resulting motive state would prompt them to act in a way designed to restore equity (i.e., fair treatment as they see it). They may decide to work less, complain more, or ask for a raise; or they may decide that they are not really as valuable to the company as they originally thought.

As an aside, it should be recognized that consonance does not require a match between the employees' perceptions of their own and other's inputs and outcomes. They might readily admit, for example, that they receive more total compensation than other—but if so, they will also feel that they deserve it for working harder. It is the *ratio*, not the absolute amounts, that defines equity. The formulas for defining the states of equity and inequity are presented below:

$$\text{State of equity:} \quad \frac{Op}{Ip} = \frac{Oo}{Io}$$

$$\text{States of inequity:} \quad \frac{Op}{Ip} < \frac{Oo}{Io}$$

$$\frac{Op}{Ip} > \frac{Oo}{Io}$$

where p is the person, and o the other or others against whom they compare the ratio of their Inputs (I) and Outcomes (O).

It should also be pointed out that what constitutes relevant inputs and outcomes vary a great deal from individual to individual. It is not just a matter of perceived effort and material compensation. An employee could consider willingness to be transferred to an undesirable location, tolerance of poor working conditions, or positive influence on other workers as part of input. The employee may regard personal freedom, desirable working conditions, a good boss, or any number of other things among outcomes. Inputs and outcomes are thus like needs—highly personal factors.

Given an inequitable situation, what will the employee do about it? Adams proposed six alternative modes of resolving inequity. When faced with inequity, the person might

1. Act to alter his or her own inputs.
2. Act to alter his or her own outcomes.
3. Cognitively distort his or her own inputs and outcomes.
4. Act on the other to change his or her inputs and outcomes.
5. Physically leave the situation.
6. Cease comparing inputs and outcomes with the other and shift to another reference.

Oddly enough, equity theorists have focused almost exclusively on alternatives 1 and 2 and monetary outcomes. Equity theory predicts that the reactions of employees to inequity will depend on not only whether they are undercompensated or overcompensated but also on whether they are paid on an hourly or piece rate basis.[72] A laboratory subject paid on an hourly basis cannot directly manipulate the monetary outcomes but can change the inputs in the form of quantity and quality of performance. An overcompensated subject is predicted to restore equity by producing higher quality and/or quantity. An undercompensated subject is predicted to restore equity by producing lower quality and/or quantity. A subject paid on a piece rate, however, can manipulate both the inputs and outcomes by means of the quantity and quality of performance. In this situation, overpaid subjects are predicted to lower their quantity of performance and increase their quality of performance, whereas underpaid subjects are predicted to increase their quantity of performance and lower the quality.

Most of the research testing equity theory has been of the laboratory variety, and the findings have generally supported equity theory predictions.[73] It should come as no surprise that the underpayment predictions have been more strongly supported than the overpayment predictions. A weakness in equity theory research has been the preoccupation with changes in the quantity or quality of performance, as we have noted, and the neglect of other common ways of resolving inequity, such as quitting and seeking a more equitable position.

The fact that behavior often changes in the direction predicted by equity theory when people are undercompensated is encouraging; that it fails to change consistently in response to overcompensation neither confirms nor refutes the theory. Equity theory is not yet explicit enough to let us predict how individuals will resolve what they perceive as inequitable situations, although efforts in this direction are being made. Goodman and Friedman, for example, found that how people deal with overcompensation inequity depends on their perception of how their performance relates to outcomes: If they think that by producing more they will get paid more (thereby increasing inequity), they will shift their emphasis to quality; if they think that quality determines their pay, they will opt for quantity.[74]

Other recent research has focused on the individual differences in how people react to conditions of inequity. One such study was reported by Vecchio.[75] He found that persons at a higher stage of moral development were more likely to react to overcompensation inequity by reducing their own outcomes. These findings suggest that, contrary to equity theory, a J. R. Ewing or an Ebeneezer Scrooge type is not likely to suffer much discomfort if he feels overcompensated. Other research has focused more on perceptions of the procedures by which outcomes are distributed rather than on equity of the outcome distribution itself. These studies of *procedural justice* suggest that employees may not be so concerned with inequity of their outcomes if they perceive that the procedures followed by management in allocating the outcomes were fair.[76]

Deci's Cognitive Evaluation Theory

Several of the theorists we have discussed distinguished between intrinsic and extrinsic motivation, but few have offered much insight into the processes that account for these motivational states. Deci's *cognitive evaluation theory* attempts to provide a better explanation than provided in past theories for the conditions that lead to intrinsically motivated behavior.[77] Deci begins by assuming that all people need to feel that they are *competent* and *control* important events in their lives. He goes on to hypothesize that persons can be intrinsically motivated to perform a task when it contributes to the fulfillment of either of these two needs. Conversely, he hypothesizes that extrinsic rewards reduce intrinsic motivation by leading the person to believe that he or she is not in control or lacks the competence to perform the task. According to Deci, workers on a piece rate incentive system, in which they receive money for each individual unit of production, may come to think of themselves more as trained seals performing for a fish than as intelligent, self-determining human beings. As a consequence of these cognitive evaluations of the self, they may cope by only working hard on the task when there are monetary incentives for their efforts.

To test this hypothesis, Deci conducted a laboratory experiment in which college students were given puzzles that were sufficiently interesting and challenging so that students worked long and hard to solve them without monetary incentives.[78] Rewarding the students with money for the completion of the puzzles was predicted to reduce their intrinsic motivation. The predictions were supported insofar as students who were paid for solving the puzzles spent less time working on them during the rest breaks than did unpaid, control subjects.

As might be expected, Deci's research and theory have not gone unchallenged.[79] Despite criticisms that other things in his research can account for his findings, the main results have been replicated in experiments even after these artifacts, as these "other things" are called, have been controlled or eliminated.[80] Serious doubts still can be raised, however, as to the relevance of such findings for actual work settings. Deci's work deals with how extrinsic incentives can lessen the motivation of those who are already motivated intrinsically, not with the more pressing issue of how to develop intrinsic motivation in the first place. Furthermore, his findings seem to apply only to situations in which people don't expect to be paid, such as psychology experiments, not to situations in which they expect to be paid as a normal return on their personal investment, such as the typical job.[81]

We should also note that the whole attempt to distinguish between intrinsic and extrinsic motivation has been questioned as a fruitless venture. According to some critics, all work motivation originates from external inducement. There are some compelling arguments for this position. Viewed historically, there is little reason to believe that people have some inborn desire to work.[82] Rather, the modern work ethic appears to have arisen as the result of cultural pressures, notably Calvinistic doctrine (the Protestant ethic that work pleases God) and social Darwinism (work has survival value). Modern society has traditionally regarded highly those individuals who succeed through hard work and condemned just as vigorously those who fail for lack of effort. An elaborate system of social rewards and punishments has evolved to ensure that these attitudes are instilled in children at an early age and retained throughout their lives.

We can assume, then, that for most people work is a means to an end rather than an end in itself. In fact, it may be a means to a lot of ends, some obvious and others quite obscure. Consider, for example, the feeling that we often refer to as *sense of accomplishment*. Isn't this very close to the idea of a basic desire to work? Probably not. In all likelihood, this feeling is the product of countless occasions in which a job well done produced favorable consequences (especially social approval) and a job poorly done produced the opposite or nothing at all. Gradually, the feelings associated with good or bad consequences become attached to the work itself and no longer require frequent external support. We recognize what kind of job we have done and reward (or punish) ourselves accordingly. Thus, an employee who appears to be working hard for the job may simply be working for rewards that are not obvious to the observer.

INTEGRATIVE MOTIVATIONAL MODELS

We chose to review 10 of the major models of work motivation, but there are even more theoretical positions we could have presented. Given this often bewildering collection of views, it is logical to ask if there is any hope of unifying what appears to be a hopelessly splintered field.

One approach might be to conduct critical experiments in which competing predictions of two or more theories are tested. Several experiments have pitted the prediction of VIE theory that higher expectancies will lead to increased performance against what appears to be the conflicting prediction of Locke's goal-setting theory that more difficult goals will lead to better performance. Other experiments have pitted the equity theory overcompensation prediction that under piece rate incentive systems people will reduce their outcomes against the VIE theory prediction that under the same conditions people will attempt to increase their outcomes. Although a single critical test is not likely to lead to a declaration of victory for one theory or the other, many experiments such as this are likely to clarify the conditions under which each theory is most predictive. Pitting one theory against another also may lead to new theories that integrate opposing views into a single framework.

Despite a lack of research to really support such attempts, a few attempts already have been made to integrate several of the motivational models within the same framework. Perhaps the most representative is Lawler and Suttle's motivation model, which uses VIE theory as the basic integrative scheme and is illustrated in Figure 3–5.[83] As can be seen from the figure, there is much more to the model than the three fundamental terms, $E{\to}P$, $P{\to}O$, and V. The other boxes contain either factors that are presumed to influence these fundamental processes (e.g., self-esteem) or presumed consequences of the fundamental processes (e.g., effort). Lines and arrows, of course, denote the path of influence.

Effort results from expectancy that effort will lead to effective performance $(E{\to}P)$; the instrumentality of effective performance for second-level outcomes such as money, supervisor praise, and so forth $(P{\to}O)$; and the valence of second-level outcomes (V) in the same manner as predicted by Vroom. The resulting level of effort determines to an extent the actual level of performance; however, performance also depends on the person's ability and the strategy chosen for carrying out the job (problem-solving approach). Ability, effort, and strategy are also seen to combine in a multiplicative fashion to effect performance. Finally, performance may produce reward. The extent to which it does, and to which individuals are able to see this relationship, depends in large measure upon organizational policy and management effectiveness. This one wavy line, therefore, summarizes many of the management issues discussed in the next two chapters (e.g., How should rewards be tied to performance? What are appropriate rewards? How is communication maximized?).

FIGURE 3-5   An Integrative Model of Work Motivation

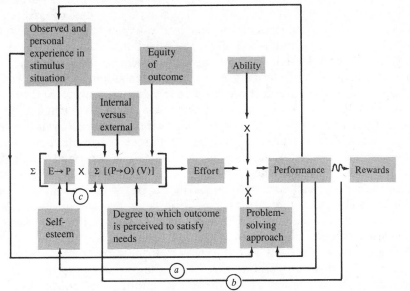

SOURCE: From Lawler, E. E., III, & Suttle, J. L. (1973). Expectancy theory and job behavior. *Organizational behavior and human performance* (p. 483). New York: Academic Press.

Our discussion to this point has focused on the central cognition Action→Reward sequence. Equally important are the factors seen to control the cognitions. By and large they are a mixture of actual experience effects (feedback from what happened in the past) and relatively stable personality characteristics. Thus, we have $E{\to}P$ expectancy dependent upon whether effort really has led to good performance in the past, colored by the person's feeling of personal adequacy (self-esteem). Likewise, $P{\to}O$ instrumentality reflects both experience with the performance-reward contingency and general belief that events in life are under personal control (internal versus external control). Valence of an outcome depends both upon how much a person thinks it will satisfy personal needs and how equitable it appears.

One final point is that feedback from either performance or the performance-reward contingency can operate on cognitive processes directly (as in loop b), indirectly (as in loop a), or both. For example, knowing how performance actually turned out affects expectancy directly (through experience) and indirectly by its influence on self-esteem (success ought to raise one's opinion of oneself).

Because the diagram in Figure 3-5 was drawn originally to illustrate the motivational aspects of VIE theory, it does not include an explicit representation of satisfaction. Elsewhere, proponents of the same theory show satisfaction flowing directly from the rewards term but influenced somewhat by equity of rewards. It is clear from Figure 3–5 that the theorists recognize the importance of both need fulfillment and equity. However, it is their contention that if an organization is run properly, satisfaction will result from good performance because both intrinsic and extrinsic rewards will be made to depend on good performance (Performance→Rewards→Satisfaction). In a poorly run organization, this relationship will not hold because the performance-rewards contingency is either absent or obscure. In short, VIE theorists see the relationship between satisfaction and performance as an index of organizational effectiveness, not, as so many human relationists believe, as a matter of satisfaction causing performance. The fact that studies have so often shown performance and satisfaction to be totally unrelated just means there are a lot of poorly run organizations. The failure of efforts to raise production by increasing satisfaction only means that management has tended to place the cart before the horse.

One of the strengths of VIE theory is that, in putting forth a comprehensive (if highly speculative) account of the cognitive processes, it affords us a useful framework (1) on which to hang everything we know about job satisfaction and performance and (2) within which to organize our empirical attack on what we don't know. By now the reader has probably observed that VIE theory is sufficiently comprehensive to accommodate virtually all the other content and process theories we have encountered thus far. It is strictly incompatible with almost none. Need satisfaction and equity theories help define valence; two-factor theory, Deci's cognitive evaluation theory, and job characteristics theory refine the reward concept through the intrinsic-extrinsic distinction; self-esteem operates on $E→P$ contingency feedback to influence expectancy.

Although Lawler and Suttle have not included goal setting within their model, others have attempted to integrate goal setting and VIE theory. Menlo, Cartledge, and Locke provide some evidence to support the notion of a two-phase process.[84] In the first phase, people choose among different task goals or, if assigned a particular goal, accept or reject the goal. Their choice is determined as VIE theory would predict, that is, by their expectancies that they can achieve each goal and the valence of goal achievement. Once a goal is set and/or accepted, goal difficulty becomes the primary determinant of performance. According to Locke, subsequent performance varies directly with the difficulty of the goal, just as goal-setting theory would predict.

Future research will undoubtedly lead to revisions in these models. In some cases, these models are so complex that they may be quite difficult to test.[85] Nevertheless, the move toward integrative approaches seems to be a step in the right direction.

APPLICATIONS

We have already discussed several of the practical implications of the various theories of work motivation. In a few cases, specific applications have followed directly from a specific theory. In most cases, practitioners have developed programs for motivating employees independently of theory or have used theory after the fact to justify the program. For each of the applications we will discuss, more than one of the theories can be used in a post hoc fashion to explain why it works or fails to work.

Management by Objectives

One implication of goal-setting theory is that managers could do a better job of planning if they knew the specific intentions of their subordinates. In fact, both might profit from an exercise designed to make the goals of each more explicit. Goal-setting theory says that actions are governed by intentions; it does not say that intentions cannot be changed or defined more clearly. The reader may recognize in this suggestion one of the major components of management by objectives (MBO), an approach to management currently enjoying widespread popularity. Although MBO and goal-setting theory developed independently, they share an emphasis on the motivational potential of goal setting. The MBO approach stresses mutual goal setting by manager and subordinate, clarity and specificity in the statement of goals, and frequent feedback concerning progress toward goals. Wherever possible, goals should be couched in terms of specific measurable outcomes (such as units produced, policies sold, product quality, accident reduction, and even worker and management satisfaction). They should be realistic and attainable.

To illustrate, a sales manager might sit down with each employee every six months and develop sales objectives for the next period. These might include the number of prospective clients to be called upon, the number of follow-ups to be made, the number of units of each item to be sold, total profit, total commission, and so on. During the period, the sales manager might monitor with them their progress toward their respective goals and perhaps consider modifications in light of unforeseen developments. At the close of the period they would review their accomplishments on each goal, and set new goals for the next period.

Clearly, goal specification is only part of what is supposed to make MBO work. Also involved are the presumed benefits of participative management (especially one's commitment to goals that one helps set), the reward value of goal achievement, the value of specific feedback for guiding future behavior, and others. Its many advocates claim that MBO has had an unparalleled record of success in application. If we subscribe to this evaluation, we must do so largely on the strength of testimonials. Scientific studies comparing MBO with other approaches using adequate controls are—to the authors' knowledge—nonexistent. Moreover, if MBO does live up to its rave notices, we have no idea what aspect(s) of it is (are) responsible. From the standpoint of humanistic theories in general, MBO is analogous to the flag, motherhood, and apple pie. Anything having so many admirable qualities simply must be good. This is not to suggest that MBO is a poor approach. The point is that MBO is a composite of many theoretical notions, each of which is supported by some scientific evidence and refuted by some. The composite has not been tested scientifically and would, in fact, be very difficult to test. Therefore, the decision to adopt or not to adopt the approach must be made on other grounds (logical, practical, intuitive, testimonial). If adopted, however, the organization should conduct its own evaluative studies to determine how effective the approach is for achieving its goals.

Job Enrichment

Another application, job enrichment, has received increased attention largely due to national surveys of job satisfaction showing that American workers are becoming increasingly unhappy with their work. One of the more controversial of these reports, published by the U.S. Department of Health, Education, and Welfare during the early 1970s, suggested that there was deep-seated discontent among American workers and that this discontent was the cause of declining productivity, increasing absenteeism, and a variety of other ills plaguing American inudstry.[86] Many organizational theorists, particularly those with humanistic inclinations, endorse the idea that workers today are alienated from their work. To support this, these theorists point to a number of changes in people and jobs that they claim are responsible for the mounting discontent. One trend, as the argument goes, has been for work to become increasingly specialized and narrow. At the same time, workers are becoming increasingly better educated and expect interesting and challenging work. The consequence of this trend is that many college-trained people now occupy jobs that underutilize their abilities and skills.

Job enrichment has been proposed as one solution to this national crisis. One of the leading proponents, Herzberg, went so far as to say that the *only* way to motivate employees is to enrich their jobs. Exactly how this should be done is not as obvious as it seems. Herzberg prefers the term *enrichment* to *job enlargement* because he feels that the two imply different means to the desired end.[87] The latter involves what he calls horizontal loading—the simple expedient of making jobs bigger by adding one dumb operation to another. The former involves *vertical loading*—a qualitative upgrading of the work. He sees horizontal loading as a serious mistake that has resulted in frequent failures. The proper approach, according to Herzberg, is to develop a specific enrichment solution for each job on the basis of careful study of that job. It may turn out that further enrichment is either impossible or unnecessary. Unlike Herzberg, most theorists seem to use the term *enlargement* generically, defining it in terms of complexity, responsibility, authority, variety, and all the other things that usually distinguish bigger from smaller jobs.

Hackman and Oldham's job characteristics model appears to provide a more useful framework for job enrichment.[88] As indicated in Figure 3–3, the core job characteristics can be manipulated via five implementation concepts. By combining different task elements previously performed by different individuals into a meaningful whole, both variety and identity can be increased. For instance, the Swedish automobile manufacturer, Volvo, has experimented with having teams of workers assemble whole components of an automobile (e.g., the engine) as an alternative to the traditional assembly line in which each individual worker is responsible for one component (e.g., the carburetor). Another implementation principle is forming natural work units. For instance, instead of randomly assigning work to secretaries in a typing pool as it occurs, give each secretary or a group of secretaries the responsibility for a particular department or group of departments. A third related principle is establishing personal and individual relationships with clients. The fourth is vertical loading in which "responsibilities and controls that formerly were reserved for management are given to the employee as part of the job" (p. 503).[89] Finally, feedback channels can be opened either through providing more frequent and immediate supervisory feedback or by establishing direct feedback from the task itself.

Job enrichment has produced mixed results, although most theorists seem to think there are at least some circumstances under which it may prove beneficial. The biggest problem is that "the case for job enlargement has been drastically overstated and overgeneralized."[90] It is definitely not the panacea for all motivational ills that some have suggested. Sometimes simply changing the job has had as great an impact as enriching it.[91] Sometimes the enriched job has exceeded the worker's capacity, producing a state known as *role overload*.[92] Undesirable consequences attributed to this state include increased tension, reduced self- esteem, reduced quality of output, and possibly even increased incidence of heart trouble. Umstot, Bell, and Mitchell found that enriched jobs led to more satisfied workers but had no effect on quantity of performance.[93] Locke, Sirota, and Wolfson found that workers in a federal agency showed large gains in productivity as the result of job enrichment, but these increases seemed to be due more to efficient work methods that accompanied the job enrichment than to increased job motivation.[94] An unexpected outcome in this study was lower job satisfaction. Workers felt that they should receive more money for their heavier workloads. Consistent with this finding, Simonds and Orife found that of 71 voluntary, intraplant job transfers, increased satisfaction resulted from moving to a more enriched job only when greater pay accompanied the move.[95]

On the basis of the available evidence, then, we are forced to conclude that, like any powerful medicine, job enrichment should be used with care. It should be undertaken only after a thorough study of the job as it presently exists, the context under which it is carried out, and the people who are likely to fill it. If implemented, its effect on satisfaction and performance should be monitored for at least several years. One should never make the mistake of assuming that job enrichment will produce greater motivation and satisfaction simply because some experts say it should, or that it represents a cheap alternative to salary increments and work force additions.

It also appears that much of the alarm raised over the increasing dissatisfaction of American workers with their jobs is somewhat overdramatized. The consistent finding in national opinion polls is that less than 15 percent of respondents indicate that they are dissatisfied with their jobs.[96] Although there was a small decline in job satisfaction during the 1970s, as measured by these polls, Organ found that this change closely paralleled the influx of younger workers into the work force.[97] Because younger workers tend to be less satisfied than older workers in any era, the entry of the baby-boom generation into the work force can easily account for the slight increase in the number of dissatisfied workers over the last decade. As the work force ages in the coming decades, we will probably observe a commensurate rise in job satisfaction. Of course, more actual dissatisfaction could be present than is revealed by available survey techniques, but we have no way of knowing that. It would appear, then, that the vast disillusionment of the American work force that makes for such good copy in magazines and newspapers is a picture that does not square with the available facts.

Behavioral Modification

Although there have been several different theories of work motivation, all share the basic notion that the cognitions and feelings of the person determine his or her behavior. Of course, these internal motivational states cannot be directly observed. They can only be inferred from the behavior of a person. The most extreme behaviorists argue that mental events like motives, thoughts, and feelings are not even suitable for scientific investigation because they are not open to public investigation. According to this position, psychologists must limit their attention to *behavior*, which is observable, and their explanation of that behavior to equally public environmental conditions. Given these limitations, behaviorists have tended to concentrate on how behavior is modified as a result of environmental manipulations. The practical application of this approach to organizations is called behavior modification (BMod).

The basic principle underlying behavior modification is that management can induce its employees to behave in ways they wish them to behave by manipulating reward structures. In Chapter 8, we will discuss in more detail the rules of instrumental conditioning, which have been derived from laboratory research with animals and applied to the workplace. There have been variations in the behavior modification programs implemented in industry.[98] The Emery Air Freight Corporation program provides a good example of behavior modification as it is typically implemented in industry.[99] There were four stages involved in the program. First, a *performance audit* was performed to determine the specific areas in which improvements in performance were needed for employees in a job. Next, supervisors set *specific goals* for improving the performance of each employee. Third, employees kept records of their own work and charted their own progress in meeting their goals. Finally, supervisors *positively reinforced* employees by praising them verbally when they met performance goals and by witholding praise (but without criticism) when they performed below standard. One focus of the program was on getting employees to use containers efficiently in packaging items for shipment. The proper way of packaging items was specified, goals were stated for improved packaging, and progress was charted. Additionally, supervisors praised workers whenever they did the job in the right way. According to Emery, the program resulted in $600,000 gross savings in 1970 and over $2 million in savings in 1975. Verbal praise is not the only reinforcer used in behavior modification. In some industrial programs, feedback on how well the person is doing is used as the reinforcer, whereas others have used money, vacation trips, time off, and even Green Stamps as reinforcement. The key principle is that reinforcers of value to the employees should be chosen.

There seems to be little doubt that behavior modification has generated a useful technology for changing behavior.[100] We must distinguish, however, between the applications associated with a theory and the explanations provided by the theory for worker behavior. The success of a behavior modification program does not prove the superiority of a radical behavioral approach over motivational theory. Indeed, from a successful program such as the one at Emery, one could just as readily claim support for Locke's goal-setting theory, Vroom's VIE theory, or Hackman and Oldham's job characteristics model. Also, a lot of things occur in behavior modification programs in addition to the reinforcement and shaping of behavior.[101] One story that has been told is of a trucking firm that attempted to reduce absenteeism among its truck drivers by setting up a system of rewards for attendance. If a truck driver showed up for work a specified number of days in a row, his or her name was placed in a lottery. The winner of the lottery won a large number of Green Stamps. Absenteeism dropped markedly as the result of the program. A careful examination of the program, however, revealed more explanations than positive reinforcement of the driver. For one thing, many of the spouses of the drivers wanted the Green Stamps and, in the hope of winning the lottery, prodded them into showing up for work each morning. The point of this illustration is that there are multiple determinants of the success of almost all behavior modification programs, and it is usually impossible to trace a program's success or failure to one and only one specific cause. Of course, from management's perspective, the important things are not why it works but whether it works and whether the benefits it yields outweigh the costs incurred. From this perspective, behavioral modification techniques have a lot to offer.

Pay as a Motivator

The most obvious means of motivating employees to perform more effectively is to provide financial rewards for their effective performance. Almost everyone gets paid for what they do in their job, and it seems logical then that financial incentives may provide a readily available, and even cheaper, means of motivating employees than such costly means as job enrichment. Most large organizations, in fact, have merit pay systems, particularly for managerial employees. It may seem strange, then, that such a widely used approach has been the object of such controversy. As we have shown, motivational theorists, most notably Herzberg, claim that financial incentives cannot motivate employees to higher levels of performance. Deci has even argued that paying persons contingent upon their performance "demotivates" them. Many need theorists have suggested that money has the potential of being a motivator for persons whose lower-order needs are most important, but for persons whose higher-order, growth needs are most important, money is not an effective motivator.

VIE theorists, on the other hand, have argued that monetary rewards can be quite effective if they are administered so that employees clearly see the relationship between performance and the reward. Both the successes and failures of monetary incentives can be accounted for in terms of the model in Figure 3–5. There is considerable evidence, albeit of variable scientific quality, that incentive plans in which pay is based on performance usually do result in higher production than straight payment systems.[102] When an incentive system fails, VIE theory provides us with two critical questions we can use to diagnose the sources of the failure: (1) Do employees expect that performing well is, in fact, related to the pay they receive $(P \rightarrow O)$? (2) Do employees have a high positive valence for the pay they receive $[V(O)]$?

For expectancies to be of sufficient magnitude to ensure that employees will exert high levels of effort on their jobs, the organization must provide feedback. It is not enough that good performance yields just rewards; the worker must be made aware and kept aware of this fact through frequent, explicit, and unambiguous feedback. Only to the extent that workers seek clear evidence that good performance pays off in raises and promotions, both for themselves and those around them, and to the extent that workers are kept abreast of how their performance stacks up relative to others will their cognitions have a chance to mirror reality. And we must always remember that their cognitions (what they think), not reality (what actually is), determine what they will do. All the effort to devise fair performance-reward contingencies is thus totally wasted because of insufficient feedback.

For pay to have high valence it must be instrumental for achieving other valued outcomes. Lawler points out that pay can be instrumental in the satisfaction of virtually all the basic needs identified by content theorists.[103] According to his model, the importance of pay to the individual depends on the importance of each of the basic needs found in Maslow's hierarchy, weighted by the instrumentality of pay in satisfying that need, summed over all the needs. Thus, an incentive plan might fail because people fail to see how pay is related to satisfaction of their foremost needs (ignorance of instrumentality) or it might fail because they see as most pressing those needs for which money is not the best route to satisfaction (need preference). There is probably little that the organization can do or should do to change the needs of workers. There is a great deal, however, that the organization can do to ensure that pay is seen as equitable, which is another determinant of valence according to at least one version of VIE theory. Above all, the organization should provide what is, in fact, fair and equitable compensation. Again, however, it is the employee's perception, not reality, that counts. Because people tend to overestimate what others earn when pay is secret, as it typically is, there is also some merit in disclosing salaries, unless the organization has a lot to be secret about.[104] Employees also may feel inequity and devalue the pay they receive if they see their performance as being evaluated unfairly. Evaluation in most jobs is a matter of someone's (usually the supervisor's) opinion. Even where objective output measures are available they are not necessarily fair, as we shall see in Chapter 5. For an incentive system to succeed, it should be based on measures of performance that are not only objectively valid but are seen by employees as valid.

In Table 3–3, Lawler has evaluated 17 pay incentive plans on the basis of his experience and a review of the research evaluating each plan.[105] As seen in the table, the best plans on some dimensions are sometimes the worst on other dimensions. Individual bonuses are the best in creating the perception that pay is tied to performance (i.e., the instrumentality of high performance for pay or $P{\rightarrow}O$). However, individual bonuses are among the worst in the negative side effects they can engender, such as "social ostracism of good performance, defensive behavior, and giving false data about performance," in their potential to encourage cooperation among employees, and in their acceptability to employees. Evidence of the low acceptability of many individual bonus plans can be found in the reaction of many public school teachers to the merit pay

TABLE 3–3   Ratings of Various Pay Incentive Plans*

		Tie Pay to Performance	Negative Side	Encourage Cooperation	Employee Acceptance
Salary Reward					
Individual plan	Productivity	4	1	1	4
	Cost effectiveness	3	1	1	4
	Superiors' ratings	3	1	1	3
Group plan	Productivity	3	1	2	4
	Cost effectiveness	3	1	2	4
	Superiors' ratings	2	1	2	3
Organizational plan	Productivity	2	1	3	4
	Cost effectiveness	2	1	2	4
Bonus Reward					
Individual plan	Productivity	5	3	1	2
	Cost effectiveness	4	2	1	2
	Superiors' ratings	4	2	1	2
Group plan	Productivity	4	1	3	3
	Cost effectiveness	3	1	3	3
	Superiors' ratings	3	1	3	3
Organizational plan	Productivity	3	1	3	4
	Cost effectiveness	3	1	3	4
	Profit	2			

*On a scale of 1 to 5, 1 = low and 5 = high.
SOURCE: Lawler, E. E., III (1982). *The strategic design of reward systems.* Publication of Center for Effective Organizations, University of Southern California.

plans proposed in several states. The typical complaint is that these plans are based on arbitrary and subjective evaluations. Moreover, in rewarding only the few teaching stars, the system may be demotivating for the large number of teachers whose performance falls short of "star quality" but who are nonetheless competent and deserving of rewards. Considering all the alternatives presented in Table 3–3, the best plans according to Lawler are based on objective measures of performance and give at least some attention to group performance.

CONCLUSIONS

People work for a number of reasons (to acquire, to achieve, to create, to earn respect, to socialize, to dominate) and not, it seems, because they possess a built-in need to work. Cultural factors and learning experiences have a lot to do with why the particular *individual* works. Thus, people may differ greatly in what—if anything—about the work situation they consider important.

Our interest in why people work stems largely from the belief that we can discover what motivates them to work *well* and what makes them *satisfied* with their work. One would expect a person to work harder and be happier about it to the extent that the work situation provided more, rather than less, of whatever it was for which he or she was working.

Some theorists internalize the above argument by seeking to translate work objects into human needs and job satisfaction into need fulfillment. Because many work objects (e.g., money) satisfy needs (e.g., food, security, status) only indirectly, this theoretical approach requires both identification of needs and a description of how work factors satisfy these needs. Maslow, Herzberg, Alderfer, Hackman and Oldham, and McClelland have all addressed these issues. Another matter of some interest is how needs (and need satisfaction) operate to influence *performance*. The usual answer is that needs both energize and direct behavior; thus, people work harder the more needy they are—particularly for things that will satisfy their needs.

Although controversy surrounds each of these theoretical notions, the work of the content theorists has raised several noteworthy points. People do seem to have multiple needs (or, if you prefer, multiple work objects) that can be met to varying degrees by the work situation. Whereas the specific consequences of ignoring these needs are not completely clear, they are in all probability bad and become increasingly worse the more widespread the neglect. It behooves any organization to keep abreast of the needs of its work force and of the extent to which these needs are being met. In composite, the content theories provide some excellent guidance regarding the needs for which to look.

Other theorists consider need satisfaction to be only part of the story. For them, job satisfaction and performance depend as well on such factors as intentions, expectations, role perceptions, abilities, outcomes, and valences. People may fail to perform because (1) they have developed either no specific goals or very inappropriate ones; (2) they have misperceived what was expected of them or the best strategy for achieving it; (3) they believe they are not equal to the task, hence effort will not yield performance, (4) they believe that performance will not be rewarded; and (5) they don't particularly value the rewards that performance brings or else consider them inequitable. We must consider all these factors individually and the *interactions* among them as well. A huge need might give a particular reward a high positive valence for an individual. Still, unless he felt there was some chance that greater effort on his part would earn him that reward, he would not try to improve his performance (as VIE theory predicts). Similarly, a woman might need money very badly and get a high-paying job. Though her need is now satisfied, she might be extremely dissatisfied because her rate of pay is lower than that of male counterparts who are working no harder than she; or her intrinsic satisfaction with the job may decrease as the result of feeling under external control of monetary incentives. As a consequence, she might, in fact, reduce her level of effort (as equity theory predicts) or exert effort only when there is a promise of money in return (as cognitive evaluation theory would predict).

Process theories, then, look well beyond need satisfaction. Their contribution lies in three main areas: (1) providing a structure within which to organize all the ideas—factual and speculative—that have appeared on satisfaction and motivation, (2) generating testable research hypotheses to increase our knowledge, and (3) emphasizing the probably complexity of human motivation in the work situation (i.e., the fact that multiple factors and complex interactions are needed to make any sort of predictions).

Taken together, the research on job satisfaction and motivation to perform clearly refutes not only scientific management's contention that individuals are motivated only by economic considerations but also the human relations position that motivated performance results directly from satisfaction. This is not to say that either money or satisfaction is unimportant, just that neither has the direct, exclusive influence suggested.

Many factors control satisfaction, including some from within the individual (ability, personality, self-perceptions) and some from the work structure. Vroom summarizes the situational factors by describing the most satisfying work role as "one which provides high pay, substantial promotional opportunities, considerate and participative supervision, an opportunity to interact with one's peers, varied duties, and a high degree of control over work methods and work pace."[106] Many of the same factors influence performance as well, although not in the same way or to the same degree. As we shall see in the next chapter, for example, interaction with a cohesive, friendly group of peers does not benefit performance as consistently as it does satisfaction. In contrast, money seems capable of exerting a more consistent effect on performance than it does on satisfaction (Herzberg's argument to the contrary notwithstanding).

In this chapter, we have focused primarily on the individual employee's needs, expectations, satisfaction, and performance. An individual employee's attitudes and behavior, however, are influenced to a large extent by the groups to which he or she belongs. We will direct our attention in the next chapter to group behavior within organizations and the influence the group has on individuals.

NOTES

1. Steers, R. M., & Porter, L. (Eds.). (1983). *Motivation and work behavior*. New York: McGraw-Hill, pp. 3–4.
2. Pritchard, R. D., Leonard, D. W., Von Bergen, C. W., & Kirk, R. J. (1976). The effects of varying schedules of reinforcement on human task performance. *Organizational Behavior and Human Performance, 16*, 205–230; Pritchard, R. D., Hollenbeck, J., & DeLeo, P. J. (1980). The effects of continuous and partial schedules of reinforcement on effort, performance, and satisfaction. *Organizational Behavior and Human Performance, 25*, 336–353.

3. Locke, E. A. (1977). The myths of behavior mod in organizations. *Academy of Management Review, 2*, 543–551.

4. Hamner, W. C., & Hamner, E. P. (1976). Behavior modification on the bottom line. *Organizational Dynamics, 4*, 8–21.

5. Merrihue, H. F., & Katzell, R. A. (1955). ERI—Yardstick of employee relations. *Harvard Business Review, 33*, 91–99; Weiss, D. J., Dawis, R. D., England, G. W., & Lofquist, L. H. (1967). *Minnesota studies in vocational rehabilitation: 22d manual for the Minnesota satisfaction questionnaire*. University of Minnesota.

6. Wanous, J. P., & Lawler, E. E., III. (1972). Measurement and meaning of job satisfaction. *Journal of Applied Psychology, 56*, 95–105.

7. Kanungo, R. N. (1982). *Work alienation: An integrative approach*. New York: Praeger Publishers.

8. Mowday, R. T., Porter, L. W., & Steers, R. M. (1982). *Employee-organization linkages: The psychology of commitment, absenteeism, and turnover*. New York: Academic Press.

9. Lawler, E. E., III, & Porter, L. W. (1967). The effect of performance on job satisfaction. *Industrial Relations, 7*, 20–28; and Locke, E. A., Cartledge, N. P., & Knerr, C. S. (1980). Studies of the relationship between satisfaction, goal-setting, and performance, *Organizational Behavior and Human Performance, 25*, 135–158.

10. Greene, C. H. (1972). The satisfaction-performance controversy. *Business Horizons, 15*(2), 31–41.

11. Nord, W. R. (1977). Job satisfaction reconsidered. *American Psychologist, 32*, 1026–1035.

12. Brayfield, A. H., & Crockett, W. H. (1955). Employee attitudes and employee performance. *Psychological Bulletin, 52*, 396–424; Petty, M. M., McGee, G. W., & Cavander, J. W. (1984). A meta-analysis of the relationship between individual job satisfaction and individual performance. *Academy of Management Review, 9*, 712–721; Iaffaldano, M. T., & Muchinsky, P. M. (1985). Job satisfaction and job performance: A meta-analysis. *Psychological Bulletin, 97*, 251–273.

13. Porter, L. W., & Steers, R. M. (1973). Organizational, work, and personal factors in employee turnover and absenteeism. *Psychological Bulletin, 80*, 151–176.

14. Chadwick-Jones, J. K., Nicholson, N., & Brown, C. (1982). *The social psychology of absenteeism*. New York: Praeger Publishers.

15. Mowday et al. *Employee-organization linkages*.

16. Kanungo. *Work alienation*.

17. Fisher, C. D. (1980). On the dubious wisdom of expecting job satisfaction to correlate with performance. *Academy of Management Review, 5*, 607–612.

18. Cherrington, D. J., Reitz, H. J., & Scott, W. E. (1971). Effect of contingent and noncontingent reward on the relationship between satisfaction and task performance. *Journal of Applied Psychology, 53*, 531–536.

19. Steers, R. M. (1975). Effects of need for achievement on the job performance-job attitude relationship. *Journal of Applied Psychology, 60*, 678–682.

20. Greene, C. H. (1972). The satisfaction-performance controversy. *Business Horizons, 15*(2), 31–41.

21. Campbell, J. P., & Pritchard, R. D. (1976). Motivation theory in industrial and organizational psychology. In M. D. Dunnette (Ed.). *Handbook of industrial and organizational psychology*. Skokie, Ill.: Rand McNally.

22. Murray, H. A. (1938). *Explorations in personality*. New York: Oxford University Press.

23. Maslow, A. H. (1943). A theory of human motivation. *Psychological Review, 50*, 370–396.

24. Wahba, M. A., & Birdwell, L. G. (1975). Maslow reconsidered: A review of research on the need hierarchy theory. In K. N. Wexley & G. H. Yukl (Eds.). *Organizational behavior and industrial psychology*. New York: Oxford University Press.

25. McGregor, D. (1960). *The human side of enterprise*. New York: McGraw-Hill.

26. Lawler, E. E., III, & Suttle, J. L. (1972). A causal correlational test of the need hierarchy in the organizational setting. *Organizational Behavior and Human*

Performance, 7, 265–287; Wahba, M. A., & Birdwell, L. G. (1975). Maslow reconsidered: A review of research on the need hierarchy theory. In K. N. Wexley & G. H. Yukl (Eds.). *Organizational behavior and industrial psychology.* New York: Oxford University Press.

27. Hall, D. T., & Nougaim, K. E. (1968). An examination of Maslow's need hierarchy in the organizational setting. *Organizational Behavior and Human Performance, 3,* 12–35.

28. Rauschenberger, J., Schmitt, N., & Hunter, J. (1980). A test of the need hierarchy concept by a Markov model of change in need strength. *Administrative Science Quarterly, 25,* 654–670.

29. Dachler, H. P., & Hulin, C. L. (1969). A reconsideration of the relationship between satisfaction and judged importance of environmental and job characteristics. *Organizational Behavior and Human Performance, 4,* 252–266.

30. Payne, R. (1970). Factor analysis of a Maslow-type need satisfaction questionnaire. *Personnel Psychology, 23,* 251–268; and Roberts, K. H., Walter, G. A., & Miles, R. T. (1970). A factor-analytic study of job satisfaction items designed to measure Maslow's need categories. *Proceedings of the 78th Annual Convention of the American Psychological Association,* 591–592.

31. Ibid.

32. Alderfer, C. P. (1972). *Existence, relatedness, and growth: Human needs in organizational settings.* New York: Free Press.

33. Scherf, G. W. H. (1974). Consumer dissatisfaction as a function of dissatisfaction with interpersonal relationships. *Journal of Applied Psychology, 59,* 465–471.

34. Alderfer. *Existence, relatedness, and growth.*

35. Herzberg, F. (1966). *Working and the nature of man* (p. 50). New York: Thomas Y. Crowell.

36. Herzberg, F. (1968). One more time: How do you motivate employees? *Harvard Business Review, 46,* 53–62.

37. Dunnette, M. D., Campbell, J. P., & Hakel, M. D. (1967). Factors contributing to job satisfaction and job dissatisfaction in six occupational groups. *Organizational Behavior and Human Performance, 2,* 143–174.

38. Schneider, J., & Locke, E. A. (1971). A critique of Herzberg's incident classification system and a suggested revision. *Organizational Behavior and Human Performance, 6,* 441–457.

39. McClelland, D. L., Atkinson, J. W., Clark, R. A., & Lowell, E. L. (1953). *The achievement motive.* New York: Appleton-Century-Crofts.

40. Atkinson, J. W., & Feather, N. T. (1966). *A theory of achievement motivation.* New York: John Wiley & Sons.

41. McClelland, D. C. (1961). *The achieving society.* New York: Van Nostrand Reinhold.

42. McClelland, D. C., & Winter, D. G. (1969). *Motivating economic achievement.* New York: Free Press.

43. Klinger, E. (1966). Fantasy need achievement as a motivational construct. *Psychological Bulletin, 66,* 291–308; and Patchen, M. (1961). *The choice of wage comparisons.* Englewood Cliffs, N.J.: Prentice-Hall.

44. Entvisle, D. R. (1972). To dispel fantasies about fantasy-based measures of achievement motivation. *Psychological Bulletin, 77,* 377–391.

45. Hackman, J. R., & Lawler, E. E., III. (1971). Employee reactions to job characteristics. *Journal of Applied Psychology, 55,* 259–286.

46. Dunham, R. B. (1976). The measurement and dimensionality of job characteristics. *Journal of Applied Psychology, 61,* 404–409; and Dunman, R. B., Aldag, R. J., & Brief, A. P. (1977). Dimensionality of task design as measured by the job diagnostic survey. *Academy of Management Journal, 20,* 209–223.

47. White, J. K. (1978). Individual differences and the job quality-worker response relationship: Review, integration, and comments. *Academy on Management Review, 3,* 267–280.

48. Hulin, C. L., & Triandis, H. C. (1981). Meanings of work in different organizational environments. In P. Nystrom & W. H. Starbuck (Eds.). *Handbook of organizational design. Vol. 2* (pp. 337–357). London: Oxford University Press.

49. Cherrington, D. J., & England, J. L. (1980). The desire for an enriched job as a moderator of the enrichment-satisfaction relationship. *Organizational Behavior and Human Performance, 25,* 139–159.

50. Locke, E. A., Carledge, N. P., & Knerr, C. S. (1980). Studies of the relationship between satisfaction, goal-setting, and performance. *Organizational Behavior and Human Performance, 25,* 135–158.

51. Latham, G. P., & Yukl, G. A. (1975). A review of research on the application of goal setting in organizations. *Academy of Management Journal, 18,* 824–845.

52. Locke, E. A., Shaw, K. N., Saari, L. M., & Latham, G. P. (1981). Goal setting and task performance: 1969–1980. *Psychological Bulletin, 90,* 125–152.

53. Tolchinsky, P. D., & King, D. C. (1980). Do goals mediate the effects of incentives on performance? *Academy of Management Review, 5,* 455–467.

54. Erez, M., & Kanfer, F. H. (1983). The role of goal acceptance in goal setting and task performance. *Academy of Management Review, 8,* 454–463.

55. Latham, G. P., Steele, T. P., & Saari, L. M. (1982). The effects of participation and goal difficulty on performance. *Personnel Psychology, 35,* 677–686.

56. Locke et al. Goal setting.

57. Ibid., p. 145.

58. See, for example, the following: Rapaport, A., & Walsten, T. S. (1972). Individual decision behavior. *Annual Review of Psychology, 23,* 131–176; Peterson, C. R., & Beach, L. R. (1967). Man as an intuitive statistician. *Psychological Bulletin, 68,* 24–46; Edwards, W. (1961). Behavioral decision theory. *Annual Review of Psychology, 12,* 473–498; and Becker, G. B., & McClintock, C. G. (1967). Value: Behavioral decision theory. *Annual Review of Psychology, 18,* 239–286.

59. Pritchard, R. D., & De Leo, P. J. (1973). Experimental test of the valence-instrumentality relationship in job performance. *Journal of Applied Psychology, 57,* 264–270; and Mitchell, T. R., & Albright, D. W. (1972). Expectancy theory predictions of the satisfaction, effort, performance, and retention of naval officers. *Organizational Behavior and Human Performance, 8,* 1–20.

60. Heneman, H. G., III, & Schwab, D. P. (1972). Evaluation of expectancy theory research on employee performance. *Psychological Bulletin, 78,* 1–9.

61. Stahl, M. J., & Harrell, A. M. (1981). Effort decisions with behavioral decision theory: Toward an individual differences model. *Organizational Behavior and Human Performance, 27,* 303–325.

62. Jorgenson, D. C., Dunnette, M. D., & Pritchard, R. D. (1973). Effects of the manipulation of a performance-reward contingency on behavior in a simulated work setting. *Journal of Applied Psychology, 57,* 271–280; Lawler, E. E., III, & Suttle, J. L. (1973). Expectancy theory and job behavior. *Organizational Behavior and Human Performance, 9,* 482–503.

63. Parker, D. F., & Dyer, L. (1976). Expectancy theory as a within-person behavioral choice model: An empirical test of some conceptual and methodological refinements. *Organizational Behavior and Human Performance, 17,* 97–117; Matsui, T., Kagawa, M., Nagamatsu, J., & Ohtsuka, Y. (1977). Validity of expectancy theory as a within-person behavior choice model for sales activities. *Journal of Applied Psychology, 62,* 764–767.

64. Matsui, T., & Ikeda, H. (1976). Effectiveness of self-generation outcomes improving prediction in expectancy theory research. *Organizational Behavior and Human Performance, 17,* 289–298.

65. Leon, F. R. (1981). The role of positive and negative outcomes in the causation of motivational forces. *Journal of Applied Psychology, 66,* 45–53.

66. Staw, B. M. (1980). Rationality and justification in organizational life. In B. M. Staw (Ed.). *Research in organizational behavior Vol. 2* (pp. 45–80). Greenwich, Conn.: JAI Press.

67. Weick, K. E. (1964). Reduction of cognitive dissonance through task enhancement and effort expenditure. *Journal of Abnormal and Social Psychology, 68,* 533–539.
68. Korman, A. K. (1976). Hypothesis of work behavior revisited and an extension. *Academy of Management Review, 1,* 50–63.
69. Dipboye, R. L. (1977). A critical review of Korman's self-consistency theory of work motivation and occupational choice. *Organizational Behavior and Human Performance, 18,* 108–126.
70. Bem, D. J. (1967). Self-perception: An alternative interpretation of cognitive dissonance phenomenon. *Psychological Review, 74,* 183–200.
71. Adams, J. S. (1965). Inequity in social exchange. In L. Berkowitz (Ed.). *Advances in experimental social psychology Vol. 2* (pp. 267–299). New York: Academic Press.
72. Lawler, E. E., III, & O'Gara, P. W. (1967). Effects of inequity produced by underpayment on work output, work quality, and attitudes toward work. *Journal of Applied Psychology, 51,* 403–410.
73. Mowday, R. T. (1983). Equity theory predictions of behavior in organizations. In R. M. Steers & L. W. Porter (Eds.). *Motivation and work behavior* (3d ed.) (pp. 91–112). New York: McGraw-Hill.
74. Goodman, P., & Friedman, A. (1971). An examination of Adams' theory of inequity. *Administrative Science Quarterly, 16,* 271–286.
75. Vecchio. R. P. (1981). An individual differences interpretation of the conflicting predictions generated by equity and expectancy theory. *Journal of Applied Psychology, 66,* 470–481.
76. Folger, R. (1984). Emerging issues in the social psychology of justice. In R. Folger (Ed.). *The sense of injustice: Social psychological perspectives* (pp. 3–24). New York: Plenum Press.
77. Deci, E. L. (1975). *Intrinsic motivation.* New York: Plenum Press.
78. Deci, E. L. (1971). Effects of externally mediated rewards on intrinsic motivation. *Journal of Personality and Social Psychology, 18,* 105–115.
79. Calder, B. J., & Staw, B. M. (1975). Self-perception of intrinsic and extrinsic motivation. *Journal of Personality and Social Psychology, 31,* 599–605.
80. Pritchard, R. D., Campbell, K. M., & Campbell, D. J. (1977). Effects of extrinsic financial rewards on intrinsic motivation. *Journal of Applied Psychology, 62,* 9–15.
81. Staw, B. M. (1977). Motivation in organizations: Toward synthesis and redirection. In B. M. Staw & G. R. Salancik (Eds.). *New directions in organizational behavior* (p. 76). Chicago: St. Clair Press.
82. Bass, B. M., & Barrett, G. V. (1972). *Man, work, and organizations.* Boston: Allyn & Bacon.
83. Lawler, E. E., III, & Suttle, J. L. (1973). Expectancy theory and job behavior. *Organizational Behavior and Human Performance, 9,* 482–503.
84. Mento, A. J., Cartledge, N. D., & Locke, E. A. (1980). Maryland versus Michigan versus Minnesota: Another look at the relationship of expectancy and goal difficulty to task performance. *Organizational Behavior and Human Performance, 25,* 419–440.
85. Lawler & Suttle. Expectancy theory, p. 502.
86. U. S. Department of Health, Education, and Welfare. (1971). *Work in America.* Cambridge, Mass: MIT Press.
87. Herzberg. One more time.
88. Hackman, J. Richard (1983). Work design. In Richard M. Steers & Lyman W. Porter (Eds). *Motivation and work behavior.* (3rd ed.). New York: McGraw-Hill, 490–516.
89. Ibid.
90. Hulin, C. L., & Blood, M. R. (1968). Job enlargement, individual differences, and worker responses. *Psychological Bulletin, 69,* 41–55.
91. Bishop, R. C., & Hill, J. W. (1971). Effects of job enlargement and job change on contiguous but nonmanipulated jobs as a function of worker status. *Journal of Applied Psychology, 55,* 175–181.

92. Sales, S. M. (1970). Some effects of role overload and role underload. *Organizational Behavior and Human Performance, 5*, 592–608.

93. Umstot, D. D., Bell, C. H., & Mitchell, T. R. (1976). Effects of job enrichment and task goals on satisfaction and productivity: Implications for job design. *Journal of Applied Psychology, 61*, 379–394.

94. Locke, E. A., Sirota, D., & Wolfson, A. D. (1976). An experimental case study of the successes and failures of job enrichment in a government agency. *Journal of Applied Psychology, 61*, 701–711.

95. Simonds, R. H., & Orife, J. N. (1975). Worker behavior versus enrichment theory. *Administrative Science Quarterly, 20*, 606–612.

96. Lawler, E. E. (1977). Satisfaction and behavior. In J. Hackman, E. Lawler, & L. Porter (Eds.). *Perspectives on behavior in organizations* (pp. 39–51). New York: McGraw-Hill.

97. Organ, D. W. (1977). Inferences about trends in labor force satisfaction: A causal-correlational analysis. *Academy of Management Journal, 20*, 510–519.

98. Hamner & Hamner. Behavior modification.

99. Ibid.

100. Ibid.

101. Locke. Myths of behavior mod.

102. Opsahl, R. L., & Dunnette, M. D. (1966). The role of financial compensation in industrial motivation. *Psychological Bulletin, 63*, 94–118; and Lawler, E. E., III. (1971). *Pay and organizational effectiveness.* New York: McGraw-Hill.

103. Lawler. Ibid.

104. Ibid.

105. Lawler, E. E., III. (1984). The strategic design of reward systems. In R. S. Schuler & S. A. Youngblood (Eds.). *Readings in personnel and human resource management* (2d ed.) (pp. 253–269). St. Paul, Minn.: West Publishing.

106. Vroom. (1964). *Work and motivation* (p. 173). New York: John Wiley & Sons.

4

Group Behavior

In the last chapter we discussed some of the alternative strategies for motivating employees to perform at high levels in their work roles. Rewarding good performance, enriching jobs, setting goals for high performance, allowing individual employees to participate in decision making, and other attempts to change employee behavior can run astray, however, when they are aimed solely at individuals and ignore the numerous face-to-face groups that make up an organization. These groups can influence the way an employee acts and feels at work as much, or more, than do the formal rules and procedures of the organization or the employee's own motives and abilities. The primary message of this chapter is that organizations can never be adequately understood or managed if they are viewed as mere collections of individuals or as faceless institutions. To effectively manage individuals in an organization, one must also manage the groups to which these individuals belong.

Group factors have not always been recognized by organizational theorists. Recall that for the scientific management theorists, the only groups worthy of consideration were those that were formally defined and recognized by management. Informal groups (those not defined by management) were regarded as counterproductive elements against which the weight of legitimate authority should be directed. The leading proponent of scientific management, Frederick Taylor, feared that workers allowed to socialize on the job would reinforce each other's laziness and resist attempts to increase their productivity.[1] The solution, according to Taylor, was to discourage workers from interacting by physically separating them and rewarding them for individual rather than group performance.

Unlike the classical theorists, the human relationists not only recognized informal group influences but emphasized them—at times, to the exclusion of all else. Nevertheless, the human relations movement introduced the important notion that informal interactions can work *for* as well as *against* the formal organization. Roethlisberger and Dickson, in direct opposition to Taylor's views, believed that if workers were isolated their productivity as well as their satisfaction would suffer.[2] The implication of this view was that management should attempt to strengthen informal relationships among employees, not discourage them.

Although we have now spent several chapters examining complications in the human relations position, the reader should not lose sight of one lasting contribution: It showed that organizations are essentially social in nature. Organizations in many of the other major industrial countries, like Japan, have recognized this for quite a while and have attempted to build and maintain strong groups of employees in their management practices. In recent years, organizations in the United States appear to have followed the example of these countries, as shown by the increased use of group-oriented management strategies like quality circles, project teams, and consensus decision making. In the present chapter, we will consider a number of questions critical to the effective management of groups in organizations: How do groups form? What types of groups are there? What are the characteristics of individuals, groups, and the environment that determine how groups behave, their effectiveness, and the satisfaction of their members? What techniques improve the effectiveness of a group's performance?

HOW DO EMPLOYEES COME TO FORM GROUPS?

Most modern organizational theorists agree that understanding the functioning of groups is a prerequisite to understanding organizations. They part company, however, when it comes to defining what a group is.[3] Indeed, Shaw lists 13 definitions, each stressing a somewhat different set of group characteristics. The essential elements seem to be captured in his definition of a group as "two or more persons who are interacting with one another in such a manner that each person influences and is influenced by each person."[4] Another characteristic of a group in an organization is that its members are typically aware of the group and their membership in it. For instance, members of a company bowling team can readily identify who is and isn't a member of the team and can see themselves as a distinct group unified by common goals. Many of the most influential groups in organizations are not formalized to this extent but *emerge* out of the day-to-day interactions that occur naturally among employees.

For persons to form a group, there first must be an *opportunity* and a *reason* for them to interact. In the absence of any other information about a collection of employees, one can usually predict fairly well which of them will form a group from knowing how physically close they are.

Many studies have shown that *proximity* and other physical features of the environment that put people in direct contact with one another provide the *opportunity* to interact and encourage group formation. Clerical workers whose desks are in the same row are more likely to interact with each other than they are with those whose desks are in separate rows.[5] Autoworkers who are seated next to each other or across from each other on an assembly line are more likely to emerge as a group than are those seated farther apart.[6] Research scientists whose offices are close are more likely to exchange information and emerge as a clique than are scientists whose offices are not within convenient walking distance.[7] By manipulating the physical environment, organizations can do a lot to either encourage or discourage interaction among employees. If an organization wants to encourage interaction among certain employees, it might design a space in which people are positioned face to face and have easy access to each other. On the other hand, if the organization wishes to discourage interaction, it should consider a space in which people do not face each other and there are barriers to interaction. Sommers calls the former a *sociopetal space* and the latter a *sociofugal space.*[8] Actually, the traditional office layout, which encloses and separates employees with rigid walls, is a good example of a sociofugal space. To facilitate communication among workers, some organizations have adopted sociopetal designs such as *landscaped offices*, which do away with rigid walls and delineate workspaces with "softer" barriers such as plants and file cabinets.

Proximity and other characteristics of the physical space may provide an opportunity for persons to interact, but they do not guarantee that a group will form. There also must be some *reason* for persons to establish a stable relationship with one another. Such a reason presents itself when people are interdependent, that is, they must cooperate with one another to achieve their individual and collective goals. Assigning a collection of workers to an extremely difficult production goal that can only be achieved through coordinated effort might be one way of inducing these workers to form closer relationships. Similarly, experiencing the same outcomes, or a *common fate*, may pull people together and facilitate the emergence of a group. An authoritarian manager who arbitrarily imposes punitive rules and procedures may unintentionally encourage the formation of strong personal relations among employees as they cope with their common fate.

Proximity, interdependence, and common fate provide an opportunity and a reason to interact, but an additional ingredient is needed for people to form an enduring relationship: Individuals must feel that they have something to gain from the relationship. The basic reason that groups form is to satisfy its members' personal goals, which may or may not be compatible with the organization's goals. Membership and participation in a group may be instrumental to fulfilling all the needs we discussed in Chapter 3. Belonging to a group can reduce anxiety and fulfill basic security and survival needs. It has been shown, for example, that a soldier's primary defense against combat stress is the support given to and received from fellow soldiers in the combat unit.[9] If the group ties are somehow weakened, the soldier is much more vulnerable. The most obvious need that groups fulfill is the need to affiliate. Maslow and other need theorists have proposed that people not only desire to have contact with others but *need* affiliation to maintain physical and psychological health. In support of need theory, research findings show signs of psychological and physiological distress among people who are isolated for long periods of time. But more than affiliation, people seek to enhance and maintain self-esteem through their group memberships. A group also may help fulfill self-actualization needs by supporting the attempts of its members to develop their potential. Toastmasters, Weight Watchers, Alcoholics Anonymous, and sensitivity groups are a few examples of groups whose primary goal is to help members improve themselves.

Another important motive for participating in groups is that the group helps define reality for its members.[10] Whereas some beliefs can easily be validated through objective means, others can never be validated in any objective fashion. An individual who thinks that the temperature is 80 degrees need only check a thermometer. On the other hand, if the person wants to determine if his or her religious beliefs are valid, there is no objective means of doing this; but the person can join a church, which surrounds him or her with believers who encourage the idea that the beliefs are correct. Past research has shown that when people have beliefs regarding important issues such as this, they often seek to validate them by affiliating with others who see things the same way. Chief executive officers always profess an aversion to being surrounded by "yes-men." Still, it is rare indeed to find CEOs who are willing to tolerate close associates who consistently dispute their decisions, opinions, or philosophies.

Not only do group members help support each other's beliefs, but people often turn to their fellow group members in deciding what to believe. Salancik and Pfeffer, in their social information processing model, propose that how an employee feels about the job is influenced more by how fellow employees feel about their jobs than by frustration or fulfillment of personal needs.[11] To test this proposition, White and Mitchell provided either a challenging or unchallenging task to persons participating in a laboratory experiment.[12] In addition, confederates of the experimenter described the task as either interesting or uninteresting. Consistent with social information processing notions, persons provided with information that the task was interesting described the task as more satisfying and challenging than did those who were provided information that the task was uninteresting. These findings seem to generalize to field settings. Griffin found that providing positive information about a job enrichment program enhanced perceptions of the job and increased satisfaction independent of actual changes in the jobs.[13] Employees are not all equally influenced by the opinions of their peers, however. One personality variable that has been found to influence the extent to which employee attitudes are shaped by the attitudes of the group is self-esteem. There is some indication that low-self-esteem persons are likely to be influenced more by the attitudes of fellow group members than are high-self-esteem persons.[14]

Once there is an opportunity and a reason for a collection of people to interact, and they feel that their important goals can be achieved through interaction, a group is likely to emerge. Groups, like individuals, do not spring into existence fully formed. Instead, they appear to pass through at least four distinct phases of development, which Tuckman called "forming, storming, norming, and performing."[15] In the forming phase, members explore their environment and seek to understand the group task and fellow group members. During this initial phase, members may engage in quite a bit of casual conversation as they assess one another and the likelihood that participation in the group will further task goals and satisfy their personal needs. As they continue to work together in performing their tasks, some interpersonal tension typically develops, and the group enters the storming phase. Groups often polarize in this phase around task and interpersonal issues as members divide into opposing camps over task strategies and leadership. If the group resolves its conflicts, it moves into the norming phase in which the members develop stable expectations regarding their respective roles. If things go well, the group develops into a cohesive entity with a unity of purpose. Having put emotional and interpersonal conflicts behind them, group members enter the performing phase in which they settle down and concentrate on their tasks. Actually, there has been little research on the sequence that groups in organizations follow as they develop from loose collectivities into cohesive teams. Much of the work on group development has been with therapy and discussion groups. There is no compelling reason, however, to expect that work groups develop any differently than other kinds of groups.

WHAT TYPES OF GROUPS FORM?

From what we have just said, it should be apparent that employees usually belong to more than one group. It is inevitable that they will belong to the functional group established formally by the organization to accomplish specific task objectives. In addition, they probably will belong to several groups that are not formally recognized but that emerge, as we have just shown, to achieve a variety of personal and task goals. Three common types of emergent groups are *instrumental, friendship,* and *self-interest* groups.

Instrumental groups emerge primarily to fulfill task goals and, as such, supplement the formal structure. The formal patterns—of interaction spelled out in lines of communication and authority, standard operating procedures, and functional groupings of employees—give the employees everything they need—from the classical standpoint—to do their jobs. Rarely is that so, however, no matter how cleverly these structural elements are conceived (see Chapter 2). Management may disseminate information through memoranda, newsletters, and even advanced-design management information systems; but the knowledge that one needs to tread softly when the boss has a hangover or to kick the stamping machine "right here" when it jams is also critical to task performance, but such knowledge rarely finds its way into the formal channels. This information follows informal routes (the grapevine) and is not always accurate, but it still may help the organization by filling the gaps left in the formal information systems. When resources are limited in an organization, as they usually are, an elaborate network may emerge in which employees bargain and negotiate for the materials they need to perform their tasks—all outside the formal system.

Friendship groups really need no illustration; they are based on purely personal attractions among a collection of employees and are familiar to everyone. Not surprisingly, people who are similar in their attitudes, personalities, abilities, race, economic status, education, sex, and age are more likely to be attracted to one another than are people who differ on one or more of these dimensions.[16]

The self-interest group emerges for the purpose of achieving objectives shared by its members. In this age of the National Rifle Association, the right-to-lifers, the Sierra Club, and Equal Rights Amendment groups, the reader should have little difficulty grasping this concept. Unions are probably the best organizational example.

DETERMINANTS OF GROUP EFFECTIVENESS

Once a group emerges or is formed by management, the question shifts to one of effectiveness. What determines how well it will carry out its tasks and accomplish its objectives? It is commonly believed that groups rarely perform more effectively than the best-performing individuals in the group and often do even worse than the average performer. Although these beliefs are not totally groundless, they are not strictly accurate, either. Groups often do perform below their potential, but nothing inherent in their groupness makes it so. They can also perform very well and, in some cases, better than their most competent members. Besides, because many tasks can be performed in no other way, organizations might as well accept the group as inevitable and seek ways to improve its effectiveness rather than to find fault with the concept.

Figure 4–1 summarizes some of the major variables proposed as causes of group performance. One obvious ingredient is the makeup of the

FIGURE 4–1   Variables Influencing Group Effectiveness and Member Attitudes

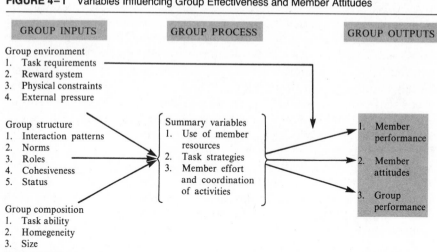

Group environment
1.   Task requirements
2.   Reward system
3.   Physical constraints
4.   External pressure

Group structure
1.   Interaction patterns
2.   Norms
3.   Roles
4.   Cohesiveness
5.   Status

Group composition
1.   Task ability
2.   Homegeneity
3.   Size

GROUP INPUTS   GROUP PROCESS   GROUP OUTPUTS

Summary variables
1.   Use of member resources
2.   Task strategies
3.   Member effort and coordination of activities

1.   Member performance
2.   Member attitudes
3.   Group performance

individuals comprising the group: the number of persons, their overall task abilities, and their homogeneity with respect to abilities, personalities, backgrounds, opinions, and other personal attributes. A group is more, however, than the simple sum of the individuals composing it. A group's effectiveness also depends upon group-level variables such as norms, roles, status hierarchy, cohesiveness, and patterns of interaction. And finally, the external environment plays an important part through variables such as task, communication network, reward system, and external pressures or threats. Environmental, personal, and structural variables can affect group outcomes both directly and indirectly. They influence outcomes indirectly through determining group process, that is, how the group uses the resources available to it, what strategy it uses in performing the task, and how effortfully and coordinatedly members perform the task. All three categories of inputs also directly influence outcomes. For example, providing efficiently designed tasks and highly capable group members is likely to benefit performance to some extent independent of the effects obtained through improving group process. In the following sections, we will consider how a group's outcomes are influenced by each of the variables listed in Figure 4–1 as well as by the process mediator.

Group Process

Group process is defined simply as all the interactions among members occurring at one point in time. In measuring group process, observations typically are made of the verbal and nonverbal communications that occur among group members. Indeed, for all practical purposes, group process is the same as interpersonal communication. When people interact

FIGURE 4–2   Model of the Communication Process

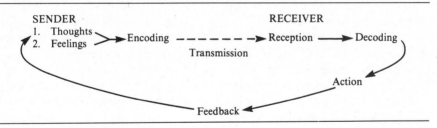

they intentionally or unintentionally exchange information and, in the process of this exchange, they develop some understanding of events happening inside and outside of the group. It seems appropriate, therefore, to begin our discussion of group process with a model of the communication process.

Figure 4–2 presents a basic model of the communication that occurs between two persons. The process begins with the thoughts and emotions of the sender of a message that are encoded (placed into symbolic form such as language) and transmitted to another individual (the receiver). The receiver must first become aware of the message being transmitted (reception) and then must translate or attach some meaning to this message (decoding). The recipient's response or lack of response to the message provides feedback to the sender of the success of the attempt to communicate.

One approach to observing group process is to record the source, the intended audience, and the duration of each communication. Later we will discuss social network analysis and sociometric techniques that can be applied to measuring patterns of communications. Additionally, several key questions should be asked regarding the characteristics of communications in the group: How often do communications break down, and where do these breakdowns occur? What group functions do communications serve? How openly do people communicate? Who influences whom in their communications?

Where Do Communications Break Down?

Communications among members of a group often fail, even in the most effective groups. Nevertheless, more effective groups probably have fewer and less serious breakdowns than do the less effective ones. Considering the several steps through which any message must pass (see Figure 4–2), it is not surprising that failures to communicate occur. Knowing how often, where, and why communications break down can tell us a lot about why a group's morale and performance are the way they are and about ways to improve them.

One source of breakdowns is the sender's failure to properly encode thoughts and feelings. A sender can be insensitive in the choice of words by failing to recognize that the same word can mean different things to different people. Moreover, a simple word can trigger anger, embarrassment, and a host of other emotions that can interfere with communications. Thus, the sender of a message needs to choose words carefully and anticipate the effect they are likely to have on the recipient.

Although words are important, people overemphasize words and forget that there are messages communicated in the way the words are delivered and the context of the delivery. People in organizations like to think of themselves as rational and usually intend to communicate rational thoughts. They sometimes fail to recognize that their emotions can "leak" into an otherwise thoughtful communication. Consider the common greeting, "Have a nice day." Depending on the intonation and phrasing with which the sender verbalizes it and the nonverbal behavior accompanying it, this simple message can be interpreted as meaning everything from "I like you and sincerely hope things go well" to "Drop dead." As Haney has stated ". . . the important issue in communication is not what the *words* mean, but what the *user* means by them" (p. 270).[17]

Even if the thoughts and feelings of the sender are properly encoded, the message may not get through to the recipient because of noise that interferes with the transmission of the message. Noise can originate from the physical environment, such as the mimeograph that is clanging away while you are trying to talk. Noise can also come in the form of competing messages. If one's secretary is busy answering the phone, it probably is not the best time to communicate an important message. To ensure that a message is successfully transmitted, the sender should pick a time and place where competition is minimal or should at least make sure of having the attention of the person to whom the message is directed.

Once accurately encoded and clearly transmitted, a communication must be received, and at this step in the process still more breakdowns occur. The thoughts and feelings of the recipient often get in the way of reception.[18] Persons who are emotionally distraught simply may not attend to as much of their environment as does a person who is less distraught.[19] Another problem is that people often fail to receive messages that are inconsistent with their expectations and desires. Consider, for example, the following parable. A supervisor has never required his subordinates to get his approval before they take the company car home. One day, he decides to implement a new policy, which requires that they first get his approval before using the cars. The policy change is communicated as part of a long memo that is sent out on Friday afternoon, just when a lot of his employees are looking forward to a weekend cruise in a company car. To the manager's surprise, he finds that several "good" employees troop off with company cars without the requisite approval. The next Monday morning, when he asks them why, he discovers that many of them simply did not receive the message. If we interpret this event in the light of the model presented in Figure 4–2, it may be that these employees did not receive the message because it was one that they neither *wanted* nor *expected*.

The next point of communication breakdown is in the decoding of the message. Although recipients may receive the words of a message accurately, they may interpret the message in a way that is contrary to the intent of the sender. Differences in such things as training, education, experience, and culture may lead to radically different interpretations of the same message. A newspaper account of an incident on a New York freeway provides a vivid illustration of this.[20] A motorist whose auto had stalled on the interstate had stopped another driver for assistance. The message conveyed was that "My car has an automatic transmission, so you'll have to get up to 30 to 35 miles per hour to get me started." In a sincere attempt to follow these instructions, the other driver backed up, accelerated to 30 miles an hour, and then collided into the rear end of the stalled car. In this example, the good Samaritan accurately received the words of the message but failed to properly decode it. The moral of the story is that a sender should never assume that recipients will attach the same meaning to a message that it is intended to have.

The final point of breakdown in the communication process is in the feedback loop. Many failures of communication could be avoided if senders simply sought feedback from the recipients. Too often, feedback is sought in the form of "Do you understand?", which many recipients are very likely to answer in the affirmative in the interest of appearing competent and knowledgeable. A better approach to seeking feedback is to ask the recipient to repeat back what was said. Still another approach is to create an open and supportive communication climate in which recipients feel free to ask questions and seek clarification.

What Functions Do Communications Serve?

Another important characteristic of communications within a group is the function they serve. Communications among group members appear to serve at least three different functions. Some communications are self-oriented in that they satisfy the individual member's own needs and appear to ignore the needs of the group. Self-oriented behavior is most frequent in the early stages of group development when members are unsure of what their relative roles should be and whether the group can satisfy their needs. Once a group clearly forms, communications tend to fall into one of two categories. Some are task oriented in that they are focused primarily on achieving the group's task goals. Others are maintenance oriented in that they are concerned primarily with maintaining good interpersonal relationships. There have been several schemes presented for measuring these two dimensions, but the best known is Bales's interaction process analysis.[21] According to the Bales scheme (see Table 4–1), each individual bit of verbal or nonverbal behavior that can elicit a

TABLE 4–1   Mean Percentage of Behavioral Acts Found for Each of the Categories in Bales's Interaction Process Analysis for Three Types of Groups

Behavioral Acts	Case Discussion Groups	Labor-Management Negotiations	Therapy Groups
1. Shows solidarity: jokes, raises others' status, gives help, rewards others	3.5	2.4	2.1
2. Shows tension release; laughs, shows satisfaction	7.0	1.2	5.6
3. Shows agreement: passive acceptance, understands, concurs, complies	16.9	10.5	5.8
4. Gives suggestion: direction, implying autonomy for others	8.0	3.0	1.1
5. Gives opinion: evaluation, analysis, expresses feeling, wish	33.4	24.5	19.8
6. Gives information: orientation, repeats, clarifies, confirms	15.5	32.7	42.2
7. Asks for information: orientation, repetition, confirmation	2.3	7.3	2.9
8. Asks for opinion: evaluation, analysis, expressions of feeling	2.2	2.2	7.3
9. Asks for suggestion: direction, possible ways of action	.7	.3	1.1
10. Shows disagreement: passive rejection, formality, withholds help	7.9	7.5	4.7
11. Shows tension: asks for help, withdraws "out of field"	2.0	1.7	4.6
12. Shows antagonism: deflates other's status, defends or asserts self	.5	4.7	2.7

SOURCE: Adapted from Bales R.F., & Hare, A.P. (1965). Diagnostic use of the interaction profile. *Journal of Social Psychology, 67,* 240.

meaningful response from another person in the group is coded into 1 of 12 categories. Half are task-oriented behaviors: giving suggestions or direction, giving opinions, giving information, asking for suggestions or direction, asking opinions, and asking for information. The other half are maintenance or socioemotional oriented: showing solidarity, showing tension release, showing agreement, showing disagreement, showing tension, and showing antagonism. Thus, if a group member said, "I think we ought to try another approach to this problem," and ended this comment with a sarcastic laugh, the comment might be scored on the Bales scheme as "giving a suggestion" and the laugh as "showing tension."

In stable and effective groups, both maintenance and task functions are served to some extent by its members. Research using interaction process analysis suggests that the preponderance of communications in most groups is of the task-oriented variety. Bales has found a similar pattern in groups as diverse as labor-management negotiation teams, psychotherapy groups, and discussion groups consisting of persons on LSD

FIGURE 4–3   Types of Messages in a Two-Person Communication Situation

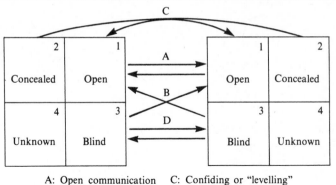

A: Open communication   C: Confiding or "levelling"
B: Leakage or unwitting   D: Emotional contagion
   revelations

SOURCE: Schein, E. H. (1969). *Process consultation: Its role in organization development* (p. 24). Reading, Mass.: Addison-Wesley Publishing. © 1969, Addison-Wesley. Reprinted with permission.

(see Table 4–1). Although the general profile varies to some degree with the task and type of members, the largest proportion of behaviors typically falls in the categories of showing agreement (16 percent), giving opinions (30 percent), and giving information (17 percent).[22] It appears from this research that the typical small-group discussion is one in which each member spends most of his or her time expressing opinions, providing information, and agreeing with others, with little time spent probing what others think or know. Given this profile, it is not surprising that the potential contributions of the quiet but capable member often are ignored by fellow group members.

How Open Are Communications among Group Members?

Still another dimension of group communication is the openness with which members communicate among themselves and others. One way of conceptualizing the communications between two persons is in terms of the Johari window, which is presented in Figure 4–3.[23] The knowledge each person has about himself is divided into four types. In the open area are those things that he knows (feelings, opinions, ideas, information he might have about the task) and is willing to share with others. In the concealed area are those things he knows but is not willing to share. The blind area consists of those things that others know but that he does not know. The unknown area consists of those things that neither the person nor the other knows. The unknown area consists in part of untapped potential, which Maslow emphasized in his discussion of self-actualization needs (see Chapter 3).

Communications among group members can be categorized according to which portions of each member's personality are in communication.

Some groups are characterized by a large amount of *open communication*. In other words, there is a free exchange of information between the "open areas," with each person openly giving and receiving information. Other types of communications are called *leakages* or *unwitting revelations* and consist of unintentional communication of things that the sender wishes to conceal. For example, one person may wish to conceal contempt for the boss but may communicate it in a negative tone of voice. A third category of communications are those in which the persons *level* with each other, that is, reveal formerly concealed information to one another. Chapter 8 discusses sensitivity groups, which attempt to create a climate in which members level with each other and, through this leveling, supposedly learn about themselves and their relations with others. Finally, there is *emotional contagion* in which two people communicate at the level of their blind areas. Consider as an example a supervisor who comes across in a hostile fashion but is unaware of how she is seen by others, and her subordinate who comes across in an equally hostile fashion and is also unaware of his abrasive manner. Each is likely to trigger an emotional response on the part of the other, but both are unlikely to see themselves as a cause of the other's response.

Groups are often believed to be more effective the more openly they communicate. This belief is somewhat simplistic. As we will discuss shortly, whether open communications improve performance or not depends on the type of task the group performs. Nevertheless, groups that have open communications are probably better off, generally speaking, than groups characterized by emotional contagion and unwitting revelations. Gibb has proposed that groups characterized by open communications are likely to have members who support each other.[24] The members of such groups are likely to listen to each other and attempt to understand each other's positions without being overly critical or controlling. On the other hand, groups characterized by defensive communications have members whose first reaction to each other is to evaluate and attempt to control.

What Is the Distribution of Communication and Influence within the Group?

Group members seldom all communicate or influence each other to the same extent. As we will discuss in the next chapter, some members of a group invariably have more influence than others. There often appears to be more than one leader, however. Some members emerge as leaders on task-related issues, whereas others may be leaders on the maintenance or socioemotional issues. In observing group communications, it is important to note who appears to wield the most influence on each dimension.

The amount of communication by each group member and perceptions of that member's influence appear to go hand in hand. When group members are surveyed as to the relative influence of members, it has been found that those members who spend the most time talking are usually seen as the most influential regardless of the value of the contributions they make to the group's performance.[25] Similarly, Schein observed that frequently

> One or more quiet members are accused by the more vocal ones of not contributing their thoughts to the discussion. In many instances, I have heard the quiet members deny this accusation, saying that they had been talking but that apparently no one had been listening to them. In most instances of this sort, I have found that the "silent member" is quite right; he had spoken several times but others had stereotyped him as silent and hence not heard what he had to say.[26]

As we have stated before, one way to improve a group's effectiveness is to create a communication climate in which the quiet but competent members are drawn out.

What Effect Does Process Have on Group Performance?

Although the various process dimensions described above provide useful assessments of groups, they do not yield much insight into the specific processes that mediate inputs to the group and the way the group performs its tasks. According to Hackman and Morris, "the impact of group interaction on group effectiveness is not direct, but instead operates by affecting three 'summary variables' that do directly determine how well a group does on its task."[27] These three summary variables are (1) the level of effort individuals exert on the task and the extent to which they coordinate their efforts, (2) how fully the group uses the task knowledge and skills of its members, and (3) the performance strategies used by members in performing the task.

One way, then, that the processes we have discussed influence the effectiveness of the group is by influencing the effort that individual group members invest in their tasks. In Chapter 3, we discussed the different characteristics of the work situation that can influence the level of employee motivation (e.g., reward system, task goals, and task characteristics). High levels of individual effort, however, may not ensure that the group will be effective in the performance of its task if the tasks require that members must also coordinate their efforts. Indeed, increasing the level of individual effort on a task might, in some circumstances, work against coordination as each member attempts to fulfill individual needs at the cost of others. Thus, Hackman and Morris include in this summary variable how well individuals coordinate their efforts as well as the individual level of effort.[28]

A second way in which group process influences group effectiveness is by determining how well the group utilizes the knowledge and skill of its members. In some cases, the group has sufficient resources to perform a task, but it assesses and weights the contributions of its members inappropriately. As we have seen, a verbally aggressive but incompetent member's ideas often appear to be given more weight by the group than the ideas of quiet but competent members. In other cases, a group might correctly identify the competent contribution but perform poorly because it fails to develop the skills and knowledge of its less competent members. Much of the training a new employee receives is conducted on the job by other members of the work group, as we will discuss in Chapter 8. It often has been observed, however, that more experienced employees have the attitude of "sink or swim" and are unwilling to assist new employees. One means of improving performance in most work groups is for the more experienced and capable members to share their expertise with others—even at the risk of some personal sacrifice.

Finally, group process influences effectiveness by shaping the strategies that members use in performing the task. Hackman and Morris define strategy as the

> collective choices made by the group members about how they will go about performing the task. Included are choices group members make about desirable performance outcomes and choices about how the group will go about trying to obtain these outcomes.[29]

Research indicates that groups often appear to desire a quick solution to problems and seldom spend time discussing alternative strategies. Groups also seem reluctant to confront conflicts in discussing a problem and often rely on majority rule or the opinions of the leader to avoid these conflicts. The best approach may be to remain flexible and switch strategies to meet the demands of the situation. Groups seldom are that flexible, however, and more often appear fixed on specific strategies without even being aware of their rigidity. Later in this chapter, when we discuss process consultation, we will discuss some attempts to improve group effectiveness by increasing member awareness of their task strategies.

The relative importance of the three summary variables depends on the nature of the group task. As we will show, on some tasks, the only critical variable is the degree of effort exerted by members. On other types of tasks, two or all three of the variables are important. In discussing the influence of the external environment, the composition of the group, and the group structure on group effectiveness, we will need to take into account the influence these inputs have on group process and the three summary variables and also the requirements of the task.

The External Environment

Now that we have discussed some of the critical processes that mediate group inputs and group performance, we will take a step back to discuss one category of inputs presented in Figure 4–1, *the external environment of the group.* Among the factors external to the group that shape the internal processes of the group and its outcomes are the task, reward system, communication network, and external pressures. Unlike many of the other variables influencing group process, the environment often can be changed by the organization; hence it often provides the most realistic means by which management can intervene to improve group effectiveness.

Task

The task that the group performs is, in all likelihood, the most important indication of how well a group performs and of the satisfaction of its members, and yet it is frequently ignored by researchers, theorists, and managers—probably because its effects are so obvious. It wouldn't surprise anyone, for instance, to find that group members behave differently when they participate in therapy sessions than they do when they are working on a crossword puzzle. In support of common sense, several experiments have shown that the type of task performed accounts for over half of the variation observed across groups, their process, and performance (of course, 50 percent still leaves plenty of room for improvement).[30]

As we mentioned earlier, there are at least two ways the task can influence the final performance of the group: (1) by influencing the motivation of its members to perform effectively on the task and (2) by imposing requirements on group process and thus moderating its effects on performance. In Chapter 3, we discussed some of the motivational consequences of task characteristics. Some of these theorists have predicted that employees with high growth needs will work harder to the extent that the task is challenging and requires the application of important abilities.[31] On tasks that are boring, inefficiently designed, extremely easy, or extremely difficult, employees often do not exert the amount of effort required for the group to perform effectively. In the latter case, employees may compensate for the lack of fulfillment in their higher-order needs by engaging in group activities. Gossip, rumors, love affairs, horseplay, and numerous other social behaviors can provide the desired relief (sometimes to the detriment of organizational goals).

The task also affects performance by imposing requirements on how group members must interact to perform the task successfully. Although tasks can be described on numerous dimensions, three dimensions have been the focus of intense scrutiny by group researchers, and they will be emphasized in the present chapter.

1. Combination of Member Contributions

One important task characteristic is the rule for combining individual contributions to the task to form the group output. Steiner distinguished four types of tasks on this basis: additive, conjunctive, disjunctive, and discretionary.[32] The relative importance of the three summary variables presented in Figure 4–1 depends on which of these four task types the group performs.

On *additive tasks*, the rule for obtaining the group's performance is to sum the performances of the individual group members. An example would be a group of sewing machine operators, each of whom is sewing a pair of pants and whose total performance is the sum of the number of pairs of pants produced. The performance of the group on this type of task depends largely on the level of effort exerted by each member and, in some cases, on the extent to which members coordinate their efforts. On a *disjunctive task*, each member contributes a performance but the group is forced to make an either-or decision and go with one and only one of the performances. An example of this type of task would be a group of managers who must choose the best applicant for a position from among a set of applicants. On this type of task, the best the group can perform is at the level of its highest performing member. On *conjunctive tasks*, the group succeeds only if all members succeed. The best the group can perform is at the level of its poorest performing member. An example of a conjunctive task would be a team of mountain climbers who are attempting to climb a mountain within a specific period of time. In the case of both conjunctive and disjunctive tasks, a particularly important process dimension is the extent to which group members use the talent available to them within the group. In the disjunctive case, the group must be able to recognize and use the best performing members. In the conjunctive task, the group must be able to identify potentially poor performers and help these members improve their performance.

In the tasks we have discussed so far, the rule for combining member performances is imposed on the group. In additive tasks, a weight of 1 is assigned to each member's contribution in forming the group's output. On conjunctive and disjunctive tasks, a weight of either 1 or 0 is assigned to each member's contribution. On the fourth type, the *discretionary task*, the group may choose its own rule and may assign any value from 1 to 0 to each member's contribution. For example, a group of four sales managers making a projection of how much demand there will be for a product might each generate an individual estimate and then average these estimates, a procedure equivalent to assigning to each member's contribution an equal weight—in this case, .25. When individual contributions are averaged, the performance of the group is largely unrelated to real group processes, except to the extent that the individual judges have been influenced by one another prior to making their estimates. When interaction is strictly precluded, this type of group is called a *nominal group*.

Additive, conjunctive, disjunctive, and discretionary tasks are all unitary; each member performs the same task, and the group performance is either one member's performance or some composite of all the performances in the group. A more common task confronting groups in organizations has a division of labor—that is, a divisible task. For example, a railroad crew might consist of an engineer, a switchman, a switchman's helper, and a brakeman, each performing a different subtask and thereby making a different contribution to the performance of the overall task. A different rule governing the combination of member outcomes to form the group product could be imposed on each subtask in a divisible task. Consequently, a divisible task is more complex than a unitary task and conceivably contains all the tasks we have discussed so far: conjunctive, disjunctive, additive, and discretionary. Potentially, a group performing a divisible task can exceed the performance of even the best individual group member, an occurrence Collins and Guetzkow call the *assembly bonus effect*. All three of the summary variables could be important in the performance of a divisible task. In particular, task strategy could play an important role insofar as the group has some discretion in how it can divide the task into subtasks.

2. Level of Coordination Required

On many types of divisible tasks, and on some unitary tasks as well, a second characteristic enters into consideration; the degree to which members are interdependent and must coordinate their efforts. Thompson distinguishes between tasks that impose pooled, sequential, and reciprocal interdependence on group members.[33] The smallest degree of interdependence, and consequently the least requirement for coordination, is found in pooled interdependence; each team member contributes to the productivity of the whole unit, but the individual members are not directly dependent on any other member. A secretarial pool that takes work as it comes but completes it independently could be considered as performing a task with pooled interdependence. With this type of interdependence, effective performance of the task depends much more on individual effort than on group coordination. An assembly line, on which each worker must coordinate activities with those on either side, illustrates a somewhat higher level: sequential interdependence. But the highest level of all is reciprocal interdependence, as in a basketball game, where success requires that team members closely coordinate their efforts.

3. Task Uncertainty

A third dimension that imposes important demands on group process is task uncertainty, which can be defined as "the difference between the amount of information required to perform the task and the amount of information already possessed."[34] This is probably the broadest and most ambiguous of the dimensions that we have applied to group tasks. Numerous task characteristics have been described as related to task uncertainty, including task complexity, goal clarity, goal-path multiplicity (the degree to which there is more than one approach to performing a task), decision verifiability (the degree to which the correctness of decisions can be determined), and decision specificity (the degree to which there is more than one correct solution). Task uncertainty generally increases as the amount of complexity and goal-path multiplicity increases and as goal clarity, decision verifiability, and decision specificity decrease.[35]

Tasks that are high on the uncertainty dimension, by definition, require members to process more information than do tasks low on uncertainty. Selecting the best job candidate from among a set of candidates should require little exchange or processing of information if the guidelines for evaluating candidates are clearly specified (e.g., grade point average of at least 3.5, engineering major, at least 25 years old, five years' job experience) and if all the data necessary to evaluate the application are on the resume. If the guidelines are not clearly specified or if the data on the person are ambiguous and incomplete, selecting the best person for the job requires considerably more information processing on the part of group members. A high degree of task uncertainty places demands on all the process dimensions that we have discussed. As the amount of information that must be processed increases, it becomes increasingly important that members exert a high level of individual effort, coordinate their efforts, use the resources of all members as completely as possible, and plan a strategy appropriate to the task.

Reward System

One of the most straightforward means available to an organization for motivating employees is to provide incentives for good performance. Partly because individualism and competitiveness are so highly valued in the United States, organizations here are prone to reward individual rather than group performance. There are two basic ways to reward individual performance. Competitive reward systems have winners and losers within the group, and one person is rewarded only at the expense of others. If the one worker producing the most in a month received a $100 bonus while all others received no bonus, this would be a purely competitive system. This type of reward system should be distinguished from individualistic reward systems, in which each group member is rewarded for individual performance independent of the performance of other group members. Although these are different systems, their effects on process and productivity seem to be similar in many respects. The indiscriminate use of either may be very destructive in its effects on group process and performance. In particular, competitive or individualistic reward systems can discourage the cooperative interaction vital to group success on tasks that require members to cooperate to accomplish task objectives. Moreover, there is always the danger that competition and individualism will degenerate into open conflict.

An example of the destructive consequences of a reward system that is incongruent with task requirements was provided by Blau in a study of the effects of an individualistic appraisal system in a public employment service.[36] The job of the employment counselors in this organization was to interview people seeking employment, obtain information on available job openings from employers, and match the best available applicants to job openings. Management implemented a system that evaluated each individual counselor on the basis of the number of clients he personally placed in jobs. For the group of counselors to maximize their collective performance, the task required that they share information about job openings. Contrary to the demands of the task, and to the detriment of the overall objectives of the employment service, the individualistic system discouraged the sharing of information and encouraged the hoarding of information.

An alternative to the individualistic and competitive systems is the cooperative system, which rewards individual employees on the basis of how their group performs. In a series of experiments conducted in university classes at Columbia in the late 1940s, Morton Deutsch found that group members rewarded for the performance of the entire group in the classes, compared to those in which members worked under a competitive reward systems, (1) were more motivated to complete their tasks, (2) were more likely to divide up the labor among group members, (3) more effectively communicated with each other, (4) were friendlier with each other, and (5) performed with higher quality and quantity.[37] Subsequent research has revealed that the effects of the reward system depend heavily on the task. A recent review of research conducted over the last three decades concluded that if the task requires cooperation, higher group performance is more likely to result from a cooperative reward structure than from either individualistic or competitive reward systems.[38] If the task does not require cooperation, it seems to make little difference whether the reward system is cooperative, competitive, or individualistic. Of course, most of the group research on reward systems has been conducted in laboratory settings and must be interpreted in that light.

Despite the possible limitations on its generalizability, the research on reward systems brings to our attention a problem critical to the successful use of incentives. On the one hand, it is important to recognize and reward individuals so that they exert maximum effort on the tasks they perform. On the other hand, many tasks require employees to coordinate their efforts. What is the resolution to these often conflicting task demands? One solution might be to have a mixed reward system, in which the individual group members are rewarded in part for the group's performance and in part for their individual performances. Some research findings, however, indicate that mixed systems are no better than individualistic or competitive systems when the task requires cooperation.[39] The issue remains unresolved, then, and an important task for future research is to determine how to design reward systems that encourage *both* individual effort and cooperation.

Physical Constraints on Communication

Often there are environmental constraints on who can communicate with whom within a group. We already have discussed one form of constraint, the physical location of group members. Equally important are the formally prescribed lines of authority and communication set forth in the classical organizational chart. An important dimension of any network of communication is the degree to which it is *centralized*, that is, the extent to which information passing from one member to another must flow through a central position in the group.

In a large amount of laboratory research conducted during the 1950s and 1960s, social psychologists attempted to assess the effects of the degree of centralization in communication networks on group functioning. In these studies, members of groups were placed in cubicles connected only by slots in the walls through which they could communicate by passing written messages to each other. Figure 4–4 shows the different communication networks imposed on groups in these studies. In the most decentralized of the four-person networks (the comcon configuration), every member could communicate directly with every other member, whereas in the most centralized network (the wheel), everyone had to go through a central person.

As might be expected, the different networks produced dramatic effects on group performance and member satisfaction. Members of decentralized networks were more satisfied with their groups than were the peripheral members of centralized networks. The only persons in centralized networks who tended to be as satisfied were those assigned to the central position. Moreover, when members of decentralized networks were given the opportunity to organize whatever network they wished, they usually stayed with a decentralized configuration.

The effects of communication networks on group performance have again been found to depend largely on the type of task.[40] In centralized networks, groups are forced to rely on one person, and their performance depends largely on the capacity of that central person to process and integrate the information held by each of the peripheral members. With simple tasks the answer to the problem is obvious. Once all the available information held by each member is pulled together, groups with centralized networks typically outperform decentralized groups on such tasks. Apparently, the centralized network allows superior coordination without overextending the central person. As the complexity of the task increases, however, the likelihood that the central person will be able to

FIGURE 4–4   Communication Networks Used in Experimental Investigations

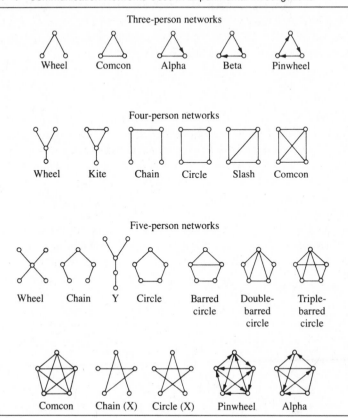

NOTE: Dots represent positions, lines represent communication channels, and arrows indicate one-way channels.

SOURCE: Shaw, M. Communication networks. (1964). In L. Berkowitz (Ed.). *Advances in experimental social psychology* (Vol. 1) (pp. 111–147). New York: Academic Press.

process and integrate all the information decreases (*channel capacity* is exceeded), and the relative performance of the decentralized configuration (which has more channel capacity) improves.

Although these findings were obtained in admittedly artificial circumstances, they appear to support a general systems principle that has implications for not only groups in real organizations but also entire organizations. Ashby's Law of Requisite Variety states that as information in the environment becomes increasingly complex, a system must become correspondingly more complex to process the information.[41] For example, corporations like General Motors and Du Pont could at one time operate quite efficiently with highly centralized organizational structures where a few people at the top of the hierarchy made all critical decisions. As product lines became increasingly diverse, the amount and complexity of the information that had to be handled eventually exceeded the capacity of these centralized structures. Not unlike the decentralized groups working on complex tasks in the laboratory, decentralized organizational structures appear to have operated more effectively in complex corporate environments than have centralized structures.[42]

External Pressures and Stress

Groups within organizations may work under a variety of external pressures and stresses, including task deadlines, crises, competition from other groups, and dangerous environmental conditions. External pressures such as these are important determinants of group process and performance. One common finding from research on groups under external threat is that, as stress increases, group leaders tend to become more autocratic and members tend to become more accepting of this leadership.[43] Whole nations as well as small groups seem more likely to succumb to dictatorships when they are under stress. The emergence of autocratic leadership is not always dysfunctional, as any soldier in combat would probably agree. There isn't much time to take a vote with "bombs bursting in air." The danger is that leaders may manufacture external threats as a ploy to obtain allegiance of group members. A recent example was the Iranian government's sanctioning of the holding of American hostages in 1979–80, which appears to have been a calculated attempt to unify the populace.

Groups in organizations often experience stress in the form of competition and conflict with other groups. Intergroup conflicts emerge for a variety of reasons, including competitive reward systems, competition for scarce resources, and various differences between group members. It is common to find rivalry and even conflict among groups performing different functions in an organization. The sales department views the production department as totally concerned with costs of production and insensitive to customer demands; the production department views the R&D department as a bunch of egghead professors with no sense of priorities. Consistent with the findings of research on other types of external pressures, groups in conflict tend to become more task oriented, autocratic, and structured. As conflict escalates, members within each group forget their individual feuds, join together to defeat the common enemy, and bring increasing pressures on members to comply with group norms.[44] At the same time that intergroup conflict is building closer relationships *within* the groups, however, it is straining relationships *between* the groups in conflict. Each sees the other in a distorted, stereotypic manner. As hostility increases, each group operates on the assumption that it is in a win-lose situation and that the other will lie, cheat, and do all manner of evil to win. These assumptions, in turn, can lead each group to behave in ways that provoke reactions in the other and thereby confirm the assumptions—because they're cheating, we must too. In short, once conflict begins to escalate, it becomes both self-fulfilling and self-perpetuating. Of course, intergroup competition and conflict do not always lessen the performance of a group. If a task requires little cooperation between groups but a large amount of cooperation within each, intergroup conflict might enhance rather than hurt overall effectiveness. If it occurs between units in an organization that must cooperate to achieve their objectives, however, intergroup conflict, in all likelihood, will harm the performance of one or both groups.

Another task situation in which external threat may harm the performance of the group is where the task requires a high degree of information processing. External threat and stress may interfere with a group's capacity to accurately receive information from its environment and to process this information in an analytical and unbiased fashion. Janis found some evidence of this in a study of well-known fiascoes in governmental decision making, such as Admiral Kimmel's failure to recognize the threat of Japan on Pearl Harbor and John F. Kennedy's decisions in the Bay of Pigs invasion.[45] According to Janis, a highly cohesive group behind each fiasco maintained its cohesiveness and the self-esteem of its members in the face of external threats through what he (and George Orwell) called *groupthink*. Groupthink is identified by several symptoms: the illusion among members that there is unanimous support for the decisions of the group, a distorted sense of invulnerability, a tendency to rationalize away errors in decision making, an elevated view of the group whereby members believe that there is a moral justification for their decisions, and a stereotyped view of outside groups. In addition to these distorted perceptions, members avoid bringing to the group information that might disrupt the esprit de corps, and individuals who dare to disagree with the group's decisions find themselves the object of ridicule and other pressures to conform. Although a group with these symptoms may appear on the surface to be highly effective, Janis proposed that it very likely is heading for a colossal error in judgment. Janis's theory has not gone without criticism.[46] Nevertheless, the groupthink notion is quite provocative and will undoubtedly receive more attention in the future.

Group Structure

A second category of inputs that determines group process and group effectiveness is the structure of the group. Earlier we defined structure as relatively stable behaviors, beliefs, and attitudes existent within a group that set it apart from other groups. Because of its structure, a group has, in a sense, an existence apart from its individual members and can maintain a distinct identity even though its membership changes. Just as the environment of the group constrains the behavior of its members, the group's structural characteristics also channel the behavior of its

TABLE 4–2 Patterns of Interactions among 12 Clerical Employees*

		Row I				Row II				Row III		
		Baldwin	Fahey	Rioux	Murray	Doherty	Rafferty	Hall	Donovan	Casey	Carey	O'Malley	Lenihan
Row I	Baldwin	—	53	23	8	0	5	2	2	0	1	1	16
	Fahey		—	26	9	0	2	3	0	2	1	0	1
	Rioux			—	75	1	4	1	2	2	1	0	0
	Murray				—	0	2	1	3	1	1	1	1
Row II	Doherty					—	24	26	18	4	8	7	2
	Rafferty						—	6	30	20	19	21	3
	Hall							—	51	7	5	3	2
	Donovan								—	3	7	1	1
Row III	Casey									—	46	42	20
	Carey										—	69	30
	O'Malley											—	53
	Lenihan												—

*The frequencies with which pairs of employees communicated during the period in which they were observed are entered in the matrix.

SOURCE: Gullahorn, J. T. (1955). Distance and friendship as factors in the gross interaction matrix. *Sociometry, 15,* 123–134.

members and influence task performance. The structural dimensions that we will discuss are patterns of interactions among members, norms, roles, cohesiveness, and status.

Interaction Patterns in Organizations

Recurring patterns of interaction among members define the boundaries of the group. The organizational chart may provide some information on who interacts with whom, but the formal chart is at best an idealized picture and at worst a total fiction. A more accurate approach to measuring interaction patterns is to observe who actually interacts with whom in the group. Gullahorn, for example, observed the interactions among 29 female employees in a large office over a two-week period, tallying every 15 minutes who was conversing with whom.[47] The frequency of conversations among the women is summarized in Table 4–2. On the basis of the interaction patterns, three groups appear to have emerged within the office. Consistent with our discussion of group formation at the beginning of this chapter, the physical proximity of the women was the major factor determining patterns of interactions. Of 1,558 interactions observed, 78 percent took place within the row in which an employee sat.

Using a quantitative technique called social network analysis,[48] data such as presented in Table 4–2 can be used to locate the informal groups within an organization and to describe their structural characteristics. The degree to which members in a group have contact with outside persons is defined as the group's *openness*. Some groups, such as the groups in rows 2 and 3, are relatively open in that members interact with persons outside their group as much as they do with persons inside the group. Other groups, such as the group in row 1, are closed in that their members have few outside contacts. There is some evidence that closed groups tend to be less creative in their problem solving, more prone to conflict and competition with other groups, and more vulnerable to groupthink.[49] Another important structural characteristic is *connectedness*, which is usually defined as the number of direct interactions among members of the group relative to the total possible interactions. The most connected groups are those in which every member frequently interacts with every other member. A related feature is the extent to which interactions consist of *two-way communication* as contrasted with *one-way* communication. Both connectedness and two-way communication have been shown to be positively related to the perceived amount of open and accurate information transfer within a group.[50] The extent to which connectedness and two-way communication facilitate the performance of a group, however, probably depends on the nature of the group task. As we stated earlier, open communication among members appears to facilitate the performance of complex tasks but may hinder the performance of a simpler task.

Norms

In stable and productive groups, members share some common expectations regarding the proper conduct of group members. These expectations are called *norms*, and they constitute another important structural dimension. Norms serve several important functions.[51] Perhaps the most important is that they allow group members to predict each other's behavior to some extent. Groups whose members do not know what to expect from each other are likely to encounter difficulties in performing their tasks and in relating to each other. Without norms, most groups would eventually dissolve.

Norms cannot be directly observed but must be inferred from the behavior and self-reports of group members. Groups have more than one norm governing the behavior of their members. There are often norms defining what type of clothing to wear, the appropriate ways to address other members, and how to distribute rewards among group members (e.g., equally, according to merit, or on the basis of need). Others govern the processes occurring in the group, particularly the strategies considered appropriate in performing the task. As noted by Feldman, norms do not exist for all behaviors that members might exhibit but only for those that are perceived as important to the group. Rubin and Beckhard found the following norms in interdisciplinary health teams consisting of physicians, nurses, and case workers:[52]

1. In making a decision, silence means consent.

2. Doctors are more important than other team members; therefore, we don't disagree with them—we wait for them to lead.

3. Conflict is dangerous. Thus it is better to avoid both task conflicts and interpersonal disagreements.

4. Positive feelings, praise, and support are not to be shared—we're all professionals here to do a job.

5. The precision and exactness demanded by our task require that we stick strictly to procedures—we don't experiment with new ways of doing things.

Particularly important are the norms defining how hard members should work and how productive they should be. In the Hawthorne studies, for instance, workers in the bank wiring room were found to stay within a range of productivity that was well below the level expected by management. Apparently the group defined for itself the productivity levels that its members should achieve, and these norms influenced the performance of most members more than management's production standards.

Norms may be measured in several ways. One common way is through observing the behavior of group members. If most members are observed to conform to some common practices and if pressures are brought to bear against members who do not conform, then these practices are defined as a norms. A more direct approach is Jackson's return potential model.[53] According to this approach, group members are asked how others in the group would react if they were to behave in certain ways. Each group member indicates how much approval or disapproval other members would show if that member were to exhibit a behavior to a specific degree. From the responses of all members of the group, a visual representation of the norm can be plotted. For example, one could use this method to measure worker norms for productivity by asking them to indicate how much they would expect other workers to approve or disapprove if they were to perform at very low, average, and very high levels. The mean level of approval and disapproval could then be plotted for each level of productivity. The results of two hypothetical groups of workers are presented in Figure 4–5.

Several useful characteristics of norms can be derived from the return potential curve, including the *intensity* of a norm (the height of the curve, both above and below the point of indifference) and the *ideal level* of a behavior (the point of maximum approval). As can be seen from Figure 4–5, Group A's norm for production is less intense than B's, but the ideal level of productivity is higher in Group B. Another important characteristic that can be derived from a survey such as this is the *crystallization* of a norm (the degree to which there are differences of opinion among members regarding how they expect the group to react to certain behaviors).

Norms serve as standards against which the behaviors of group members are judged, and those who deviate from the norms of the group are likely to find both subtle and overt pressures brought to bear against them by fellow group members. In the bank wiring room group in the Hawthorne plant, those who exceeded the production norm were labeled *rate busters* and were punished in various ways, including verbal criticism and *binging* (a sock on the arm). Those who fell too far below the productivity level considered to be ideal were labeled as *chislers* and also received disapproval from the group.

Not only do group members pressure deviants in the group to conform, but individual members seem only too willing to succumb to these pressures. In a series of classic experiments in social psychology, Asch found that close to two thirds of group members conformed to obviously incorrect majority opinions.[54] Conformity to group norms may represent *compliance* as members yield to pressures in order to avoid punishments and obtain rewards.[55] When others are not around to reward or punish them, group norms lose their power to influence those who merely show compliance. Other members may *internalize* norms; in other words, they actually come to believe that what the group wants them to do is proper or correct. A member who has internalized a norm will conform to it regardless of whether he or she is likely to gain rewards or avoid punishments

FIGURE 4–5   Norms for Production in Two Groups

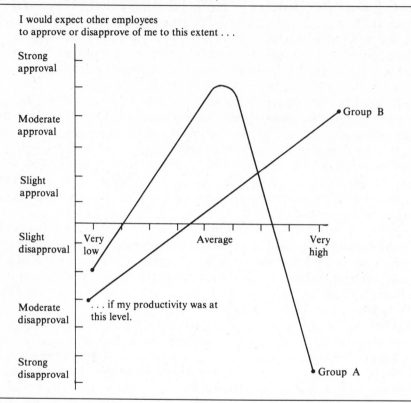

through conformity. The ultimate objective of most attempts by groups to *socialize* their members is probably to induce members to internalize group norms, but it is likely that compliance is most frequently achieved.

Roles

Norms apply to behaviors expected of all members of the group. Each member, however, is expected to behave in some ways that differ from the behaviors of other group members. The persistent pattern of behavior that results from these expectations is called a *role*. Some roles that are performed by group members are formally defined by the organization. Other roles, however, may emerge from more informal interactions.

The more people interact, the more specialized the role structure of the group tends to become. Evidence of this was provided by Bales who observed groups of students discussing human relations cases.[56] After each of the discussion sessions, group members selected the member they liked the most, the member who had the best ideas, and the members who provided the best guidance. After the first session, the same group member tended to be seen as the best liked and the one with the best ideas and guidance. As the meetings progressed, however, the members began to make distinctions among *task* and *socioemotional* roles. The members ranked highest on ideas and guidance (task roles) tended to be ranked among the least liked (socioemotional role). Only rarely did one group member occupy both roles and emerge as both a task and socioemotional leader. Rather, these two leadership roles appeared to become specialized.

Social network analysis, which we described earlier, can identify other roles. At least five different roles have been distinguished. *Liaisons* are not members of any group but who have contact with members of two or more separate groups and serve the function of coordinating these groups. *Isolates* have few or no relationships with others. *Stars* have a relatively high number of interactions with other persons. *Bridges* or *linking pins* are members of multiple groups and can serve much the same function as liaisons. The various roles that informally emerge in a group can serve valuable functions. Liaisons and linking pins can provide an avenue for communications with other groups in the organization. Even isolates can serve a function if their isolation is seen as an example of what can happen if a member violates group norms.

Katz and Kahn have presented a model of the process by which roles emerge in groups and organizations.[57] They posit that each member of an organization has a *role set*, a group of other persons who communicate either explicitly or implicitly their expectations for what the focal person should be doing. The role set *sends* or communicates role expectations by conveying subtly or not so subtly what the focal person should be doing. The role set may include peers, subordinates, supervisors, spouses, children—in short, anyone, inside or outside the organization, who expects specific behaviors of the focal person and has the opportunity to communicate these expectations. The focal person's perception of what the role set expects is the *received role*. Whether or not the role occupant actually performs the role in the way that others desire depends in large part on whether the role occupant accurately perceives their expectations. Past findings indicate that there is plenty of room for improvement here as subordinates are often quite inaccurate in their perceptions of what their supervisors expect of them.

In complex organizations, there is frequently some stress associated with the sending and receiving of roles. Katz and Kahn distinguish between two major role stressors: ambiguity and conflict.[58] *Role ambiguity* results when the expectations sent to a particular role occupant are incomplete or unclear. For example, new members of a group often experience role ambiguity because veteran members of the group fail to show them the ropes. It is often the case, however, that group members know what is expected of them by other persons, but the expectations are incompatible and conflicting. *Role conflict*, as this type of role stress is termed, exists in three forms. *Person-role conflict* occurs when the values or other personal characteristics of the role occupant conflict with the expectations of others: A group member is expected by other group members to cheat on an expense account, in conflict with his or her moral standards. *Intrarole conflict* occurs when incompatible behaviors are expected of a role occupant by different persons or the same person in a role set: A first-line supervisor is caught between his subordinates, who expect him to treat them as his equals, and his boss, who expects him to "crack the whip." The third type of role conflict is *interrole conflict*, in which a person must perform two incompatible roles: The role of manager in a firm conflicts with the roles of parent and spouse.

From past research, it seems clear that the more role conflict and ambiguity a focal person experiences, the more dissatisfied he or she is with the job and the more job-related tension he or she feels.[59] The consequences of role conflict and ambiguity for group performance, however, are not particularly clear. For a group to perform adequately, there should be some degree of clarity and consistency in the communication of role expectations, but there are limits to how far one can and should structure roles. It is unlikely that we can ever specify in minute detail the what, when, and how of most jobs, particularly those that are relatively complex. Moreover, trying to specify in detail what each group member is expected to do just might, on some tasks, lead to group rigidity and reduce the group's capacity to respond rapidly to unforeseen events. As we mentioned earlier in our discussion of Ashby's Law of Requisite Variety, complex tasks that require cooperation may need to be relatively "loose" in their internal structure to effectively perform the task. Some evidence of this was found by Burns and Stalker in a classic study of electronic firms in Britain.[60] They concluded from their findings that in changing conditions the more effective firms are likely to have *organic organizational structures* in which there is ambiguity and even confusion in the definition of job duties. Despite the lack of clarity, an organic structure appears better able to meet the demands of an unstable environment than a *mechanistic structure* in which there is a clear and orderly delineation of responsibilities.

Group Cohesiveness

Another structural dimension is group cohesiveness. As the term indicates, this is the degree to which group members stick together or, if one prefers jargon, it is the "resultant of all forces acting on group members to remain in or leave the group."[61] There seem to be two primary forces that keep groups together. First, members stay with a group as long as it helps them to achieve their goals. Once that ceases, the group is likely to lose some of its appeal. A second force is the personal attractiveness of members for one another. Cohesiveness is measured by asking members to rate the attractiveness of the group and their desire to remain as members or by asking members to nominate those group members with whom

FIGURE 4–6   Sociograms of Two Work Groups in a Research Laboratory

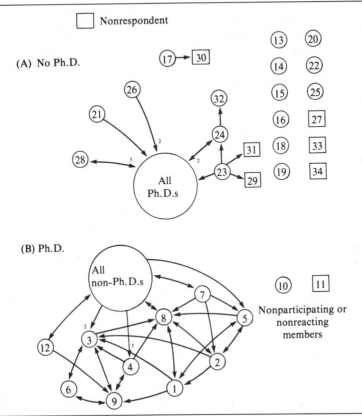

Note: All workers were asked to choose the others with whom they would most like to socialize. Lines with single arrows denote unilateral choices. Lines with double arrows denote mutual choices. Numbers indicate the number of choices made where more than one. Numbers 1 and 2 in circles represent the research directors.

SOURCE: Allen, T. J., & Cohen, S. I. (1965). Information flow in research and development laboratories. *Administrative Science Quarterly, 14,* 12–20.

they would most like to work or socialize. Using the latter approach, a group is said to be cohesive to the extent that members show a large number of reciprocated or mutual nominations. Allen and Cohen used this procedure with technicians and Ph.D. scientists in a research laboratory.[62] As may be seen in the *sociogram* presented in Figure 4–6, the Ph.D. scientists formed a more cohesive group than the technician group. When asked to choose the persons with whom they most like to socialize, there were no mutual choices among the technicians compared to six mutual choices among the Ph.D.s.

Among the factors that seem to induce high cohesiveness are group success in achieving goals, small group size, external threats, and perceptions of group members that they are similar to one another in beliefs, backgrounds, and other characteristics.[63] Cohesion has several important effects on the behavior of group members. In highly cohesive groups, members tend to pressure each other to conform to group norms to a greater extent than do members of low-cohesive groups.[64] Likewise, as cohesion increases, group members are also more likely to conform to group norms. Members of cohesive groups not only seem to conform more to group norms, but they are less likely to blame the group for their misfortunes. This was recently demonstrated in a study in which members of groups that were low in cohesion were shown to blame the group for task failures and to assume personal responsibilities for task success.[65] In contrast, members of cohesive groups were not affected in their assignment of responsibility by their success or failure on the tasks. In cohesive groups, persons were more willing to assume personal responsibility for failure and more willing to give credit to fellow group members for task successes. In several other respects, members of cohesive groups seem to interact in a more cooperative and congenial fashion. Members of cohesive groups are also more likely to personally identify with their groups, enjoy the company of other group members, and assist one another than are members of noncohesive groups. Finally, group cohesiveness appears to be associated with lower anxiety and stress among members.[66]

If cohesion leads to so many positive group processes, one would expect that it also would enhance the performance of the group. The relationship is not that simple, however. Stogdill reviewed this research and found that cohesiveness was related to poorer performance or had no relationship to performance about as many times as it was related to improved performance.[67] It seems that, again, one must take into account the nature of the task. Group cohesiveness appears likely to improve performance on tasks in which anxiety has a significant detrimental effect on performance (e.g., military combat) and on tasks in which members are required to coordinate their activities to a high degree.[68] The clearest evidence, however, seems to be that cohesion affects performance primarily through influencing the degree to which members conform to group norms. Members of highly cohesive groups tend to differ less in their performance than do members of less cohesive groups due to the greater conformity of members in cohesive groups to productivity norms.[69] Thus, management should not expect that improved productivity will necessarily result from improved group cohesiveness—it all depends on the group's norm for productivity. An increase in the cohesion of a group could result in a highly productive group (if the norms support high production) or in a very unproductive group (if the norms support a low level of production). One might expect, for example, that increased cohesion would have the effect of increasing the performance of Group B in Figure 4–6 to a greater extent than it would Group A.

Status

Our last type of structural factor, *status*, refers to the rank or worth of a group member as perceived by other members. It may result from one's own efforts (*achieved status*) or from factors that are totally outside the person's control (*ascribed status*). Race, sex, religion, national origin, and color are all possible sources of ascribed status. Rarely do all persons in the group have the same status. Usually a *status hierarchy* exists on which persons can be ordered from most to least valued on the basis of their perceived prestige, importance, and utility to the group. Similar to norms and roles, status depends on the perceptions and values of the group—what one group considers to be of high value may be considered worthless by another group. Because the status hierarchy is not always obvious, either to insiders or to outsiders, it is often reinforced by symbols. The offices of employees with high status may have rugs on the floor and their names on the door; employees of moderate status may only have their names on the door; a low-status employee may not even have a door, much less a rug.

As an example of a status hierarchy, consider the hypothetical management team described in Table 4–3. The overall status of a member of this team is a function of her ranking on each of several dimensions. The most obvious is formal position (president, vice president, division manager, etc.), but informal factors such as age, seniority, and education enter in as well. If the assumption is made that all dimensions are equally important in Table 4–3, overall status is indicated by the sum of the employee's rankings on the different dimensions. As shown in the table, the employee in this group who holds the highest formal position, the president, also has the highest overall status. The overall status of some of the other members, however, is inconsistent with their formal status. *Status congruence* is an important characteristic of the status hierarchy and reflects the extent to which the positions a person occupies on the various dimensions are consistent. In the example, the president has the highest status congruence, but the project engineer has the lowest. Another example would be a competent female hired into an all-white male group where status derives from being male and being competent. The status incongruence could disrupt communications and evoke tension among members as they face the dilemma of whether to relate to the newcomer as a low-status female or as a high-status expert.[70] A second characteristic is *status discrepancy*, or the extent to which a person's overall status in one group is inconsistent with status in another. Thus, a college professor might occupy a high-status position in his main line of work but a very low one in his National Guard unit. Of course, status discrepancy is more likely to create problems for the group in which the person occupies the low-status position than for the group in which he or she occupies a

TABLE 4–3 Rankings of Managerial Team Members on Status Dimensions

| | Rankings on Status Dimensions | | | | |
	Formal Position	Age	Seniority	Education	Overall Status
President	1	1	1	1	1
Senior vice president	2	3	6	7	4
Vice president	3	5	3	4	3
Division manager	4	7	4	5	5
Department manager	5	8	5	8	8
General supervisor	6	6	7	6	7
Supervisor	7	2	2	3	2
Project engineer	8	4	8	2	6

higher one. A third characteristic of a status hierarchy is the level of *status consensus*, or the degree to which members of a group agree on the relative status of each member. Low consensus can originate from disagreements among members as to the importance of the various status dimensions. Such would be the case in the group illustrated in Table 4–2 if some members considered age to be the most important factor and others stressed education. Low consensus also can originate from disagreements among group members on how they rank members on a factor. All members, for instance, might agree that education is important but might differ in their perception of the status of individual members on this dimension. For some, a degree from Harvard might be considered a higher educational attainment than a degree from Stanford, whereas others might hold the opposite opinion. Although there are exceptions, effective groups are likely to have members who are low in status discrepancy, high in status congruence, and who agree on the relative status of members in the group.[71]

Despite the negative effects of low consensus on group effectiveness, there are also risks associated with a well-articulated status hierarchy. Not surprisingly, a high-status person influences decision making, resource allocation, and communication flow in a group more than a low-status person does.[72] This shouldn't cause alarm as long as the higher-status persons are also the most capable members for the task at hand. For one thing, a group may consider task ability to be less important than other status dimensions (e.g., seniority, race) or it may assume mistakenly that a high-status person's competence on one task generalizes to most other tasks—the old halo effect. In either event, the ideas and opinions of high-status persons may be overutilized, whereas those of low-status persons may be underutilized.

In essence, differences in status tend to create a centralized network of communication. Higher-status persons have been found to initiate and receive more communications than do lower-status members.[73]

Consistent with this finding, group members have been shown to prefer communicating with members of higher status than with lower-status members.[74] As we have already shown, however, a centralized flow of communication is not a particularly effective way to use group resources when the task at hand is complex and requires a large amount of information processing. Moreover, communications directed to higher-status persons are often quite distorted since lower-status persons offer mostly praise, respect, agreement, and other positive messages to their superiors and filter out bad news. This is one reason that top officials often are the last to know when an organization is headed for a crisis.

There is probably little that the organization can do to change the status hierarchy, other than make people aware of its existence and the influence it can have on interpersonal relations. Managers should at least be made aware, however, of the effects that their status can have on their communications with subordinates, particularly the stifling effects that their mere presence can have on the generation and evaluation of ideas during problem-solving discussions. Also, the leader can assume responsibility for seeing that the ideas of low-status members are given full consideration by the group.

Group Composition

The structure of a group makes it something more than the individuals that constitute it. Nonetheless, it is still made up of individuals. The third category of inputs in Figure 4–1, then, concerns the characteristics of a group's members. We will address three questions concerning the characteristics of group members. First, do members have the *abilities* necessary to perform the task, and is the group using those abilities fully? Second, does the group possess the right mix of persons—is it too homogeneous or not homogeneous enough? Finally, does the group have too many or too few members? In the present section, we examine some of the effects of ability, homogeneity-heterogeneity, and size.

Task Ability

Not surprisingly, groups tend to perform better the higher the task abilities of their members. Yet, group performance is often far below the level of performance one would expect from the aggregate of individual abilities. Steiner expressed this failure of groups to achieve their potential as:

Actual productivity = Potential productivity − Process loss[75]

The failure to achieve potential is the result of losses or deficiencies on the three process dimensions that we discussed previously: effort or coordination of effort, utilization of individual abilities, and task strategies (see Figure 4–1). The type of process loss most likely to occur depends on the task.

Groups performing additive tasks often fail to perform up to their potential because their members exert insufficient effort and because they do not properly coordinate their efforts. A simple illustration of this was provided over 50 years ago by a German psychologist, Rigelmann, who compared individuals and groups performing a rope-pulling task.[76] Eight men pulling together exerted only about four times as much force as an individual working alone, not eight times as much—which one would expect if their individual efforts combined in a purely additive fashion. In situations such as this, people probably do not feel as directly responsible for the outcome as they are when working alone, and thus they are less inclined to give total effort. They also are likely to fail in coordinating their efforts—in this case, pulling the rope.

In tasks requiring greater levels of coordination than the simple additive variety, all three group process dimensions can affect performance. It should be harder, then, to predict how well the group will do from individual abilities. Jones found some evidence for this in a study of the relationship between team success and the ability of team members in professional sports.[77] Nearly 90 percent of the variation in the performance of baseball teams was predictable from measures of member skill, compared to only 35 percent of the performance of basketball teams. The difference obviously reflects the difference in coordination required by tasks in the two sports. For the same reason, one wouldn't expect a Pro Bowl football team, consisting of the best players in the league, to beat a Super Bowl championship team. Even though the average ability of the Pro Bowl team is probably greater, the members would not be as used to playing together as a team and would show greater process losses.

Homogeneity-Heterogeneity

Group members who are homogeneous with regard to their personalities, values, attitudes, and backgrounds are more likely to work harmoniously than heterogeneous ones. Nevertheless, there is a down side to homogeneity. Group members may work together so harmoniously that they fail to explore alternative approaches to problems and duplicate each other's strengths and weaknesses. The effects of homogeneity and heterogeneity again depend on the task.

On most types of tasks, with the exception of conjunctive tasks and many types of additive tasks, increased heterogeneity has the potential for improving a group's performance if it is associated with more diverse task resources. The "College Bowl" quiz show, for instance, matches one team against another in what is essentially a disjunctive task. Questions are asked on a variety of topics, and the first member of a team who presses a button and answers the question correctly wins points for his or her team. An effective team is not likely to consist of all physics or English majors but is probably quite heterogeneous with regard to the areas of expertise of its members. A heterogeneous group is also more likely to have the talents needed for the various subtasks on a divisible task. At least two studies have found that interdisciplinary research teams whose members differ in their strategies for tackling technical problems and their general styles of problem solving are superior in their performance to teams whose members are similar in their strategies and styles.[78]

Although heterogeneity may increase the potential performance of the group, heterogeneity also puts some strain on personal relationships among its members. Whether heterogeneity hurts or helps the performance of a group seems to depend on whether it leads to substantive conflict (disagreement on task-related issues) or *affective conflict* (conflict over purely personal issues). Guetzkow and Gyr observed 72 decision-making conferences and found that group effectiveness was positively related to the amount of substantive conflict but negatively related to the amount of affective conflict.[79] The practical implication of these findings is that the leader of a heterogeneous group may have to be quite skilled in handling disagreements and interpersonal conflict for the group to perform up to its potential.

Group Size

Another factor that appears to be an important determinant of group process and performance is the number of persons in a group. Adding members to a group should increase the group's potential on most tasks. The more people there are working on an additive task, the more total resources there are available and the better the group should be able to perform. On a disjunctive task, more people means a greater likelihood that someone in the group will be able to solve the problem and, on a divisible task, a greater opportunity for specialization. Only in the case of the conjunctive task would one expect size to have an adverse effect: Adding more people to a mountain-climbing team would only increase the risk of winding up with someone even slower than the slowest current member.[80]

Even though adding more members typically increases the group's overall performance on most types of tasks, groups do not perform as well as they should. Moreover, groups seem to perform increasingly below their potential as the size of the group increases. For example, Ingham and Levinger found that dyads pulling a rope pulled at 93 percent of individual capacity, triads at 85 percent, and groups of eight at only 49 percent.[81] This failure to achieve potential, called *social loafing*, has been demonstrated in a wide variety of tasks.[82] In addition to inhibiting individual performance, large group size has been associated with low job satisfaction, high absence rates, high turnover, and frequent labor disputes. Porter and Lawler proposed that these effects of large group size were mediated by low cohesiveness, task specialization, and disruptions in communication.[83] Other research has shown that members of groups that are too large relative to the demands of the task are less likely to participate and assume responsibility for the fate of the group than are members of groups that are too small relative to task demands.[84]

Although groups can be too small, it appears that being too big is the more serious problem. The solution is that organizations should carefully examine task demands and avoid both overstaffing and understaffing.

INTERVENTIONS TO IMPROVE GROUP PERFORMANCE

Now that we have surveyed a number of variables that can influence group process and performance, we must ask what practical suggestions can be gleaned from all this material. Hackman and Morris propose three interventions, each focused on deficiencies in one of the three process areas.[85] If task strategy seems to be a problem, then an attempt should be made to change the group norms that control choice of strategy. If lack of effort is indicated, then one of the techniques designed to improve motivation should be considered. If lack of knowledge and skills is evident, then a carefully designed and validated selection or training program should be implemented. We will discuss some of the specific techniques relevant to each of these three categories of interventions.

Interventions to Modify Group Strategy

We will discuss two primary approaches to modifying a group's task strategies: process consultation and technologies for group problem solving.

Process Consultation

In process consultation, the members of the group diagnose their problems in working together and implement solutions to these problems. Although a process consultant usually assists the group in making this diagnosis, the consultant's role is to help the client organization gain insight into its own group processes, not to recommend a particular diagnosis or solution. Schein lists three broad categories of process interventions that the consultant may use: *agenda setting, survey feedback*, and *counseling*.[86] Agenda-setting interventions attempt to focus attention on internal processes that are critical to task success but are normally ignored by the group. For instance, at the end of each meeting, a group might be asked to spend a few minutes reviewing what happened during the meeting. How openly did they communicate? What task strategies did they employ? How effectively did they use member resources?

Survey feedback typically involves the use of a questionnaire or series of interviews to gather data on how group members see their process problems. The process consultant might well ask members to describe and evaluate the group on many of the input and process dimensions found in Figure 4–1. The results of the survey are then presented to the group for discussion and solicitation of ideas. Ideally, survey feedback brings to the surface problems that have been hampering the group's performance but that members have been unwilling to discuss. Whether or not a group can handle feedback and reach constructive solutions rests heavily on the skills of the process consultant.

The third intervention approach calls for the coaching or counseling of individuals or the entire group by the consultant. The consultant might, for instance, take a directive manager aside and tell him or her that their style is inhibiting open discussion of common problems by the management team. If, in fact, the manager wishes to get their views on these problems, the consultant might coach him or her in ways to make the style more effective to that end.

Because process consultation encompasses a wide range of activities, it is difficult, if not impossible, to draw sweeping conclusions about the effectiveness of the technique. One recent review concluded that many of the common process consultation techniques seem to increase cohesiveness and satisfaction of group members.[87] The evidence is considerably weaker, however, insofar as group performance is concerned.

Technologies for Group Problem Solving

In contrast to the rather flexible format of process consultation, a number of highly structured programs have been devised for improving the way groups attack problems and make decisions. All of these technologies are similar in that they try to minimize specific barriers to group problem solving: pressures to uniformity (e.g., groupthink), tendencies to avoid expressing disagreement, tendencies to argue for the sake of winning the argument rather than solving the problem, tendencies to be solution minded without first examining alternatives, and dominance of group discussion by a few individuals. They differ, however, in the extent to which they allow group members to interact freely.

One technology that encourages open but structured interaction among group members is *consensus decision making*. With this technique, group members are told to avoid either arguing for their own individual positions or agreeing just to avoid conflict. Instead, they are told to discuss a problem until all members can at least accept the rationale of the majority decision, even if they aren't in total agreement. They are not permitted to use conflict resolution techniques such as majority vote, averaging, or trading. Although it is not a universal prescription, the consensus technique has proven superior to the unstructured approach in several studies.[88]

Whereas the consensus decision-making technique instructs the whole group, other approaches concentrate more on the leader of the group in suggesting ways to counteract some of the liabilities of group problem solving. For instance, the late N. R. F. Maier suggested that leaders should be trained to act as coordinators, rather than as directors, of the group's discussion.[89] Specifically, leaders should be trained to avoid stating their own opinions, to delay the group's evaluation of alternatives until all alternatives are generated, and to protect minority points of view within the group. Maier and his associates have conducted a large number of laboratory experiments showing that groups with leaders exhibiting these behaviors perform better than those with more directive leaders.

A third technique that encourages free interaction is *brainstorming*. Members of brainstorming groups are instructed to generate as many ideas as possible, no matter how extreme or outlandish these ideas may be, without evaluating either their own ideas or the ideas of others. Research on brainstorming has failed to support its effectiveness as a group problem-solving technique. In comparison to brainstorming groups, more high-quality ideas result if individuals are simply instructed to brainstorm silently and the individual contributions are collated to form the group product.[90] The group in this case is only a nominal one, given that the members do not actually interact.

Findings that nominal groups were more effective than interacting ones led to the development of a fourth approach, the *nominal group technique*.[91] As we just noted, this one differs from the others in that interaction among members is discouraged. Members are first instructed to generate ideas silently without discussing their ideas with each other. The ideas are then recorded in round-robin fashion for everyone to see, followed by a discussion of the alternatives in which members are allowed to clarify but not evaluate them. Finally, everyone votes on the best alternatives (e.g., the top five), and these votes are tallied. There may be additional rounds for voting and discussion before the group arrives at a final product.

From the research on the relative effectiveness of the different group problem-solving technologies, it appears that structured, noninteractive techniques are superior to unstructured, interactive ones.[92] Also, it appears that groups in which the problem-solving process is structured are more likely to implement the solution than are those using more unstructured techniques.[93]

Even if groups do not use a specific technique, they should at least spend some time planning their task strategies before beginning a problem. In support of this suggestion, Hackman, Weiss, and Brousseau found that groups that were required to spend a few minutes discussing and planning their task strategy performed better than groups that tackled the problem without a strategy session.[94] A preliminary strategy session was only effective, however, if group members did not share the same task information. If all group members had the same information, discussion of strategy appeared to detract somewhat from effective performance. Recent findings reported by Guzzo suggest that, in their preliminary discussion of strategy, group members should forego expressing their feelings about the issues at hand.[95] Research groups that vented their feelings about a problem before attempting to solve it subsequently performed more poorly on the task than did groups that delayed expression of feelings until after the task was completed.

Improving Group Performance through Selection of Its Members

As we have stated, groups generally perform better the more capable their members are. This suggests that one can implement procedures to improve group performance. First, analyze the job and establish criteria of success. Second, estimate the personal attributes required in the job. Third, measure applicants on these attributes and validate whether they indeed predict job performance. Finally, use measures that are valid predictors of success to screen and select group members.

We will not go into a full discussion of the issues and research related to these procedures. We will save this until Chapter 7. One approach to selection and placement that we will discuss here is the use of peer nomination and assessment to select team members. Three methods of peer assessment have appeared in the literature. Peer nomination is essentially an election, with members voting on which members are the best on an attribute such as leadership. In peer ratings, group members evaluate everyone else in the group on the attribute by using some kind of rating scale. Finally, in peer rankings, members rank order all members on the attribute in question. Peer nominations generally appear to be highly valid in predicting performance on tasks relevant to the attributes in question. Peer ratings are somewhat less valid, and peer rankings have not been researched enough to justify any conclusions at the present time.

The research demonstrating the validity of peer nominations suggests that allowing a team to select its own members could be a fruitful approach to enhancing the performance of the team.[96] Not only do members appear capable of making valid judgments about the task abilities of their peers, but they are probably the best judges of which of their peers they can work best with. Consequently, teams that select their own may be able to coordinate their efforts as well or even better than teams in which more traditional selection methods are used. This is only a hypothesis, however, which has yet to be fully tested. In one of the few studies evaluating the effects of self-selection, Van Zelst examined the performance of 74 carpenters and bricklayers, before and after using self-selection to form work crews in a residential housing development.[97] The workers were asked to pick their first three choices for a work partner. On the basis of this procedure, 50 workers were assigned to teams consisting of either their first or second choices. After teams were formed in this manner, the labor and material costs per row of houses dropped significantly. In a second study, self-chosen crews increased their efficiency of production so much that every 29th house could be built from the savings from the previous 28.[98]

Another more recent example of self-selection was in the pet food plant of General Foods in Topeka, Kansas. The organization of this plant was based largely on the concept of *team management*. Teams consisting of 7 to 14 workers were formed, and each team was given the responsibility of screening and selecting new members. According to Walton's account of the Topeka project, a consequence of having employees select their own subordinates and co-workers was that they were highly committed to the success of the persons they selected.[99] This was not a true experiment, however, so we have no way of knowing whether self-selection was any more effective than a traditional selection approach would have been. Moreover, questions have been raised as to whether the glowing picture painted by Walton of the Topeka project might not be a bit too rosy. Nevertheless, this and other studies suggest that allowing groups to select their own members is at least not as disastrous as commonly believed.

Despite the evidence in favor of self-selection by teams, this is not a widespread practice. A major concern, which a recent experiment supported, is that the procedure will disrupt relations among group members.[100] Another fear is that team members may violate fair employment guidelines and show bias against applicants who differ in their sex, race, or age from the majority of the group. Despite these possible drawbacks, self-selection seems to be an approach that can in some circumstances facilitate the formation and development of effective teams.

Interventions to Improve Group Performance through Work Restructuring

Another intervention suggested by Hackman and Morris is to restructure jobs to motivate employees and to better coordinate their efforts. One approach is job enrichment, which we discussed in Chapter 3 and is typically aimed at individual workers. A broader approach, that often includes job enrichment as one of several components, is the *sociotechnical* approach to job design and organizational development (see Chapter 7 for a definition of organization development). The sociotechnical approach was begun at the Tavistock Institute in England in the early 50s and has as its main aim forging better fits between the technological, structural, and social subsystems constituting an organization. Most sociotechnical interventions focus on redesigning work procedures and relationships to fit a technology. Relatively few have attempted to redesign the technology to fit the social system.[101]

Trist and Bamforth provided one of the best illustrations of the sociotechnical approach in a study they conducted with a British Coal Mining Company in the early 1950s.[102] Coal mining in this particular mine had been conducted by teams of six workers, two workers to a shift. Each team had selected its own members and did all its own work. When a shift changed, the next two men would take up where the last shift had left off. The miners were paid on the basis of the productivity of the total team. After World War II, a new technology was introduced in which each shift specialized in one aspect of the mining process. One shift extracted the coal, the second shoveled coal into the conveyer, and the third would advance mining equipment farther into the mine. Moreover, the new technology required that men work farther apart than they previously had, and it led to greater specialization in job duties and pay rates. Numerous problems arose as a consequence of the technological change, as evidenced in a rate of productivity that was far lower than anticipated and in an increasing rate of absenteeism. According to Trist and Bamforth's explanation, the technological change disrupted the social system, and the new social relations imposed by the technology were incompatible in many respects with the demands of the task. Miners preferred doing the whole task, not one small part of the task. Also, the social isolation of the new procedure left the miners without the social support they needed to efficiently perform the dangerous tasks they were assigned. Many of the older miners also felt status incongruence as new miners were hired and placed on higher-status jobs. Additionally, the individual pay rates fostered an individualism that was inconsistent with the requirement that miners coordinate their efforts across and within shifts.

The problem facing the Tavistock Institute was how to implement work arrangements that would retain the best of the old social arrangements while maintaining the efficiencies of the new technology. The solution they arrived at was to form each shift of workers into an *autonomous work group* and to assign to the group the whole job, not one phase of the job. Each shift would begin wherever the previous shift had stopped in its work. This necessitated the training of team members so that they would have all the skills needed to perform the jobs. Each group also decided for itself how members would be allocated to jobs during each shift. Finally, all members of a shift team were to share equally in a common paynote. After implementing the integrated mining procedures, productivity rose and absenteeism dropped dramatically. One can only speculate as to the degree that the intervention itself led to these effects. As in most studies evaluating sociotechnical interventions, there was no control organization against which to compare the effects of the intervention. Nevertheless, the results of this and similar studies suggest that the sociotechnical approach has considerable potential for improving the effectiveness of groups in organizations.

CONCLUSIONS

Organizations can be viewed as consisting of numerous small face-to-face groups, some formally created by the organization and others emerging from the daily interactions of employees. In a sense, the emergent groups in an organization constitute microcosms of the larger, formal organization. They have their own leadership, rules, and division of labor, and these may or may not be compatible with the leadership, rules, and division of labor imposed by the formal organization. Further, the influences that emergent groups have on their members can equal or surpass that of the formal organization.

Persons come to form a group as the result of factors that provide both an opportunity to interact, such as proximity, and a reason to interact, such as common fate and interdependence. The basic reason groups form, however, is to satisfy the needs of its members. When it ceases to fulfill these needs, it is unlikely to survive as a group. The types of groups in organizations can be distinguished on the basis of the types of needs or goals they fulfill: *Instrumental groups* are primarily concerned with accomplishing task objectives, *friendship* groups consist of purely personal relationships among persons who are attracted to one another, and *self-interest* groups consist of persons who band together to achieve explicit objectives held in common.

Groups often have been viewed as rather irrational and inefficient. According to the classical theorists, an organization is best managed as a set of vertical relationships between supervisors and individual subordinates. If lateral and horizontal relationships emerge that are not formally defined by this structure, they are likely to hinder the achievement of organizational objectives. Another common view is that a group usually performs far below the level of its most proficient members. Although this often does occur, groups can perform their tasks effectively and on occasion can perform at a level that meets or exceeds the best members. Effectiveness is determined by three different categories of inputs: *environment, group structure*, and *group composition*. The effects of these inputs are mediated by at least three categories of process variables: *effort or coordination of effort, utilization of individual abilities*, and *task strategies*.

Throughout this chapter we have developed several themes. One of these is that the task is perhaps the most important determinant of a group's effectiveness. The task influences the performance of the group directly (through its effect on the motivation of its members) and indirectly (through its control of processes required for the group to perform effectively). Furthermore, the group is effective only to the extent that the environmental, individual, and group inputs match task requirements. Another theme is that although groups tend to perform more effectively on most tasks as member ability, heterogeneity, and size (up to a point) increase, they usually fail to achieve the productivity levels they are capable of achieving.

To improve group performance, we first should determine the specific processes responsible for poor performance. If member effort is the problem, then *motivational strategies* such as job enrichment, reward systems, and goal setting should be considered. If insufficient knowledge and skills of members is the problem, then *reconstructing the group* with more capable members and training members in the requisite skills are appropriate interventions. Finally, if the wrong task strategies are being employed by members, some thought should be given to *changing the norms* that prevent members from adopting the correct strategies. Research indicates that noninteractive, structured problem-solving techniques, such as the nominal group technique, may be quite effective in improving the performance of groups on problem-solving tasks.

Of course, there are no simple solutions to improving group effectiveness. Groups are complex systems and, as in all complex systems, any one output such as performance usually has multiple causes. Few failures of groups to perform effectively are likely to be due only to member effort, task strategies, or insufficient task ability. To properly diagnose a group's ineffectiveness and to reach solutions to its problems, we must attempt to untangle a complex and interwoven set of determinants—a difficult undertaking but by no means impossible.

Whatever the cause of a group's effectiveness, primary responsibility rests with the formal leader of the group. The superior of the group serves as a critical link between the larger organization and the group of employees under his or her supervision. It is appropriate, therefore, to turn our attention to the function of management: In other words, what makes managers effective or ineffective?

NOTES

1. Taylor, F. W. (1911). *The principles of scientific management.* New York: Harper & Row.
2. Roethlisberger, F., & Dickson, W. (1939). *Management and the worker.* Cambridge, Mass.: Harvard University Press.
3. Shaw, M. E. (1976). *Group dynamics: The psychology of small group behavior.* New York: McGraw-Hill.
4. Ibid., p. 11.
5. Gullahorn, J. T. (1955). Distance and friendship as factors in the gross interaction matrix. *Sociometry, 15,* 123–134.
6. Walker, C. R., & Guest, R. H. (1952). *The man on the assembly line.* Cambridge, Mass.: Harvard University Press.
7. Keller, R. T., & Holland, W. E. (1983). Communicators and innovators in research and development organizations. *Academy of Management Journal, 26,* 742–749.

8. Sommer, R. (1969). *Personal space: The behavioral basis of design.* Englewood Cliffs, N.J.: Prentice-Hall.

9. Greenbaum, C. W. (1979). The small group under the gun: Uses of small groups in battle conditions. *Journal of Applied Behavioral Sciences, 15*, 392–405.

10. Festinger, L. (1954). A theory of social comparison processes. *Human Relations, 7*, 117–140.

11. Salancik, G., & Pfeffer, J. A. (1978). A social information-processing approach to job attitudes and task design. *Administrative Science Quarterly, 23*, 224–253.

12. White, S. E., & Mitchell, T. R. (1979). Job enrichment versus social cues: A comparison and competitive test. *Journal of Applied Psychology, 64*, 1–9.

13. Griffin, R. W. (1983). Objective and social sources of information in task redesign: A field experiment. *Administrative Science Quarterly, 28*, 184–200.

14. Jewell, L. N., & Reitz, H. J. (1980). *Group effectiveness in organizations.* Glenview, Ill.: Scott, Foresman.

15. Tuckman, B. W. (1965). Developmental sequence in small groups. *Psychological Bulletin, 63*, 384–399.

16. Lincoln, J. R., & Miller, J. (1979). Work and friendship ties in organizations: A comparative analysis of relational networks. *Administrative Science Quarterly, 24*, 181–199.

17. Haney, W. V. (1973). *Communication and organizational behavior* (3d ed.). Homewood, Ill.: Richard D. Irwin.

18. Easterbrook, J. A. (1959). The effect of emotion on cue utilization and the organization of behavior. *Psychological Review, 66*, 183–201.

19. Ibid.

20. Haney, *Communication and organizational behavior*, p. 246.

21. Bales, R. F. (1950). *Interaction process analysis: A method for the study of small groups.* Reading, Mass.: Addison-Wesley Publishing.

22. Hare, A. P. (1976). *Handbook of small group research* (pp. 62–69). New York: Free Press.

23. Schein, E. H. (1969). *Process consultation: Its role in organization development.* Reading, Mass.: Addison-Wesley Publishing.

24. Gibb, J. R. (1961). Defensive communication. *Journal of Communication, XI* (3), 141–148.

25. Bottger, P. C. (1984). Expertise and air time as bases of actual and perceived influence in problem-solving groups. *Journal of Applied Psychology, 69*, 214–221.

26. Schein. *Process consultation.*

27. Hackman, J. R., & Morris, C. G. (1975). Group tasks, group interaction process, and group performance effectiveness: A review and proposed integration. In L. Berkowitz (Ed.). *Advances in experimental social psychology* (Vol. 8) (p. 345). New York: Academic Press.

28. Ibid., p. 65.

29. Ibid.

30. Hackman, J. R. (1968). Effects of task characteristics on group products. *Journal of Experimental Social Psychology, 4*, 162–187; and Morris, C. G. (1966). Task effects on group interaction. *Journal of Personality and Social Psychology, 5*, 545–554.

31. Katz, D. (1964). The motivational basis of organizational behavior. *Behavioral Science, 9*, 131–146; and Alderfer, C. (1972). *Existence, relatedness, and growth: Human needs in organizational settings.* New York: Free Press.

32. Steiner, I. D. (1972). *Group process and productivity.* New York: Academic Press.

33. Thompson, J. D. (1967). *Organizations in action.* New York: McGraw-Hill.

34. Galbraith, J. D. (1977). *Organization design* (p. 38). Reading, Mass: Addison-Wesley Publishing.

35. Fiedler, F. E., & Chemers, M. M. (1974). *Leadership and effective management* (pp. 66–68). Glenview, Ill.: Scott, Foresman.

36. Blau, P. M. (1954). Cooperation and competition in a bureaucracy. *American Journal of Sociology, 59*, 530–535.
37. Deutsch, M. (1949). An experimental study of the effects of cooperation and competition upon group process. *Human Relations, 2*, 199–232; and Deutsch, M. (1949). A theory of cooperation and competition. *Human Relations, 2*, 129–152.
38. Johnson, D. W., Maruyama, G., Johnson, R., Nelson, D., & Skon, L. (1981). Effects of cooperative, competitive, and individualistic goal structures on achievement: A meta-analysis. *Psychological Bulletin, 89*, 47–62.
39. Rosenbaum, M. E., Moore, D. L., Cotton, J. L., Cook, M. S., Hierser, R. A., Shovar, M. N., & Gray, M. J. (1980). Group productivity and process: Pure and mixed reward structures and task interdependence. *Journal of Personality and Social Psychology, 39*, 626–642.
40. Shaw, M. E. (1964). Communication networks. In L. Berkowitz (Ed.). *Advances in experimental social psychology* (Vol. 11) (pp. 111–147). New York: Academic Press.
41. Ashby, W. Ross. (1956). *An introduction to cybernetics.* London: Chapman and Hall.
42. Chandler, A. D., Jr. (1962). *Strategy and structure: Chapters in the history of the American industrial enterprise.* Cambridge, Mass.: MIT Press.
43. Isenberg, D. J. (1981). Some effects of time pressures on vertical structure and decision-making accuracy in small groups. *Organizational Behavior and Human Performance, 27*, 119–134; Smart, G., & Vertinsky, I. (1977). Designs for crisis decision units. *Administrative Science Quarterly, 22*, 640–657; and Torrance, E. P. (1961). A theory of leadership and interpersonal behavior under stress. In L. Petrullo and B. M. Bass (Eds.). *Leadership and interpersonal behavior* (pp. 100–117). New York: Holt, Rinehart & Winston.
44. Blake, R. R., & Mouton, J. S. (1961). Reactions to intergroup competition under win-lose conditions. *Management Science, 7*, 420–435.
45. Janis, I. L. (1972). *Victims of groupthink.* Boston: Houghton Mifflin.
46. Katz, D., & Kahn, R. L. (1978). *The social psychology of organizations* (2d ed.). New York: John Wiley & Sons.
47. Gullahorn. Distance and friendship.
48. Tichy, N., & Fombrun, C. (1979). Network analysis in organizational settings. *Human Relations, 32*, 923–965; and Schwartz, D. F., & Jacobson, E. (1977). Organizational communication network analysis: The liaison communication role. *Organizational Behavior and Human Performance, 18*, 158–174.
49. Ziller, R. C. (1965). Toward a theory of open and closed groups. *Psychological Bulletin, 64*, 164–182.
50. O'Reilly, C. A., III, & Roberts, K. H. (1977). Task group structure, communication, and effectiveness in three organizations. *Journal of Applied Psychology, 62*, 674–681.
51. Feldman, D. C. (1984). The development and enforcement of group norms. *Academy of Management Review, 9*, 47–53.
52. Rubin, I., & Beckhard, R. (1974). Factors influencing the effectiveness of health teams. In D. A. Kolb, I. M. Rubin, & J. M. McIntyre (Eds.). *Organizational psychology: A book of readings* (2d ed.) (pp. 202–212). Englewood Cliffs, N.J.: Prentice-Hall.
53. Jackson, J. (1965). Structural characteristics of norms. In I. D. Steiner & M. Fishbein (Eds.). *Current studies in social psychology.* New York: Holt, Rinehart & Winston.
54. Asch, S. E. (1951). Effects of group pressure upon the modification and distortion of judgments. In H. Guetzkow (Ed.), *Groups, leadership, and men* (pp. 177–190). Pittsburgh: Carnegie Press.
55. Kelman, H. (1958). Compliance, identification, and internalization: Three processes of attitude change. *Journal of Conflict Resolution, 2*, 51–60.
56. Bales, R. F., & Slater, P. E. (1966). Role differentiation. In T. Parsons, R. F. Bales, et al. (Eds.). *The family, socialization, and interaction process* (pp. 259–306). New York: Free Press.
57. Katz, D., & Kahn, R. L. (1978). *The social psychology of organizations* (pp. 186–221). (2d ed.). New York: John Wiley and Sons.

58. Ibid.
59. Fisher, C. D., & Gitelson, R. A. (1983). A meta-analysis of the correlates of role conflict and ambiguity. *Journal of Applied Psychology, 68*, 320–333.
60. Burns, T., & Stalker, G. M. (1961). *The management of innovation*. London: Tavistock.
61. Shaw, M. (1976). *Group dynamics: The psychology of small-group behavior* (p. 446). New York: McGraw-Hill.
62. Allen, T. J., & Cohen, S. I. (1969). Information flow in research and development laboratories. *Administrative Science Quarterly, 14*, 12–20.
63. Lott, A. J., & Lott, B. E. (1965). Group cohesiveness as interpersonal attraction: A review of relationships with antecedent and consequent variables. *Psychological Bulletin, 64*, 259–309.
64. Festinger, L., Gerard, H., Hymovitch, B., Kelley, H. H., & Ravens, B. (1952). The influence process in the presence of extreme deviates. *Human Relations, 5*, 327–346.
65. Schlenker, B. R., & Miller R. S. (1977). Group cohesiveness as a determinant of egocentric perceptions in cooperative groups. *Human Relations, 30*, 1039–1055.
66. Shaw. *Group dynamics*, pp. 197–201.
67. Stogdill, R. M. (1972). Group productivity, drive, and cohesiveness. *Organizational Behavior and Human Performance, 8*, 26–43.
68. Greenbaum, C. W. (1979). The small group under the gun: Use of small groups in battle conditions. *Journal of Applied Behavioral Sciences, 15*, 392–405.
69. Seashore, S. E. (1954). *Group cohesiveness in the industrial work group*. Ann Arbor: University of Michigan Press.
70. Fairhurst, G. T., & Snavely, B. K. (1983). Majority and token minority group relationships: Power acquisition and acommunication. *Academy of Management Review, 8*, 292–300.
71. Collins, B., & Guetzkow, H. (1964). *A social psychology of group processes for decision making* (pp. 98–100). New York: John Wiley & Sons.
72. Shaw. *Group dynamics*, pp. 246–247.
73. Ibid.
74. Ibid.
75. Steiner. *Group process and productivity*.
76. Ingham, A. G., Levinger, G., Graves, J., & Peckham, V. (1974). The Ringlemann effect: Studies of group size and group performance. *Journal of Experimental Social Psychology, 10*, 371–384.
77. Jones, M. B. (1974). Regressing group on individual effectiveness. *Organizational Behavior and Human Performance, 11*, 426–451.
78. Pelz, D. C. & Andrews, F. M. (1966). *Scientists in organizations: Productive climates for research and development*. New York: John Wiley & Sons; and Smith, C. G. (1971). Scientific performance and the composition of research teams. *Administrative Science Quarterly, 16*, 486–495.
79. Guetzkow, H., & Gyr, J. (1954). An analysis of conflict in decision-making groups. *Human Relations, 7*, 367–382.
80. Steiner. *Group process and productivity*.
81. Ingham et al. Ringlemann effect.
82. Latane, B., & Nida, S. (1981). Ten years of research on group size and helping. *Psychological Bulletin, 89*, 308–324.
83. Porter, L. W., & Lawler, E. E., III. (1965). Properties of organizational structure in relation to job attitudes and job behavior. *Psychological Bulletin, 64*, 23–51.
84. Ibid.
85. Hackman & Morris. Group tasks.
86. Schein, E. H. (1969). *Process consultation: Its role in organizational development*. Reading, Mass.: Addison-Wesley Publishing.

87. Kaplan, R. E. (1977). The conspicuous absence of evidence that process consultation enhances task performance. *Journal of Applied Behavioral Science, 13*, 346–360.

88. Hall, J., & Watson, W. H. (1971). The effects of a normative intervention on group decision-making performance. *Human Relations, 23*, 299–317; Hall, J., & Williams, M. S. (1970). Group dynamics training and improved decision making. *Journal of Applied Behavioral Science, 6*, 27–32.

89. Maier, N. R. F. (1967). Assets and liabilities in group problem solving: The need for an integrative function. *Psychological Review, 74*, 239–440.

90. Bouchard, T. J., Jr., & Hare, M. (1970). Size, performance, and potential in brainstorming groups. *Journal of Applied Psychology, 54*, 51–55; and Campbell, J. (1968). Individual versus group problem solving in an industrial sample. *Journal of Applied Psychology, 52*, 205–210.

91. Delbecq, A. L., Van De Ven, A. H., & Gustafson, D. H. (1976). *Group techniques for program planning: A guide to nominal group and delphi processes.* Glenview, Ill.: Scott, Foresman.

92. Ibid.

93. White, S. E., Dittrich, J. E., & Lang, J. R. (1980). The effects of group decision-making process and problem-solving complexity on implementation attempts. *Administrative Science Quarterly, 25*, 428–440.

94. Hackman, J. R., Brousseau, K. R., & Weiss, J. A. (1976). The interaction of task design and group performance strategies in determining group effectiveness. *Organizational Behavior and Human Performance, 16*, 350–365.

95. Guzzo, R. A., & Waters, J. A. (1982). The expression of affect and the performance of decision-making groups. *Journal of Applied Psychology, 67*, 67–74.

96. Kane, J. S., & Lawler, E. E. III. (1978). Methods of peer assessment. *Psychological Bulletin, 85*, 555–586.

97. Van Zelst, R. H. (1952). Sociometrically selected work teams increase productivity. *Personnel Psychology, 5*, 175–185.

98. Van Zelst, R. H. (1952). Validation of a sociometric regrouping procedure. *Journal of Abnormal and Social Psychology, 47*, 299–301.

99. Walton, R. E. (1983). From Hawthorne to Topeka and Kalmar. In W. L. French, C. H. Bell Jr., & R. A. Zawacki (Eds.). *Organizational development: Theory, practice, & research* (pp. 292–300). Plano, Tex.: Business Publications.

100. De Nisi, A. S., Randolph, W. A., & Blencoe, A. G. (1983). Potential problems with peer ratings. *Academy of Management Journal, 26*, 457–464.

101. Pasmore, W., Francis, C., Halderman, J., & Shani, A. (1982). Sociotechnical systems: A North American reflection on empirical studies of the 70s. *Human Relations, 35*(12), 1179–1204.

102. Trist, E., & Bamforth, K. (1951). Some social and psychological consequences of the long-wall method of coal-getting. *Human Relations, 4*(1), 1–8.

5

Leadership and Supervision

In the last two chapters we observed that healthy organizations are usually characterized by a motivated, satisfied work force and effective work groups. Research and theory have provided at least a rough idea of what conditions—cognitive and otherwise—are associated with this happy state of affairs when it exists. Favorable conditions, however, do not just materialize out of thin air. The success or failure of an organization to achieve its goals and to fulfill the needs of its members are usually attributed, rightly or wrongly, to the few people who occupy positions of leadership. Whatever the reasons—and they range from formal authority to personal qualities to situational variables—some people lead; many others follow. Leadership influence may be great or small; it may be compatible or incompatible with the goals of the organization; and it may operate through designated or unrecognized leaders.

It is our purpose in this chapter to examine the leadership process from several different angles. In the first part of the chapter, we will discuss some basic terms. First, we will define what we mean by *leadership*: In what forms does it exist in organizations? Is it the same as supervision and management? Next, we will distinguish between leadership and leadership *effectiveness*. In most of our discussion in this chapter, we will be concerned with explaining and predicting why some leaders are more effective than others and what, if anything, an organization can do to improve the effectiveness of its leaders. What personal traits should an organization look for in selecting and placing people in leadership roles? How should they train people to behave in leadership roles? How can the situation be engineered to maximize leader effectiveness? We will discuss the continuing efforts of researchers and theorists to find answers to these and other questions.

A FEW BASIC DISTINCTIONS

Leadership versus Supervision

Most current definitions of leadership involve interpersonal influence. People are said to occupy a role of leadership to the extent that they try to influence other people to act or think in certain ways. People *are* leaders to the extent that they actually are successful in their attempts to influence others. Persons who occupy leadership roles but exert little actual influence are often called *nominal leaders*.

Throughout this chapter, we will use the terms *leadership, supervision,* and *management* almost interchangeably. They are not entirely synonymous, however, in that both supervision and management carry more of the connotations associated with the leadership role. Supervisor or manager usually refers to people who occupy formally held positions of leadership. They may or may not be the people who exert the greatest influence. The most influential member of the group may not be its appointed leader but an individual who has emerged from the ranks by virtue of his or her behavior. It is important, then, to distinguish between *appointed* and *emergent* leadership, just as in the last chapter we distinguished between formal and informal (or emergent) groups.

Leadership versus Leader Effectiveness

Another important distinction that is often obscured in discussions of underlying processes is between *leadership* and *leader effectiveness*. The behavior and attitudes of other persons in response to the leader's attempts to influence them defines leadership, whereas *effectiveness* is dependent upon how well the group achieves its objectives. By definition, leaders are people who attempt to influence others in some way, whether through persuasion, example, force, or one of the many other available strategies. The roles that leaders occupy, however, usually involve a lot more than just trying to influence people. Typical functions include planning, problem solving, and decision making. For this reason, a leader may be influential without being effective in performance of the total managerial role. Many an excellent leader, from an influence standpoint, has led the group right down the tubes as a result of poor planning or decision making: General Custer seemed to have many willing followers. On the other hand, it is impossible to be effective without influence as long as the task requires a group effort.

Criteria for Leader Effectiveness

How do we know whether an individual is effective or not in a leadership role? This is not an easy question to answer because there are several different criteria of success, and they do not always agree. The *performance* of the leader's work group as measured on such objective dimensions as quantity, equality, profitability, and costs would appear to be the logical index of a leader's effectiveness. Although it may seem obvious that a results orientation is the most appropriate, one must realize that objective measures are not always available, and when they are it is often impossible to identify the *leader's contribution* to performance.

In most large organizations, persons in leadership roles seem to acquire reputations as highly effective, moderately effective, or ineffective leaders as the result of *subjective* judgments by their bosses, their peers, and their subordinates. These constitute the *multiple constituencies* of a leader. To acquire a reputation as an effective leader, a person in the leadership role must somehow meet, at least to some extent, the expectations of all three constituencies. This is often difficult, because subordinates, peers, and superiors frequently expect somewhat different things. Some evidence of this was provided by Tsui in a study of over 300 middle-level managers in a *Fortune* 500 corporation.[1] Tsui found that in evaluating the effectiveness of a manager on the dimensions presented in Table 5-1, the superior of the manager emphasized entrepreneurial activities, peers were more concerned with the manager's performance as liaison and spokesperson, and subordinates were most concerned with the manager's leadership, resource allocation, and environmental monitoring. Only 11 percent of the managers were rated highly by all three constituencies (peers, bosses, and subordinates) on how effectively they carried out their role activities. Those that were rated highly by all three groups, however, were more likely to be promoted and receive merit salary increases than were those receiving high ratings from only one or two of their constituency groups.

The subjective judgments of bosses, peers, and subordinates are all important determinants of the reputation that a person in a leadership role develops. The reputation acquired may have very little to do with performance on more objective dimensions, however. Subjective judgments also suffer from many potential biases, which we will have more to say about in Chapter 6. Although subjective judgments can be improved, the conflicting expectations and objectives that exist in most complex organizations make it extremely difficult and often impossible to develop a single criterion for determining the effectiveness of a person in a leadership role. Nevertheless, many of the theories of leadership that we will discuss falsely assume that objective measures of performance and superior, subordinate, and peer views of effectiveness all come together neatly to form a single, unidimensional criterion of success. When readers ultimately begin to consider what approach to management is best for them, they would do well to begin by asking what the objectives of their constituencies are and how they can best reconcile the differences that invariably exist among these objectives.

TABLE 5–1   Mintzberg's Classification of Managerial Roles

Role	Description	Identifiable Activities from Study of Chief Executives
Interpersonal		
Figurehead	Symbolic head; obliged to perform a number of routine duties of a legal or social nature	Ceremony, status requests, solicitations
Leader	Responsible for the motivation and activation of subordinates; responsible for staffing, training, and associated duties	Virtually all managerial activities involving subordinates
Liaison	Maintains self-developed network of outside contacts and informers who provide favors and information	Acknowledgments of mail; external board work; other activities involving outsiders
Informational		
Monitor	Seeks and receives wide variety of special information (much of it current) to develop through understanding of organization and environment; emerges as nerve center of internal and external information of the organization	Handling all mail and contacts categorized as concerned primarily with receiving information (e.g., periodical news, observational tours)
Disseminator	Transmits information received from outsiders or from other subordinates to members of the organization; some information factual, some involving interpretation and integration of diverse value positions of organizational influencers	Forwarding mail into organization for informational purposes, verbal contacts involving information flow to subordinates (e.g., review sessions, instant communication flows)
Spokesperson	Transmits information to outsiders on organization's plans, policies, actions, results, etc.: serves as expert on organization's industry	Board meetings; handling mail and contacts involving transmission of information to outsiders
Decisional		
Entrepreneur	Searches organization and its environment for opportunities and initiates "improvement projects" to bring about change; supervises design of certain projects as well	Strategy and review sessions involving initiation or design of improvement projects
Disturbance handler	Responsible for corrective action when organization faces important, unexpected disturbances	Strategy and review sessions involving disturbances and crises
Resource allocator	Responsible for the allocation of organizational resources of all kinds—in effect the making or approval of all significant organizational decisions	Scheduling; requests for authorization; any activity involving budgeting and the programming of subordinates' work
Negotiator	Responsible for representing the organization at major negotiations	Negotiation

SOURCE: Mintzberg, H. (1973). *The nature of managerial work* (pp. 92–93). New York: Harper & Row. Copyright © 1973 by Henry Mintzberg. Reprinted by permission of Harper & Row, Publishers, Inc.

Alternative Approaches to Leadership

Most theories of leadership effectiveness are descendents of commonsense ideas that have been around for ages. In Chapter 2, we pointed out that there are really only a few fundamentally different ideas in this regard.

One view is that leaders are born, not made. That is, some people can lead and some can't, regardless of how hard they try, how smart they are, or how many Dale Carnegie courses they have taken. This we have referred to as *trait theory*, because effective leadership is seen to depend on relatively stable characteristics of the *individual*.

The second commonsense idea is that there are effective and ineffective ways to manage that almost anyone can learn: You too can win friends and influence people. All one has to do is learn to behave in the proper way. This we have designated *behavioral theory* because effective leadership is seen to depend on specific patterns of behavior that the individual can modify. It is what the person does, not what he or she is, that counts.

Finally, there is the commonsense idea that anyone can win with a winner; no one can win with a loser. That is, what the leader is or does is less important than the *situation*. An effective leader has managed to be in the right place at the right time. *Situational theory,* therefore, focuses on characteristics outside the individual entirely. One would expect situational theory to be extremely popular among proven managerial failures.

Few present-day theorists would deny that there is an element of truth in all three of these commonsense notions. The difference between theoretical positions is primarily one of emphasis. Trait theories stress stable traits; behavioral theories, leadership style; and situational theories, environmental factors (such as the task and subordinates). Each attempts to see how much of the total variation in observed managerial effectiveness can be attributed to one of these sets of factors. Some of the more advanced models try to include several sets of factors. Fiedler's contingency theory and the Vroom and Yetton model, both of which we shall examine in some detail momentarily, are the most prominent examples of this multifactor approach. Much of the remainder of this chapter will be spent looking at each of these alternative approaches to leadership in more detail.

Trait Theories of Leadership

Although often referred to as trait theory, it is somewhat misleading to call this approach to leadership a theory. What it really represents is an assumption, usually implicit, that a leader's behavior and effectiveness depend primarily on enduring characteristics of the individual. According to the popular stereotype, the effective leader possesses traits of self-confidence, aggressiveness, a high need for achievement, above-average intelligence, above-average height, a physical appearance that is attractive and exudes authority, and the proper race and gender (Caucasian male).[2] Of course, stereotypes of the successful leader do not necessarily reflect reality. Psychologists have conducted many studies over the last

40 years to determine what traits are really associated with becoming a leader and performing the leadership role effectively. The primary contribution of this research has been to debunk many of the commonsense conceptions of effective leaders. Nevertheless, a few traits have been found to relate to leadership and leader effectiveness, and it is worthwhile for us to scan the evidence on each of the major trait categories.

Research on Leadership Traits.

Physical Traits.   Despite the advice that abounds in the self-help literature on how to "dress for success" or create a "power image," there is little evidence of any universal principles for creating the right physical image. Research on such physical characteristics as height, weight, and general appearance has been generally inconclusive.[3] Physical appearance does appear to play an important role in the first impression people form of a manager (and is therefore emphasized by those who "package" our would-be political leaders as well as by those who make the selections).[4] The right appearance probably does help in getting a managerial job, and it may help in establishing an initial power base, but the image fades fast if there is nothing to back it up. The way a person looks is not likely to be as important in the long run as how competently he or she performs the leadership role.

Sex and Race.   Managerial positions are occupied mostly by white males. Does this mean that white males are inherently superior as leaders? The available evidence suggests that there is still some bias against women and minorities as managers, but that they can be just as effective in managerial roles as white males.[5] Undoubtedly, some women and minority group members encounter unusual difficulties in some organizations when placed in positions of leadership. A few studies have shown that men who have never worked for a woman are quite negative in their attitudes toward women managers. However, those men who have worked for a female manager are considerably more positive in their attitudes toward women as managers.[6] Women and minorities often must work doubly hard to gain the acceptance of subordinates, peers, and superiors, and these problems should not be underestimated. Nevertheless, there is no solid reason to believe that any sex or ethnic group is inherently deficient in leadership potential; problems of acceptance are just as appropriately viewed as an indication of deficiencies in the organization or the people led as in the would-be leader.

Intelligence.   Unlike physical traits, sex, and race, the mental ability of the leader appears to be positively related to leadership effectiveness. The relationship is not a large one. In a summary of the research on leader intelligence, Ghiselli found that mental ability tests correlate with measured proficiency of executives, middle managers, and supervisors with coefficients on the order of .25, thus accounting for only 6 percent of the variation in proficiency.[7] The findings of some studies suggest that the actual relationship between intelligence and leadership effectiveness is curvilinear.[8] Not only can too little intelligence prove a handicap; too much can be equally detrimental to overall effectiveness. Although there is little research on this, it seems likely that the optimal intelligence level of the leader is determined by the intelligence of the followers. It seems that a leader should be more intelligent than the followers—but not too much more intelligent.

Personality Traits. There have been numerous attempts to find the critical personality traits distinguishing effective leaders from ineffective leaders. In the typical study, managers are given standardized personality inventories, which provide scores on a variety of trait dimensions (e.g., achievement orientation, self-confidence, and dominance). An examination is then made of how effective managers differ from less effective managers on these various dimensions. Representative of the personality trait research are Nash's research with the Strong Vocational Interest Blank, Miner's work with his Sentence Completion Test, Gough's research with the California Psychological Inventory (CPI), and McClelland's research with the Thematic Apperception Test (TAT).

Nash concerned himself mainly with *managerial interests* as measured by a popular inventory (questionnaire) known as the Strong Vocational Interest Blank.[9] He found that effective managers differed from ineffective ones in their preferences for activities that are somewhat risky, involve independent and intense thought, and allow them to interact with and dominate others. The effective manager disliked close or detailed tasks and preferred physical and social over aesthetic or cultural forms of recreation.

John Miner developed the Miner Sentence Completion Scale to measure the trait he considers critical to success in management—the motivation to manage.[10] A person with a high motivation to manage purportedly possesses the following characteristics:

1. A favorable attitude toward authority.
2. A desire to compete against others.
3. Assertiveness—a desire to take charge and make decisions.
4. A desire to exercise power—feels comfortable rewarding and punishing subordinates.
5. A desire to stand out from the group and draw the attention of others.
6. Takes a positive view of routine administrative chores.

Miner and his associates have reported the findings of several studies in which they found that a high motivation to manage was related to managerial success in large bureaucratic organizations. On the basis of two decades of research with his Sentence Completion Test, Miner concluded that college students' motivation to manage has declined by about 35 percent since the early 1960s and continues to decline by about 3 percent a year. In one sample of graduate and undergraduate students, he found that only 8 percent had a motivation to manage that reached the level of the average business manager. We should note, however, that Miner's research has been criticized for the low reliability of his measure (see the chapter on selection for a discussion of reliability).

Another standardized test used in research on leader traits is the California Psychological Inventory (CPI). Gough developed a special scale from the CPI to measure managerial potential and found that it correlated .20 with performance ratings of a sample of military officers.[11] Persons scoring high on the managerial potential scale tended to describe themselves with such traits as self-confident, clear thinking, and goal oriented.

Finally, McClelland and Boyatizis (1982) found that scores on the TAT were correlated to a small degree with the levels of promotion attained 8 and 16 years later by a sample of 237 AT&T managers.[12] The most successful managers appeared to be those with a moderate to high nPow and a low nAff. Need for achievement was related to success only for lower-level managers. In another study, Stahl used an entirely different measure of these same traits and found, similar to McClelland and Boyatizis' findings, that successful managers tended to have high nPow.[13]

The most consistent findings from this and other research on the traits of effective managers appear to be that the successful manager is self-confident, dominant, active, energetic, and achievement oriented.[14] The picture one often gets from examining the research on leader traits seems very close to the popular (if not entirely flattering) stereotype of the hard-working, money-hungry, power-mad business tycoon. Fortunately, the evidence suggests that even if such tendencies exist, they in no sense constitute a universal prescription for success.

Problems with Universal Traits.   Despite the occasional observation of a relationship between standardized trait measures and criteria of managerial effectiveness, the findings do not justify sweeping generalizations about the traits of the successful manager. One problem with this research is the tendency to define the effectiveness of a manager in terms of the level to which he or she has risen in the company. Even if every vice president in the country had some characteristic pattern of traits, it would not prove that such traits are critical for the role of vice president. Suppose, for example, top management preferred to fill managerial positions with people just like themselves. In time, this would produce a rather stereotyped managerial personality by virtue of selection bias rather than by any demonstrable superiority. If you consider this proposition idle speculation, reflect on the reluctance with which minority groups, women, men with long hair or unconventional modes of dress, and other unconventional people have been accepted into the management fraternity.

Another problem is the growing body of evidence suggesting that even if general personality characteristics do turn out to be related to leadership, they will never account for much of the variation in effectiveness. Leader traits are probably of some importance but only in conjunction with follower traits, organizational climate, and a lot of other factors. It is unlikely, in other words, that a universally effective profile of traits for managers exists. Korman concluded his review of the literature on the prediction of managerial performance with the comment that selection research has really contributed very little to our understanding of leadership behavior.[15] At the very best, traits such as these probably account for less than 10 percent of the observed differences in managerial effectiveness.

Even if traits were strongly related to managerial effectiveness, it is unlikely that we could measure many of these traits adequately. There are considerable problems with the measurement of personality traits, which will be taken up in Chapter 7. One, however—the problem of intentional distortion or faking—should be mentioned here. Self-report questionnaires such as the Strong Vocational Interest Inventory are easily faked. That is, a person can readily misrepresent interests, self-assurance, and so forth when it is in his or her best interest to do so—such as when seeking a managerial position. It is conceivable that once the desired traits become widely known, every managerial applicant who fills out a self-report inventory will be found to have them. Whether faking is, in fact, a serious and widespread problem has not been firmly established (see Chapter 7). It remains, however, a *potential* problem with any self-report personality inventory.

A final problem with prescribing universal traits is that there are serious questions as to whether the so-called personality traits differentiating effective and ineffective managers are the *causes* of their relative effectiveness or the result of other factors. Most studies are of a *concurrent* nature. In other words, the traits of the more effective managers currently employed in an organization are compared with those of the less effective ones. In this type of study, any observed differences between the two groups of managers can be explained by a host of other factors besides personality traits. For instance, the finding of a positive correlation between self-confidence and leader effectiveness has led some to agree that the self-confidence trait *causes* the success. Yet, as we saw in Chapter 1, one could just as validly conclude that the success causes the self-confidence or that both self-confidence and success originate from some third variable, such as leader intelligence.

Applications.

Tailor-Made Selection Instruments. The trait theory approach seems to show real promise in one way. If, instead of trying to find universally desirable traits, we concentrate on the traits required for *particular managerial positions* in specific organizations, the outlook becomes much brighter. For one thing, this approach in effect holds constant such factors as organizational climate and employee characteristics. For another, it makes possible direct evaluation of the items used to measure the traits: One can simply keep adding and eliminating test items (or whatever predictive scales are used) until a set is obtained that is highly related to the criterion of managerial effectiveness for that particular position. Just such an approach was used very successfully by the Standard Oil Company of New Jersey (SONJ, now Exxon Corporation) in a program designed to identify potential managers early in their careers.[16] In the initial studies, 443 managers took tests of verbal ability, inductive reasoning, and management judgment; inventoried their managerial attitudes; and underwent a personality measure, the Guilford-Zimmerman Temperament Survey. As shown in Table 5–2, a prospective manager who scored in the top 20 percent on the tests they developed had over 20 times as great a chance of being in the top third on managerial success as one who scored in the bottom 20 percent. According to one description of their results,

> Successful executives in the SONJ organization have shown a total life pattern of successful endeavors. They were good in college, are active in taking advantage of leadership opportunities, and see themselves as forceful, dominant, assertive, and confident.[17]

Of course, a drawback to this approach is that it requires development of a unique set of predictive items for each distinguishable management category. What works for department managers at Standard Oil may be less useful for vice presidents and totally useless for *any* managerial level at Shell Oil. The greatest strength of specific application of personality theory is therefore also its greatest weakness: It recognizes that every managerial job may require different personal traits.

Assessment Centers. Another current application of trait theory to the selection of managers is the assessment center approach. In an assessment center, candidates for managerial positions participate in exercises designed to draw out behavior indicative of managerial traits. For example, in one assessment center candidates perform four types of exercises that are typical of assessment center tasks.[18]

1. *In-basket exercise:* Candidates are given two hours to process and respond in writing to 40 realistic memoranda.
2. *Leadership problem:* The candidate and two assistants, who are actually confederates of the assessors, are given one hour to solve

TABLE 5–2 Relations of Scores on the Early
Identification of Management Potential
(EIMP) Test to Managerial Success

Rank on Test	Rank on Managerial Success			
	Low 1/3	Middle 1/3	High 1/3	N
1–44	0%	5%	95%	44
45–88	2	23	75	44
89–132	5	38	57	44
133–176	10	45	45	44
177–220	25	55	20	44
221–265	40	47	13	45
266–310	53	38	9	45
311–355	56	33	11	45
356–399	64	29	7	44
400–443	79	21	0	43
N	148	148	147	443

SOURCE: Sparks, C. Paul. (1983). Paper-and-pencil measures of potential. In G. F. Dreher & P. Sackett (Eds.). *Perspectives on employee staffing and selection* (p. 357). Homewood, Ill.: Richard D. Irwin.

a problem. One assistant plays the role of a disagreeable but competent individual, and the other an agreeable but incompetent
one.

3. *Problem-solving exercise:* Candidates must decide between two
   alternative courses of action and give a 30-minute formal presentation defending their decision.

4. *Leaderless group discussion:* All candidates participate in two
   different discussion sessions, one in which each person is assigned a role, and the other in which no roles are designated.

On the basis of their performance on these tasks, participants are evaluated on traits such as organizing and planning, perception and analysis,
decision making, decisiveness, leadership, sensitivity to people, oral communications, written communications, and adaptability. This, of course,
is but one example of an approach that has become extremely popular in
industry for selecting, training, and evaluating managers. It has been estimated that over 1,000 such programs were in place by the mid- 1970s.[19]
The specific traits, exercises, and objectives vary from organization to
organization. In Standard Oil of Ohio's assessment center, for example,
candidates are evaluated on amount of participation, oral communication, personal acceptability, impact, quality of participation, personal
breadth, orientation to detail, self-direction, relationship with authority,
originality, understanding of people, and drive. Those run by the Internal
Revenue Service examine decision making, decisiveness, flexibility, leadership, oral communications, organization, planning, perception, analytic ability, persuasiveness, sensitivity to people, and stress tolerance.[20]

Assessment center trait ratings have been used quite successfully to predict whether a candidate will be subsequently promoted to high-level management positions in an organization. Questions have been raised, however, regarding the utility of assessment procedures. In the much-heralded AT&T program, trait ratings have been shown to predict managerial success over periods as long as eight years. However, Henrichs found that one could predict just as well using information in the candidates' personnel files.[21] These findings raise some doubts as to whether assessment centers are worth the effort, particularly if the considerably cheaper alternative of assessing paper credentials can achieve the same degree of prediction. Some studies have supported the use of assessment centers by showing that their benefits outweigh their costs. Moreover, managers have expressed a great deal of confidence in their utility. Whether they are, in fact, worth the investment cannot be answered conclusively at this point. Considering that managerial selection is only one of their potential uses, their future appears promising. For present purposes, it is sufficient to note that assessment centers represent an extension of the idea that traits can be used with some degree of success to predict managerial effectiveness in *particular managerial positions.*

Summary of the Trait Approach. The trait approach to leadership became popular during the 1930s and 1940s, when selection, particularly by means of psychological tests, seemed to hold the answer to all organizational problems. Neither it nor the emphasis on selection has retained its dominant position in the field. Few psychologists still believe that we either can or should fill the ranks of management exclusively on the basis of test scores. Although there have been a few consistent relationships found between leadership effectiveness and traits such as intelligence, need for achievement, self-confidence, and assertiveness, the correlations are quite small. Another challenge to the trait approach has come from theorists outside industrial and organizational psychology. In recent years, some social psychologists have disputed that personality traits are stable across situations and thus capable of governing behavior to any important extent.[22] The current vogue in much of the research on personality is to show how situations can account for the behavior of a person better than paper-and-pencil measures of traits. However, a more moderate position and, we believe, a more fruitful one is to determine how situations and traits *interact* to affect leadership effectiveness. From this viewpoint, trait measures may help us understand leadership processes but are far from the total answer.

Behavioral Theories of Leadership

Partly as the result of their disenchantment with trait approaches and partly because of a larger behavioral trend in psychology, some theorists sought to understand leadership effectiveness by analyzing what leaders actually do. What specific behaviors, they asked, distinguish effective from ineffective leaders? Much of the work stemming from this approach has been of a descriptive nature. Researchers have sought to capture the essential activities of people in leadership roles, the behavior patterns or styles through which they operate in these roles, and the specific means by which they attempt to influence others. Leadership thus becomes a matter of activities that influence others. Defined in this way, the goal of research and theory becomes to identify effective behavior patterns or styles of management rather than personal traits.

The Manager's Job. In studying the behaviors related to managerial effectiveness, the logical place to start is the manager's job. Most people would probably agree that managers develop, discipline, motivate, and coordinate the activities of their subordinates. It turns out that supervising is just one of many roles that a manager must perform. Mintzberg presented 10 roles that he considered common to the work of managers. These roles are listed and defined in Table 5–1.[23] Although Mintzberg's classification scheme was based on an intensive analysis of only four executives, later studies with larger groups of managers have provided more substantive support for his model.

Mahoney, Jerdee, and Carroll identified eight basic managerial functions that overlap to some extent with Mintzberg's managerial roles. Going a step farther than Mintzberg, they were able to determine the average percentage of time managers spent on each one.[24] Their results for 452 managers in 13 companies were as follows:

Managerial Activity	Percentage of Time Spent
Planning	19.5%
Investigating	12.6
Coordinating	15.0
Evaluating	12.7
Supervising	28.7
Staffing	4.1
Negotiating	6.0
Representing	1.8

The relative emphasis placed upon each of the various activities by a particular manager varies, naturally, with all the idiosyncratic conditions included in the organizational climate. It also varies quite systematically with the level of the manager. Mahoney, Jerdee, and Carroll found that low-level managers tend to see *supervision* as their primary function, whereas high-level managers look upon themselves more as *planners* than supervisors. At all levels, however, *supervision* and *planning* were seen to outweigh by far the other functions as primary role descriptions.

FIGURE 5–1   Continuum of Leadership Behavior

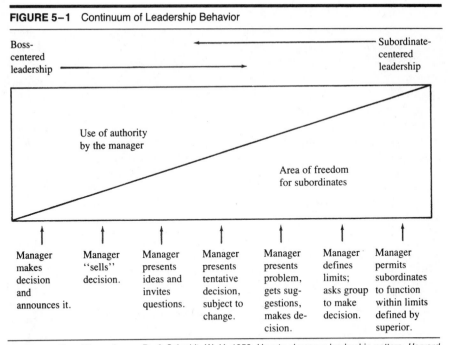

SOURCE: From Tannenbaum, R., & Schmidt, W. H. 1958. How to choose a leadership pattern. *Harvard Business Review, 36,* 95–101.

Styles of Leadership.   As we discussed in the previous section, supervising people is not the only activity required of a manager, but it is often the most important one. Understanding how managers carry out their supervisory activities thus becomes a very critical issue. For some, supervision is a matter of tight control, coercion, and explicit direction; for others, it involves shared responsibility, open communication, and a group orientation. A person's *style of leadership* is the composite of the way he or she looks at and behaves in the leader role. The most popular way of looking at styles is in terms of continua or dimensions that summarize a lot of specific behaviors. The three dimensions that have received the greatest attention from psychologists are an autocratic or democratic continuum, initiating structure, and consideration.

Autocratic versus Democratic Styles of Leadership.   Since the earliest days of the human relations movement, organization theorists have made a sharp distinction between democratic and autocratic styles. The former was touted as the hallmark of enlightened human relations management, whereas the latter was looked upon as an undesirable link with the past. Basically, the distinction was then and is now between the leader who shares the decision-making function (democratic) and the one who doesn't (autocratic), that is, between *participative* and *nonparticipative* management. As usually conceived today, participation is a matter of degree rather than an all-or-none proposition. Managerial behavior patterns lie on a continuum from democratic (or subordinate-centered) at one end to authoritarian (or boss-centered) at the other (see Figure 5–1).[25]

For all its early rave notices, participative management has not proven to be a consistently superior style. In a recent review of the effects of participative decision making, it was reported that only 22 percent of the studies concerned with performance clearly supported a democratic style as more effective than an autocratic style. Fifty-six percent found no difference or an equivocal difference in the effectiveness of the two styles, whereas 10 percent found that an autocratic style was more effective than a democratic style. When worker satisfaction, rather than performance, was the main criterion, results did favor the participative style: 60 percent showed that democratic leadership was more conducive to job satisfaction than was autocratic leadership, 30 percent showed no difference or an equivocal one, and only 9 percent showed an advantage for the autocratic style.[26]

From these findings, then, a participative leadership style seems more likely to increase the job satisfaction of employees than it does their performance. Many questions remain unanswered, however. Past research has tended to focus on the ends of the continuum represented in Figure 5–1 and has tended to ignore the effects of less extreme democratic or autocratic styles. Also, the effects of participative and autocratic leadership seem to depend on a number of situational variables including (1) task structure, (2) group and organizational size, (3) extent to which leader and followers possess expertise, and (4) needs and values of the leader and followers. For example, an autocratic leader may impose on the group a relatively centralized network of communication, which, as we discussed in Chapter 4, seems best suited for structured, routine tasks where efficiency is the primary goal. On the other hand, a participative leader is more apt to wind up with a decentralized network of communication, which is more appropriate for complex tasks. A participative style also seems more appropriate when the effectiveness of the decision requires that subordinates accept the decision and be willing to work hard to implement it. The danger of participation is that it may reduce efficiency and, occasionally, the internal harmony of the group. This is because a participative style is likely to encourage the expression of more diverse opinions among subordinates than an autocratic style does, hence more time-consuming conflict and confusion in the decision-making process. Not that conflict is necessarily bad; a certain amount of it may foster a genuine exchange of information and new approaches to problems. Harmony, after all, can reflect indifference as well as closeness in interpersonal relationships. Later, when we examine Vroom and Yetton's model of leadership, we will discuss in more detail the various situational factors that influence the success of various gradations of participative and autocratic styles.

Initiation of Structure and Consideration. A popular view of leadership has been a one-dimensional distinction between employee versus task orientations. According to this view, a supervisor is concerned totally with the task or with people or else compromises to some degree between task and people. Any effort expended on organizing, planning, controlling, and directing must be at the expense of establishing rapport with subordinates and attending to their needs and feelings. Likewise, to exert effort on developing close, friendly relations with the group must be at the expense of the task. This popular way of looking at management behavior turns out to be inaccurate. Years of research by several widely respected teams of social scientists have produced a quite different picture of management style.[27] The consensus is that at least two dimensions are necessary to provide an adequate description of leadership behavior. Surprisingly enough, there has been very close agreement among most research groups as to the minimum number of basic dimensions (two) and the definition of these dimensions.

The first dimension has been called leader *consideration*. As might be guessed, it "includes behavior indicating mutual trust, respect, and a certain warmth and rapport between a supervisor and his group."[28] Leaders who are high on this dimension are often characterized by participative decision making and two-way communication. Other terms describing this dimension include *employee-centered supervision, supportiveness,* and *concern for people*.

We will refer to the other dimension as *initiating structure*, although it also has been called *production-centered supervision, goal orientation,* and *concern for production*. It is defined in terms of behavior "in which the supervisor organizes and defines group activities and his relation to the group."[29] To the extent that a manager assigns tasks, plans ahead, and emphasizes production—in short, tries overtly to achieve organizational goals—he or she is exhibiting the structure dimension.

Consideration and *initiating structure* are widely accepted descriptions of leadership behavior, thanks largely to the work of John Hemphill, Ralph Stogdill, and their associates. Their initial studies led to the definition of the terms and the development of techniques to measure them. Starting with a pool of 1,800 descriptions of specific managerial behaviors, these investigators were able to classify the items reliably into 10 basic categories, which they used to describe the behavior patterns of a large number of actual leaders (each leader was scored on each behavior category). Finally, they applied a factor analysis (see Chapter 7) to the questionnaire results and differences obtained on all 10 scales. In other words, the 10 seemingly different behavior categories were really just various combinations of two independent factors: consideration and initiating structure. Knowing this, it was possible to develop a new

TABLE 5–3   Ohio State Leadership Scales (Selected Initiating Structure and Consideration Items)

Item*	Early† LBDQ	Revised‡ LBDQ	SBDQ§	LOQ‖
Initiating structure:				
1. He makes his attitudes clear to the group.	X	X		
2. He rules with an iron hand.	X		X	X
3. He speaks in a manner not to be questioned.#	X			X
4. He schedules the work to be done.	X	X		
5. He maintains definite standards of performance.	X	X		
6. He emphasizes the meeting of deadlines.	X		X	X
7. He encourages the use of uniform procedures.	X	X		
8. He lets group members know what is expected of them.	X	X		
9. He sees to it that the work of group members is coordinated.	X			
10. He offers new approaches to problems.			X	X
11. He insists that he be informed on decisions made by foremen under him.			X	X
12. He lets others do their work the way they think best. (R)			X	X
13. He needles foremen under him for greater effort.			X	X
14. He encourages overtime work.			X	X
15. He stresses being ahead of competing work groups.			X	X
Consideration:				
1. He does personal favors for group members.	X		X	X
2. He is easy to understand.	X		X	
3. He refuses to explain his actions. (R)	X	X	X	X
4. He acts without consulting the group. (R)	X	X	X	X
5. He backs up the members in their actions.	X		X	X
6. He treats all group members as his equals.	X	X	X	X
7. He is friendly and approachable.	X	X	X	
8. He makes group members feel at ease when talking with them.	X		X	
9. He puts suggestions made by the group into operation.	X	X	X	X
10. He gets group approval on important matters before going ahead.	X		X	X
11. He refuses to give in when people disagree with him. (R)			X	X
12. He demands more than we can do. (R)			X	X
13. He helps his foremen with their personal problems.			X	X
14. He criticizes his foremen in front of others. (R)			X	
15. He stands up for his foremen even though it makes him unpopular			X	X
16. He rejects suggestions for changes. (R)			X	X
17. He changes the duties of people under him without first talking it over with them. (R)			X	X
18. He treats people under him without considering their feelings. (R)			X	

TABLE 5–3 *(concluded)*

Item*	Early† LBDQ	Revised‡ LBDQ	SBDQ§	LOQ‖
19. He tries to keep the foremen under him in good standing with those in higher authority.			X	
20. He "rides" the foreman who makes a mistake. (R)			X	
21. He stresses the importance of high morale among those under him.			X	

*Some SBDQ and LOQ items are listed under nearly identical or similar LBDQ items. For administration to workers, SBDQ items are usually modified (see Fleishman, 1969, 1973, for examples). The symbol (R) designates a reflected item (reversed scoring).
†From Halpin, 1957. (Also in Halpin and Winer, 1957).
‡From Stogdill, 1963.
§From Fleishman, 1957a.
‖From Fleishman, 1957b.
#Noted as a reflected consideration item on the LOQ.
SOURCE: From Schriesheim, C., & Kerr, S. 1974. Psychometric properties of the Ohio State leadership scales. *Psychological* Bulletin, 81, 757.

questionnaire to measure these two dimensions explicitly. The resulting instrument, known as the Leadership Behavior Description Questionnaire (LBDQ), is shown in its various forms in Table 5–3.[30]

In marked contrast to the view of leadership as varying along a task–employee orientation continuum, consideration and initiating structure appear to be independent aspects. That is, a manager who behaves in a highly considerate fashion does not necessarily do so at the expense of structuring the situation. The manager can be oriented toward accomplishing organizational goals, provide a high degree of structure for the group, and still be highly considerate of the needs of the work group.

The original LBDQ and several similar scales are presented in Table 5–3. The LBDQ, the revised LBDQ, and the Supervisory Behavior Description Questionnaire (SBDQ) require that people acquainted with the manager, such as subordinates, peers, or supervisors, describe the frequency with which the manager exhibits behaviors that fall under the consideration and initiation of structure categories. The fourth version of the scale, the Leadership Opinion Questionnaire (LOQ), is similar in content to the LBDQ but requires that the manager describe him or herself.[31]

Subsequent research with the LBDQ and its different versions have shown consistently that employees who are satisfied with their jobs have supervisors who they describe as highly considerate.[32] Although the strength of the relationship between consideration and satisfaction has varied to some degree across studies, it is almost always positive in direction. The relationship between consideration and subordinate performance, however, has not been shown as clearly. Survey studies have usually found that higher consideration on the part of the supervisor is associated with higher performance, but the relationship is usually quite small in size and often statistically nonsignificant.

The correlations found between initiating structure and both satisfaction and performance have varied considerably from study to study.[33] The relationship between initiating structure and subordinate satisfaction and between initiating structure and subordinate performance is positive in some studies, negative in others, and at or close to zero in the remainder.

One source of the confusion is that the different versions of the LBDQ seem to measure somewhat different aspects of initiating structure. Negative relationships between initiating structure and subordinate satisfaction are more likely to be found with the SBDQ, probably because of the presence of some punitive items (e.g., "He rules with an iron hand"). Positive relationships are more likely to be found when initiating structure is purged of these items (as in the revised LBDQ).

Differences in leadership scales can account for some, but not all, of the inconsistencies in findings for initiation of structure. Differences between studies in the tasks, subordinates, organizations, and leader attributes also seem to account for many of the discrepancies. Professional, technical, or managerial employees working on nonroutine tasks tend to be more satisfied with a highly structuring supervisor than do blue-collar employees working on routine tasks. Whereas the former seem to like a supervisor who reduces some of the ambiguity in their roles, the latter may view a structuring style as adding routine to an already overroutinized position. The *path-goal* theory of leadership, a contingency view that we will discuss later in this chapter, presents one possible interpretation of the moderating effects of occupational level, task structure, and other situational variables.[34]

A particularly interesting question in research on the LBDQ has been what combination of initiating structure and consideration is most conducive to subordinate satisfaction and performance. A popular theory is that the single most effective leadership style is high on both initiating structure and consideration. The best known proponents of this view are Blake and Mouton, who have built an elaborate commercial program for organizational development around the notion of two independent management factors—*concern for people* and *concern for production.*[35] Using these factors to define two principal coordinates, Blake and Mouton constructed a matrix by dividing each dimension arbitrarily into nine equal steps. The resulting grid thus defines 81 distinguishable management styles. The ideal style is represented by the 9,9 cell (maximum concern for people and production), and the very worst by 1,1 (little concern for either). In application, the Blake-Mouton approach seeks first to locate managers of an organization on the grid (as indicated by their present behavior); then it undertakes to change their behavior in the 9,9 direction through an intensive training program.

Recent evidence tends to refute the notion that a 9,9 (or a high initiating structure, high consideration) combination is the best combination for all situations. The best style combination seems to depend on the situation. For example, Fleishman and Harris conducted a study at International Harvester in which they found that the apparent effects of initiation of structure (as measured by the SBDQ) on the number of labor grievances and the rate of employee turnover (both very costly symptoms of dissatisfaction) depended on supervisor consideration.[36] For supervisors low on consideration, increased structuring was associated with increases in both grievances and turnover. For supervisors who were high on consideration, however, degree of structure appeared largely unrelated to turnover or grievances. This and other studies have refuted the notion that one must be high on both structure and consideration to maximize subordinate satisfaction and performance.[37] It appears that even a 1,1 style (i.e., low emphasis on both productivity and people) could conceivably be effective with some subordinates and tasks.

Considering these findings, one must view with skepticism the rather extravagant claims made by promotors of a 9,9 style. Nevertheless, Blake and Mouton's grid program has probably been of some value, if for no other reason than it encourages whole organizations to take a close look at their management practices. The mere fact that an organization agrees to undertake a critical self-analysis of its management implies that it has already taken a big step in the right direction. How much more the grid exercise itself contributes is debatable.

Leader Influence and Power.   An essential aspect of leadership is influence, as we discussed at the beginning of the chapter. Yet research on leadership style and the day-to-day role activities of leaders typically lacks explicit descriptions of how leaders attempt to change the behavior and attitudes of others. Knowing that a leader "schedules the work to be done" or "treats all group members as his or her equal" does not tell us much about how the leader attempts to improve the performance of a poor performer or maintain the performance of good workers.

Bases of Power.   French and Raven define the power of a person in an organization as the amount of influence or control he could exercise over others if he wanted to.[38] According to French and Raven, three bases of power derive from the position the person occupies:

1. *Reward power*, or the ability to control the administration of incentives.

2. *Coercive power*, or the ability to control the administration of punishment.

3. *Legitimate power*, or the authority vested in a position by organizational policy or social agreement.

For example, person A has power over person B to the extent that A occupies a recognized position of authority and can mete out rewards and punishments to B. A branch manager who has the complete authority to hire, fire, set pay rates, and establish working conditions for branch employees would have tremendous power over them—tremendous, but not necessarily complete, for two more bases of power derive chiefly from the leader personally.

4. *Referent power*, or the extent to which subordinates wish to identify with the leader.

5. *Expert power*, or the extent to which a leader is perceived by subordinates as knowledgeable.

Power can be measured in several different objective and subjective ways, each of which carries a somewhat different meaning. A manager's reward, coercive, and legitimate powers can be described in such objective terms as the number of people supervised, level in the hierarchy, degree of control over budgets, and authority to hire and fire. They can also be described in terms of how the manager and superiors, peers, subordinates, or a panel of impartial observers view the manager's influence in these matters. In the case of expert and referent power, subjective measurement is really the only plausible alternative. From the standpoint of predicting behavior, it could be argued that subjective measures are most useful for all five power bases because actually perceived, not real, power counts. If, for example, you think you control a person's rewards and that person agrees with you, you will both act as though you did even if the control really lies elsewhere.

If we do choose the subjective approach to power measurement, there is still the matter of deciding what questions to ask and of whom to ask them. Table 5–4 presents some of the alternative choices. The most common alternative is to measure power in terms of the resources that the manager perceives as available. An example, which has actually been carried out, sought to find out how various organizational factors such as management philosophy influence a manager's perception of his or her own power. Not surprisingly, the higher the level of the manager in an organization, the more access to legitimate, reward, and coercive means of influence he or she typically perceives.[39] Holding a high-level position does not ensure that the manager will have expert and referent power, as can be seen in the failures of several recent American presidents. A manager shouldn't expect the organization to supply expert and referent power; those must be earned by demonstrating to subordinates and oth-

---

TABLE 5–4   Alternative Approaches to Measuring Supervisor Power and Influence Tactics

---

Supervisor's self-perceived power
  1. Referent power—"My personality allows me to work well in this job."
  2. Expert power—"My ability gives me an advantage in this job."
  3. Legitimate power—"My position gives me a great deal of authority."
  4. Coercive power—"I can punish employees at lower levels."
  5. Reward power—"I can reward persons at lower levels."

Supervisor's self-perceived influence tactics
  1. Friendliness—"I acted in a friendly manner before making my request."
  2. Bargaining—"I offered to pitch in with my subordinate's work if he would do what I wanted."
  3. Reason—"I used logical arguments in order to convince my subordinate to do what I wanted."
  4. Coalitions—"I obtained the support and cooperation of my other subordinates to back."
  5. Assertiveness—"I demanded in no uncertain terms that my subordinate do exactly what I wanted."
  6. Sanctions—"I threatened my subordinate with an unsatisfactory performance appraisal unless he did what I wanted."
  7. Higher authority—"I appealed to higher management to get them to put pressure on my subordinate."

Subordinate self-reported reasons for compliance
  1. Expert power—"I have confidence in his knowledge and good judgment and trust that his direction will be right."
  2. Coercive power—"He can penalize or make things difficult for those who do not co-operate with him."
  3. Legitimate power—"He has the right, considering his job as my supervisor, to expect that his direction will be followed."
  4. Reward power—"He can provide benefits and rewards to those who cooperate with him."
  5. Referent power—"I respect him personally and want to act in a way that merits his respect."

---

ers that the manager is, in fact, worthy of their respect and trust. One interesting issue in the research is just what effect allowing subordinates to participate in decision making has on self-perceived power. The common idea is that participation lessens power, but at least one study has shown that this generalization is somewhat simplistic. Although high-ranking managers perceived their expert and coercive powers to be *lower* under participative than under directive management policies, low-ranking managers saw their power as *greater* under participative policy.[40]

Another approach to measuring power is to examine the tactics and strategies that people perceive the manager to use in attempting to influence others. Kipnis has found that influence tactics can be distinguished along the lines of the categories found in Table 5–4.[41] A third approach has been to ask subordinates to rate why they comply with their manager. For example, one might ask subordinates to think of the times they typically comply with their manager and to indicate just why they comply. Is it because of the rewards and punishments the manager has available, or personality, position, or expertise?

Leadership As an Increment in Influence.   Earlier we differentiated management and supervision from leadership, stating that leadership involves interpersonal influence that goes beyond merely carrying out the duties of the position. Katz and Kahn suggested that a manager who successfully influences people in the organization doesn't really exert *leadership* if, in complying with management's wishes, these people are just going along with the routine directives of the organization. According to their analysis, leadership is an *increment in influence* over and above mechanical compliance with routine directives.[42] The ability to rise above mechanical compliance depends to a large extent on the referent and expert powers of the manager.

A similar theory was presented by Jacobs, who distinguished among three types of influence in organizations.[43] *Power* he defined as influence resulting from the capacity to deprive another of rewards or to inflict costs in the form of punishment (note that his use of the term is more narrow than the way we defined power in the previous section). A manager who relies exclusively on these means of influence can often obtain compliance but only with close supervision and surveillance. *Authority*, the second type of influence, results from an implicit agreement among subordinates that compliance with a supervisor's wishes is needed to achieve objectives. Subordinates comply with a supervisor's wishes because they recognize his or her legitimate right to supervise, but they are not likely to go beyond minimal requirements of the task and display creativity or spontaneity. *Supervision* usually involves the exercise of power and authority. The third type of influence, *leadership*, results from a two-way interaction in which the subordinates comply with the manager's influence attempts because they respect the manager's competence and other personal characteristics (i.e., expert and referent powers), not because they fear punishment, desire a reward, or submit to a status differential (i.e., coercive, reward, and legitimate powers). Jacobs predicts that a manager's effectiveness depends more on how much leadership is exercised than on how much authority and power is wielded.

Ivancevich and Donnelly tested the incremental influence notions of Jacobs and of Katz and Kahn by examining the correlations between the perceived power of sales supervisors and the performance of their subordinates.[44] Their findings appear to support the incremental influence hypothesis of Katz and Kahn and Jacobs. The more expert and referent power the salespeople attributed to their supervisor, the better they performed on six of eight indexes of sales performance. In only one of eight cases was reward power related to performance, and in no case was a significant correlation found between performance and either coercive or legitimate power.

VDL Theory.   Graen and his associates built upon Jacob's distinction between leadership and supervision in their vertical dyad linkage

(VDL) model.[45] According to the VDL model, a manager's job is too demanding to devote equal time and effort to each individual subordinate. Invariably, a manager differentiates between subordinates, developing close relations with a select few (in-group) whose competence is trusted and maintaining more distant, formal relations with the remainder (out-group). In interactions with the in-group, the manager is more likely to wield referent and expert power, communicate openly, and allow participation in decision making. Members of the in-group reciprocate by showing commitment to group goals and a high degree of self-motivation. In essence, the manager's relationship to the in-group is one of *leadership* as defined by Jacobs. On the other hand, the relationship to the out-group is one of *supervision*. With the out-group, the manager relies on the formal employment contract. In exchange for fulfilling the requirements of the job, the manager sees that the subordinate has secure employment, receives monetary compensation, and receives other benefits accruing from fulfillment of the contract. The out-group members may dutifully fulfill this contract, but they do not develop the degree of commitment or involvement found among in-group subordinates.

A recent study conducted by Vecchi & Gobdel is typical of the research that has been conducted to test the VDL model.[46] Tellers in several branch offices of a bank were asked whether they were a trusted assistant (IN) or merely a hired hand (OUT) in their relationships with the branch manager. Consistent with Graen's predictions, those who described themselves as belonging in the IN group had higher performance ratings, greater satisfaction with the supervisor, and expressed less desire to quit.

Unfortunately, the present contribution of the VDL model to the understanding of leadership is quite limited. For one thing, the study described above as well as most of the tests of the VDL model have relied on self-reports to assess the relationship between the manager and each subordinate. As we will discuss later in this chapter, self-report measures of leader behavior often appear to have little relationship to the actual behavior of the leader. Also, at least two important questions have not been addressed by the model and past research: Are leaders who form an in-group any more or less effective than leaders who do not differentiate among subordinates? What should a leader do to effectively manage the problems that often result from real or perceived preferential treatment?

Despite its present limitations, the VDL model highlights an important and ubiquitous phenomenon. Persons in leadership roles do not act the same way with all subordinates, as is often assumed in the leadership theories we have discussed.

The Detrimental Effects of Power.   A common theme in the leadership literature is that the exercise of referent and expert powers increases the effectiveness of the leader. Kipnis has proposed that distinctly negative consequences can result from a situation in which the only means of influence over subordinates are rewards, punishments, or one's position.[47] In a series of laboratory and field studies, Kipnis has provided evidence for the following sequence of events:

1. Supervisors will tend to use whatever resources for influence that are made available to them. When they have the power to give pay raises, to deduct pay, as well as to train, to transfer, and to fire workers, they use them in preference to personal persuasion (which, to be effective, requires that supervisors have expert and referent power to back them up).

2. A supervisor who has reward and coercive power tends to perceive subordinates who comply as doing so because of his or her power and not because of good intentions.

3. Supervisors who possess reward and coercive power are less likely to see their subordinates as possessing high ability, are more likely to perceive themselves as possessing high ability, and less likely to develop close relationships with the subordinates. In contrast to supervisors with high coercive and reward power, supervisors without these means of influence have a more positive view of subordinates, whom they tend to see as more self-motivated.

The research of Kipnis and his associates illustrates a paradox in the exercise of power. The more power a supervisor has, the more he or she may be able to induce subordinates to comply. But in doing so, the supervisor may become distrustful of subordinates and thereby sow the seeds that will later flower into poor leader-member relations and, eventually, reduced power and effectiveness.

Kipnis is concerned with the corrupting influence of the presence of power. Some evidence shows, however, that a *lack of power* can cause problems as well. Greene and Podsakoff found that after the withdrawal of a bonus plan in which supervisors could recommend monetary rewards, the supervisors were perceived by their subordinates to have less reward power, less referent power, and less influence on higher management, but *more* coercive power.[48] Supervisors appeared to have compensated for their loss of reward power by making more use of punishments to induce subordinates to follow their directives.

The research on the effects of power on the way supervisors wield their influence suggests that organizations *should* provide supervisors with the rewards, punishments, and legitimacy necessary to carry out their duties. At the same time, they should be encouraged to avoid overuse of these means of influence and to develop their expert and referent powers. This is easier said than done and may require formal training in leadership skills (which we will discuss in Chapter 8).

Criticisms of Research on Leadership Behavior. Research on leadership styles, power, and influence has yielded some useful measurement instruments, but it has also come in for its share of criticism. First, research on styles of leadership at one time was intended to find the one or two dimensions that could capture the essence of effective leadership. More recently, the scales that have emerged from these efforts, such as the LBDQ, have been criticized for being too simple and crude to adequately measure something as complex as leader behavior. Research efforts now appear to be in the direction of developing more complex scales. In one of the older programs of research on leadership, Taylor developed the Four-Factor Theory Questionnaire (FFTQ), which measured four dimensions of leader behavior: (1) supervisory support (friendly and easy to approach), (2) goal emphasis (encourages people to do their best), (3) work facilitation (provides help in scheduling work), and (4) interaction facilitation (encourages people to work as a team).[49] In recent years, additional style dimensions have been proposed. Bass and Valenzi set forth five styles of leadership;[50] Stogdill, in his revisions of the LBDQ, added 10 more dimensions to the 2 found in the original LBDQ;[51] Yukl went even further and presented a taxonomy of no less than 19 managerial behaviors![52] There haven't been enough studies conducted with these new instruments to provide definite conclusions regarding their relative validity. The authors of these instruments appear to have taken a step in the right direction, however, in examining other leader behaviors besides those concerned with supervision of subordinates.

A second complaint is that it is impossible to tell from the correlational studies (the ones that most clearly support style theory) whether results attributed to consideration and structure are *caused by* or are the *cause of* these behaviors. Managers might show a lot of consideration because workers are productive and happy; they might initiate structure because things are going badly.[53] Likewise, subordinates might view their supervisors as experts and as likeable because they have succeeded. All we know for sure is that certain states of satisfaction and performance seem to go with certain leader behavior patterns.

A third criticism of the research on leadership style is that many of the dimensions found by factor analysis reflect intuitive notions of the person who rates the leader more than actual leader behavior. One view is that people have personal notions (implicit theories) of what leader behaviors tend to occur together and how they are related to the effectiveness and satisfaction of the work group.[54] When describing the behavior of a leader, the observer falls back on these notions. For instance, conventional wisdom has it that a supervisor who is "friendly and approachable" will also frequently "do personal favors for group members" and show other consideration behaviors listed in Table 5–3. Consequently, a specific leader who is friendly and approachable may be rated by an observer as doing personal favors regardless of whether the leader ever exhibited this type of behavior. Thus, according to this view, factors of consideration and initiating structure, as well as different types of power and influence, emerge as independent clusters of behaviors as a result of logical notions in the rater's head as to what leader behaviors go together, and they have little to do with actual relationships among behaviors.

Summary of the Behavioral Approach to Leadership. The shortcomings notwithstanding, the research on leader behavior has shown that *how* the leader carries out the functions of the leadership role is as important, and in many situations more important, as personal traits in determining effectiveness. If trait theory implies that selection is the key to managerial success, research on leader behavior tends to emphasize training. Once the proper behaviors are known, managers can supposedly be taught to use them. Thus, numerous training programs have been marketed to acquaint managers with the importance of consideration and to show them how to develop a more considerate style of management. Less attention is usually paid to initiating structure, because it is assumed that past training and experience have, if anything, overemphasized this factor already. Furthermore, there is some evidence to support the human relations view that consideration, participativeness, and supportiveness are the most important facets of leadership as long as employee satisfaction is the primary goal. It is less clear what it takes to maximize their productivity.

The bulk of the evidence, therefore, suggests that there is no one best way of leading. One difficulty, once again, is that success or effectiveness can be defined in different ways (the old criterion problem). Another source of complexity is that the effects of leader behavior appear to be moderated by a host of other variables, notably personality, which we discussed earlier, and situational factors, which we take up next.

Situational Approaches to Leadership

Whether we view leadership in terms of the traits or the behavior of the leader, attention is still focused on the person in the leadership role as the cause of work group effectiveness. If a work group is ineffective, it is because the leader has in some way failed. If the work group succeeds, this success is attributed to the leader's behavior and/or enduring traits of leadership. As discussed earlier, these views tend to place too much emphasis on the leader and too little on the nature of the situation in which the leader must function. In reaction to the limitations of the trait and behavioral views of leadership, some theorists have called attention to the situation as the primary determinant of what the leader does and of effectiveness as a leader.

FIGURE 5-2 A Situational View of Leader Behavior

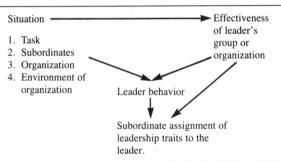

The Effect of the Situation on Leader Behavior and Effectiveness. Although we have discussed several style theories of leadership, only a few organizational theorists have expressed radical situational views. One reason for this may be that few managers are likely to pay much attention to theorists who tell them that what they do doesn't make much difference, regardless of the possible validity of this view. In this section, we will discuss some of the major elements of the situational view.

Figure 5-2 attempts to pull several radical situational views together into one model. In a sense, one could call this a leaderless theory of leadership. According to this model, the effectiveness of the group or organization and the leader's own behavior are both caused by situational forces that the leader has little control over. Despite the actual failure of the leader to affect the performance of the group, however, subordinates tend to see the leader as one of the primary causes of their successes and failures. If the group succeeds, they are likely to view the leader as a major reason for their success, particularly if his or her behavior has the appearance of things leaders should do. If the group fails, however, they are likely to blame the leader for this failure and to see him or her as lacking traits of leadership. "Successful leaders" have managed to be in the right place at the right time and have cultivated the image of an effective leader among followers. Now we will examine each of these links in the model separately in light of the available evidence.

Situation → Leader Behavior. Contrary to the trait theorists, who view leadership style as stable across situations, the radical situational view is that leadership style changes with the situation. Consistent with this view, there is an increasing amount of research showing that people can change their leader behavior rather drastically as a function of changes in the task, subordinates, and performance of the group. People in leadership roles have been found to show higher consideration, less initiation of structure, and less close supervision for subordinates they consider competent than for those they consider incompetent.[55] They also have been shown to change their behavior quite dramatically in response to changes in tasks. On highly complex tasks, they tend to become more structuring and task oriented than on simple tasks.[56] Similarly, as subordinate performance decreases, people in leadership roles tend to become less considerate and less structuring.[57] Finally, people in leadership roles are more participative when their followers show initiative, offer ideas, and set goals than when their followers are passive, request instructions, and are unquestioning.[58]

Leaders do not just respond mindlessly to situational variables. Instead, the responses of leaders to the situation appear to be mediated by their interpretation of these situations. Green and Mitchell recently presented an attributional model of leader-member interactions in which they proposed that leaders' explanations of a cause of performance determine how they respond to subordinates.[59] If the leader attributes the cause of a performance to factors external to the subordinate (e.g., the task, working conditions), the leader will focus action on the situation by changing the task or improving working conditions. A fundamental error that leaders (and everyone else as well) tend to make in attributing causality, however, is the tendency to ignore the effects of the situation and to place an inordinate weight on the subordinate as a cause of what they observe. Green and Mitchell propose that "because a leader is more likely to explain member performance with internal causes than external causes, leader behavior is more likely to be directed at the member than at situational factors" (p. 451). The implication of this tendency is that leaders will tend to ignore the effect of the situation despite its large impact on both their own behavior and the performance of their groups. It is much more common to hear a manager blame poor group performance on subordinate laziness or irresponsibility than on the absence of challenge in the job or the type of supervision provided. Thus, it appears that managers are more participative and considerate when subordinates perform at high levels because they have attributed the good performance to the competence and motivation of the subordinates. On the other hand, when subordinates perform poorly, managers are more structuring and punitive because they have attributed the performance to the low ability or motivation of the subordinates. Because leaders tend to place the responsibility for outcomes on people, the important influence of impersonal or situational factors tends to be ignored. Paradoxically, it is the situation that can be changed with the fewest repercussions.

Situation → Group and Organizational Effectiveness. Another assumption implicit in both the trait and behavioral views of leadership is that leaders make a difference in how well a group or organization performs. Some theorists have attacked conventional wisdom and suggest that the effectiveness depends mainly on the situation in which the group or organization finds itself and very little on the leader. Studies of the effects of *managerial succession* have often been cited as support for the radical situational view. The typical study of this type examines the relationship between changes in the leader and variations in the performance of a group or organization to determine how much of the variation in performance can be attributed to who is in the leadership role. Most of the early studies appear to support a radical situational view. Lieberson and O'Connor examined 167 business firms in 13 industries over a 20-year period and found that, compared with factors such as economic cycles, the changes in top-level executives had very small effects on organizational performance.[60] Allen, Panian, and Lotz examined the relationship between turnover in managers of major league baseball teams and the performance of the teams for all major league teams between 1920 and 1973.[61] As any baseball fan would have guessed, owners were more likely to fire the manager the more games the team lost during the previous season. Contrary to what owners and fans typically hope for, however, managerial turnover did not appear to have much effect on team performance. Rather, the best single predictor of performance in any one season was how well the team performed the previous season. In a study more relevant to industrial supervision, Rosen examined the effects of changes in supervisors on performance of work crews in a furniture manufacturing plant. Again, compared to other variables, who the particular supervisor was made very little difference in how well the work groups performed.[62]

Recently, these studies of managerial succession have been criticized for both conceptual and methodological errors. Using a different statistical approach to examining the effects of changes in managerial succession, Weiner and Mahoney found that who the chief executive officers of firms were appeared to be a major determinant of their profitability.[63] Smith, Carson, and Alexander pointed out that most previous studies had not looked at the previous success of the new leader as a predictor of future performance.[64] They found, in a study of Methodist churches, that a changeover in ministers appeared to increase the effectiveness of churches (i.e., increased giving, membership, and property development), particularly if the minister had been successful in a previous church. A large number of isues are unresolved in the research on managerial succession, but it seems accurate to conclude that the situational view is supported insofar as many situational factors beyond the control of the leader can account for a large part of the effectiveness of the group or organization. Nevertheless, an increasing amount of research supports what most people have known all the time: who the leader is does make a difference and sometimes may be the major determinant of performance.

Effectiveness→ Subordinate Attributions of Causality.   According to the radical situational view, people cling to the belief that the leader determines events and not vice versa.[65] There are several possible reasons why people tend to attribute the cause of group and organizational effectiveness to the leader. The person in the leadership role serves as a convenient scapegoat in times of failure and as a symbol of success when things are going well. So strong is our belief in the causal importance of leadership that our perceptions of how a leader behaves in a situation can be influenced more by how well the group or organization performs than by the leader's actual behavior. In one series of studies, subjects rated the same leader under different sets of instructions: Some were told that the group performed at a high level and others that it had been a failure.[66] Those who believed the group had done well rated the leader as showing more initiating structure and consideration behaviors than did those who believed the group had failed.

One explanation for such findings is, as we noted before, that people rely on personal theories in describing leaders. Because people probably believe that a successful group is more likely to have an active, strong leader (i.e., high on both initiating structure and consideration) than does a group that fails, they are inclined to let this theory color their description of the leader's behavior. If the group succeeds, then the leader is seen as active, strong, and generally responsible for its performance; if it fails, then the leader is seen as weak, passive, and responsible for its failures. Attributions such as these may fulfill a need to see order in the environment. It is more gratifying to believe that the leader is in control of the situation than to see ourselves and the leader as at the mercy of external forces.

Persons in leadership roles seldom sit back and passively accept whatever explanations subordinates, peers, and superiors use to explain events. They often attempt to manage the impressions others have of the performances of their group or organization. Consciously or unconsciously, they may attempt to create the impression that they are responsible for the successes and not responsible for the failures. For example, several studies have shown that CEOs credit themselves (e.g., their past decisions) when the firm is doing well but blame declining performance on the environment of the firms (bad economic times, policy of the federal government).[67] In all likelihood, these are planned and conscious attempts to win the confidence of shareholders by convincing them that they "can cope with an unruly environment." According to Pfeffer, "Successful leaders, as perceived by the members of the social system, are those who can separate themselves from organizational failures and associate themselves with organizational successes."[68]

It is interesting to compare the attributions posed by subordinates of the leader for the causes of performance with the explanations provided by the leader, which we discussed earlier. Leaders are likely to attribute the cause of their subordinates' performance to factors internal to the subordinates. On the other hand, the subordinate is likely to attribute the causes of his own performance to factors in the situation, particularly the leader. According to Green and Mitchell, "This basic difference in causal explanations and resultant leader behavior serves as a major source of leader-member conflict and miscommunication."[69]

Implications for Effective Leadership. The obvious implication of a radical situational view of leadership is that one does not have to worry about who the leader is or what the leader does. To ensure effective performance of the work group, one instead should pay attention to the design of tasks, selection of subordinates, reward systems, organizational structures, and other situational factors. In this respect, the scientific management and classical theorists might be considered radical situationalists, although their prescriptions would probably differ from those advanced by the modern proponents. An example is Weber's theory of the bureaucratic ideal, which states that effective organizations are more likely to have well-designed tasks, procedures, and rules than they are to have charismatic leaders. The manager is there to see that the bureaucracy runs, and if given enough legitimate, reward, and coercive power, there is no need for "leadership."

Viewed from the perspective of the person in the leadership role, a radical situational approach implies that successful leadership is more a matter of impression management than of how the role is performed. The "effective" manager can create the right image and induce the belief in superiors, subordinates, and peers that he or she is responsible for the success of the group but not for its failures.[70]

Limitations on a Radical Situational View of Leadership. The radical situational view provides a counterweight to balance the aforementioned overemphasis in the popular mind on the leader's role in group effectiveness. Just as the trait and behavioral theories were clearly too narrow, however, so too is the situational view in its radical form. As we have already shown, there appears to be ample research evidence to show that the leader *does* make a difference in how effectively groups and organizations perform. Although situational factors are often more important than either supervisors or subordinates think they are, they are not the whole story.

A more moderate situational view, put forth by Kerr and Jermier, holds that the leader can influence the satisfaction and performance of subordinates but only in some situations.[71] The effects predicted in their model are summarized in Table 5–5. The basic idea is that there are two types of situational variables: neutralizers and substitutes. *Neutralizers* are so called because they can prevent the leader from having either a negative or positive influence on subordinate satisfaction and performance. For example, if physical barriers separate superior and subordinates and prevent them from communicating, then it is almost

---

TABLE 5–5   Specific Substitutes and Neutralizers: Supportive and Instrumental Leadership

	Substitute or Neutralizer	Supportive Leadership	Instrumental Leadership
A.	**Subordinate characteristics**		
1.	Experience, ability, training		Substitute
2.	"Professional" orientation	Substitute	Substitute
3.	Indifference toward rewards offered by organization	Neutralizer	Neutralizer
B.	**Task Characteristics**		
1.	Structured, routine, unambiguous task		Substitute
2.	Feedback provided by task		Substitute
3.	Intrinsically satisfying task	Substitute	
C.	**Organization characteristics**		
1.	Cohesive work group	Substitute	Substitute
2.	Low position power (leader lacks control over organizational rewards)	Neutralizer	Neutralizer
3.	Formalization (explicit plans, goals, areas of responsibility)		Substitute
4.	Inflexibility (rigid, unyielding rules and procedures)		Neutralizer
5.	Leader located apart from subordinates with only limited communication possible	Neutralizer	Neutralizer

SOURCE: Yukl, G. A. (1981). *Leadership in organizations* (p. 163). Englewood Cliffs, N.J.: Prentice-Hall.

impossible for leaders to affect subordinate performance through either supportive or instrumental leadership. Other situational variables are *substitutes* in that they do not prevent a leader from influencing subordinates, but they make such behaviors redundant and possibly harmful. Thus, subordinates who form a cohesive team or who have a strong professional orientation may be self-managing and may not need a leader to either structure their tasks or attend to their needs. One of the authors is acquainted with a manufacturing plant in Houston that appears to have provided just such a substitute for formal leadership. Workers in this plant have been organized into small teams that make most of the day-to-day decisions, including the hiring, firing, and disciplining of their own. There are no first-line supervisors in this plant and, given the tight control that the teams appear to exert over their own operations, such supervision would probably be counterproductive.

The research testing Kerr and Jermier's model suggests that the extent to which situational variables act as substitutes or neutralizers depends on the specific organization. One study, conducted with nurses in a community hospital, provided strong support only for the prediction that a high degree of formalization renders instrumental leadership unnecessary.[72] Another study, also conducted in a hospital setting, provided somewhat stronger support for the model.[73] Task, work group cohesion, and worker education were all found to substitute for the head nurse's leadership behavior in much the way Kerr and Jermier predict. However, a third study has found that providing rewards contingent on good performance is associated with good performance and high satisfaction even in situations that Kerr and Jermier predict would neutralize or substitute for these leader behaviors.[74] The findings, then, are mixed in their support of Kerr and Jermier's model and indicate that this model will require modifications. Nevertheless, the idea of searching for situations in which leadership behavior will and will not affect work group outcomes seems a more realistic starting point than concentrating exclusively either on the situation or the leader's behavior and traits.

Contingency Theories of Leadership

As we have just seen, some theorists have stressed the traits of the leader, others the behaviors of the leader, and a few the leader's situation as the primary cause of effectiveness. Our contention was that each of these factors has some influence on leader effectiveness, but none is sufficient to account for it completely. An alternative approach states that the effectiveness of the leader is contingent on some combination of leader traits, leader behavior, and the situation. There have been numerous isolated efforts to tie situational factors into trait or behavior theories. Only three fairly comprehensive contingency theories have emerged: Fiedler's contingency theory, House's path-goal theory, and Vroom and Yetton's prescriptive decision model.

Fiedler's Contingency Theory. Fiedler's model is the only contingency model that has examined the interplay of all three factors: traits, behaviors, and situations of the leader.[75] His contention is that the critical aspect of a situation from a leadership standpoint is favorableness or the degree to which the situation makes it easy for the leader to manage. Three main factors combine to determine a situation's favorableness: task structure, leader-member relations, and position power. It is easier to be a leader, Fiedler argues, when the group to be led is faced with a clearly outlined task (high task structure), when it has great respect for its leader (good leader-member relations), and when the leader has a considerable amount of reward, coercive, and legitimate powers (position power), than when the opposite conditions obtain. Also, the high degree of control over events that the leader has in this situation leads to less anxiety and greater feelings of certainty that the task will be completed than is the case when leader-member relations are poor, the task is unstructured, and there is little position power. If, as a first approximation, we identify situations according to whether they are high or low on these

TABLE 5–6   Predictions of Fiedler's Contingency Theory for Leader Effectiveness in Each of the Eight Situational Octants

Situational Favorability	Octant	Leader- Member Relations	Task Structure	Power	Effective Leader?
High favorability	1	Good	Structured	Strong	Low LPC
	2	Good	Structured	Weak	Low LPC
	3	Good	Unstructured	Strong	Low LPC
Moderate favorability	4	Good	Unstructured	Weak	High LPC
	5	Poor	Structured	Strong	High LPC
	6	Poor	Structured	Weak	High LPC
	7	Poor	Unstructured	Strong	High LPC
High unfavorability	8	Poor	Unstructured	Weak	Low LPC

three dimensions, we end up with the eight categories found in Table 5–6. Octant 1 represents the most favorable set of conditions, octant 8 the worst, and the others rank somewhere between. The specific ordering of octants is based on the assumption that *leader-member relations* is the most important factor, *task structure* next, and *position power* the least. To complete the picture, Fiedler has developed procedures (mainly questionnaires) for measuring situations on each of these three dimensions.

The behavior and effectiveness of the leader depend upon the combination of leader personality and the situation's favorableness. The personality trait by which Fiedler distinguishes between leaders is the concern they have for maintaining good interpersonal relations relative to completing the task. This dimension is measured with a questionnaire known as the Least Preferred Co-Worker (LPC) index, which requires a leader to rate, on several trait dimensions, the person with whom he or she has had the most difficulty working. The rationale is that a leader whose highest priority is accomplishing a task will evaluate the least-preferred co-worker on the basis of how that person helped to achieve task goals. Consequently, a leader will tend to rate the person with whom he or she had difficulties very low on a large number of trait dimensions. By contrast, a leader who places highest priority on good interpersonal relations will not weight the co-worker's contribution to task success as heavily. Compared to the task-oriented leader (who is inclined to give the LPC low ratings), then, the relationships-oriented leader is inclined to view the LPC more favorably. The theory is, then, that the LPC measure measures the rater more than it does the rated. A high-LPC leader is supposedly people oriented, whereas a low-LPC leader is task oriented.

The contingency model has been tested in over 178 studies conducted in all sorts of groups all over the world—the Belgian navy, high school basketball teams, Japanese students.[76] In addition to an enviable travel opportunity, this work has afforded Fiedler some support for his contingency model. By and large, the studies have examined the correlation between the LPC measure and performance measures in situations typifying each of the eight conditions. The model predicts a positive correlation between LPC and performance in the middle octants, indicating that relationships-oriented leaders are more effective in these situations. A negative correlation between LPC and performance is predicted in the extremely favorable and unfavorable octants, indicating that a more task-oriented leadership is effective in these situations. Recent summaries of the research on Fiedler's model seem to justify three conclusions: (1) the pattern of results generally provides support for all but octant 2 predictions, (2) laboratory tests of the model provide more consistent support than the field research, and (3) the model leaves a lot of the variance in leader effectiveness unexplained.[77]

Despite the general support for the predictions, Fiedler's theory is very controversial. Both the theory itself and the supporting evidence have been sharply criticized. The most thorough critiques have come from Graen and his co-workers and from Ashour.[78] Among other things, they contend that many of the results offered as evidence for the model have failed to meet scientific standards for reliability. Further, the specific definition of favorableness has changed from study to study and often, it seems, on the basis of the results that favorableness is supposed to help predict. It is hard, then, to tell how meaningful the supporting evidence really is. Other criticisms have been leveled against the various measures used to define situational features (i.e., leader-member relations, position power, and structure) and the LPC index of leadership style.[79] Perhaps the most damning criticisms have been aimed at the LPC measure.[80] Fiedler himself has seemingly changed his views several times on what the LPC is, viewing it one time as a measure of leader style and more recently as a measure of leader needs.[81]

For all these objections, Fiedler's contingency model continues to stimulate controversy and research. Because it has not been an overwhelming success in predicting leadership effectiveness, the reader may justifiably ask why it merits so much attention. One reason is that it is intuitively appealing. Another is that it is more comprehensive than most other leadership models. Probably the best reason is summed up in the old adage: Theories are never destroyed by contradictory evidence; only by better theories. Even most of Fiedler's critics seem to feel that the contingency model represents a good first approximation—that it should be improved upon rather than scrapped entirely.[82]

If trait theory stresses selection of leaders and behavioral theory stresses training, what are the practical implications of Fiedler's contingency theory? Because it includes more factors than either of the other types of theory, it obviously affords more options as well. Suppose, for example, there was reason to suspect that the management of an organization was not as effective as it might be. First, we might try to diagnose the problem using the contingency approach. This we could do by measuring each manager's style (using the LPC index) together with the situation in which the manager was operating (in terms of position power, leader-member relations, and task structure). If the contingency theory is correct, the problem could well turn out to be a serious mismatch between the traits of the leader and situations.

Having diagnosed the problem, the second step would be to try to change something so as to achieve a better match. Here, again, we would have several options. We could transfer people, shift leaders around, hire new ones, or reorganize groups. We could try to change leaders' styles to better suit the occasion, e.g., counsel or train them in the appropriate behavior. Or we could go to work on the situation, attacking the problem through any or all of the three situational factors. This, incidentally, is the approach preferred by Fiedler.[83] Organizations could be engineered to suit the available leadership by adjusting each manager's position power, task structure, and leader-member relations in accordance with his or her style. They might, for example, increase (or decrease) the manager's formal authority by changing the decision-making power or the number and rank of the people supervised. They could give the manager more (or less) specific operating instructions. They could try to improve the manager's rapport with workers through some sort of group training exercises or by changing the composition of the group. The creative reader can probably think of dozens of specific examples for each of these solutions.

Path-Goal Theory Applications to Leadership.   As we mentioned in Chapter 3, VIE theory is, in the opinion of many industrial and organizational psychologists, the most comprehensive and valid theory of work motivation. It is not surprising, then, that efforts have been made to extend the basic VIE ideas to leader behavior. In this context, it is often referred to as path-goal theory. The general orientation of path-goal theory is that one does not need to really add much to basic theories of work motivation to understand and predict effective leadership. An effective leader, from the perspective of path-goal theory, *motivates* employees to perform at high levels. In turn, motivation increases just as VIE theory predicts with increases in (1) the subjective probability that effort will result in effective performance, (2) the instrumentality of effective performance for valued outcomes, and (3) the valence of these outcomes. In addition to examining the effects of leader behavior on subordinate motivation, VIE theory also has been used to predict just how leaders choose from among alternative leadership styles. Let us consider each of these applications of VIE theory.

Prediction of Leader Behavior.   According to VIE theory, a leader will adopt whatever style is thought to have the best chance of producing the desired outcomes. Thus, if primarily interested in production and believing that a directive style will maximize production, the leader is likely to choose a directive style of managing. If interested primarily in the morale of subordinates and believing that a considerate approach will yield the highest morale, the leader will use that style. In short, everything we said about VIE theory in connection with workers can be applied to leaders. The only differences are in the kind of outcomes, instrumentalities, and expectancies considered.

Nebeker and Mitchell have made a good start toward identifying some of these elements as applied to leadership.[84] They were able to predict extremely well the extent to which supervisors in naval aviation and public works maintenance crews exhibited certain kinds of leadership behaviors (e.g., treating subordinates as individuals and supervising subordinates' ongoing activities). The supervisors behaved much as VIE theory predicts, that is, they chose to lead in a way they anticipated would allow them to achieve valued objectives.

Predictions of Subordinate Motivation and Satisfaction.   House and his associates have presented a path-goal theory to predict the effects of leader behavior on subordinate satisfaction and motivation.[85] In their view, an essential function of a leader is to enhance the motivation and job satisfaction of subordinates by (1) increasing subordinate expectancies that the exertion of effort will lead to effective performance and valued outcomes and (2) increasing the valence of the outcomes given to the subordinate for good performance. Another key proposition is that the leader's behavior should complement the situation to provide what is missing or to reduce frustrating barriers to performance. Predictions have been derived from these basic propositions concerning four dimensions of leader behavior: (1) directiveness (structuring), (2) supportiveness (consideration), (3) participativeness, and (4) achievement orientation.[86]

1. *Leader directiveness.* If the task is highly structured, then the subordinate knows what to do to succeed. Directive, structuring leadership would tend to be seen as redundant at best and, at worst, a cruel imposition of control. Such leadership probably would be seen as useful, however, in an unstructured task where the subordinate is likely to have low expectancies that efforts will accomplish task goals or achieve valued outcomes. The prediction, then, is that task structure should influence (moderate) the effects of leader directiveness on subordinate performance and satisfaction. In support of this prediction, more directive leaders have been found to have more satisfied subordinates in unstructured tasks; but leader directiveness has been found to be associated with lower subordinate satisfaction on more structured tasks.[87] The hypothesized effects on performance have not been found, however.

2. *Leader supportiveness.* Another prediction from path-goal theory is that supportive, considerate leadership will be associated with higher job satisfaction when the job is dissatisfying than when it is intrinsically satisfying. A similar prediction is that supportive or considerate leadership will show a more positive relationship to job satisfaction when the task is stressful than when it is nonstressful. In the case of a dissatisfying task and a stressful task, supportiveness complements the situation by providing rewards (praise, emotional support, etc.) where there are few intrinsic rewards. Again, the research generally has tended to support the predictions.[88]

3. *Leader participativeness.* A third prediction involves the degree to which the leader is participative. The job satisfaction resulting from participative leadership should depend on both the structure of the task and the authoritarianism of the subordinates. Authoritarianism is a personality trait that purportedly measures the extent to which persons submit to authority figures. High-authoritarian subordinates prefer to be controlled by their environment, whereas low-authoritarian subordinates value their independence. According to House, low-authoritarian subordinates are more satisfied with a job when the supervisor allows them to participate in decisions regarding the job than when the supervisor is nonparticipative. Moreover, the low-authoritarian subordinate values participation for its own sake, not for its effects on goal achievement. On the other hand, the job satisfaction of an authoritarian subordinate is enhanced by participation only in unstructured tasks. Participation enchances satisfaction among these subordinates only to the extent that it increases their expectancies that their efforts will result in task success. Schuler supported these predictions in a study of 353 employees in a manufacturing plant.[89] However, this is only one study, and until more research is conducted, we will reserve judgment on the validity of House's predictions for leader participativeness.

4. *Achievement-oriented leadership.* An achievement-oriented leader, according to House and Mitchell,

> sets challenging goals, expects subordinates to perform at their highest level, continuously seeks improvement in performance, and shows a high degree of confidence that the subordinates will assume responsibility, put forth effort, and accomplish challenging goals.[90]

The path-goal theory prediction is that achievement-oriented leadership will cause subordinates to have more confidence in their own ability and that this will cause them to increase their efforts to succeed. Again, however, this expectation holds only for unstructured tasks where subordinate expectancies are likely to be low. Despite one study by House and Mitchell that partially confirmed this hypothesis, there is still little evidence on which to evaluate it.[91]

In general, then, the evidence tends to support several path-goal theory predictions regarding job satisfaction. Further, some recent evidence supports House's contention that subordinate expectancies mediate the effects of leader behavior on subordinate satisfaction.[92] The relationships reported between leadership style and job satisfaction are not particularly strong, however, and are subject to other interpretations. Also, because most of the evidence is correlational, one is again faced with the indeterminancy of cause-effect relationships.

Contributions of Path-Goal Theory.   Despite its weaknesses, path-goal theory seems to hold some promise as a contingency theory of leadership. It has proven to be a useful framework for explaining some of the inconsistencies in the research on the Ohio State scales (LBDQ and SBDQ) that we discussed earlier in this chapter. Also, the model has clear implications for improving leadership. It might be, for example, that leaders sometimes form erroneous impressions of the relationship between their behavior and their own desired outcomes. A leader might believe that directive supervision will increase the subordinates' satisfaction when, for the particular task, it tends to have the opposite effect. Confronted with evidence as to the true situation, the leader might be inclined to alter leadership style. Or it might be that leaders and subordinates attach quite different values to various outcomes. Knowing this, it might be possible to arrive at some sort of compromise goals to which the manager could adapt his or her behavior. The point is that incorporating both leader and subordinate behavior within a common theoretical framework (VIE theory) encourages us to look at leader-member interactions. Some of these undoubtedly play a major role in the manager's effectiveness, the subordinates' attitudes and motivation, and the group's success.

Vroom and Yetton's Model of Leadership.   If failure to provide specific managerial prescriptions is a major weakness of many contingency models, such is certainly not the case with our third contingency theory—the Vroom-Yetton model.[93] The latter was developed explicitly to help managers deal with practical, real-life problems. Similar to Fiedler's theory, it assumes that different situations call for different actions. Unlike Fiedler's theory, it attempts to spell out in very concrete terms the situational possibilities and the acceptable response alternatives. In essence, the Vroom-Yetton model provides a taxonomy of problem types, a procedure for identifying a particular problem within this scheme, and a set of behavioral alternatives for each problem so identified.

Somewhat similar to the Tannenbaum and Schmidt continuum that was presented in Figure 5–1, Vroom and Yetton present five levels of participative decision making that range from the most autocratic (AI) to the most participative (GII in the case of groups and DI in the case of individuals). These five alternative decision methods are presented in Table 5–7 and are self-explanatory. In deciding among these alternative leadership approaches, Vroom and Yetton believe the leader should carefully

TABLE 5–7 Decision Methods for Groups and Individual Problems

Group Problems	*Individual Problems*
AI. You solve the problem or make decision yourself, using information available to you at the time.	AI. You solve the problem or make the decision by yourself, using information available to you at the time.
AII. You obtain the necessary information from your subordinates, then decide the solution to the problem yourself. You may or may not tell your subordinates what the problem is in getting the information from them. The role played by your subordinates in making the decision is clearly one of providing the necessary information to you rather than generating or evaluating alternative solutions.	AII. You obtain the necessary information from your subordinate, then decide on the solution to the problem yourself. You may or may not tell the subordinate what the problem is in getting information from him. His role in making the decision is clearly one of providing the necessary information to you, rather than generating or evaluating alternative solutions.
CI. You share the problem with the relevant subordinates individually, getting their ideas and suggestions without bringing them together as a group. Then *you* make the decision, which may or may not reflect your subordinates' influence.	CI. You share the problem with your subordinate, getting his ideas and suggestions. Then you make a decision, which may or may not reflect his influence.
CII. You share the problem with your subordinates as a group, obtaining their collective ideas and suggestions. Then you make the decision, which may or may not reflect your subordinates' influence.	GI. You share the problem with your subordinate, and together you analyze the problem and arrive at a mutually agreeable solution.
GII. You share the problem with your subordinates as a group. Together you generate and evaluate alternatives and attempt to reach agreement (consensus) on a solution. Your role is much like that of chairman. You do not try to influence the group to adopt "your" solution, and you are willing to accept and implement any solution which has the support of the entire group.	DI. You delegate the problem to your subordinate, providing him with any relevant information that you possess, but giving him responsibility for solving the problem by himself. You may or may not request him to tell you what solution he has reached.

SOURCE: From Vroom, V. H., & Yetton, P. W. A normative model of leadership styles (p. 133). In K. N. Wexley & G. A. Yukl (Eds.). *Organizational behavior and industrial psychology*. New York: Oxford.

diagnose the situation in terms of eight basic attributes, which are shown at the top of Figure 5–3. Using a few basic assumptions, plus the available evidence on each attribute, Vroom, Yetton, and Jago were able to logically derive 18 distinct kinds of problems, shown as numbered endpoints in Figure 5–3.[94] The logic process is also represented here in the form of a decision-tree. If attribute A does not apply (the *no* branch in the tree), then we can skip attributes B–D on logical grounds and ask whether or not E applies. If it does not, we arrive at our first problem type

FIGURE 5–3   Decision-Process Flow Chart for Both Individual and Group Problems

A. Is there a quality requirement such that one solution is likely to be more rational than another?
B. Do I have sufficient information to make a high-quality decision?
C. Is the problem structured?
D. Is acceptance of decision by subordinates critical to effective implementation?
E. If I were to make the decision by myself, is it reasonably certain that it would be accepted by my subordinates?
F. Do subordinates share the organizational goals to be attained in solving this problem?
G. Is conflict among subordinates likely in preferred solutions? (This question is irrelevant to individual problems.)
H. Do subordinates have sufficient information to make a high-quality decision?

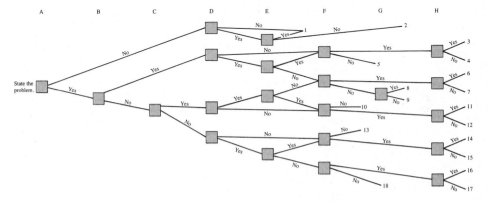

The feasible set is shown for each problem type for group (G) and individual (I) problems.

1	G: AI, AII, CI, CII, GII I: AI, DI, AII, CI, GI	7	G: GII I: GI	13	G: GII I: CI
2	G: GII I: DI, GI	8	G: GII I: CI	14	G: CII, GII I: DI, CI, GI
3	G: AI, AII, CI, GII, GII I: AI, DI, AII, CI, GI	9	G: CI, CII I: CI	15	G: GII, GII I: CI, GI
4	G: AI, AII, GI, GII, GII I: AI, AII, GI, GI	10	G: AII, CI, CII I: AII, CI	16	G: GII I: DI, GI
5	G: AI, AII, GI, GII I: AI, AII, GI	11	G: AII, CI, CII, GII I: AII, CI, GI	17	G: GII I: GI
6	G: GII I: DI, GI	12	G: AII, CI, CII, GII I: DI, AII, CI, GI	18	G: CII I: CI

SOURCE: From *Leadership and decision making* by Victor H. Vroom and Phillip Yetton. Pittsburgh: University of Pittsburgh Press, 1974, 194. Copyright 1973 by University of Pittsburgh Press. Reprinted by permission.

(1). A type 1 problem is one in which neither the course of action taken nor the support of subordinates in this decision matters much insofar as the quality and acceptability of the decision are concerned.

Underlying the decision logic presented in Figure 5–3 are 10 contingency rules that (1) ensure a high quality or rational decision and (2) increase the acceptability of the decision to subordinates. Quality and acceptance of the decision are protected by eliminating decision

---

TABLE 5–8   Rules Underlying the Vroom/Yetton/Jago Model

---

1. *The Leader Information Rule:*
   If the quality of the decision is important and the leader does not possess enough information or expertise to solve the problem by himself, then AI is eliminated from the feasible set.

2. *The Subordinate Information Rule:*
   (applicable to individual problems only) If the quality of the decision is important and the subordinate does not possess enough information or expertise to solve the problem himself, then DI is eliminated from the feasible set.

3a. *The Goal Congruence Rule:*
   If the quality of the decision is important and the subordinates are not likely to pursue organization goals in their efforts to solve this problem, then GII and DI are eliminated from the feasible set.

3b. *The Augmented Goal Congruence Rule:*
   (applicable to individual problems only) Under the conditions specified in the previous rule (i.e., quality of decision is important, and the subordinate does not share the organizational goals to be attained in solving the problem), GI may also constitute a risk to the quality of the decision taken in response to an individual problem. Such a risk is a reasonable one to take only if the nature of the problem is such that the acceptance of the subordinate is critical to the effective implementation and prior probability of acceptance of an autocratic solution is low.

4a. *The Unstructured Problem Rule (Group):*
   In decisions in which the quality of the decision is important, if the leader lacks the necessary information or expertise to solve the problem by himself and if the problem is unstructured, the method of solving the problem should provide for interaction among subordinates. Accordingly, AI, AII, and CI are eliminated from the feasible set.

4b. *The Unstructured Problem Rule (Individual):*
   In decisions in which the quality of the decision is important, if the leader lacks the necessary information to solve the problem by himself and if the problem is unstructured, the method of solving

the problem should permit the subordinate to generate solutions to the problem. Accordingly, AI and AII are eliminated from the feasible set.

5. *The Acceptance Rule:*
   If the acceptance of the decision by subordinates is critical to effective implementation and if it is not certain that an autocratic decision will be accepted, AI and AII are eliminated from the feasible set.

6. *The Conflict Rule:*
   (applicable to group problems only) If the acceptance of the decision is critical, an autocratic decision is not certain to be accepted and disagreement among subordinates in methods of attaining the organizational goal is likely, the methods used in solving the problem should enable those in disagreement to resolve their differences with full knowledge of the problem. Accordingly, AI, AII, and CI, which permit no interaction among subordinates, are eliminated from the feasible set.

7. *The Fairness Rule:*
   If the quality of the decision is unimportant, but acceptance of the decision is critical and not certain to result from an autocratic decision, the decision process used should permit the subordinates to interact with one another and negotiate over the fair method of resolving any differences with full responsibility on them for determining what is equitable. Accordingly, AI, AII, CI, and CII are eliminated from the feasible set.

8. *The Acceptance Priority Rule:*
   If acceptance is critical, not certain to result from an autocratic decision and if (the) subordinate(s) is (are) motivated to pursue the organizational goals represented in the problem, then methods which provide equal partnership in the decision-making process can provide greater acceptance without risking decision quality. Accordingly, AI, AII, CI, and CII are eliminated from the feasible set.

9. *The Group Problem Rule:*
   If a problem has approximately equal effects on each of a number of sub-

TABLE 5–8 *(concluded)*

ordinates (i.e., is a group problem) the decision process used should provide them with equal opportunities to influence that decision. Use of a decision process such as GI or DI which provides opportunities for only one of the affected subordinates to influence that decision may in the short run produce feelings of inequity reflected in lessened commitment to the decision on the part of those "left out" of the decision process and, in the long run, be a source of conflict and divisiveness.	10. *The Individual Problem Rule:* If a problem affects only one subordinate, decision processes which *unilaterally* introduce other (unaffected) subordinate, decision processes which constitute an unnecessary use of time of the unaffected subordinates and can reduce the amount of commitment of the affected subordinate to the decision by reducing the amount of his opportunity to influence the decision. Thus, CII and GII are eliminated from the feasible set.

SOURCE: Vroom, V. H., & Jago, A. (1974). Decision making as a social process: Normative and descriptive models of leader behavior. *Decision Sciences*, (October), 748.

alternatives that would threaten either of these outcomes. These 10 rules are presented in Table 5–8. Rules 1 through 4 are intended to protect the quality of the decision, and rules 5 through 8 its acceptability. Rules 9 and 10 allow the elimination of group decision making when we are dealing with a task in which only one subordinate will be affected, or it may allow the elimination of individual decision making when the task effects more than one individual.

Once one has applied the 10 decision rules, one is left with a feasible set of solutions. After applying all the rules protecting quality and acceptance, one could end up with a situation in which AI, AII, CI, CII, GII (as well as GI and DI) are all feasible (as in problem type 1). In cases such as this where more than one option is feasible, the leader's choice among the alternatives must be based on whether the leader thinks making the decision in a timely fashion or developing subordinate decision-making skills is the more important consideration. If making a time-efficient decision is more important, then the leader should choose the most autocratic alternative within the feasible set. If development of subordinates is more important, then the leader should pick a more participative decision strategy. Other problems (i.e., routes through the decision tree), of course, call for more restrictive behavioral alternatives. Problem type 7 calls for only one response, full participation of the individual (GI) or group (GII). In this case, all alternatives other than GI and GII threaten the quality or acceptability of the solution. Despite their time-consuming nature, these are the only logical choices available.

To test the model, Jago and Vroom asked managers to describe a decision they made that turned out successfully and another that was a failure.[95] Their descriptions of these incidents were then classified as to the problem type and the feasible solution set for that type by the model. Of the successful decisions, the actual decision method used by the leader was in the feasible set prescribed by the model 65 percent of the time and was outside the set only 29 percent of the time. Of the unsuccessful decisions, 71 percent were outside the model's prescription, and only 35 percent were inside. In a recent laboratory test of the model, Field gave five problems that varied along the attributes in the Vroom and Yetton model to small groups.[96] The leader of each group was instructed to follow one of the five decision styles specified in the model across all five problems. Generally, when the leader used a decision process that the model defined as effective, the group was more successful in solving the problems than when the leader used a process that was defined as ineffective. Other evidence supportive of the model has been presented by Jago.[97]

The Vroom-Yetton model has been used to train managers in diagnosing the situation and in choosing the preferred style. First, the trainee responds to 30 to 54 hypothetical decision-making situations that vary along the eight situational attributes. After considering each case, the trainee is asked to state which decision method to use if he or she were the leader in that situation, and the answer is compared to those prescribed by the model. Managers in these training programs tend to respond to the situational attributes much as prescribed by the model — but with one notable exception. Rather than using participative decision-making techniques when conflict among subordinates is likely (as specified by rule 6), managers tend to use more autocratic styles.

It is still too early, of course, to evaluate the Vroom-Yetton model as an aid to managerial decision making. As the reader undoubtedly realizes, it is not an easy matter to verify the superiority of one approach over another in even a single situation. It will probably be many years before all the predictions of this model have received enough attention to warrant an estimate of its overall adequacy. Undoubtedly, in the process of testing these hypotheses, some of the initial assumptions will have to be revised. Even if it proves wrong in many of its predictions, however, this model is a distinct improvement over most other theories in the industrial-organizational field, because it is precise enough to allow rigorous testing of its predictions. Also, because it is based almost entirely on available *empirical* evidence rather than a set of esoteric theoretical constructs, it can be easily changed in light of new evidence. From a practical standpoint, prescriptions are sufficiently explicit to be applied readily in the real world. As understanding of leadership behavior grows, the model can serve as a handy mechanism for implementing the new information. What is learned can be put quickly to use.

Other Contingency Approaches. Fiedler's contingency theory, Vroom and Yetton's decision theory approach, and House's path-goal theory are contingency theories of leadership that have received considerable attention from scholars. Other contingency theories presented have received considerable attention from managers and trainers but have generated much less research. Two that we will discuss are Reddin's 3-D model and Hersey and Blanchard's situational leadership theory. Both essentially took Blake and Mouton's managerial grid dimensions and added a contingency variable.

Reddin's 3-D Model. Reddin distinguished between the same four basic types of leadership styles that Blake and Mouton presented in their Managerial Grid® model.[98] A leader may be high on both relationship orientation and task orientation, high on one and low on the other, or low on both. In addition to these dimensions, Reddin has added an effectiveness dimension.

The essential statement of Reddin's model is that each of the four leadership types in the grid can be implemented effectively or can be implemented ineffectively. A leader who is high in both task and relationships orientation may be effective if seen by subordinates as being both organized and supportive but ineffective if seen as overstructuring and insincere. The high-task and low-relationship leader can be effective if leadership style facilitates achievement of organization goals but ineffective if seen as autocratic and interested only in short-run goals. High-relationships–low-task leaders can be effective if seen as trustful and concerned but ineffective if seen as "country club managers" and unwilling to make hard decisions. Finally, a low-task–low-relationship leader can be effective if seen as appropriately delegating work and maintaining distance but ineffective if seen as abdicating responsibilities and retired on the job. Reddin has constructed a test of leadership that purports to measure these eight types.

Hersey and Blanchard's Situational Leadership Model. Similar to Reddin, Hersey and Blanchard build on the Blake and Mouton approach, but the third dimension that they add is that of *maturity* of followers. Maturity is defined as "the capacity to set high but attainable goals (achievement-motivation), willingness and ability to take responsibility, and education and/or experience of an individual or a group."[99] According to Hersey and Blanchard, followers are never totally mature or totally immature—they are only mature or immature with regard to some task. They propose that a leader should reduce task orientation and increase relationships orientation as the maturity of followers increases, up until the group reaches a moderate level of maturity. From this point on, a leader is more effective when decreasing both task and relationships behavior. Thus, the most effective style for a highly mature group is a low-relationships–low-task orientation. For a moderately mature group, it is a high-relationships–low-task orientation. A somewhat less than moderate level of maturity calls for a high-task–high-relationship orientation. Finally, a highly immature group needs a leader who is high in task orientation and low in relationship orientation.

Validity of the Reddin and the Hersey and Blanchard Approaches.   Neither of these approaches has generated much in the way of research, so there is very little empirical basis for saying they are valid or invalid. Graeff has criticized the Hersey and Blanchard model for several conceptual weaknesses, however, including the ambiguity of the maturity dimension. Also, he notes that the model is based on a misstatement of past research. Hersey and Blanchard claim that past studies have found a curvilinear relationship between follower effectiveness and both leader task orientation and leader relationship orientation. Graeff notes that there is little evidence to support this contention.

At the present time, about all we can say about these two popular approaches is that they need to be tested empirically. Until such research can be conducted, these models should be used with extreme caution, if at all.

CONCLUSIONS

Generally speaking, organizations are successful to the extent that they are able to get their people working together in pursuit of common organizational goals. Such concerted effort depends heavily upon the perceptions of individual organization members, as we discussed in the last chapter. This chapter has focused on leadership as another important contributing factor. Leaders, after all, play a major role in the shaping of employee attitudes and behavior as well as in the actual planning and organizing of work. There have been four major approaches to understanding and predicting leadership effectiveness, and they differ mainly in the emphasis placed—traits, behaviors, situations, or combinations of these three factors—as causes of the leader's behavior and the performance of the work group or organization.

Trait theory emphasizes the importance of personal characteristics and implies that the way to develop excellence in management is through selection based upon desirable traits. In support of a trait approach, effective leaders tend to be intelligent, self-confident, assertive, and high on need for achievement. However, traits account for only a small proportion of variance in leader effectiveness. Also, different organizations and different levels of management require different profiles of traits for effective management.

Behavior theory emphasizes specific behaviors of the leader, with the implication that training, not selection, offers the best route to managerial effectiveness. The activities in which managers engage have been found to vary considerably from manager to manager. Among the leading functions performed by managers are supervising the work of others and planning. Some six or eight other functions also have been identified, but these tend to vary a great deal with individual management positions. The planning function becomes progessively more important relative to the supervisory function as one moves up the organizational ladder.

In understanding why managers are effective or ineffective in the performance of their roles, knowing what they do is not as important as knowing the style with which they carry out their responsibilities. The degrees to which the leader allows subordinates to participate in decision making, structures their work roles, and is considerate of their needs and feelings are the three dimensions of leadership style that have received the most attention. Recently, it has been suggested that more, rather than fewer, dimensions are necessary to describe observed differences in style. How these basic dimensions (whether 1 or 2 or 4 or 10) relate to effectiveness is a debatable matter. The more participative, considerate styles seem to produce greater employee satisfaction and commitment to group goals. It is not clear whether they also increase productivity. It is difficult to reach any conclusion about structured, directive styles because the relationship to satisfaction and productivity varies considerably with the situation.

Another behavioral approach to leadership has been to examine the specific means that leaders use to influence their subordinates. *Power* has been viewed as the composite of a leader's potential to reward, punish, exercise legitimate authority over, and command the respect of subordinates (through the leader's expertise and personality). It should be recognized that power in this sense describes the influence the leader *could* exert; not necessarily that which he or she does exert. Individuals exercise considerable control over their leadership roles, even in highly structured organizations, through their ability to acquire *expert* and *referent* power. It is not yet known what, if any, personal characteristics make a leader most acceptable in the eyes of subordinates. This may depend a great deal upon the personal characteristics of the followers. A widely held view is that effective leadership results from an increment in influence over and above the influence resulting from coercive, reward, or legitimate power. Indeed, a distinction has been made between supervision that results from the exercise of legitimate, coercive, and reward powers and leadership associated with the use of referent and expert powers. This view is compatible with a human relations view but has not received much attention in the research on leadership.

A third view of leadership is that the situation, including characteristics of the subordinates, the task, and the organization, not only shapes the behavior of the leader but also serves as the primary cause of group effectiveness. In its most radical form, this view holds that leadership is a fiction people create to explain organizational events. In a less extreme form, the situational view is both logically reasonable and consistent with a great deal of evidence. Clearly, leader behavior is affected by situational factors such as the task structure, the competence of subordinates, and the performance of the group, even if all the facts on how it works are not yet known. Furthermore, it seems clear that the situation can, in some cases, substitute for or even neutralize the leadership of the person in the supervisory role.

Neither personality, behavior, nor the situation alone seem capable of explaining all the observed differences in leadership effectiveness, however. Consequently, most theorists are beginning to explore combined effects, and one type of theory (the contingency view) has taken situational interaction as its principal point of focus.

In Fiedler's version of contingency theory, highly favorable or unfavorable conditions call for a directive style; intermediate conditions require a participative approach. Possible routes to managerial improvement range from reorganizing work groups and altering power relationships to training supervisors. In spite of its somewhat less than dramatic track record in predicting the success of actual groups, Fiedler's theory has shown signs of promise. The key to its ultimate value probably lies in better measurement techniques for both situational and leadership factors.

A second theoretical position, which combines elements of contingency theory with the cognitive explanatory notions of VIE theory, is known as the path-goal model. It holds that the appropriateness of a leader behavior is dictated by its effect on subordinate perceptions of the effort-performance and performance-reward contingencies. Predictions are made regarding which combinations of situational variables and leadership styles are most likely to be effective. Leader behavior is seen to affect satisfaction and performance through its effects on worker expectations. Another aspect of path-goal theorizing seeks to explain why leaders behave as they do. It holds that the leader, like everyone else in the work group, acts to maximize chances of obtaining desired outcomes. In the leader's case, this means adopting a style that one believes will result in the highest production, morale, esteem, or whatever it is one wants from the work group.

A third, more explicit, version of contingency theory is the Vroom-Yetton model, which considers five alternative behavioral styles in conjunction with eight problem attributes. From a set of empirically based assumptions, feasible behavioral alternatives are derived from each of 18 specific problem types. Although the validity of these prescriptions remain to be verified, the model is couched in terms that are specific enough to permit rigorous testing. Such clarity also makes it an extremely useful *practical* tool through which the manager can apply the best available knowledge to the immediate problem.

A major limitation of all four approaches to leadership that we have discussed is that they view causality as moving in one direction only. Either the leader or the situation was presented as the prime determinant of the performance and satisfaction of followers. It is clear from past research, however, that *repicrocal causality* characterizes the leadership process.[100] In other words, leadership involves a give and take between supervisor, subordinates, and other situational factors—that he or she, they, and the situation are involved in a complex interplay of influences that eventuates (in some still poorly understood way) in group success or failure. Although each of the four approaches to leadership has contributed in some way to what is known about leadership, future models are likely to incorporate this dynamic view of the leadership process to a much greater degree.

The reader may find this chapter a bit disconcerting. If it has shattered cherished beliefs about what it takes to lead, that is all to the good. A lot of such beliefs in organizations today sorely need to be challenged. If it has replaced these beliefs with a sort of hopeless feeling that nobody knows much about effective leadership, that is unfortunate but only a few steps from the truth. What is known is that effective leadership is not simply a matter of dynamic personality, good humanitarian instincts, or favorable circumstances. It is not *simply anything*. Now that we are beginning to realize how complex leadership really is, we are finally on the road toward understanding how to make it more effective. But the road is long, and our journey has barely begun.

NOTES

1. Tsui, A. S. (1984). A role set analysis of managerial reputation. *Organizational Behavior and Human Performance, 34*, 64–96.
2. Campbell, J. P., Dunnette, M. D., Lawler, E. E. III, & Weick, K. D. (1970). *Managerial behavior, performance, and effectiveness* (pp. 7–8). New York: McGraw-Hill; and Quinn, R. P., Tabor, J. M., & Gordon, L. K. (1968). *The decision to discriminate: A study of executive selection*. Ann Arbor, Michigan: Institute of Survey Research.
3. Stogdill, R. M. (1974). *Handbook of leadership: A survey of theory and research* (p. 74). New York: Free Press.
4. Dipboye, R. L., Fromkin, H. L., & Wiback, K. (1975). Relative importance of applicant sex, attractiveness, and scholastic standing in evaluation of job applicant resumes. *Journal of Applied Psychology, 60*, 39–43.
5. Adams, E. F. (1978). A multivariate study of subordinate perceptions of and attitudes toward minority and majority managers. *Journal of Applied Psychology, 63*, 277–288.
6. Ezell, H. F., Odewahn, C. A., & Sherman, J. D. (1981). The effects of having been supervised by a woman on perceptions of female managerial competence. *Personnel Psychology, 34*, 291–299.
7. Ghiselli, E. E. (1966). *The validity of occupational aptitude tests*. New York: John Wiley & Sons.
8. Stogdill. *Handbook of leadership*, p. 78.
9. Nash, A. N. (1963). *Development and evaluation of a strong vocational interest blank for differentiating between potentially effective and less effective business managers*. Unpublished doctoral dissertation, University of Minnesota.
10. Miner, J. B. (1978). Twenty years of research on role motivation theory of managerial effectiveness. *Personnel Psychology, 31*, 739–760.
11. Gough H. G. (1984). A managerial potential scale for the California Psychological Inventory. *Journal of Applied Psychology, 69*, 233–240.

12. McClelland, D. C., & Boyatizis, R. (1982). Leadership motive pattern and long-term success in management. *Journal of Applied Psychology, 67,* 737–743.

13. Stahl, M. J. (1983). Achievement, power, and managerial motivation: Selecting managerial talent with the job-choice exercise. *Personnel Psychology, 36,* 775–784.

14. House, R. J., & Baetz, J. L. (1979). Leadership: Some empirical generalizations and new research directions. In B. Staw & L. Cummings (Eds.). *Research in organizational behavior* (Vol. 1). Greenwich, Conn.: JAI Press.

15. Korman, A. (1968). The prediction of managerial performance: A review. *Personnel Psychology, 21,* 295–332.

16. Sparks, C. P. (1983). Paper-and-pencil measures of potential. In G. Dreher & P. Sackett (Eds.). *Perspectives on employee staffing and selection* (pp. 349–368). Homewood, Ill.: Richard D. Irwin.

17. Campbell et al. *Managerial behavior,* p. 169.

18. Cohen, S. L., & Sands, L. (1978). The effects of order of exercise presentation on assessment center performances: One standardization concern. *Personnel Psychology, 31,* 35–47.

19. Bass, B., & Barrett, G. (1981). *People, work, and organizations: An introduction to industrial and organizational psychology* (p. 409). Boston: Allyn & Bacon.

20. Moses, J. L., & Bynham, W. C. (1977). *Applying the assessment center method.* New York: Pergamon Press, p. 193.

21. Hinrichs, J. R. (1978). An eight-year follow-up of a management assessment center. *Journal of Applied Psychology, 63,* 596–601.

22. Mischel, W. (1968). *Personality and assessment.* New York: John Wiley & Sons.

23. Mintzberg, H. (1973). *The nature of managerial work.* New York: Harper & Row.

24. Mahoney, R. A., Jerdee, T. H., & Carroll, S. J. (1965). The job(s) of management. *Industrial Relations, 4,* 97–110.

25. Tannenbaum, R., & Schmidt, W. H. (1958). How to choose a leadership pattern. *Harvard Business Review, 36,* 95–101.

26. Locke, E. A., & Schweiger, D. M. (1978). Participation in decision making: One more look. In B. M. Staw (Ed.). *Research in organizational behavior* (pp. 269–339). Greenwich, Conn.: JAI Press.

27. Stogdill, R. M., & Coons, A. E. (Eds.). (1957). *Leader behavior: Its description and measurement.* Research monograph, *88,* Columbus: Ohio State University, Bureau of Business.

28. Fleishman, E. A., & Harris, E. F. (1962). Patterns of leadership behavior related to employee grievances and turnover. *Personnel Psychology, 15,* 43–56.

29. Ibid.

30. Schriesheim, C. A., & Kerr, S. (1974) Psychometric properties of Ohio State leadership scales. *Psychological Bulletin, 81,* 756–765.

31. Stogdill, *Handbook of leadership.*

32. Schriesheim, C., House, R., & Kerr, S. (1976). Leader initiation of structure: A reconciliation of discrepant research results and some empirical tests. *Organizational Behavior and Human Performance, 15,* 297–321.

33. Ibid., pp. 297–362.

34. House, R. J. (1971). A path-goal theory of leader effectiveness. *Administrative Science Quarterly, 16,* 321–328.

35. Blake, R. R., & Mouton, J. S. (1969). *Building a dynamic corporation through grid organization development.* Reading, Mass.: Addison-Wesley Publishing.

36. Fleishman, E. A., & Harris, E. F. (1962). Patterns of leadership behavior related to employee grievances and turnover. *Personnel Psychology, 15,* 43–56.

37. Larson, L. L., Hunt, J. G., & Osborn, R. N. (1976). The great hi-hi leader behavior myth: A lesson from Occam's razor. *Academy of Management Journal, 19,* 628–641; and Nystrom, P. C. (1978). Managers and the hi-hi leader myth. *Academy of Management Journal, 21,* 325–331.

38. French, J. R. P., & Raven, B. H. (1959). The bases of social power. In D. Cartwright (Ed.). *Studies in social power.* Ann Arbor, Mich.: Institute for Social Research.

39. Kahn, R. L., Wolfe, D., Quinn, R. P., Snoek, J. D., & Rosenthal, R. A. (1964). *Organizational stress: Studies in role conflict and ambiguity.* New York: John Wiley & Sons.

40. Dieterly, D. L., & Schneider, B. (1974). The effect of organizational environment on perceived power and climate: A laboratory study. *Organizational Behavior and Human Performance, 11*, 334–335.

41. Kipnis, D., Schmidt, S. M., & Wilkinson, I. (1980). Interorganizational influence tactics: Explorations in getting one's way. *Journal of Applied Psychology, 65*, 440–52.

42. Katz, D., & Kahn, R. L. (1977). *The social psychology of organizations* (p. 928). New York: John Wiley & Sons.

43. Jacobs, T. O. (1971). *Leadership and exchange in formal organizations.* Alexandria, Va.: Human Resources Research Organization.

44. Ivancevich, J. M., & Donnelly, J. H. (1974). Leader influence and performance. In E. A. Fleishman and A. R. Bass (Eds.). *Studies in personnel and industrial psychology* (p. 339). Homewood, Ill.: Dorsey Press.

45. Dansereau, F., Graen, G., & Haga, W. J. (1975). A vertical dyad linkage approach to leadership within formal organizations: A longitudinal investigation of the role-making process. *Organizational Behavior and Human Performance, 13*, 46–78.

46. Vecchi, R. P., & Gobdel, B. C. (1984). The vertical dyad linkage model of leadership: Problems and prospects. *Organizational Behavior and Human Performance, 34*, 5–20.

47. Kipnis, D. (1976). *The powerholders.* Chicago: University of Chicago Press.

48. Greene, C. N., & Podsakoff, P. M. (1981). Effects of withdrawal of a performance-contingent reward on supervisory influence and power. *Academy of Management Journal, 24*, 527–542.

49. Bowers, D. G., & Seashore, S. E. (1966). Predicting organization effectiveness with a four-factor theory of leadership. *Administrative Sciences Quarterly, 11*, 238–263.

50. Bass, B. M., & Valenzi, E. R. (1974). Contingent aspects of effective management styles. In J. G. Hunt & L. L. Larson (Eds.). *Contingent approaches to leadership.* Carbondale: Southern Illinois University Press.

51. Stogdill. *Handbook of leadership.*

52. Yukl, G. A. (1981). *Leadership in organizations* (pp. 121–125). Englewood Cliffs, N.J.: Prentice-Hall.

53. Lowin, A., & Craig, J. R. (1968). The influence of level of performance on managerial style: An object lesson in the ambiguity of correlational data. *Organizational Behavior and Human Performance, 3*, 440–458.

54. Rush, M. C., Thomas, J. C., & Lord, R. G. (1977). Implicit leadership theory: A potential threat to the internal validity of leader behavior questionnaires. *Organizational Behavior and Human Performance, 20*, 93–111.

55. Lowin & Craig. Influence of level of performance.

56. Barrow, J. C. (1976). Work performance and task complexity as causal determinants of leader behavior style and flexibility. *Journal of Applied Psychology, 61*, 433–440.

57. Farris, G. F., & Lim, F. G. (1969). Effects of performance on leadership, cohesiveness, influence, satisfaction, and subsequent performance. *Journal of Applied Psychology, 53*, 490–497.

58. Crowe, B. J., Bochner, S., & Clark, A. W. (1972). The effects of subordinates' behavior on managerial style. *Human Relations, 25*, 215–237.

59. Green, S. G., & Mitchell, T. R. (1979). Attributional processes in leader-member interactions. *Organizational Behavior and Human Performance, 23*, 429–459.

60. Lieberson, S., & O'Connor, J. F. (1972). Leadership and organizational performance: A study of large corporations. *American Sociological Review, 37*, 117–130.

61. Allen, M. P., Panian, S. K., & Lotz, R. E. (1979). Managerial succession and organizational performance: A recalcitrant problem revisited. *Administrative Science Quarterly, 24*, 167–180.

62. Rosen, N. A. (1969). *Leadership change and work group dynamics.* Ithaca, N.Y.: Cornell University Press.

63. Weiner, N., & Mahoney, A. (1981). A model of corporate performances as a function of environmental, organizational, and leadership influences. *Academy of Management Journal, 24,* 453–470.

64. Smith, J. E., Carson, K. P., & Alexander, R. A. (1984). Leadership: It can make a difference. *Academy of Management Journal, 27,* 765–776.

65. Calder, B. J. (1977). An attribution theory of leadership. In B. M. Staw & G. R. Salancik (Eds.). *New directions in organizational behavior* (pp. 179–204). Chicago: St. Clair Press.

66. Mitchell, T. R., Larson, J. R., & Green, S. G. (1977). Leader behavior, situational moderators, and group performance: An attributional analysis. *Organizational Behavior and Human Performance, 18,* 254–268.

67. Salancik, G. R., & Meindl, J. R. (1984). Corporate attributions as strategic illusions of management control. *Administrative Science Quarterly, 29,* 238–254; Bettman, J. R., & Barton, A. W. (1983). Attributions in the boardroom: Causal reasoning in corporate annual reports. *Administrative Science Quarterly, 28,* 165–183; and Staw, B. M., McKeachnie, P. I., & Puffer, S. M. (1983). The justification of organizational performance. *Administrative Science Quarterly, 28,* 582–600.

68. Pfeffer, J. (1977). The ambiguity of leadership. *Academy of Management Review, 2,* 104–112.

69. Green & Mitchell. Attributional processes, p. 451.

70. Pfeffer. Ambiguity of leadership.

71. Kerr, S., & Jermier, J. M. (1978). Substitutes for leadership: Their meaning and measurement. *Organizational Behavior and Human Performance, 22,* 375–403.

72. Howell, J. P., & Dorfman, P. W. (1981). Substitutes for leadership: Test of a construct. *Academy of Management Journal, 24,* 714–728.

73. Sheridan, J. E., Vredenburgh, D. J., & Abelson, M. A. (1984). Contextual model of leadership influence in hospital units. *Academy of Management Journal, 27,* 57–78.

74. Podsakoff, P. M., Todor, W. D., Grover, R. A., & Huber, V. L. (1984). Situational moderators of leader reward and punishment behaviors: Fact or fiction? *Organizational Behavior and Human Performance, 34,* 21–63.

75. Fiedler, F. E. (1978). The contingency model and the dynamics of the leadership process. In L. Berkowitz (Ed.). *Advances in experimental social psychology* (pp. 59–112). New York: Academic Press.

76. Fiedler. F. E. (1971). Validation and extension of the contingency model of leadership effectiveness: A review of empirical findings. *Psychological Bulletin, 76,* 128–148.

77. Strube, M. J., & Garcia, J. E. (1981). A meta-analytic investigation of Fiedler's contingency model of leadership effectiveness. *Psychological Bulletin, 90,* 307–321; Vecchio, R. P. (1983). Assessing the validity of Fiedler's contingency model of leadership effectiveness: A closer look at Strube and Garcia. *Psychological Bulletin, 93,* 404–408; and Peters, L. H., Hartke, D. D., & Pohlmann, J. T. (1985). Fiedler's contingency theory of leadership: An application of the meta-analysis procedures of Schmidt and Hunter. *Psychological Bulletin, 97,* 274–285.

78. Graen, G., Alvares, K. M., Orris, J. B., & Martella, J. A. (1970). Contingency model of leadership effectiveness: Antecedent and evidential results. *Psychological Bulletin, 74,* 285–296; and Ashour, A. S. (1973). The contingency model of leadership effectiveness: An evaluation. *Organizational Behavior and Human Performance, 9,* 339–355, 369–376.

79. Mitchell, T. R., Biglan, A., Oncken, G. R., & Fiedler, F. E. (1970). The contingency model: Criticism and suggestions. *Academy of Management Journal, 13,* 253–268.

80. Evans, M. G., & Dermer, J. (1974). What does the least preferred co-workers scale really measure? *Journal of Applied Psychology, 59,* 202–206.

81. Fiedler. Contingency model.

82. Korman, A. K. (1973). On the development of contingency theories of leadership: Some methodological considerations and a possible alternative. *Journal of Applied Psychology, 58*, 384–387; and Ashour. Contingency model.

83. Fiedler, F. E. (1965). Engineer the job to fit the manager. *Harvard Business Review, 43*, 115–122.

84. Nebeker, D. M., & Mitchell, T. R. (1974). Leader behavior: An expectancy theory approach. *Organizational Behavior and Human Performance, 11*, 355–367.

85. House, R. J. (1971). A path-goal theory of leader effectiveness. *Administrative Science Quarterly, 16*, 321–328.

86. House, R. J., & Mitchell, T. R. (1975). Path-goal theory of leadership. In K. N. Wexley & G. A. Yukl (Eds.). *Organizational behavior and industrial psychology* (pp. 177–186). New York: Oxford Press.

87. Schriesheim, C. A., & DeNisi, A. S. (1981). Task dimensions as moderators of the effects of instrumental leadership: A two-sample replicated test of path-goal leadership theory. *Journal of Applied Psychology, 66*, 589–597.

88. House & Mitchell. Path-goal theory of leadership.

89. Schuler, R. S. (1976). Participation with supervisor and subordinate authoritarianism: A path-goal theory reconciliation. *Administrative Science Quarterly, 21*, 320– 325.

90. House & Mitchell. Path-goal theory of leadership, p. 455.

91. Ibid.

92. Fulk, J., & Wendler, E. R. (1982). Dimensionality of leader-subordinate interactions. *Organizational Behavior and Human Performance, 30*, 241–264.

93. Vroom, V. H., & Yetton, P. W. (1973). *Leadership and decision making.* Pittsburgh: University of Pittsburgh Press.

94. Vroom, V. H., & Jago, A. G. (1974). Decision making as a social process: Normative and descriptive models of leader behavior. *Decision Sciences, 5*, 743–769.

95. Vroom, V. H., & Jago, A. G. (1978). On the validity of the Vroom-Yetton model. *Journal of Applied Psychology, 63*, 151–162.

96. Field, R. H. G. (1982). A test of the Vroom-Yetton normative model of leadership. *Journal of Applied Psychology, 67*, 523–532.

97. Jago, A. G. (1979). *Leadership: Perspectives in theory and research.* Unpublished manuscript, University of Houston.

98. Reddin, W. J. (1967). The 3-D management style theory. *Training and Development Journal, 21*(4), 8–17.

99. Hersey, P., & Blanchard, K. H. (1982). *Management of organization behavior: Utilizing human resources* (2d ed.) (p. 161). Englewood Cliffs, N.J.: Prentice-Hall.

100. Greene, C. N. (1979). The reciprocal nature of influence between leader and subordinate. *Journal of Applied Psychology, 60*, 187–193; and Herold, D. M. (1977). Two-way influence processes in leader-follower dyads. *Academy of Management Journal, 20*, 224–237.

6

Work Description and Performance Evaluation

Implicit in our discussion of organization theories was the assumption that performance—of individuals, groups, or whole organizations—is, in fact, measurable. A moment's reflection, however, should convince the reader that it is no simple matter to measure performance accurately. For one thing, it is not always clear what constitutes good work behavior. What, for example, distinguishes an outstanding secretary from a mediocre one? Is the best salesperson always the one with the highest record of gross sales? Can we judge the performance of a baseball manager purely on the basis of the team's winning percentage? In each of these examples—and indeed in most jobs—there is considerable room for debate as to the appropriate criteria.

Even if we knew what to measure there is no assurance that we could measure it adequately. Jobs vary considerably in this respect. Some, particularly routine production jobs, permit relatively pure measurement of output; others, particularly higher-level managerial jobs, have no clearly defined link with production. Thus it becomes necessary to rely on subjective judgment—usually supervisory ratings.

Since we cannot take evaluation for granted, we must spend some time examining the various ways that the problem has been approached. We shall review both objective and subjective evaluation procedures later in this chapter. First, however, it would be well to deal with two important preliminary questions: Why is performance evaluation so important in the first place, and how does it relate to the equally important matter of job description? We shall consider these topics in reverse order.

DESCRIPTION OF WORK ROLES

Job Description and Performance Evaluation

Performance evaluation is any systematic attempt to gauge how well a person is doing a job. Clearly, evaluation would be impossible or meaningless without some explicit specification of what one is expected to do. Unless the person being evaluated and the person rendering judgment agree on what the job entails, there is little chance for a fair or accurate appraisal. Thus *job description* is a prerequisite for performance evaluation.

There are numerous other reasons why accurate description of job characteristics is important. It is essential for the development of effective selection, placement, training, and compensation programs. Unless we know what we are selecting, training, or compensating people *for*, we can scarcely hope to realize much benefit from such procedures. Job description is also essential for the evaluation of selection, placement, and training programs, and for the recruiting of new employees. In fact, there is hardly a personnel function that is not dependent to some extent on how well work roles are spelled out. Efforts on the part of the federal government to combat unfair discrimination in employment and promotion have relied heavily on job description requirements, as we shall see in the next chapter.

Although precise job description is essential for modern management, it raises an interesting dilemma with respect to management philosophy. It will be recalled that a major distinction between the old classical philosophy of management and the modern humanistic viewpoint was the emphasis placed on structure—the organization of work. Rigid, explicit definition of everyone's duties was the cornerstone of the bureaucratic model. The humanistic philosophy stressed individual responsibility, creative expression, and self-determination in job definition, that is, "the worker makes the job." Rigid job description, therefore, seems directly at variance with the trend toward individual growth and participative management. If individuals or work groups were allowed to divide up the work as they saw fit, duties and responsibilities would be in a constant state of flux. Formalized job descriptions would be meaningless and, if used as a basis for personnel decisions, grossly unfair. This is not a trivial dilemma, and it has no absolute solution. At a practical level it means that management must try to be as explicit as possible about work roles without locking individuals into totally restrictive, predetermined patterns.

While the dilemma may be insolvable, it is subject to compromise. Several techniques can be used to minimize its practical impact. One is to recognize the changeable nature of job characteristics and consider job description as a record of—rather than a prescription for—work behavior. Thus job description is viewed as a continuing organizational activity; not a rigid organizational blueprint. Another compromise approach is to specify jobs in terms general enough to permit some latitude in execution. Consider, for example, the job of *loss claims clerk* at the Fictitious Mutual Insurance Company. A highly specific (and restrictive) description might read as follows: "Checks loss claim forms for completeness and accuracy; collects additional information as needed; figures deductible amounts (percentages); searches the insured's file for claim and premium history; prepares report for the claims adjuster." The same job could be described somewhat less restrictively by citing general skills or capabilities required. For example: "Requires ability to perform arithmetic operations, calculate percentages, check figures for accuracy, communicate effectively with clients, prepare written reports; experience in reading legal documents." An even less restrictive description might be phrased in terms of the objectives of the job. For example: "Assists claims adjuster in gathering, verifying, and preparing materials on the basis of which decisions regarding loss claim payments are made."

Each of the above descriptions is accurate; however, each stresses a different aspect of the job: specific duties, requirements, or objectives. By including the more general aspects in the description, one can see both how the job is done and and how much latitude there might be for doing it *differently.* As a practical matter, it is important to recognize that job descriptions should be written somewhat differently for different purposes. Certain features (such as skill requirements) are particularly important for recruiting or selection; others (such as operational sequences) are essential for training; still others (such as how the job relates to other jobs or families of jobs) are useful for placement and promotion decisions as well as for general personnel planning purposes. A description that emphasizes personal qualifications and hence is oriented toward selection or recruiting functions is known as a *job specification.* The personal characteristics themselves are called *job requirements.*

Approaches to Job Description

Given that it is important to describe precisely what is expected of people in various work roles, the next problem is how to accomplish such descriptions. There are two broad approaches to job description. One is to make use of standard job classification systems, shaping or matching the to-be-described jobs to the standard definitions. The other is to analyze jobs as they exist, writing job descriptions on the basis of *job analysis* data. Since the standard descriptions are usually only rough approximations of the jobs that exist in any particular organization, it is usually desirable to carry out job analyses within the organization. Standard systems provide useful guidance in developing new jobs or revising old ones. They are also helpful as a first step in the process of analyzing existing jobs.

The most widely used standard system is furnished by the U.S. Training and Employment Service (USTES). This federal agency attempts to survey, analyze, and classify the nation's population of jobs on a periodic basis. Results of the survey appear in the *Dictionary of Occupational Titles* (DOT), which lists and briefly defines about 22,000 current job titles.[1] Over the years, USTES has developed a number of adjuncts to its basic system, all aimed at increasing the standardization and precision of its procedures and descriptions. The ideal would be an integrated set of analytic procedures, descriptive terms, rules for combining those terms into task statements, and schemes for classifying jobs that would apply to *any* job whatsoever and would leave almost *nothing* to the interpretation of the analyst. With such a system, anybody could describe any job, and the resulting description would have the same precise meaning to everyone.

To appreciate the full scope of USTES's efforts toward this ideal, consider the material assembled in their analysis schedule shown in Figure 6–1. The six *worker trait scales* shown in item 6 are based upon a factor analysis of 4,000 jobs listed in the DOT. Thus they represent a fairly comprehensive set of dimensions through which one can indicate how much of various characteristics a person should have to do well on the specified job. Each level of each scale has a precise definition: GED (general educational development) 1, for example, refers to the 10 percent most highly educated people in the work force. The three *work-performed* scales (item 5) each refer to a large collection of very precise terms or procedures. Each of 100 general *work fields* (e.g., Cooking—food preparation) has a list of possible "method verbs" (e.g., basting, frying, measuring) and "machines, tools, equipment, and work aids" (e.g., forks, pots, ovens) that apply to it. The product or object of that work (MPSMS) is indicated by reference to another long list of precise terms organized by work fields (e.g., bread, meals, pasteries). The *worker functions*, which we shall explore more fully in a moment, refer to a list of general operations that can be performed on *data, people,* and *things*. Now, once the work performed has been described on these three scales (item 5), a statement can be written, again according to very precise rules, to yield the *job summary* (item 4). Everything is then coded numerically for proper filing in the DOT.

The advantages of a standardized set of descriptions and description rules, particularly when based upon a limited number of common dimensions (function or worker characteristics that cut across job categories), is obvious. Besides aiding the job analyst and contributing to all the personnel functions described earlier, it gives people a common language with which to communicate about work. Even more important, it shows both the worker and the organization how jobs are *related* to one another. Thus the individual is better able to develop a career plan and to make reasoned decisions; the organization is better able to see logical progressions and to formulate overall personnel strategies. Standardized, dimensional descriptions give work structure a dynamic quality.

FIGURE 6-1 First Section of the USTES Schedule Using the Job of *Dough Mixer* as an Illustration

---

U.S. Department of Labor
Manpower Administration

OMB 44-R0722

Estab. & Sched. No. 522-146-3-10

JOB ANALYSIS SCHEDULE

1. Estab. Job Title DOUGH MIXER
2. Ind. Assign. (bake. prod.)
3. SIC Code(s) and Title(s) 2051 Bread and other bakery products

---

Code 520.782

WTA Group Oper. Control p. 435

4. JOB SUMMARY:

Operates mixing machine to mix ingredients for straight and sponge (yeast) doughs according to established formulas, directs other workers in fermentation of dough, and cuts dough into pieces with hand cutter.

5. WORK PERFORMED RATINGS:

| | D | P | (T) |
Worker Functions	Data	People	Things
	5	6	2

Work Field 146 - Cooking, Food Preparing

M.P.S.M.S. 384 - Bakery Products

DOT Title

Ind. Desig.

6. WORKER TRAITS RATINGS:

GED   1 (2) 3 4 5 6

SVP   1 2 3 (4) 5 6 7 8 9

Aptitudes G 3 V 3 N 3 S 3 P 3 Q 4 K 3 F 3 M 3 E 4 C 4

Temperaments D F I J (M) P R S (T) V

Interests   (1a) 1b 2a 2b 3a 3b 4a (4b) 5a (5b)

Phys. Demands S L M (H) V 2 (3)(4) 5 (6)

Environ. Cond. (I) O B 2 3 4 (5) 6 7

SOURCE: U.S. Department of Labor (1972). *Handbook for analyzing jobs.* Washington, D.C.: U.S. Government Printing Office, p. 42.

Even the USTES system, however, falls far short of our ideal. The main problem with this or any standardized system, of course, is that it cannot encompass *all* the nuances of any specific job. The duties of a sheet metal worker or secretary in one company may be quite different from those in another. If people are hired on the basis of the standard descriptions, therefore, they may be unsuited for what they really are expected to do. For this reason it is important to conduct one's own job analysis—to describe the jobs as they actually exist. We turn, therefore, to the question of how job analysis is actually carried out.

Job Analysis

This is any systematic procedure aimed at collecting information about how jobs are done and what personal characteristics they require. The first step in the search for such information is usually the review of available literature about the job: previous job descriptions; standard (e.g., DOT) descriptions; descriptions of closely related jobs. Ultimately, however, the search must lead directly to the job itself as it is currently performed. There are numerous specific methods for carrying out such analyses. Some focus primarily on the capabilities and behaviors required of the worker (*worker-oriented* methods), whereas others are more concerned with the nature and goals of the work itself (*work-oriented* methods). Many also try to reflect how *important* particular elements are to the total job and how *often* each is required. Besides these general features, the specific analytic features can be distinguished on the basis of two fundamental characteristics: (1) the *source* of information and (2) the *form* in which data are gathered.

1.   *Sources.* We can distinguish three very different sources of information. One is *the person engaged in doing the job:* We can watch and record what the worker does, have the worker prepare a diary on what he or she does, or ask questions about what he or she does. The second possible source of information is someone, other than the job incumbent, who is presumed to be an expert on that job (usually a supervisor). The third source is *personal experience:* The analyst can learn to do the job and then record observations of how it is done.

2.   *Forms of inquiry.* We can also distinguish three basic means of tapping into these sources of information. The first is the *self-report* approach, whereby the source individual records in some structured fashion an impression of what the job entails. This, of course, can itself take several different forms: diaries, questionnaires, checklists. Next we have the *interview* approach, whereby the analyst interacts directly with the source individual. Interviews can also be conducted in a variety of ways: structured around a list of specific questions; open-ended, or largely unstructured; administered in groups or carried out individually. Finally, there is the *critical incident* technique, which we first encountered in

Chapter 3, whereby the source individual cites specific behavioral incidents that were particularly important for successful (or unsuccessful) completion of the job. Critical incident data are usually gathered as narrative accounts, classified, and analyzed for content in an effort to pinpoint behavior crucial for success or failure.

It is possible to identify a lot of different job analytic procedures by applying the above forms of inquiry to the three potential sources of information. In actual practice, it is usually desirable to use several combinations of these techniques, for each has its limitations.[2] We shall not burden the reader with a history of all the specific methods that have been devised or with the multitude of detailed forms that have been developed to assist the analyst in carrying out these procedures. Such information is readily available in any advanced text.[3] Rather, we shall concentrate on the limitations or potential difficulties inherent in the various sources of information and forms of inquiry. The aim is to put the reader in a better position to judge the suitability of any procedure, should the need arise to conduct an analysis.

First, let us consider the potential sources of information. Job incumbents should be in the best position to know what their job is all about. Still, they can give a very distorted picture of what is really essential about their work. Most people like to feel that what they do is important. Some like to think that they alone know the secret to doing the job properly or that there is much more to the job than appearances would indicate. The simpler the job, the greater is the temptation for an incumbent to dress it up in order to maintain self-respect. Consider, for example, a hypothetical widget assembler whose sole responsibility consists of inserting and tightening four machine screws in the widgets as they reach his position on the assembly line. Asked to describe his job, he would probably mention how important it is not to strip the screws or overtighten them, how essential it is to watch for misaligned screw holes, and a number of other obvious or nonessential details. The result, of course, would be an overly complicated job description. Conversely, the incumbent very often *neglects* important aspects of the job, either because they have become so routine that they are no longer noticed or because their importance isn't realized. Finally, the worker may distort the description by including his or her own idiosyncratic ways of doing the job. These might include shortcuts that would create problems for less skilled workers or merely nonessential habits that have been acquired.

The "expert" source of information may no longer be as expert as he or she was when doing, rather than supervising, the job. The job may have changed since then. Or some of the critical details may have been forgotten. Still, qualified or not, the "expert" will more than likely insist that he or she is knowledgeable. To do otherwise, after all, would be to admit ignorance of what is being supervised.

The main problem with having the analyst learn the job is that even fairly simple jobs can take a long time to learn, at least to a reasonable level of proficiency. Furthermore, the analyst may become so involved in *doing* that he or she has difficulty with the *observing:* Some objectivity may be lost in being too close to the work.

All the above difficulties, of course, can be minimized, provided the analyst recognizes their potential existence. Several sources rather than one could be used. For example, independent descriptions from several incumbents and a supervisor could be combined. Or he or she might check out the descriptions given by others by doing the job personally. Finally, potential biases can be reduced to some extent by using a structured form of inquiry.

Naturally, each form of inquiry has its potential shortcomings, too. Highly structured self-report techniques or interviews require that the analyst know a fair amount about the job in the first place. Otherwise, the questions asked may not hit all the relevant points. Open-ended approaches, on the other hand, make it easy for the information source to commit all the sins we have just outlined. The critical incident approach is very effective in identifying behaviors that are particularly important for good or poor performance. It ignores, however, all the routine things a person must do in the course of performing the job. It would be difficult to write a complete set of job specifications solely on the basis of critical incident data.

Once again, the solution appears to lie in the use of multiple techniques.[4] Self-report questionnaires should include opportunities for the respondent to add information that is missed by the structured items. Interviews should be oriented around the questions that are known in advance to be critical but should be flexible enough to permit exploration of other leads that arise during the discussion. What we are saying, in essence, is that the analyst should not rely exclusively on any one approach. He or she should consider what the job information is to be used for, what sort of precision is needed, what kinds of error are tolerable, and then design the approach accordingly. Whatever approach is chosen, the analyst should do the utmost to measure the *job* rather than the individual doing it. If he or she observes, observe with this in mind; if he or she interviews, tease out the idiosyncratic from the essential by careful questioning. Even if he or she uses a *worker-oriented* method, focus on those behaviors that any worker in that job would be expected to carry out.

Job Analysis Systems.   Our description of job analysis to this point has been very general; our purpose was to summarize the various options from a logical perspective without reference to any specific system. Such principles apply whether one wishes to devise one's own procedure or to choose from among the standard systems already available. In this section, we shall review a few examples of these standard approaches to job analysis: functional job analysis (FJA),[5] the U.S. Air Force Task Inventory Method (TI/CODAP),[6] the Position Analysis Questionnaire (PAQ),[7] and the ability requirements approach.[8] While these are certainly not the only standard approaches, they are among the most commonly used; also they illustrate rather nicely some of our earlier distinctions.

Before proceeding with the descriptions, however, it might be well to dispose of one initial question: What are the pros and cons of standard systems *in general*? The main advantage, of course, is that such methods have had the benefit of years of research and refinement. While much still remains to be learned about the detailed nature of their validity, accuracy, and usefulness,[9] each has survived the test of application in a wide variety of work settings. As we shall see, having a "track record" makes any procedure less susceptible to criticisms of arbitrariness and unfairness. In addition, it permits use of the data produced by the analysis for purposes that require *comparisons* among jobs, organizations, or even geographical regions. Salary administration is a good case in point: It would be hard to evaluate the comparable worth of a machinist in Muskegon versus a plumber in Peoria unless both jobs were analyzed using the same approach. On the other hand, the down side of standard systems is that they never capture *all* the critical details of any particular set of jobs in any particular organization. A customized approach is usually better able to do that albeit at much greater expense.

1. Functional Job Analysis (FJA). Functional job analysis is an important element in the USTES system, as we saw in Figure 6–1. Essentially, it consists of (1) a standardized language to describe what workers do and (2) a means of evaluating the level and orientation of what they do. The basic unit of analysis is the task—an action or action sequence organized over time and designed to contribute a specific end result to the accomplishment of an objective. The basic premise underlying FJA is that, while tasks may be described in an infinite number of ways, they are reducible to a few basic behavior patterns, or functions. These functions vary in complexity (level) and are directed (oriented) toward one of three possible objects: *data, people,* or *things.* The entire system is summarized in Figure 6–2. The level of complexity of each function has been quantified by Fine and Wiley, as illustrated for the *data* functions in Table 6–1. Orientation is estimated as a percentage (e.g., 10 percent data, 60 percent people, 30 percent things orientation).

To illustrate how the FJA system might be used, consider our lowly widget assembler. His job might be described as 90 percent manipulating (function) things (screws with screwdriver) and 10 percent taking instructions (function) from people (supervisor). Both of these are at a fairly low level of complexity. Thus we know basically what he does, to what, and at what level of complexity.

There is some evidence to suggest that FJA is at least a *reliable* ap-

FIGURE 6-2 Summary Chart of Worker Function Scales

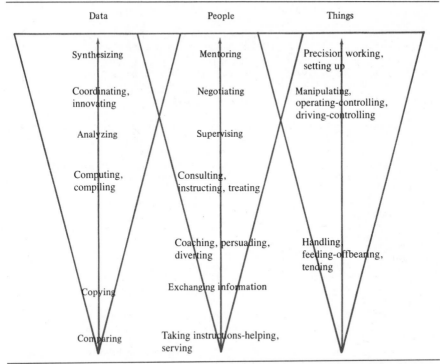

Note: Each successive function reading down typically involves all those that follow it. The functions separated by a comma are separate functions on the same level separately defined. They are on the same level because empirical evidence does not make a hierarchical distinction clear.

The hyphenated functions—*Taking instructions-helping, operating-controlling, driving-controlling,* and *feeding-offbearing,*—are single functions.

Setting up, operating-controlling, driving-controlling, feeding-offbearing, and *tending* are special cases involving machines and equipment of *Precision working, Manipulating,* and *Handling,* respectively, and hence are indented under them.

SOURCE: From Fine, S. & Wiley, W. W., (1971). An introduction to functional job analysis: A scaling of selected tasks from the social welfare field (p. 31). Kalamazoo, Mich.: W. E. Upjohn Institute for Employment Research.

proach (i.e., different analysts will arrive at comparable descriptions). Also, a recent study has shown that the "people" and "data" scales provide a useful means of indexing the features of work that underlie job enrichment efforts (e.g., perceived *autonomy, variety, task significance*—see Chapter 3).[10] Whether or not it provides a sufficiently *complete* description remains to be seen. We know that it is possible with other methods to provide plenty of detail without capturing the essence of what people do—thus missing the forest for the trees. Maybe FJA gives us a glimpse of the forest.

2. Air Force Task Inventory Method (TI/CODAP).[11] In contrast to FJA, which seeks to map all jobs onto a small set of common

TABLE 6-1   Complete Definitions for the Six Levels of the Data Function Scale

Level	Definition
1	Comparing: Selects, sorts, or arranges data, people, or things, judging whether their readily observable functional, structural, or compositional characteristics are similar to or different from prescribed standards.
2	Copying: Transcribes, enters, and/or posts data, following a schema or plan to assemble or make things and using a variety of work aids.
3A	Computing: Performs arithmetic operations and makes reports and/or carries out a prescribed action in relation to them.
3B	Compiling: Gathers, collects, or classifies information about data, people, or things, following a schema or system but using discretion in application.
4	Analyzing: Examines and evaluates data (about things, data, or people) with reference to the criteria, standards, and/or requirements of a particular discipline, art, technique, or craft to determine interaction effects (consequences) and to consider alternatives.
5A	Innovating: Modifies, alters, and/or adapts existing designs, procedures, or methods to meet unique specifications, unusual conditions, or specific standards of effectiveness within the overall framework of operating theories, principles, and/or organizational contexts.
5B	Coordinating: Decides time, place, and sequences of operations of a process, system, or organization, and/or the need for revision of goals, policies (boundary conditions), or procedures on the basis of analysis of data and of performance review of pertinent objectives and requirements. Includes overseeing and/or executing decisions and/or reporting on events.
6	Synthesizing: *Takes off in new directions* on the basis of personal intuitions, feelings, and ideas (with or without regard for tradition, experience, and existing parameters) to *conceive new approaches* to or statements of problems and the development of system, operational, or aesthetic "solutions" or "resolutions" of them, typically outside of existing theoretical, stylistic, or organizational context.

SOURCE: From Fine, S. A. & Wiley, W. W. (1971). An introduction to functional job analysis: Methods for manpower analysis. Monograph No. 4. Kalamazoo, Mich.: W. E. Upjohn Institute for Employment Research.

descriptions, the *TI* approach is concerned only with precise descriptions of the requisite tasks using whatever descriptors seem most appropriate. It is also *work-oriented*, whereas *FJA* is more *worker oriented*; it combines checklist, open-ended questionnaire, and observation interview methods; and recent versions incorporate a number of computer-based refinements (the CODAP acronym). The resulting procedure goes somewhat as follows: First, a preliminary task inventory is constructed from whatever literature is available on the set of jobs to be analyzed. Next, experts are consulted to edit (add to, subtract from) the items on the preliminary inventory. Third, the resulting 200 to 300 items are grouped under major functional categories (or "duties"). An example of the preliminary inventory for one such duty is shown in Figure 6-3. Fourth, the preliminary inventory is pretested using experienced incumbents who check each task that applies to their job. As illustrated in Figure 6-3, they also are encouraged to add items that they feel are important but that do not appear on the form.

FIGURE 6–3 Examples of Tasks Contained in Two Duties for the Airman Supply Career Field

Listed below are a duty and the tasks which it includes. Check all tasks which you perform. Add any tasks you do which are not listed. Then rate the tasks you have checked.	CHECK	TIME SPENT	TNG & EXP
DUTY: PROCESSING PROPERTY FOR STORAGE	√ if done	1 Small Amt. 2 Below Av. 3 Aver. 4 Above Av. 5 Great Amt.	1 Small Amt. 2 Below Av. 3 Aver. 4 Above Av. 5 Great Amt.
TASKS INCLUDED IN ABOVE DUTY			
1. Examine property items received for presence of gasoline, oil, hydraulic fluid, or indications of corrosion			
2. Drain gasoline, oil, or hydraulic fluid from equipment to be stored			
3. Use proper methods to clean and dry property items preparatory to storage			
4. Accomplish corrosion-control measures on property to be stored			
5. Enclose desccants and containers to avoid moisture accumulation and damage during storage			
6. Use appropriate methods and materials to wrap and package property for storage			
7. Identify and label packages, crates, or boxes			
8. Segregate property according to type and grade for routing to storage areas			

SOURCE: From Morsh, J. E. An analysis of jobs—Use of the task inventory method of job analysis. USAF Technical Report WADD-TR-61-113.

The final version of the inventory is constructed on the basis of the pretest results and given to a large sample of job incumbents. The format is the same as that used in the pretest (i.e., as shown in Figure 6–3). Once again, the respondent can add information that is not covered by the questionnaire.

The TI system is as thorough and relevant as any technique now available; hence it is a good model to follow in designing one's own approach.

By combining several sources (experts and incumbents) and procedures (interview and open-ended questionnaire), by pretesting the inventories, and by using a large number of respondents for each job, the approach overcomes most of the shortcomings inherent in each component technique. It is, however, a "brute force" approach: It requires a lot of people and a fair amount of time. Thus it would be difficult to implement in anything but a large organization. It illustrates very nicely our cardinal principle that should be followed in any job analysis: Since each source and procedure is deficient by itself, the only safe bet is to *combine* them in a manner that will minimize the individual deficiencies. This may require a certain amount of ingenuity on the part of the person designing the analysis.

3. The Position Analysis Questionnaire (PAQ).[12]

As in the FJA, the underlying philosophy in the PAQ is that all jobs can be reduced to a set of behavioral job *elements*, each of which can be defined in terms of a set of basic *dimensions*. The PAQ is a structured instrument composed of 194 of these elements classified into six major categories, or *divisions:* information input (35 elements), mediation process (14), work output (49), interpersonal activities (36), work situation and job context (19), and miscellaneous aspects (41). The analyst describes a job by rating, usually on a six-point scale, how much of each of these elements it entails. For example, one of the information-input elements is use of written materials; one of the mediation process elements is use of mathematics; one of the work-output elements is use of keyboard devices. Considering only these three items for purposes of illustration, the job of statistical clerk might be judged 3 in use of written materials, 5 in use of mathematics, and 4 in keyboard devices. The profile of these ratings would define the job.

Research by E. J. McCormick, the originator of this instrument, and his colleagues has shown that the 194 items in the PAQ can be represented by 32 dimensions underlying the divisions, or 13 more general factors underlying the whole business (see Table 6–2). Moreover, ratings of particular jobs in terms of these elements is quite reliable over raters— that is, different analysts arrive at much the same descriptive values for the same job. These and other research findings suggest, first, that the concept of a common structure underlying all jobs is a reasonable one and, second, that measurement of jobs in terms of this structure is feasible.[13] A third feature emphasized by the developers is that the dimension scores provide a *valid* representation of the requirements for various jobs. Since the topic of validity doesn't come up until the next chapter, we cannot examine their claim very thoroughly here. Let us just say that they related PAQ measures to scores made by people in various jobs on a common aptitude test battery and found reasonably good agreement between certain test score differences and PAQ differences across jobs. For exam-

TABLE 6–2   The 12 Most Clearly Defined Overall Factors Represented by the PAQ*

1. Having decision, communicating, and general responsibilities.
2. Operating machines or equipment.
3. Performing clerical-related activities.
4. Performing technical-related activities.
5. Performing service-related activities.
6. Working regular day versus other work schedules.
7. Performing routine or repetitive activities.
8. Being aware of work environment.
9. Engaging in physical activities.
10. Supervising or coordinating other personnel.
11. Public or customer-related contacts.
12. Working in an unpleasant, hazardous, or demanding environment.

*A 13th factor was left unnamed since it was not clearly interpretable.
SOURCE: From McCormick, E. J. & Ilgen, D. (1980). Englewood Cliffs, N.J.: Prentice-Hall.

ple, if bricklayers had lower verbal test scores than English teachers on the average, as one would expect, the PAQ would tend to show that the job of bricklayer also "scored" lower on verbally oriented dimensions. Not everyone is as impressed with this argument as the developers. Still, the attempt to establish validity empirically is well beyond what most other systems have done, and the PAQ has become widely recognized as a sensitive and comprehensive way to describe work. The only question, really, is whether it is too sensitive and comprehensive. For some purposes, such as developing training or selection requirements or trying to make compensation systems equitable, the level of detail provided is very useful. For others, such as developing a meaningful description or overall concept of what a job entails, this same detail— even with the various interpretative analyses that are now available[14]— can be a bit overwhelming.

One other difficulty with the PAQ is that for some jobs, notably those at the professional and managerial levels, many of the 194 items simply do not apply. This can be a problem because it can lead to a gross overestimation of the instrument's measurement capabilities.[15] If, for example, 90 percent of the items were clearly not applicable to a particular job, two people doing the analysis independently would show very high agreement if they simply agreed that most of the items were irrelevant! And this would be true even if they were in total disagreement on the 10 percent of the items that were actually *informative*. To combat this problem, a new version of the PAQ (the PMPQ or Professional and Management Position Questionnaire[16]) has been developed. It includes some different items (a total of 197) and leads to the set of factors shown in Table 6–3. Comparing these with the PAQ factors (Table 6–2) makes it obvious that the two versions address quite different job content domains; hence the PAQ is not nearly as universal as it was originally intended to be.

TABLE 6–3   The 10 Principal Factors Represented in the PMPQ

1. Personal job requirements.
2. Planning and decision making.
3. Complex analysis and communications.
4. Technical activities.
5. Processing of information/data.
6. Relevant experience.
7. Interpersonal activities.
8. Special training.
9. Communicating/instructing.
10. Second language usage.

SOURCE: Mitchell, J. L., & McCormick, E. J. 1980). *User's Manual for the Professional and Managerial Position Questionnaire, System IV.* West Lafayette, Ind.: Purdue Research Foundation.

4. Job Requirements Approach.   A relatively new approach, which has proven particularly useful in the domain of *physical* characteristics, involves a direct frontal attack on job *requirements*. Except for one section in the USTES description, most systems try to deal with what people *do* in a job and then derive a set of requirements to spell out what personal qualities it takes to do that job proficiently. The ability requirements approach analyzes the job by looking at the requirements directly. To even begin to do this, of course, presupposes knowledge of the domain of human abilities that a job might require. There would be little point, for example, in describing requirements on dimensions for which we have no good measures (e.g., personal charm) or even good evidence that the ability exists (e.g., clairvoyance).

A recent book by Fleishman and Quaintance[17] summarizes the work that has been done to date charting the various domains of human performance. Collectively these taxonomies yield some 40 to 50 basic task requirements. To illustrate how the approach is actually implemented, however, we shall limit the discussion to one domain: *physical* abilities.

Some years ago, Fleishman described the domain of physical abilities, using a factor analytic approach. He identified nine major dimensions: dynamic strength, trunk strength, static strength, explosive strength, extent of flexion, dynamic flexion, gross body coordination, gross body equilibrium, and stamina. Applying this structure to the work setting, the analyst develops scales for each dimension, choosing benchmark tasks to illustrate the range of conditions represented (e.g., lifting a 100-pound carton of canned beans to shoulder height might anchor the top of the trunk strength scale). The analyst then describes each job in terms of its profile on these scales. In some cases, the measures can be fairly objective (e.g., the 100-pound carton that must be lifted can be weighed), while in others they call for subjective ratings.[18]

Although still evolving, this general approach has already seen application in a variety of physical work contexts: fire and police departments, a grocery chain, a major communications company, oil field operations. The biggest difficulty encountered so far is that of establishing good scales with appropriate reference tasks, a chore that must be repeated in each new work setting. Unless care is used in this initial phase of the process, the measures obtained may prove unreliable. However, results to date have been encouraging, particularly considering the prominence of physical abilities in the whole issue of sex discrimination.[19] Certain jobs have traditionally been reserved for males on the assumption that they were physically too demanding for most women. That may in fact be true in some cases, but it is also a convenient excuse for excluding perfectly capable women in many others. It is easy to see how a physical requirements analysis can settle the issue for any given job, and the Fleshman-Hogan approach has proven its worth in meeting this need.[20]

The logic of the requirements approach to job analysis is not limited to physical abilities. As we shall see in the next chapter, many other domains of human capability have been defined, at least roughly, in an effort to improve selection and placement decisions.

COMPENSATION AND JOB WORTH

One aspect of a job that is of particular interest to anyone potentially or actually associated with it is its rate of pay. The topic of compensation falls logically between that of job description and performance evaluation. What a person is paid should depend in part upon how much the job itself is worth and in part upon how much the individual contributes to that job through performance. All too often in practice these relationships are not clearly specified. Compensation systems have a habit of growing "like Topsy" rather than according to logical plan. They are often shrouded in secrecy and for good reason: It is hard to defend the indefensible. The potentially dire consequences for satisfaction and performance of ill-defined, irrational, misunderstood, or downright inequitable pay systems were spelled out in Chapter 3.

Clearly, then, at least half the task of developing an acceptable compensation system lies in deciding how much each job in the organization is worth. Needless to say, an accurate job description—particularly one that breaks each job into a set of common elements as in the PAQ/PMPQ— is an essential first step in that direction. Once we know *what* people do, there remains the task of putting a dollar value on it. Since this is more appropriately a topic in personnel management than in personnel *psychology*, only the rudiments of the process will be covered here.

The question of how much various kinds of work are worth is a very fundamental philosophical one. The whole labor movement was based on the premise that actual *production* work was worth more, relative to *work management* and *capital investment functions*, than it was receiving. Managers and owners, of course, have always argued the importance of their roles: Whereas a common laborer is easily replaced by another common laborer (or, if the laborer gets too expensive, by a machine), it is not as easy to replace a capable manager or a group of investors. There is, of course, no absolute answer to the question of job worth criteria. In practice, it must be resolved by some sort of compromise among the competing value systems involved. Collective bargaining is obviously one mechanism by which a compromise is reached.

Another is the adoption of some coherent and equitable system for weighting various considerations. At the broadest level, we can distinguish three main sets of considerations: *internal, external,* and *individual* equity factors.[21] Taking them in reverse order, *individual* factors are those brought to the workplace by the employee—seniority, performance, skill, etc. *External* factors are those over which neither the individual nor the employer has much control—minimum wage and overtime pay laws, labor market conditions, salaries paid by competitors, etc. *Internal* equity refers to the value for the employer of work actually done in various jobs—the fact that a production or sales position, for example, is inherently more valuable than a mail clerk position. It is important to recognize that these three concepts are distinct and, in practice, often difficult to reconcile. Universities, for example, must pay higher salaries to professors of medicine, law, and accounting than to professors of English, history, or sociology due to *external* considerations (the former professions command higher average salaries in the general labor market). However, the *internal* worth of instruction in English is at least as high for the university's educational mission as that of accounting, and an eminent senior historian should merit salary treatment in preference to a brand-new law professor by virtue of their respective *individual* contributions. Were a university to rely entirely on internal considerations, it would have very happy historians but no one to teach law courses. Were it to emphasize external factors, it would probably develop first-rate professional schools at the expense of the liberal arts. Were it to focus exclusively on individual factors, it would wind up with a few old, distinguished professors in each department and not enough total faculty to carry out any of its programs effectively.

With these distinctions in mind, our attention for the rest of this section will be directed chiefly toward *internal* equity considerations, particularly as they relate to the current controversy known as the *comparable worth* issue.

Job Evaluation Methods and Internal Equity

According to Bass and Barrett, four such methods can be distinguished: *ranking, classification, factor comparison,* and the *point system.*[22] Whichever of these is adopted, it should always involve participation by committee representatives of all interested parties (organized or unorganized labor, management, personnel, the various divisions or departments, and so on). Such a committee must establish the standards or criteria to be used in the evaluation and then proceed with the application of these criteria to the jobs. (All this, of course, presupposes that the organization has progressed beyond the rigid tenets of classical management theory to the point of accepting at least minimal participation).

The procedures differ with respect to how judgments of worth are made, given a set of agreed-upon criteria. *Ranking*, as it suggests, requires that the committee simply put all the jobs in rank order from most to least valuable. Each job is considered as a unit (it is not broken into dimensions). *Classification* is similar except that it requires the initial specification of a set of ordered worth categories into which jobs are then sorted. Once ordered or classified, a pay scale (or range of values) is applied to each rank (or category).

The *factor comparison* and *point* systems are similar to each other and different from the others in that both involve evaluating jobs in terms of underlying factors or common dimensions rather than as complete entities. Thus, in order to carry out an evaluation, it is necessary to determine three things: (1) what common factors underlie the set of jobs to be evaluated, (2) how much of each factor is present in each job, and (3) how much each level of each factor is worth.

The factor comparison and point methods differ mainly in terms of how question 3 above is answered. In the factor comparison approach, a small sample of *key* (representative) jobs is selected, and each is assigned what is agreed upon as an equitable salary range. Salary levels are then set for the other jobs by comparison of their factor composition with that of the key jobs. Suppose, for example, the widget assembler was a key job paying $5.00 per hour. Of this, 50 percent (or $2.50) was for a *physical demands* factor, 33 percent (or $1.67) was for a *working conditions* factor, and 17 percent (or $.83) was for a *skill* factor. Now, all jobs having comparable physical demands would be awarded $2.50 for this factor, all with comparable working conditions would earn $1.67 for this factor, and so on. The total salary for a particular job would be the sum of all its factor values.

In the point method, each possible level of each factor is first evaluated in terms of *points*. Physical demands, for example, might be judged to exist at four levels worth 40, 30, 20, and 10 points, respectively; skill at five levels worth 50, 40, 30, 20, and 10 points, respectively; and so on. Next, each job is evaluated on the basis of the points it accrues for its particular level of each factor. The widget assembler might get 30 points for physical demands, 20 points for working conditions, and 10 points for skill. Only after the total point value has been established for all jobs are the points converted to dollars. If each point were set to equal 8.34 cents per hour, for example, the widget assembler would earn about $5 per hour

(60 points × 8.34 cents). Briefly, then, the point system sets up an internally consistent evaluation structure within which jobs are located before any consideration is given to money. *The whole structure* is then converted to money. Any new job need only be fitted into the structure, and its pay rate is determined automatically. Any change in the point-dollar conversion would affect all jobs proportionately.

The advantages of the factor-based methods over the others are obvious. In particular, they should tend to produce more objective, more consistent, more complete estimates of a job's internal worth. The only disadvantage would seem to be the rather involved procedures necessary to carry out the evaluation task properly. There are probably many instances in which the increased precision is simply not worth the trouble. In relatively small organizations, for example, where there are few job categories and they differ greatly from each other, overall ranking might be a perfectly adequate technique. Also, any potential advantage in the more elaborate procedures is lost if the common factors are not identified and measured accurately. If, for example, we fail to include in our point estimation a very critical characteristic of some particular job (for example, friendliness in the case of a receptionist), we could arrive at a gross underevaluation. This kind of possible distortion serves to underscore the importance of good analytical job descriptions. The more accurately the job is described, the less likely it is that something will be left out or weighted improperly in the job evaluation.

Recent years have seen job evaluation and the search for internal equity take on a considerably expanded sense of urgency by virtue of court rulings involving fair employment practices legislation. The concept set forth in these laws is essentially that, within an organization, equal work should warrant equal pay (i.e., there should be internal equity). Persons should not be paid less because they are female, black, old, and so on, so long as they are doing the same work as others in the same jobs. However, the interpretation has in some cases gone a step further in recognizing that no two positions are *exactly* alike and that in fact, females and minority group members have often been channeled into lower-paying jobs—a clearly discriminatory practice. This liberal interpretation requires, therefore, that employers pay comparable wages for jobs of *comparable worth* to the organization. How does one establish *comparable worth*? How, for example, does one compare a traditionally "male" job such as oilfield roustabout with a traditionally "female" job such as clerk-typist? (The former, incidentally, generally pays much more than the latter.) The reader should realize by now that systematic job evaluation, and the factor-based methods in particular, offer an excellent—and legally defensible—answer to such questions. Physical demands and a rigorous environment contribute the most to the worth of the oilfield job; certain knowledge and skill requirements tend to dominate the clerk-typist job. Once the organization has established the worth of these dimensions and their various levels, it has constructed a basis for comparison that is largely independent of male-female stereotypes or other irrelevant considerations. If the clerk-typist job comes out lower in pay, it is because the composite value of its elements to the organization is lower than that of the oilfield job, not because women are willing to work for less money than men.

Market Surveys and External Equity

What if it happens that women *are* willing to work for less than men? Or that in a particular labor market it is very difficult to find people willing to endure the hardships of life in the "oilpatch," and financial inducement is the only way to keep the drills drilling and the pumps pumping? Naturally, one cannot ignore the pressures of supply and demand, of competitive rates, of collective bargaining agreements, and of other external factors if one is to stay in business. The law recognizes this reality.

It is not, however, always an easy matter to determine the external worth of all the jobs in an organization or to track the inevitable changes that occur over time. Most organizations of any size conduct periodic surveys of what they consider to be their primary labor markets for the particular types of people they need. The scope may range from a reasonable commuting distance to the entire world, depending on the availability of talent. In addition, many industries, professions, nonprofit organizations, and government agencies monitor trends in various segments of the labor force, and these reports are also available to the employer. The American Psychological Association, for example, conducts an annual survey of its membership to determine the prevailing salaries for the main psychological specialties (e.g., clinical, I/O, experimental), regions of the country, places of employment (e.g., industry, academic, government), and so on, and the results are published for the benefit of employers and job seekers. Thus a potential employer need only consult the *American Psychologist* to find an externally equitable rate for a prospective hire.

If establishing external equity poses some difficulty, it is nothing compared to the problem of reconciling external with internal considerations. In the last section, the internal equity story ended with the internally coherent system being converted to money (e.g., points to dollars). Left unsaid was the fact that the resulting *internal* compensation structure may deviate considerably from the pattern obtained through *external* salary surveys. Computer programmers may be less valuable to the company than executive secretaries but, because the demand for programmers in recent years has so far outpaced the supply, their market value— particularly in some locations—may exceed that of *any* secretarial category. Thus the internal and external prescriptions are in this case directly in conflict. How is it resolved? Unfortunately, there is no universal answer. Typically, the two systems are juggled in an ad hoc fashion until they fall roughly into line. According to the opinion of at least one knowledgeable source, "When external and internal equity considerations are in conflict, we suspect, though lacking scientific evidence, that external equity takes precedence."[23]

PERFORMANCE EVALUATION AND INDIVIDUAL EQUITY

A worker's compensation, we said, should reflect not only how much the *job* is worth but how much he or she is worth in that job. Pay systems based on this general philosophy are known as *incentive systems*. Naturally, performance is not the only possible basis for pay; neither is pay the only possible reward for performance. Still, the logic of incentive compensation is rather widely accepted. We mention it here only as a vivid illustration of the importance of accurate performance evaluation. Without it, incentive systems make no sense. Indeed, the main shortcoming of most ineffective incentive plans is their reliance on poor or irrelevant measures of performance. On the other hand, accurate performance evaluation can make incentive systems work, at least to the extent that the employees understand the performance-reward contingency.

There are, of course, many other reasons why accurate performance evaluation is important. It provides critical information for personnel decisions such as who should be promoted, terminated, transferred, counseled, or trained. It is essential for the evaluation of selection and training programs: If the program is good, it should result in improved performance. Finally, as we saw in the last two chapters, performance evaluation serves as one of the two main dependent variables in research on organizational and management processes. That is, theoretical notions such as valence or expectancy are tested in terms of how they affect performance (and satisfaction).

None of these important functions can be carried out very well without some sort of dependable measures of performance. Thus, for example, a test used to select people, a program used to train them, or a theory used to predict what will motivate them may appear much better or worse than it really is simply because performance criteria are too insensitive or irrelevant to indicate the true effect. It becomes extremely important, therefore, to consider at this point how performance should be evaluated. The word *should* is significant here because so few organizations actually pay the matter of performance evaluation the attention it deserves. Two basic issues must be dealt with if performance is to be evaluated properly. The first is the question of what constitutes good or poor job behavior. What should be the basis on which a worker's performance is judged? What, in other words, are the *criteria* of job performance? The second is the question of how to measure the criteria once we have identified them.

Performance Criteria

Strictly speaking, we could say there are as many potential bases for evaluating job performance as there are job descriptions. Were it feasible to do so, we could establish standards for every aspect of every job and judge the individual according to whether he, or she met, fell short of, or exceeded these standards. Such an approach, of course, would be impractical and unnecessarily detailed. It would also be the ultimate in thoroughness.

At the other extreme, we could judge everyone's performance on a *single* criterion: perhaps an overall rating by one's supervisor, or some index of how much one's performance has contributed to the goals of the organization (gross sales, in the case of a salesperson). Underlying this approach is the idea that in the final analysis there is some universal scale of goodness on which anyone's performance of any job could be located. This *ultimate criterion*, however, can never be measured directly. Therefore, we must estimate where people belong on it by using purely subjective judgment or whatever other means we can contrive. Even if we try to take into account a lot of aspects of performance, the object is still to combine the information into an overall assessment—an estimate of the ultimate criterion.

Most actual evaluation procedures fall somewhere between these two extremes. As a rule they assume that we can describe performance adequately using a relatively small number of common dimensions or features that apply to any job. There is considerable disagreement as to whether these dimensions should be considered as separate criteria of job performance or as elements used to estimate a single ultimate criterion. The latter position, known as the *composite-criterion* approach, requires that all the measures eventually be combined into a single composite score; the former, or *multiple-criterion* approach, allows performance to be expressed separately in terms of each criterion dimension. Suppose, for example, we used accident rate, output quantity, output quality, and work attitude as performance criteria. In the multiple-criterion approach, we would describe a person's performance as a profile of scores on these dimensions: One might rank high in attitude and output rate but poor in output quality and accident rate. In the composite-criterion approach, the scores would all be combined into a single performance index. Thus the person's deficiencies in the safety and quality areas would serve to offset a good attitude and rate of production record in the final evaluation.

While debate continues as to which is the better evaluation philosophy conceptually, in practice both multiple and composite criteria are useful for different purposes. If, for instance, we want to use the assessment to establish an incentive pay system, we must ultimately arrive at a single

scale. If, instead, our purpose is to evaluate training or selection procedures, we may well prefer the diagnostic information provided by multiple criteria. Either way, we would actually *measure* performance in terms
of several intermediate criteria—whether or not we combined them later
on. In the case of nonmanagement jobs, the factors most commonly represented include some index of (1) quantity of output, (2) quality of output,
(3) learning ability, (4) work habits and attitudes, (5) facility in interpersonal relationships, (6) safety, and (7) judgment or problem-solving
ability.

Supervisory criteria are considerably less universal and depend, to a
great extent, upon the general philosophy of management of the organization. Implicit in each theory of leadership, for example, is a somewhat
different set of criteria. Quite frequently, management performance is
evaluated subjectively on an overall basis simply because no one knows
what the appropriate components are. Some attempts have been made to
specify general supervisory criteria. One, for example, lists (1) establishment of an effective climate for work, (2) ethics in managing subordinates, (3) self-development, (4) personal maturity and sensitivity, (5)
knowledge and execution of corporate policies and procedures, and (6)
technical job knowledge.[24] While these may indeed be important aspects
of supervision, they are certainly not easy to pin down when it comes to
measurement. What is considered an effective work climate for one person may be total chaos for another. Since there are no objective definitions for most of these criteria, it is questionable whether they are as
meaningful as the *blue-collar* criteria.

There is one serious problem in evaluating performance—blue- or
white-collar—on the basis of a few common dimensional criteria. It is the
danger that the evaluation will be incomplete or distorted because it fails
to recognize important *unique* features of particular jobs and people. Suppose, for example, the job of widget inspector requires that a person be at-
tentive, accurate, dependable, and little else. Is it appropriate to down-
grade a widget inspector's performance because she doesn't speak to
anyone, doesn't learn things quickly, and gives every indication of hating
her work? Obviously not. If, therefore, common dimensions are used, they
should at least be weighted differentially to take into account specific job
requirements.[25] Closely related to the specificity problem is the fact that
dimensional criteria are often stated in rather vague or general terms
(see, for example, the aforementioned supervisory criteria). They thus
lend themselves to biases in measurement. Suppose, for example, a supervisor was partial toward a particular subordinate. It would be much
easier for the supervisor to rate the subordinate excessively high on such
global characteristics as quality of work or interpersonal relations than it
would be to misrepresent the frequency with which the worker produced
defective products or caused friction within the work group.

Both of the above difficulties can be minimized by careful selection and definition of criterion dimensions. It is essential that criteria be developed on the basis of a thorough study of major job categories and that the resulting dimensions be expressed in as explicit a form as possible. This usually means that the criteria should represent actual *behavior* that distinguishes good from poor performance. In other words, we must be sure our criteria include all the critical aspects of all the jobs and that we leave little room for interpretation of these criteria. Certainly one of the best ways to find out what the most important aspects of job behavior are is through use of the oft-mentioned *critical incident* technique.[26] To illustrate how this procedure might be used to identify criteria, we shall relate an actual case history from the experience of one of the authors. This particular example also illustrates a few of the problems discussed above—it is a fairly typical case.

A large insurance company engaged the author to review its selection procedures for clerical workers. It was soon discovered that evaluation of these procedures was impossible because the performance criteria were so poor. Annually, each clerical employee was rated on a scale from 0 (*unacceptable*) to 4 (*outstanding*) on each of seven criteria: volume of work, quality of work, self-development, dependability, willingness, personal acceptance, and maturity. A composite evaluation was then computed by simply adding up all seven ratings. Each criterion dimension was thus weighted equally regardless of the job. To make matters worse, supervisors were required to use a "forced-rating" procedure on the overall evaluation. This is similar to grading on a curve: A certain percentage of subordinates are force-rated into each category (e.g., 10 percent *outstanding*, 20 percent *above average*, 30 percent *average*, and so on). Faced with this impossible situation, the supervisors merely decided which employees were most useful to them (for whatever reasons), rated each *outstanding* or *above average* on the composite evaluation, and then filled out the component scales so as to add up to the already determined composite. Since the most useful people were usually those in the more skilled positions, the net result was that people in low-level jobs were always rated low—irrespective of how they performed—and those in higher-level jobs were always rated high—also irrespective of their performance. The overall evaluation was thus virtually meaningless, and the component scales were something less than that.

To rectify the situation, a complete overhaul was done on the evaluation system. The objective was to develop a set of criteria that would encompass all critical job behaviors and a procedure that would encourage honest assessment of these behaviors. The first step was to gather critical incident data from a large sample of clerical supervisors via interviews. Each supervisor was asked to relate specific episodes involving employees that he considered illustrative of especially good or poor clerical behavior. The resulting tape-recorded incidents were analyzed for content and sorted into categories on the basis of similarity. Sample statements were then selected from each category, preserving insofar as possible the original wording, and assembled into a preliminary questionnaire, as shown in Table 6–4.

Even a cursory look at the various jobs included by this company in the clerical category suggested that different jobs would have different profiles of critical behavior. Hence the next step was to determine the relative *importance* of each item for each job category. The preliminary questionnaire was given to several supervisors of each type of clerical job, with instructions to distribute 200 points over these items in accordance with the importance of each behavior for performance of that particular job (see instructions in Table 6–4). The result was a separate profile of weighted statements for each job.

The third step was to minimize the number of items necessary to describe clerical performance completely. Without going into details, the procedure used to do this involved the statistical technique of *factor analysis* (see Chapter 3). The final set of criterion behaviors is illustrated in Table 6–5, together with the weighted value of each item, for the job of *reinstatement clerk*. The same items were used for all clerical jobs, each of which, like the reinstatement clerk example, had its own profile of importance weights.

The procedure by which this set of criteria is now used to evaluate clerical performance is very simple for the supervisor. All he or she does is check whether or not each item is typical of the employee's behavior. The resulting pattern of checked items is then scored by computer, using the weights established for that employee's job, and stored in the computer. In this way, the supervisor is relieved of the task of actually *evaluating* subordinates (or rather, juggling scale ratings to match a preconceived overall value). Instead, the supervisor merely *describes* their behavior, and the evaluation is done. Performance evaluation should thus be less subject to distortion, more job-related, and above all, more complete than with the old method.

Performance Measurement Techniques

The end product of the example just given was a measurement procedure known as a *weighted checklist*. It is but one of many techniques used to measure performance on the chosen criteria. Most of these techniques fall into one of two broad categories defined according to the objectivity of the measurement process: *objective* versus *subjective* measures. We should recognize at the outset, however, that the distinction is not as clear-cut as it seems. Few methods for evaluating performance are inherently either totally objective or subjective. *Objectivity* refers to the extent to which measures are independent of human judgment. We say that a report or measurement of an event is *objective* insofar as it would remain the same regardless of who made the observation. Different observers, on the other hand, would be likely to render different *subjective* reports of the same event.

When applied to performance evaluation techniques, objectivity usually reduces to how much latitude for interpretation is permitted by the specific device (questionnaire, checklist, production log, etc.) used to take the measurement. Some are very rigid: There is little room for observer judgment in a *count* of how many units a worker produced. Some are clearly subjective: A general *rating* of how well a person gets along with fellow workers is usually a matter of pure judgment. However, *ratings* and even *counts* can be more or less subjective. We might ask a supervisor to rate a worker's ability to get along by considering how often the worker was involved in instances of friction; or we might have the supervisor report a worker's output by estimating (rather than counting) productivity. The point is, neither the general kind of criteria nor the general kind of measurement technique used determines the objectivity of performance measures, although some are more conducive to objectivity than others. It is the *specific device and criterion* that define objectivity. Thus when we classify graphic-rating procedures as subjective, for example, the reader should realize that they can be more or less subjective, depending upon how they are worded.

Objective Measures

These measurement scales are usually implied directly by the criteria on which performance is evaluated. For example, *output quantity* can obviously be measured by counting units produced, orders written, or revenue generated. *Quality* can be gauged by counting defective units produced or the frequency with which prescribed standards are met. *Dependability* can be expressed in terms of absenteeism and tardiness figures; *accidents*, by recorded accident rates; and so on. There is little point in listing all the possible measures that could be taken. More important, the reader should recognize that objective measurement demands clear, unambiguous specification of the criteria. If we have that, objective measurement is always possible. Without it, objective measurement is out of the question.

It is commonly assumed that objective measures are inherently superior to subjective ones, that by their very nature they provide a fairer and more accurate mans of evaluating performance. Bass and Barrett, however, present a rather convincing argument to the contrary.[27] It is their contention that relying completely on objective measures often gives an incomplete or distorted picture of what the individual has actually accomplished. Production, sales, and accident data, for example, can all be at least partially determined by factors beyond the employee's control. Low production by an assembly-line worker may reflect social pressures rather than incompetence or indifference. Low sales volume may reflect a poor sales territory. A high accident rate may reflect faulty equipment or

TABLE 6–4 Portion of the Initial 50-Item Evaluation Form Used to Obtain Weightings for Specific Clerical Jobs

Supervisor's Name: Date:

Job Title and Grade Level:

Department:

Instructions: Distribute 200 points over the following 50 items by entering any number from 0–200 in the space to the right of each item. Please rate the importance of the behavior, ignoring the positive or negative wording of the statement.

	Points (0–200)
A. Knowledge and Skills	
1. Knows where to go for necessary information	_____
2. Knows all the procedures involved in job	_____
3. Learns procedures and changes in procedures quickly	_____
4. Is willing and able to make decisions	_____
5. Understands how the whole unit (department, etc.) operates	_____
6. Organizes work or information well	_____
7. Handles pressure easily; meets deadlines	_____
8. Catches mistakes of others	_____
9. Is able to analyze situations capably	_____
10. Does a good job of training new people	_____
11. Notices details (e.g., minor discrepancies)	_____
12. Uses good English	_____
13. Is well versed in technical terminology	_____
14. Anticipates boss's needs	_____
15. Communicates effectively	_____
B. Initiative and self-development	
1. Looks for better ways to do things	_____
2. Seeks to learn new skills or otherwise expand capabilities	_____
3. Asks questions when unsure	_____
4. Begins new work without being told	_____
5. Goes one step beyond requirements of job	_____
C. Enthusiasm; work orientation; attitude	
1. Helps others when caught up with own work	_____
2. Finishes work quickly and looks for more	_____
3. Continues beyond normal working hours if necessary to finish job	_____
4. Is tardy or absent more often than necessary	_____
5. Is away from desk more than necessary	_____
6. Talks excessively about personal matters with other employees or on the phone	_____
7. Requires more supervision than should be necessary	_____
8. Daydreams excessively	_____
9. Willingly carries out unusual or unpleasant duties	_____
10. Complains a lot to other employees about job	_____
11. Cares for and maintains equipment	_____

Employee's Performance Appraisal
(Salary grade 1–8)

Name   Date:

Department:

Instructions: Check those statements that are *typical* of the employee's behavior on the job. Leave blank those statements that are *not typical* of the employee or are irrelevant for his or her job.

		Check
1.	Knows all the procedures involved in the job	12.5
2.	Organizes work or information well; is good at analyzing things	8.4
3.	Catches mistakes of others or takes notice of important details and discrepancies	3.8
4.	Does a good job of training new people	1.8
5.	Is well versed in technical terminology	0.5
6.	Uses good English; spelling	0.8
7.	Understands how the whole unit (department) operates	3.0
8.	Handles pressures easily; meets deadlines	3.3
9.	Anticipates boss's needs	0.0
10.	Is willing and able to make decisions	3.3
11.	Looks for better ways to do things	2.0
12.	Finishes own work quickly and looks for more or seeks to help others with theirs	2.3
13.	Goes one step beyond requirements of job	1.0
14.	Asks questions when unsure	4.0
15.	Learns or "catches on" quickly	5.0
16.	Seeks to learn new skills or otherwise expand capabilities	2.8
17.	Willingly carries out unusual or unpleasant duties when necessary	1.3
18.	Cares for an maintains equipment	0.5
19.	Continues beyond normal working hours if necessary to finish job	0.5
20.	Is rarely tardy or absent without good reason	6.4
21.	Seldom does disruptive or nonproductive things such as wandering about the office, daydreaming, carrying on long personal conversations, complaining	5.6
22.	Keeps confidences and loyalties	1.0
23.	Responds well to criticism and supervision	2.0
24.	Gets along well and cooperates with fellow employees; is considerate	1.3
25.	Is courteous and tactful in dealings with the public, agents, or others outside the office	2.5
26.	Is looked upon by others as a leader	0.5
27.	Communicates effectively	1.0
28.	Turns out a large volume of work or doesn't let work pile up	13.4
29.	Does an accurate or high-quality job	9.5

poor working conditions. In short, objective measures only eliminate the biases and errors of human judgment, not biases and errors in general. There remains the possibility of distortion due to contamination and deficiency in the criterion measures. *Contamination* refers to the inclusion of extraneous factors, such as the above-mentioned social pressures and sales territory differences; *deficiency* refers to the exclusion of important aspects of performance. If we demand total objectivity in our measures, we may miss a lot of important things that people do in their jobs that are accessible only through human judgment. There is no objective measure for the smile on the face of the effective receptionist.

Another problem with objective measures is that they tend, in practice, to be far more ambiguous and far less reliable than they appear on the surface.[28] Consider a seemingly straightforward measure—*absenteeism*. Should it include every occasion when a person is not physically at work, whatever the reasons or circumstances, or just the ones that are unjustified? If we count only the unjustified ones, then what are the acceptable justifications, and who determines whether the particular instance qualifies? Would everyone making this judgment call it the same way? What if no one checks? What about sick leave provisions in union contracts (a time-off allowance that is often viewed as implicit vacation)—should that be counted, or only the time in excess of it? And, if it is not counted, then do nonunion or salaried employees also receive the same dispensation? Our nice, neat objective measure quickly deteriorates into a welter of options and opinions; the numbers that appear at one time and place in our personnel files may mean something quite different from those recorded somewhere else.

Subjective Measures

The most completely subjective approach is to allow the evaluator total freedom in describing how subordinates have performed. This is a completely *unstructured* technique. Its main disadvantage (and perhaps its main advantage as well) is that it produces highly idiosyncratic evaluations. Two evaluators might say entirely different things about the same worker. Similarly, the same evaluator might say entirely different things about two equally effective workers, one of whom is liked better than the other. This approach might be useful as a basis for counseling as, for example, in the MBO system discussed in Chapter 3. It would be difficult to use as a basis for an incentive pay system, or as a means of evaluating selection programs, or for any other purpose in which people are *compared*.

All the other techniques are designed to minimize the idiosyncrasies (particularly the errors and biases) inherent in subjective measurement. They all impose some degree of structure on the way in which the evaluator expresses a judgment: They try to make subjective measurement to some extent objective. Before presenting the principal techniques, it might be well to consider a few of the biases and errors they are designed to minimize. These are all distortions that are known to occur very frequently in any sort of subjective judgment task.

The first is the *halo effect*, which we encountered earlier. It is the tendency to let our impression of one aspect of a person's performance color our evaluation of others—or, even worse, our overall evaluation. The halo effect can be negative or positive. We might, for example, inflate or depress our judgment of an individual's quality of work based on whether we considered that person to be nice or obnoxious. Athough it has been recognized for at least 65 years as one of the foremost problems in human judgment, the halo concept is not as simple a matter as was originally believed.[29] Several ways have been used to measure it, and each seems to emphasize a different part of the total judgmental process.[30] This is perhaps best illustrated by Cooper[31] in a recent article that attempts to explain the halo effect in terms of how people process information (see Figure 6–4). He concludes that there are actually five main sources of error or bias involved plus one component that reflects *true* intercorrelation among the characteristics that the rater is judging! How large this "true" component is relative to the error components is currently being debated in the literature.[32] Regardless of where the controversey leads, however, it is safe to say that halo error will continue as the number one target for improvement in performance ratings.

A second common bias is the *central tendency* error, in which the evaluator tends to avoid extremely high or low evaluations. The result is that good performance may show up somewhat lower than it should, and poor performance somewhat higher.

Closely related to the central tendency bias are errors of *leniency* and *stringency*—the tendency for an evaluator to judge everyone's performance either consistently high or low. An example of the former is the supervisor who prides herself on "having only top-notch people in my outfit." Equally as familiar is the hard-nosed perfectionist who views everyone as seriously deficient one way or another. The obvious result of such biases is consistent over- or underevaluation of an entire group.

A fourth set of biases involves the sequence, order, or timing of evaluations. We might call them *context effects*. People very rarely, if ever, make judgments on an absolute basis. *Good* or *poor* usually reduce to *how* good or *how* poor something is relative to others (relative to some context). Not all context items, however, have an equal impact on the judgment of a particular item. For example, we tend to weight things that have occurred recently more heavily than past events. Also, very extreme or exceptional events have a disproportionate effect. Context effects can show up in many ways in subjective performance evaluation. For example, we might rate someone too high or too low on one trait because we judged that person as very good or very poor on the previous one. Or, we might rate him up or down on everything because of the contrast between his

FIGURE 6–4 A Sequential Model of the Rating Process

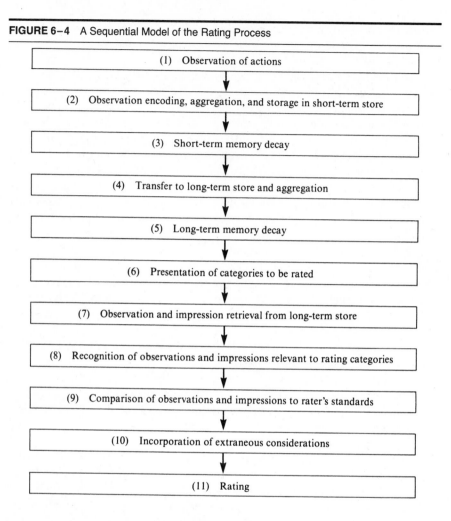

| (1)   Observation of actions |
| (2)   Observation encoding, aggregation, and storage in short-term store |
| (3)   Short-term memory decay |
| (4)   Transfer to long-term store and aggregation |
| (5)   Long-term memory decay |
| (6)   Presentation of categories to be rated |
| (7)   Observation and impression retrieval from long-term store |
| (8)   Recognition of observations and impressions relevant to rating categories |
| (9)   Comparison of observations and impressions to rater's standards |
| (10)   Incorporation of extraneous considerations |
| (11)   Rating |

performance and that of an extremely poor or outstanding worker who happened to be rated just before him.

A final set of biases is that characteristic of the *rater*. Everyone has likes and dislikes when it comes to other people. Often we prefer in others characteristics that we see in ourselves. Obviously any such preferences can bias any subjective evaluation of the other person. Instances of systematically biased judgments attributable to racial, sex, age, religious, political, and even attitudinal differences are too commonplace to require further description. The reader is undoubtedly familiar with the nature and history of various forms of discrimination in the workplace. An interesting comparison involving rater biases is offered by studies in which the same behavior is judged by individuals viewing it from different vantage points: the *employee* who produced the behavior, *peers*, and *supervisor*. By and large, there is fair agreement between overall supervisory and peer ratings but very little between either of these and self-ratings. In many instances, peers and supervisors seem to focus on different aspects of behavior.[33] As an aside, it is worth noting that peer ratings have proven more reliable and predictive than the typical supervisory ratings,[34] although modern organizations—being creatures of classical thought—rarely consider using any judgments other than those produced by supervisors. Even more heretical than peer evaluation is the idea that *subordinates* might have something useful to say about the performance of their bosses. If we can divorce ourselves from our classical heritage for just a moment, it should be perfectly obvious that different sources are appropriate for different kinds of information. As Latham and Wexley note, self-evaluation is most appropriate where an employee works alone or possesses a rare skill, especially as part of a system that stresses goal setting. Peer appraisal is probably the best source of information on how a person *really* does a job, provided the jobs involved offer considerable peer interaction. Subordinate appraisals probably tell us some important things about how (and even how well) the manager managed and are especially useful where the organization stresses the building of teamwork. Supervisory ratings are best when a major emphasis is placed on the manager's role in developing talent. Naturally, the best of all possible worlds would be that in which a composite picture of performance is constructed from multiple information sources.[35]

Conceptually, all the subjective procedures are very simple; hence each need be described only briefly here. They are not nearly so simple in implementation. Before undertaking any major evaluation program, therefore, the reader should refer to a more thorough account of the operational details of these procedures.[36] As we shall see in a moment, there are a number of specific evaluation methods all designed, one way or another, to structure the evaluator's responses. Most of these procedures stem from one of the following philosophies of measurement:

1. *Comparative judgment.* Individual performance is best judged relative to that of other individuals. This means that the standards used in evaluation are based directly upon group norms.

2. *Absolute judgment.* Individual performance is best judged against relatively fixed, independently determined standards. If these standards are in some way tied to group norms, the correspondence is established separately from the actual judgment process.

3. *Behavioral description.* Individual performance is best judged through careful observation of what people do rather than through on-the-spot *evaluation* of performance. Thus *evaluation* of behavioral items is carried out separately from the determination of whether or not the items actually *occur.*

Simply, then, the role of the evaluator or judge in the performance evaluation process is seen in the three philosophies as (1) that of making direct comparisons among employees, (2) that of judging individuals independently against fixed standards, and (3) that of describing relevant aspects of the performance itself. The specific manner in which these principles are implemented is the basis on which the various methods of performance evaluation are distinguished. We turn, therefore, to a brief consideration of these procedures.

Comparative Judgment Procedures

The principal comparative judgment methods are the *ranking* and *forced-distribution* procedures. A third, *paired-comparisons*, is too cumbersome for most practical purposes in that it requires every individual to be compared with every other individual in a pair-wise fashion (e.g., if 100 people were to be evaluated it would require 4,950 judgments). Moreover, the procedures for data analysis require a level of sophistication beyond the present book.[37] Thus we shall confine our attention to the other two methods.

Ranking, of course, requires that the evaluator merely rank all subordinates from best to worst. It may be done separately for different traits or on an overall basis. Either way it is a rather gross procedure that becomes progressively more cumbersome—and probably less accurate—as the number of people to be evaluated increases.

The *forced-distribution* procedure should be familiar to all readers who have been exposed sometime during their academic history to grading on a strict curve. Performance categories (letter grades, poor-fair-good-excellent categories, and so on) are determined in advance, and a fixed proportion of the people being evaluated are assigned to each category on the basis of comparative merit. Thus, for example, the top 10 percent might be judged excellent; the bottom 10 percent poor, irrespective of the absolute level of group performance. In essence, the forced-distribution procedure is just an extension of the ranking procedure in which points of demarcation are located on the rank scale to define preset categories.

The main argument for comparative judgment procedures is that they minimize the influence of evaluator biases such as *central-tendency* and *leniency* errors. However, as the number of people to be judged increases, the methods become increasingly cumbersome. As this happens, the evaluator is likely to do an increasingly less conscientious job of evaluation. Suppose, for example, a manager had only three individuals to rank order. The manager would probably spend considerably more time weighing their comparative merits than if they were part of a work group composed of 100 subordinates, all of whom had to be ranked.

Another problem specific to the forced-distribution approach is that it assumes the "true" criterion measures are normally distributed within the group being evaluted. While this may be true for the *population* from which the group is drawn, it is not necessarily so for the group itself. For example, consider a pool of 15 typists employed at United Widget. In the general *population* of typists, it could easily be that exactly 10 percent would qualify as outstanding Widget typists, 10 percent would be unsatisfactory, and so on, in accordance with the familiar bell-shaped curve. However, for any number of possible reasons, 10 of the 15 typists in the pool at any given time might be from the top 20 percent of the general population. Therefore, the forced distribution of evaluations would not correspond to the actual distribution of talent, and a large proportion of the typists would receive unfair ratings. This danger becomes more pronounced the fewer people there are to be evaluated and the less random the procedures are by which these people have been chosen from their respective populations.

Absolute Judgment Procedures

These methods generally take the form of one or another kind of structured *rating*. They are by far the most commonly used of the formal evaluation methods. In all such procedures, each individual is judged on some absolute scale or set of scales, as illustrated on the typical form in Figure 6–5. Theoretically, judgment of each aspect of performance should be independent of all the others, even if the aspects are to some extent interrelated themselves, and that of each individual should be independent of all the other individuals. As we saw in the insurance company example and in our discussion of context biases, however, it rarely works out that way. The structure may encourage independent judgments, but it certainly does not guarantee it. Halo effects, personal biases, context effects, central-tendency errors, and all the rest can still occur.

One might wonder, in view of all these difficulties, whether rating scales have any redeeming virtues at all—whether there are *any* conditions under which they might prove useful. While it would be difficult to give a categorical answer to these questions, a case has been made for seeking to rectify the faults rather than writing off ratings scales entirely. Numerous suggestions have been made of ways to improve the rating procedure. One possibility is to do a more systematic job of *training* potential users. Another is to *translate* vague, global scales (such as dependability) into a series of graded behavioral statements (such as "Could be expected to be late to work at least once every week"). A third approach involves *corrective procedures* of various kinds applied to the obtained scale values themselves. Techniques are available, for example, to help partial out some of the systematic rater biases such as leniency or central-tendency error. Still another possibility is to use *multiple raters* in the hope of improving reliability.

While the issue is certainly far from resolved, recent evidence does seem to indicate that the rating scale concept is a viable one, given that sufficient care is taken in its implementation. Campbell et al.,[38] for example, describe an approach to management evaluation based on the

FIGURE 6–5   Examples of Typical Rating Scales for Certain Rating Factors
(Multiple-Step Scales Usually Have Anywhere from Five to Nine Categories)

A. Graphic rating scale
(rater places check mark on scale)

Job knowledge

Exceptionally good	Above average	Average	Below average	Poor

B. Multiple-step rating scales
(rater marks one category)

Dependability

☐	☐	☐	☐	☐
Unsatisfactory Requires constant supervision to insure that directions are followed	Below average Requires considerable supervision. Does not always follow directions	Average Requires average or normal supervision	Above average Can usually be depended upon to complete assignments	Outstanding Needs virtually no supervision; completely reliable

Quantity of work

☐	☐	☐	☐	☐
Consistently exceeds job requirements	Frequently exceeds job requirements	Meets job requirements	Frequently below job requirements	Consistently below job requirements

Job knowledge

☐	☐	☐	☐	☐
Thorough knowledge	Knows his job well	Average	Below average	Unsatisfactory

SOURCE: McCormick, E. J., & Tiffin, J. (1974). *Industrial Psychology* (6th ed.), (p. 196). Englewood Cliffs, N.J.: Prentice-Hall. Copyright © 1974 by Prentice-Hall. Reprinted by permission.

"retranslation method" of Smith and Kendall,[39] which they feel has great promise. The essential difference between this and other rating scale approaches is that its scales are oriented toward critical behaviors rather than abstract dimensions or traits. The development of scales is an involved process that includes (1) collecting a large number of critical behaviors (incidents)—good and bad—associated with various jobs,

(2) organizing these incidents into labeled categories, (3) having a second group of knowledgable people assign the incidents to the labeled categories—the "retranslation" step—to see how good the original classification was, and (4) having a third group of people assign scale values to the surviving items in each category to serve as anchors or reference behaviors. The end result is thus a number of *behaviorally anchored rating scales* (BARS), which evaluators then use in making their assessments. An illustration of a BARS scale for the dimension *meeting day-to-day deadlines* is shown in Figure 6–6. Since the benchmarks are all expressed in very concrete, job-related terms, the evaluator can presumably rate performance quite objectively. We say *presumably* because some questions have been raised as to whether the modest increase in objectivity and precision is worth the effort.[40] Latham and Wexley, however, have developed a modified version of BARS, called (*behavioral observation scales* (BOS), which they claim overcomes most of the shortcomings in BARS.[41] This particular approach to ratings, incidentally, incorporates much of the behavioral description philosophy to which we now turn our attention.

Behavioral Description

Three techniques designed to yield actual description of the performance in question are the *forced choice, weighted checklist*, and *critical incident* methods.

Forced choice procedures and *weighted checklists* are the most highly structured techniques of all. Both are aimed at minimizing rater biases of all kinds by requiring the evaluator to focus on very specific attributes or items of behavior. The forced choice method is similar to the familiar multiple-choice testing procedure: The evaluator must choose from a set of descriptive adjectives or statements the one that best (or least) describes the behavior of the person being evaluated. A whole series of these multiple-choice items is usually presented, covering all aspects of the person's performance. Typically, the items are presented in blocks, or sets of alternatives, each member of which is equivalent to the others in *favorability* but different in its ability to *discriminate* on the dimension of interest. Suppose, for example, it had been established that people who were judged to be *excellent* supervisors were also said to show "personal interest" in their subordinates, while those judged *average* or lower were not. "Shows personal interest" would be a highly *discriminating* item for a forced-choice block to evaluate supervisors. Suppose, further, that "is very articulate" does not discriminate among good and poor supervisors. If it were also shown that "shows personal interest" and "is very articulate" are regarded by potential evaluators as desirable traits of roughly equivalent degree, the pair would constitute a good forced choice block. Put to use in a supervisor's effectiveness scale, an evaluator would

FIGURE 6–6   Department Manager Job Behavior Rating Scale for the Dimension
Meeting Day-to-Day Deadlines

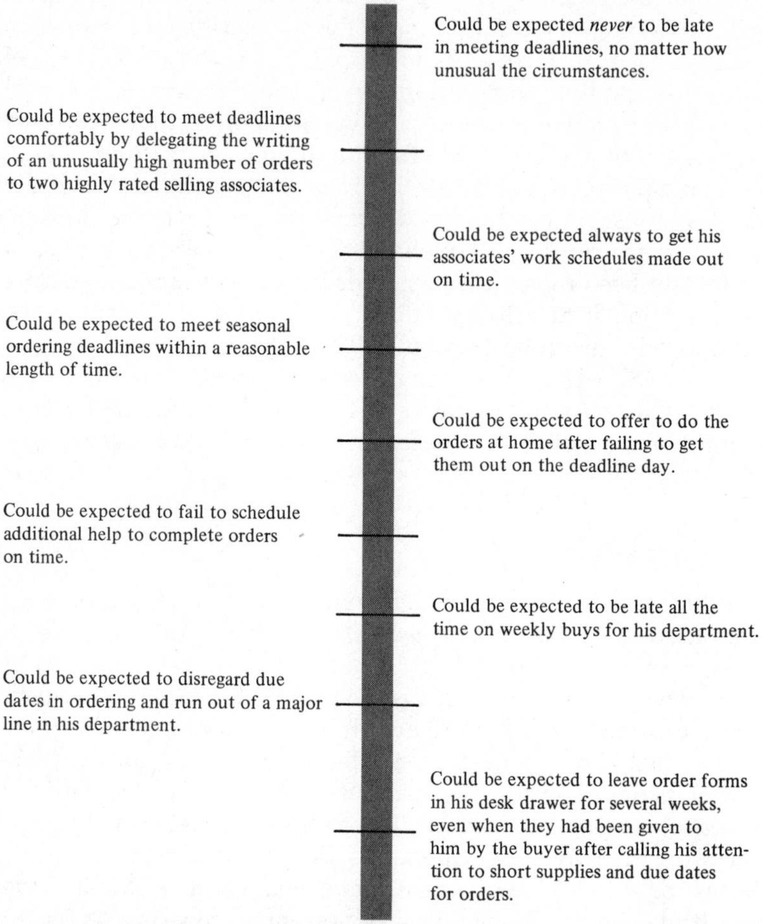

Could be expected *never* to be late
in meeting deadlines, no matter how
unusual the circumstances.

Could be expected to meet deadlines
comfortably by delegating the writing
of an unusually high number of orders
to two highly rated selling associates.

Could be expected always to get his
associates' work schedules made out
on time.

Could be expected to meet seasonal
ordering deadlines within a reasonable
length of time.

Could be expected to offer to do the
orders at home after failing to get
them out on the deadline day.

Could be expected to fail to schedule
additional help to complete orders
on time.

Could be expected to be late all the
time on weekly buys for his department.

Could be expected to disregard due
dates in ordering and run out of a major
line in his department.

Could be expected to leave order forms
in his desk drawer for several weeks,
even when they had been given to
him by the buyer after calling his attention to short supplies and due dates
for orders.

SOURCE: From Campbell, J. P., Dunnette, M. D., Lawler, E. E. III, & Weick, K. E. Jr. (1970). *Managerial behavior, performance, and effectiveness*, (p. 122). New York: McGraw-Hill.

produce a more positive rating of a supervisor if he or she checked "shows personal interest" than "is very articulate."

Obviously, a great deal of preliminary research must be undertaken to establish the *favorability* and *discriminability* of each item and to compose the blocks. The intended result of all this effort is an instrument that minimizes biases such as the halo effect (since the rater cannot guess which alternative is most favorable) while providing maximum sensitivity to *real* performance differences.

In the weighted checklist format, the descriptive items are simply listed and the evaluator checks any that apply. This approach was illustrated in the insurance company example given earlier (see Table 6–5). Like the forced choice method, the weighted checklist takes much of the actual *evaluative* process out of the rater's hands. Usually, as in the earlier example, each item is weighted according to its importance for the particular job, and computation of the overall evaluation is done automatically rather than by the rater personally. Thus, the rater who wishes to bias the result must know how much each descriptive statement contributes to the final score. This could probably be done to some extent, but it would be a lot more difficult than in the ranking or rating methods.

The main difficulty with both forced choice and weighted checklist methods is that a considerable amount of research is required to develop a good set of items and weight them properly. Obviously, if the items are poorly worded, fail to represent the job adequately, or fail to recognize the importance of critical behaviors, the final evaluation cannot hope to be accurate.

The *critical incident* approach has already received more than its share of description. In evaluation, the procedure is used as a structured method for recording what employees actually *do* that makes their performance above or below average. The supervisor simply keeps a record (usually on a daily or weekly basis) of specific instances of excellent or poor behavior observed in subordinates. Then, when it comes time for evaluation, the supervisor does not need to rely on memory or some general intuitive impression of how the individual performed. Obviously, such data can help the evaluator make an unbiased appraisal if so inclined. However, it would not be difficult to distort the records by selecting the incidents in accordance with personal biases. We are more likely, after all, to see the good and overlook the bad in people whom we have already decided are superior workers.

It might be well to close our discussion of performance evaluation with one important, if very general, observation. In and of themselves, *procedures*—structured or otherwise, good or poor—cannot ensure accurate, fair, or unbiased evaluation. All they can do is help the conscientious, fair-minded supervisor do a more accurate, a fairer, and a less biased job of evaluating people. If the supervisor is neither conscientious nor fair-minded, *no* subjective procedure has much chance of yielding an accurate appraisal. The emphasis in performance evaluation, therefore, should be upon educating the supervisor in the importance of conscientious performance evaluation, in the potential sources of bias, and in the procedures through which their effects can be minimized.[42] In other words, the supervisor's cooperation and enthusiastic support are essential to the success of any evaluation program. Since people tend to support what they help create, it would be well to include the supervisors themselves in the actual development of any comprehensive program. The reader will recognize this as one of the guiding principles in the insurance company example presented earlier.

CONCLUSIONS

Virtually every other aspect of personnel management and research is dependent upon adequate description of jobs and evaluation of performance. One cannot recruit, select, train, or counsel employees effectively unless he or she has a clear picture of each work role. Similarly, he or she cannot provide feedback, reinforce work outcome expectancies, or develop equitable reward systems unless there is a sound basis for distinguishing good from poor performance. The researcher cannot devise and test new ideas for selection, training, motivation, and the like unless he or she, too, has good work role descriptions and performance criteria.

Job description is generally accomplished through use of standard *classification systems* (e.g., the *DOT*), systematic *job analysis* procedures, or both. Of the various analytic procedures developed, the most useful seem to be based upon the concept of common dimensions that underlie all jobs. Description in dimensional terms allows meaningful comparisons and contrasts to be drawn among job and job classes. Foremost among these dimensional techniques is McCormick's approach, which is built around an instrument known as the PAQ. This device and its first cousin, the PMPQ, enable the analyst to describe any job in terms of the extent to which it exhibits, in his or her estimation, each of 190 plus behavioral elements.

One characteristic of jobs that is of considerable practical as well as theoretical interest is rate of pay. Although many external equity factors such as collective bargaining agreements, labor market conditions, and the general economy help to set pay scales, organizations should try to be as consistent as possible in salary administration. This follows from our previous discussion of motivation and satisfaction: Without a coherent compensation system it is difficult to create any realistic work reward expectancies or equity concepts in the minds of the employees. Coherence or internal equity can only be achieved through some form of systematic *job evaluation*. Available procedures include *ranking, classification, factor comparison,* and *point systems*. Of these, the two latter methods appear most consistent and free of bias in that they, like dimensional job analysis, are based upon characteristics shared by many jobs. Thus value is assigned to levels of common dimensions (strength, education, responsibility requirements, etc.) and *combined* to yield overall job worth, rather than being assigned directly to the job itself.

It also follows from various theories of motivation and job satisfaction that rewards should be based at least in part upon performance, a major component of individual equity. Unfortunately, there is little consensus on the appropriate *philosophy* for evaluating performance (whether it should be represented as one or many criteria), or on the proper kinds of *criteria* (objective or subjective), or on the ways in which these criteria should be measured. It is often argued that where they are accessible, objective measures of work input constitute the most defensible performance criteria. In all too many cases, however, such measures are not available, are incomplete, or are confounded with other factors over which the employee has no control. Thus even objective measures are subject to serious faults.

Subjective procedures are prone to a variety of well-established errors of human judgment (e.g., the halo effect, errors of central tendency, leniency). A number of techniques have been devised to help the evaluator combat these tendencies. Some are based on direct *comparison* of worker performance, some on absolute judgment with reference to *fixed standards*, still others on systematic description of work *behavior*. The most commonly used of these approaches are *ranking* procedures, *rating* scales, *weighted checklists, forced choice checklists*, and the *critical incident* technique. None guarantees bias-free evaluation of performance although, in the hands of the conscientious evaluator, the behavioral description methods (i.e., the last three above) seem capable of minimizing bias. They too, however, have their problems, the most notable of which is the substantial time and effort required for development of a good instrument.

Since one cannot rely exclusively on the measuring device to remove biases and distortions from subjective evaluation, every effort should be made to solicit the cooperation and support of the people who do the evaluating. They should be made aware of the importance of the evaluation process, apprised of the potential sources of error in their judgments, instructed carefully in the use of the evaluation instrument, and encouraged to participate in the development and evaluation of each step in the process.

NOTES

1. United States Training and Employment Service, (1972). *Dictionary of occupational titles* (4th ed.). Washington, D.C.: U.S. Government Printing Office.
2. Bernardin, H. J., & Beatty, R. W. (1984). *Performance appraisal: Assessing human behavior at work*. Belmont, Calif.: Kent.
3. McCormick, E. J., & Ilgen, D. (1980). *Industrial psychology*. Englewood Cliffs, N.J.: Prentice-Hall, is a good example; also Levine, E. L. (1983). *Everything you always wanted to know about job analysis*. Tampa: Mariner; also Bernardin & Beatty, *Performance appraisal*.
4. Levine, E. L., Ash, R. A., hall, H. L., & Sistrunk, F. (1981). *Evaluation of seven job analysis methods*. Law Enforcement Assistance Administration, Grant No. 79-DF-AX-0105.
5. Fine, S. A., & Wiley, W. W. (1974). An introduction to functional job analysis. In E. A. Fleishman & A. R. Bass (Eds.), *Studies in personal and industrial psychology*. Homewood, Ill.: Dorsey Press.
6. Morsh, J. E. (1964). Job analysis in the U.S. Air Force. *Personnel Psychology, 17,* 7–17; also Christal, R. E. (1974). The U.S. Air Force occupational research project. *JSAS Catalog of Selected Documents in Psychology, 4,* 61.
7. McCormick, E. J., Jeanneret, P. R., & Mecham, R. C. (1972). A study of job characteristics and job dimensions as based on the position analysis questionnaire (PAQ). *Journal of Applied Psychology Monograph, 56,* 347–86.

8. Fleishman, E. A., & Hogan J. C. (1978). *A taxonomic method for assessing the physical requirements of jobs.* Technical Report. Washington, D.C.: Advanced Research Resources Organization; also Fleishman, E. H., & Quaintance, M. K. (1984). *Taxonomies of human performance.* New York: Academic Press.

9. Zedeck, S., & Cascio, W. F. (1984). Psychological issues on personnel decisions. *Annual Review of Psychology, 35,* 461–518.

10. Rousseau, D. M. (1982). Job perceptions when working with data, people, and things. *Journal of Occupational Psychology, 55,* 43–52.

11. Christal. U.S. Air Force occupational research project.

12. Available from the University Book Store, West Lafayette, Indiana 47906.

13. McCormick, Jeanneret, & Mecham. A study of job characteristics and job dimensions as based on the Position Analysis Questionnaire (PAQ), 347–386.

14. For example: PAQ Services, Inc., P.O. Box 3337, Logan, Utah 84321.

15. Cornelius, E. T., DeNisi, A. S., & Blencoe, A. G. (1984). Expert and naive raters using the PAQ: Does it matter? *Personnel Psychology, 37,* 453–464; also Harvey, R. J., & Hayes, T. L. (1986). *Monte Carlo baselines for interrater reliability correlations using the position analysis questionnaire.* Rice University Technical Report, Houston, TX., January, 1985.

16. Mitchell, J. L., & McCormick, E. J. (1979). *Development of the PMPQ: A structural job analysis questionnaire for the study of professional and managerial positions.* PPMQ Report No. 1. Lafayette: Purdue University Department of Psychological Sciences.

17. Fleishman & Quaintance, *Taxonomies of human performance.*

18. Fleishman & Hogan. *Taxonomic method.*

19. Hogan, J. C., & Fleishman, E. A. (1979). An index of the physical effort required in human task performance. *Journal of Applied Psychology, 64,* 197–204.

20. Reilly, R. R., Zedeck, S., & Tenopyr, M. L. (1979). Validity and fairness of physical ability tests for predicting performance in craft jobs. *Journal of Applied Psychology, 64,* 262–274.

21. Wallace, M. J., Jr., & Fay, C. H. (1983). *Compensation theory and practice.* Belmont, Calif.: Kent.

22. Bass, B. M., & Barrett, G. V. (1972). *Man, work, and organizations.* Boston: Allyn & Bacon.

23. Ibid., p. 144.

24. Peres, H. (1962). Performance dimensions of supervisory positions. *Personnel Psychology, 15,* 405–10.

25. It should be noted that some studies have found that weighting items for specific jobs adds little to the usefulness of the evaluation system when it is actually implemented. The authors believe, however, that a critical consideration is the homogeneity of the job population.

26. Latham, G. P., & Wexley, K. N. (1982). *Increasing productivity through performance appraisal.* Reading, Mass.: Addison-Wesley Publishing.

27. Bass & Barrett. *Man, work and the organization.*

28. Landy, F. J. (1985). *Psychology of work behavior.* Homewood, Ill.: Dorsey Press; also Saal, F. E., Downey, R. G., & Lakey, M. A. (1980). Rating the ratings: Assessing the psychometric quality of rating data. *Psychological Bulletin, 88,* 413–428.

29. Bernardin & Beatty. *Performance appraisal;* also Zedeck & Cascio, Psychological issues in personnel decisions.

30. Saal, Downey, & Lakey. Rating the ratings.

31. Cooper, W. H. (1981). Ubiquitous halo. *Psychological Bulletin, 90,* 218–244.

32. Zedeck & Cascio. Psychological issues.

33. Cambell, J. P., Dunnette, M. D., Lawler, E. E., III, & Weick, K. E., Jr. (1970). *Managerial behavior, performance, and effectiveness.* New York: McGraw-Hill; also Holzbach, R. L. (1978). Rater bias in performance ratings: Superior, self, and peer ratings. *Journal of Applied Psychology, 63,* 579–88.

34. Wherry, R. J., & Fryer, D. H. (1949). Buddy ratings: Popularity contest or leadership criterion? *Personnel Psychology, 2,* 147–59.

35. Latham & Wexley. *Increasing productivity.*

36. See, for example, Henderson, R. (1980). *Performance appraisal: Theory to practice.* Reston, Va.: Reston Publishing; also Bernardin & Beatty, *Performance appraisal.*

37. The interested reader should consult Nunnally, J. C. (1978). *Psychometric theory* (2d ed.). New York: McGraw-Hill.

38. Campbell et al. *Managerial behavior, performance, and effectiveness.*

39. Smith, P. C., & Kendall, L. M. (1963). Retranslation of expectation. *Journal of Applied Psychology, 47,* 149–55.

40. Schwab, D. P., & Heneman, H. G. III. (1975). Behaviorally anchored rating scales: A review of the literature. *Personnel Psychology, 28,* 549–562.

41. Latham & Wexley. *Increasing productivity.*

42. Beer, M. (1981). Performance appraisal: Dilemmas and possibilities. *Organizational Dynamics,* Spring, 24–36.

7

Attraction, Selection, and Placement

At the very beginning of the book we distinguished two main perspectives on human behavior: one concerned with *general characteristics,* the other with *individual differences.* Most of the material presented thus far clearly belongs in the former category. We have sought to understand how people or organizations in *general* function. It is now time to turn our attention to the other approach and consider how people *differ* from one another. While the individual difference perspective has implications for many—if not all—organizational functions, its major impact has been felt in the area of selection and placement. How are decisions made through which specific people assume specific roles in specific organizations? And from a practical standpoint, how can these decisions be optimized?

BACKGROUND

Individual Choice and Recruiting

The traditional way of looking at the selection and placement functions has been exclusively from the standpoint of the *organization;* i.e., how does management get the right people into the right jobs? The assumption is that there are a number of people available for every job, some are better qualified than others, and the trick is to recruit, select, and place the best of the lot in each position. As we shall see later in the chapter, there are a number of problems with this simple logic even when the assumption of favorable labor market conditions does, in fact, hold. Often, of course, it does not. Even more important, how many people are available for any particular job is in large measure determined by the organization's success in making the position attractive—irrespective of the general labor market and trends in job or career preferences.

For these and many other reasons, a strictly organizational viewpoint offers an incomplete account of how people are—or could be—selected and placed. For the last decade or so, psychologists and managers alike have been forced to realize that the selection process is a two-way street.[1] People are not just grist for the organizational selection mill. They too have preferences, gather information, form opinions, and make decisions designed to achieve their employment goals.

Compared to what we can say about the employer's side of the process, however, our discussion of the individual's approach to the employment decision and of its implications for recruitment is necessarily limited. The handful of available studies has been reviewed by Wanous[2] with respect to three main issues: (1) how individuals come to prefer or choose particular organizations, (2) how accurate the information is on which they base such choices, and (3) what role recruiting practices play in these decisions and in their consequences. Most of the studies were limited in that they involved relatively small samples of college-educated people who were making their first real entry into the job market. Moreover, they differed widely in the behavior measured and theoretical issues addressed. Some were concerned chiefly with the cognitive processes responsible for the perceived attractiveness of organizations; others focused on the effort to enter, or actual choice among organizations; a few even considered what happened to the perceptions or behavior of individuals after they were hired.

Obviously, one cannot draw very firm conclusions on the basis of such limited and diverse research efforts. Still, a few promising generalizations seem to be emerging. From a theoretical standpoint, contrasting views have held that the decision to join a particular organization is either an unprogrammed one based upon the rather impulsive consideration of only a few dominant factors, or a rational, comprehensive one involving the systematic integration of all valued factors. The distinction is much the same as that between people as "satisficers" and as expectancy-valence aggregators (VIE theory), which we encountered in earlier chapters.

In the present context, the evidence tends to support the more rational-comprehensive view. The typical study involves ratings by graduating college or professional students of the likelihood (*expectancy*) that particular organizations or jobs will provide specified attractiveness factors (starting salaries, advancement opportunities, etc.) and of the personal importance (*valence*) attached to each. Some form of VIE model is then used to integrate these factor estimates into an overall attractiveness score for each organization as considered by each student. Finally, depending upon the study's objective, the attractiveness estimates are used to predict expressed organizational preferences, effort to enter, or actual choice of employment, usually by means of correlation indexes or the proportions of choices forecast accurately by the model.

Several studies of this sort have produced organizational choice predictions of around 80 percent accuracy: Students wound up choosing employers consistent with their combined valence-expectancy estimates 8 times out of 10. Of course, we cannot know how much better the prediction was than would have occurred with unprogrammed or other strategies, since none of the studies involved such direct comparisons. Further, the predictions of overall preferences and effort spent to enter particular organizations was not nearly as accurate as for actual choice behavior. Still, it would appear that the participants in these studies considered a number of factors before reaching their decisions. Whether prospective blue-collar workers or experienced employees are as rational in their approach to organizational entry as these college graduates is a moot question.

Of somewhat greater practical significance are studies concerned with the individual's pre- and postemployment perceptions. How accurate is the information on which choices are based, and what happens if reality fails to live up to prior expectations? A consistent finding is that, save for very concrete extrinsic factors such as pay and working hours, prospective employees hold unrealistically high expectations of the organizations to which they seek entry.[3] This distortion may be particularly high for disadvantaged and/or minority group applicants. Thus it is not surprising that, just as consistently, postentry attitudes toward the organization and general levels of work satisfaction decline markedly over the months and years following employment. It seems that in forming inflated expectations individuals set themselves up for disappointment.

Self-delusion, however, is only part of the story. Organizations do much to reinforce the optimism of those they are seeking to attract through recruiting practices that provide selected, slanted, or downright dishonest information. Consider, for example, the military recruiting materials that one encounters daily on billboards, in magazines, and in radio and television commercials. One would scarcely suspect from this information that military organizations exist for the purpose of fighting wars, or that the job entails killing people and risking one's own life if the occasion so demands. Little is said about the rigors of basic training, the intellectual level of one's probable cohorts, or the limitations on one's personal freedoms. Instead we see bright, energetic people learning new skills and traveling to exotic places.

Recruiting practices have traditionally sought to present the organization in its most favorable light with the idea of maximizing the available pool of talent or attracting the best candidates. What this strategy fails to consider is the potential impact of heightened expectations on the satisfaction and retention of those ultimately hired. Disillusionment resulting in poor morale and high turnover could easily offset whatever improvement the recruiting strategy brought about in the quality of hirees. On the other hand, there is always the fear that too much realism in recruiting—particularly where competitors are not so candid—could be disastrous: Our volunteer army might not survive a recruiting campaign featuring Vietnam war pictures and interviews with disabled veterans. Keeping them and satisfying them becomes rather trivial if you can't attract them in the first place.

What then is an appropriate strategy? While the evidence is still sparse, a growing body of research data suggests that the long-run benefits of realistic job information may outweigh the short-run advantages of biased recruiting. Several studies have indicated that providing prospective or newly hired employees with realistic job previews reduces their expectations in the specific areas described, with consequent improvement in their work attitudes.[4] And, even more important, it increases their survival rates.[5] Surprisingly, the realism does not seem to hurt recruiting efforts seriously, although it was reported in two studies to have increased the rate at which offers were refused.[6] In others, however, the refusal rate remained the same or actually declined. All things considered, then, the fears surrounding realistic recruiting do not appear justified, whereas the promise of reductions in false expectations, disillusionment, and turnover seems very real. Most organizations would be well advised to review their recruiting strategies.[7]

We are still, of course, a long way from completely understanding how people go about making job choices and why they prefer one organization or another. In a sense, the problem is a special case in human motivation, a topic that we found earlier to be quite complicated. The factors that drive people to seek employment and guide their selection processes are undoubtedly just as complex as those involved in choosing a level of work effort. Be that as it may, one aspect of the organizational entry problem stands out as a persistent, important, and unresolved practical difficulty: People tend to enter jobs with unrealistic expectations based on incomplete or inaccurate information. Part of the problem, we have seen, lies in misleading recruiting strategies. But that is probably not the whole story. Much needs to be learned about where—and how readily—the information necessary to make reasoned job decisions is available (if, indeed, it is available at all). Where does the responsibility lie for providing this information? With government? Our educational systems? The business community? Do prospective employees distort the facts, even when they are available, to fit their own personal stereotypes or needs? If so, should job and career counseling pay more attention to decision processes than to detailed job descriptions? The problems associated with inflated expectations and poor entry decisions require that more effort be directed toward answering questions such as these.

Individual Differences and Personnel Decisions

It is apparent that while there are great similarities among people, there are great differences among individuals on almost any personal characteristic one might care to name. Some, such as weight and height, are easily observed and measured. No one questions their existence or the fact that people differ on them. Others, such as skills, intelligence, motivation, aptitudes, and the like, are more controversial. They are not directly observable and are often extremely difficult to measure. Psychologists with an individual difference orientation assume that people differ on these behavioral or cognitive traits much as they do on the easily observed physical ones. In most cases, this means that if one were to measure a large number of people on a particular trait (height, mechanical aptitude, or whatever), a few would score very low, a few would score very high, and the rest would be distributed around the middle. The resulting frequency distribution would approximate the familiar bell-shaped curve illustrated in Figure 7–1. It is generally assumed that such measures (hence each person's relative standing on the bell curve for that trait) are fairly stable. Were this not the case, there would be little point in trying to use individual differences as a basis for selection or placement: The best person for a particular job today might be the very worst person tomorrow. How stable some of these traits are—how much people can improve their relative standings—is an age-old issue that may well never be completely resolved. The reason is that it has implications for such socially volatile questions as whether race and sex differences in various abilities (notably intelligence) are genetic or acquired.[8] The religious fervor with which this argument has been joined, even by supposedly objective scientists, plus the difficulty of obtaining incontrovertible evidence for either position forces this pessimistic outlook. It is important, however, to divorce the question of stability from that of causation. Whether for reasons of heredity, early experience, social disadvantage, nutrition, or whatever, the evidence strongly supports the assumption that many trait measures remain quite stable over extended portions of a person's adult life. From a practical standpoint, this means that such measures are potentially useful for selection and placement.

A final assumption underlying the individual difference approach to selection and placement is that if people differ reliably on any trait we should be able to *measure* these differences. Naturally we cannot measure psychological ones directly; only through their manifestations in behavior or verbal report. For example, we infer that person A is higher in numerical aptitude than person B either by comparing their performance on a standard set of number problems or by asking them a standard set of questions about their experience with numbers (grades in mathematics courses, interest in working with numbers, etc.).

We assume, then, that individuals differ in a relatively stable manner on a lot of basic traits and that these differences are measurable. The reader will recall that we reached much the same conclusion about jobs: Each has its own configuration of basic requirements. The classic problem in organizational selection and placement is to decide which of the available people to hire and into what jobs to put them.

FIGURE 7–1   A Normal Distribution of Scores on a Hypothetical Trait

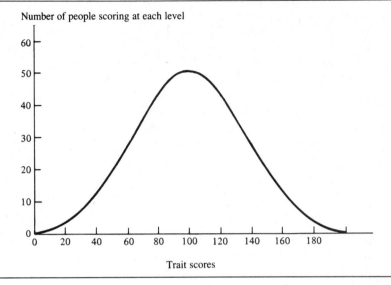

Number of people scoring at each level

Trait scores

At first glance, it probably seems that a good person-job fit is the *only* plausible rationale for hiring people, and were we blessed with trait measurements of unquestioned accuracy and a world without prejudice or disadvantage, that would undoubtedly be so. Unfortunately, we have not found utopia. Our instruments are not perfect, and they have not always been used fairly. Achieving a best fit from the employer's standpoint can mean excluding from employment disproportionate numbers of minority group, female, and older workers. And many of those so excluded may be little, if any, less promising than those hired. Thus considerations such as the fairness and social consequences of employment decisions have been added to the list of selection objectives, at times in direct conflict with the best-fit objective.

In the next section, we shall deal with the selection and placement topic from the traditional standpoint of the organization, that is, as though the best-fit objective were the only consideration. Then, in the following section, we shall broaden our perspective to include the other considerations, with the concept of *fairness* serving as the vehicle for discussion.

TRADITIONAL CONCEPTS

Selection and Placement

There are essentially two ways to match people and jobs on the basis of individual difference measures. Although similar in many respects, they differ considerably in philosophy. *Selection* represents a *job-centered* philosophy; *placement,* a *person-centered* philosophy. That is, in selection we start with the job requirements. We try to find the person who best fits them from among those who apply, hire that person, and reject everyone else. In placement, we start with the people whom we have already hired or intend to hire. We survey their traits, look at the available jobs, and try to arrive at the best match *given these people and these jobs.*

The difference between these philosophies is not at all trivial. For example, one (selection) implies that job characteristics are relatively fixed; hence we should try to hire people who possess a specific mix of traits. The other (placement) suggests that we might choose people on the basis of more general considerations and still achieve a good person-job fit. Perhaps a good illustration of this distinction is found in the drafting of professional football players. Some coaches consistently seek specialists who can fill *existing positions* (such as drop-back quarterbacks and wide receivers). Others consistently opt for superior athletes on the assumption that they can be placed effectively *somewhere.* There are times, of course, when placement is the only possible approach as, for example, when the number of applicants is equal to or less than the number of positions to be filled.

Despite these and other important differences, most of the material in the chapter applies to both selection and placement. Because it is a little simpler from the conceptual standpoint, we shall focus on the selection process.

Conceptual Basis of Selection

One attempts to predict how a person will behave or perform in the future on the basis of information available in the present. The predictive information is usually some sample of present or past behavior: test scores, interview responses, work history, and so on. As we said earlier, it is typically assumed that individual differences on such behavior samples reflect relatively stable *trait* differences. A person scores high on a manual dexterity test (behavior sample) in part, at least, because he or she possesses a lot of something called *manual dexterity* (a trait). If this trait is also important for some particular job, say that of widget assembler, then knowing the person's manual dexterity score should help in predicting success in assembling widgets. Of course, job performance usually depends on far more than a single trait. Just because a person is *capable* of assembling widgets rapidly doesn't necessarily mean that he or she *will.* The person may lack motivation, for example, or may tend to be extremely careless. The more of thse traits we can identify and measure, the better should be our prediction.

Prediction, then, depends to a great extent upon our ability to identify and measure relevant traits. As we just saw, traits are not actually measured directly but are *inferred* from behavior samples. Therefore, if we hope to do a better job of selecting people than we could do by chance, we must consider explicitly or implicitly at least three classes of information: (1) behavior samples, which are known as *predictors* (e.g., test scores, work histories); (2) *traits,* which the predictors are presumed to tap (e.g., manual dexterity, intelligence); and (3) *job specifications,* which we hope to match up with the traits. If we are successful in achieving a good match, the chances are the people selected will do well on the job. We can never really know this, however, unless we obtain one more class of information: (4) *criterion* measures of the sort discussed in the last chapter (for example, performance evaluation and job satisfaction data). In fact, it is best if we measure how well people perform at several different points in time after their selection. The reason is that criterion scores have been shown to change a great deal in some jobs over at least the first few months of employment.[9] Thus someone may perform very well relative to others after a few weeks but very poorly later on.

Most so-called selection *models* or strategies are described and evaluated in terms of relationships that exist among these four classes of information. As illustrated in Figure 7–2, predictors and criterion measures are the behavioral endpoints of the selection process. We use the former to predict the latter. The bracketed items (traits and job requirements) are somewhat theoretical intervening aspects of the process that help us conceptualize what we are doing when we relate predictors and criteria. The manual dexterity test predicts widget assembly performance, we theorize, because the job of widget assembler involves fine manual operations for which the trait of dexterity is relevant.

Not every selection strategy makes use of all four categories of information to the same extent. Some concentrate almost exclusively on the behavioral endpoints; others focus on traits. To illustrate how strategies may vary in this regard we shall contrast two extreme cases, which, for expository convenience, we shall label the *actuarial* and *diagnostic* approaches.

Actuarial Approach

One strategy for selection in effect does away with the bracketed terms in Figure 7–2. It is possible to develop a rather impressive selection procedure on a strictly empirical basis without regard for traits or job requirements. All one needs to do is start with a large pool of potentially predictive items (e.g., test questions), find out which ones do in fact distinguish between people who do well and poorly on the job, keep those items, and discard all the rest.[10] The result is a selection device (e.g., a test) that can pick with some degree of precision who will succeed and who will fail but without offering any inkling as to the reasons why.

There are several very serious difficulties with this approach.[11] From

FIGURE 7–2 A Summary of the Four Major Classes of Components Involved
in the Selection Process

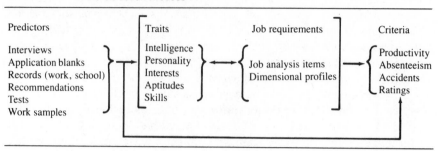

a practical standpoint, it can be very costly and time consuming. For example, it is often necessary to go through a huge number of items, people, and repetitions in order to arrive at a good set of predictors. Further, any change in the job or the people applying for it can destroy the predictiveness of the device. Since we don't know *why* it is predictive, we have no way of estimating the conditions under which its predictiveness might change. We are obliged, therefore, to keep repeating our empirical evaluation. Finally, the actuarial approach can obscure unfair and illegal discriminatory practices. If, for example, an organization were hostile toward certain racial groups, any item associated with a person's ethnic background (such as "What foods do you prefer?") would likely be predictive of success. Since there would be no indication *why* the item was predictive, a highly discriminatory practice would appear in the guise of a benign — even laudable — objective selection procedure.

There are other grounds on which to condemn strict actuarial prediction that are of a more technical nature. We need not go into them here. Suffice it to say that there is good reason to be dubious of this approach.

Diagnostic Approach

The alternative strategy uses all the information in Figure 7–2. Predictors are developed on the basis of trait and job requirement considerations even if their value is ultimately established in terms of criterion measures. That is, we start with a job analysis and then proceed to develop a theory regarding what traits are most important based on this analysis. We next devise predictors to tap these traits and only then compare predictor scores with measures of criterion performance. In this way, we test both our predictors and our theory.

Clearly, diagnostic selection depends on several relationships rather than just one. Besides the predictor-criterion linkage involved in actuarial prediction, we must worry about how the predictors relate to the traits, how the traits relate to the job, and how the job characteristics are represented in the criteria. Errors can occur at each of these points as well as in the measurement operations themselves. That is, we might fail to select the best people because (1) we have unreliable measures of predictors and/or criteria, (2) our job description is inaccurate, (3) our predictors fail to measure the traits we think they do, (4) the traits we consider important for the job aren't—or some we have neglected are, or (5) our criteria do not adequately represent what people are supposed to do on the job. Not only can such errors reduce the effectiveness of selection, they can fool us into thinking that our selection process is either better or worse than it really is. For example, we might actually be doing a good job of selection and not realize it because of deficiencies in our criterion. Or, we might be doing a very poor job of it even though we seem to be measuring important traits with some precision.

The point is, effective selection is not just a matter of *predictor* qualities. It requires in addition that we have good job descriptions, a good theory as to relevant traits, good evidence that our predictors measure these traits, and good criteria. Indeed, it makes no sense to speak of a good *predictor* without considering what the predictor is good *for*. Obvious though it may seem, this point is all too often either ignored or misunderstood. People involved in selection often speak of the "excellent test battery" or the "highly effective interview format" they are using, as though the worth of such predictors were a purely intrinsic matter. Predictors must be good for an explicit *something* (a specific trait, a specific job criterion) or they are most assuredly good for nothing.

Evaluating Selection Procedures

By what logic, then, do we declare a selection procedure good or poor? It should be obvious from the foregoing discussion that there are several answers to this question. Each of the potential sources of error is a potential source of evaluative information. Consider the following illustration. We wish to hire some new widget assemblers (the incumbents having left in protest over their overexposure in the foregoing pages). We decide that the fine *manipulative movements* required by the job constitute the chief determinant of success, that *manual dexterity* is the key trait, and that the tweezer manipulation test is a good index of this trait. Our criterion is the *number of widgets assembled* per day after 90 days on the job.

A complete evaluation of this procedure would require that we satisfy ourselves on at least the following points: (1) that the tweezer test does, in fact, measure dexterity—hence we are really measuring the trait or *construct* of interest; (2) that the dexterity construct does, in fact, cover most of the important *content* of the job—that is, widget assemblers do little more than make fine manipulative movements; (3) that rate of production is, in fact, a true representation of the assembler's worth in that job; (4) that people who score high on the tweezer test maintain higher production rates than people who score low—that is, the tweezer test *predicts* performance; and (5) that tweezer scores and production-rate figures are reliable—that is, a person's "reading" on them tends to remain the same.

It is easier to satisfy some of the above requirements than others. Statistical techniques have been devised to estimate the *reliability* of predictors and criteria, (5 above), as well as *predictive validity* (4 above) and—more indirectly—the *construct validity* (1 above) of predictors. *Content validity* (2 above) and *criterion relevance* (3 above) can only be appraised on logical grounds. Before becoming overly distressed by this barrage of new terms, the reader should recognize that all we are really saying is that evaluation is a matter of establishing various kinds of *validity* and *reliability* for the selection procedures. We proceed now to discuss these concepts.

Reliability

Reliability refers to consistency in measurement. We say that a procedure for measuring something is *reliable* to the extent that it yields the same reading each time it is applied to the same thing. Put another way, it is the extent to which measurements are free from capricious fluctuation (or random error). For example, we could probably measure the length of a room more *reliably* (with less variability) using a yardstick than by pacing it off.

When we try to measure a trait, it is reasonable to assume that part of the obtained score represents the amount of the trait present at that moment and part is due to other factors. Suppose we were to give a student 25 arithmetic problems and she got 80 percent of them right. Her true capability for solving problems might be at the 90 percent level. The fact that her score was only 80 could have been due to (1) distraction in the test situation, (2) lack of sleep the night before, (3) an unusually hard sample of problems, (4) failure to practice on similar problems before the test, or any of a number of other extraneous factors. In combination, these other factors are responsible for the capricious fluctuation in our measures—they constitute the error component. The greater the contribution of these extraneous factors to the total score, the greater the unreliability of the trait measurement.

It is not possible, of course, to separate the true trait component from the error component of a single score. We can only estimate their relative contribution statistically by taking the same measurement more than once and comparing the results. The usual way this is done in estimating reliability is to take two presumably comparable measurements from each of a large number of people. We might, for example, give our 25-problem arithmetic test to 100 students and then follow it up with another 25-problem test of similar items. To the extent that the students' relative standing on the two tests remained the same (those who scored high on the first scored high on the second; low on the first, low on the second, etc.), we would conclude that our measurement instrument was reliable. A statistic that is commonly used to summarize the degree of correspondence is known as the *correlation coefficient* (*r*). It can assume values from 0.0 (indicating no correspondence at all) to 1.0 (indicating perfect agreement between the two sets of scores). We shall discuss correlation more fully later on.

There are several common ways to estimate reliability, all of which involve taking two measures from the same people and correlating the results. They differ, in a *logical* sense, with respect to which extraneous factors wind up in the overall reliability estimate as part of the error component. In a *procedural* sense, they differ in terms of what items are included in the first and second measurements, and whether or not the two measurements are taken at the same time.

1. Test-Retest Method. Exactly the same measurement instrument (test) is given twice to the same people, either in immediate succession (*immediate test-retest*) or separated by a time interval (*delayed test-retest*). Whatever changes occur in the people or the test situation between the first and second administration will show up in the error estimate. Peculiarities in the instrument itself, such as a lot of unusually hard items, will contribute (erroneously) to the "true" score component since they will be present equally on both administrations. The immediate test-retest method generally produces the highest estimate of reliability, since virtually everything present during the first administration is also present during the second. Thus few extraneous factors have a chance to operate. Of course, since people may *remember* how they responded the first time, this estimate is probably unrealistically high. The test-retest estimate is often referred to as the *coefficient of stability*.

2. Subsample Methods. Several techniques involve a *single* administration of the measurement instrument. Part of the items (the first half; every other one) are used to compute one measure for each person tested; the rest are used to compute the other. Thus we have *split-half* and *odd-even* methods in which scores on two subsamples of the same instrument are correlated. Another technique in this category (*item reliability*) involves correlating performance on *each item* with the overall test scores. One would consider most reliable those items that distinguish between good and poor performers on the overall test. Since all these methods are aimed at estimating how consistent the instrument is in what it measures (i.e., the extent to which various parts measure the same thing), the resulting index is often referred to as the *coefficient of internal consistency*. Naturally, all extraneous factors associated with the people or test situation will show up as "true" score rather than error since they would all be present equally on both subsamples (i.e., a person who was tired or distracted on the odd items would be just as tired or distracted on the even ones). Variations in item content, however, show up in the error component and reduce the estimated reliability.

3. Parallel Forms Method. The third principal method derives from a combination of the considerations involved in the first two. Like the subsample approach, different sets of presumably comparable items enter into the two measures. Like the test-retest approach, the two constitute full-length sequential measurement instruments that can be administered on either an *immediate* or *delayed* basis. The delayed parallel forms procedure probably yields the most realistic estimate of reliability in that virtually all the extraneous factors contribute to the error component as they should. This means, of course, that the *coefficient of equivalence,* as it is called, tends to be lower than the others.

It is important to appreciate these different ways of estimating reliability, particularly when the measuring instrument of concern is a standardized, marketed test. The test user should always obtain from the publisher information regarding the manner in which reliability was established. Since those who market tests often like to present their wares in as favorable a light as possible, the published reliability figures may turn out to be based on immediate test-retest procedures. The reader will recognize that such estimates ignore many potential sources of error.

Validity

If reliability refers to how well a procedure *measures,* validity refers to how well it measures *what it is supposed to measure.* Obviously, if it is a poor measuring instrument (unreliable, in other words), it cannot measure *anything* well. No procedure can be valid unless it is reliable. It can, however, be reliable (measure *something* consistently) but not valid for the intended purpose (what it measures well is irrelevant). We might, for example, measure people's height very reliably with a ruler. If, however, we were interested in assessing manual dexterity or predicting job performance, our reliable ruler measurements would be of little use—they would be *invalid* for these purposes.

As we saw a moment ago, the concept of validity is applicable at several points in the selection process. In practice, however, it is generally reserved for relationships involving *predictors* (see Figure 7–2). Each of these relationships represents a different measurement objective; hence each involves a somewhat different kind of validity. A predictor's *construct validity* refers to how well it measures the traits (e.g., manual dexterity, intelligence) it is supposed to measure. Its *content validity* refers to its *representativeness* as a behavior sample. Does it, for example, cover all aspects of the job for which it is being used to select people? Obviously, a good job analysis is important for establishing content validity.

Predictive validity and concurrent validity both involve the relationship between predictors and criteria. *Predictive validity* refers to how well the predictor forecasts criterion measures (job performance, satisfaction, etc.). Do applicants who score high on the predictor actually turn out better on the job? *Concurrent validity* refers to the correspondence of predictor and criterion scores for job *incumbents* rather than *applicants*. Do incumbents who score high on the predictor also do better on the job?

A final validity concept, that of *face validity,* refers to the predictor's appearance. A predictor (or selection procedure) has face validity to the extent that it *looks* as if it measures what it purports to measure. A common typing test, for example, has high face validity as a measure of one's ability to use a typewriter. In fact, any such *job-sample* test has high face validity. By way of contrast, many personality tests disguise what they are trying to measure in order to prevent people taking them from intentionally misrepresenting themselves. Such tests have very low face validity. In the case of personnel selection, there is usually little difference between the face validity of a procedure and its content validity. If a sample of behavior is representative of tasks involved in some particular job, it will usually look relevant for that job.

Since it is a purely subjective concept, face validity has never been considered very important for selection. Naturally, it is far more important for a predictor actually to *measure* what it is supposed to rather than to *look* as if it does. Face validity is clearly no substitute for the other kinds. It can be important, however, in one respect. Face validity can have a considerable impact on the manner in which applicants approach the selection process. If they consider the predictor irrelevant, as they probably will if it has low face validity, they may view the whole process as unfair or capricious. Therefore they may put forth little effort to do well, believing the situation to be hopeless. This is particularly likely if the applicants are already apprehensive about seeking employment. Minority group members and people with little education or employment experience tend to approach the whole situation with a mixture of fear, suspicion, and anxiety. The more straightforward and understandable the selection procedure is, the more comfortable the applicants will feel and the more likely they will be to behave normally. Thus, while face validity cannot substitute for predictive validity, it can contribute indirectly to the predictive worth of a selection procedure. It is an important aspect of selection from the employee's vantage point.[12]

The fact that validity is defined in so many conceptually distinct ways has led to a great deal of confusion and misunderstanding, particularly among those charged with formulating, enforcing, or simply trying to abide by fair employment legislation (a topic considered later in this chapter). If fairness requires valid hiring and promotion practices, then it would be nice to have some unequivocal rule for deciding what is and isn't valid. That psychologists have failed to produce such a rule is obvious because no single evaluative procedure could cover all the facets of validity that we have just examined.

It has recently been suggested that part of the confusion stems from the implication that we are dealing with alternative *kinds* of validity, and that some kinds are inherently better than others. A more appropriate way to look at it is that validity refers to the *meaning* that one can safely attribute to a set of measures.[13] And meaning obviously depends upon the context within which the measures are to be used: An intelligence test can have meaning purely as an index of some general intellectual trait or as a predictor for the selection of managers. Different methods are required to establish its meaning (or validity) in these different contexts. It makes no more sense to consider one kind of validity superior to another than it does to claim that a chain saw is superior to a paring knife.

Validity Measurement

Viewed in the above manner, each validity concept implies a somewhat different approach to measurement. *Face validity,* of course, is typically not measured at all. It could be, perhaps, by pooling the judgment of experts using some sort of rating procedure, but to the authors' knowledge this has not been done.

Content Validity

This is established logically rather than quantitatively. One simply attempts to spell out the correspondence between elements of the job (usually drawn from the job analysis) and elements of the predictors. Naturally, the more comprehensive and explicit the analyses, the more meaningful can be the expression of content validity. Ideally, one might be able to indicate the proportion of job elements represented in the predictor set.

Construct Validity

Since it involves relationships between predictors and unobservable *traits,* construct validity can only be established indirectly. One procedure relies upon the method of factor analysis (see Chapter 3), which, it will be recalled, permits us to describe any large set of complex measures in terms of a smaller set of underlying dimensions or factors. If we factor analyze a large set of predictor scores, then we can regard the resulting factors as indicative of basic traits measured by the predictors. Loadings of predictors on these factors (correlations between predictors and underlying factors yielded by the factor analysis) indicate the extent to which each predictor is related to each trait construct. In other words, the factor analysis procedure provides estimates both of what the traits are and how closely the predictors relate to them.

Criterion-Related Validity

Estimation of criterion-related validity is based on the correlation between predictor and criterion scores. This index of agreement, which will be explained in a moment, is known as the *validity coefficient*. In the case of *predictive* validity, predictor scores are obtained from job applicants before they are hired, criterion scores are taken at some reasonable time after they are hired, and the two sets of scores are compared. Several conditions should be met if the estimate is to be an accurate one. First, all applicants should be hired regardless of predictor scores (or, if too many apply, selection should be on a random basis). If, instead, only people with high predictor scores are selected, it becomes very difficult to show a valid relationship even if one exists. This is because the range of scores to be used in the correlation is severely limited—a condition that necessarily reduces the coefficient of correlation. Although it is possible to compensate for this limitation by a statistical correction used in computing the correlation coefficient (*correction for attenuation*), one cannot put as much faith in this corrected estimate as in an estimate based on a full range of scores.

Second, every effort should be made to use reliable, relevant criteria. This is easier said than done, particularly if evaluation is subjective and the evaluators are aware of the predictor scores. For example, a supervisor who knows that one of the ratees had a high test score and another a low test score when hired may very well treat the two people differently and see the former as the more able worker even if their performance is indistinguishable. Such criterion contamination, which was discussed in the last chapter, can lead to spuriously high validity coefficients.

Third, some method should be used to compensate for the fact that initial validity coefficients tend to be spuriously high because of unique characteristics of the validation sample. That is, where we compute a predictor-criterion correlation for a specific group of people, some of what we obtain is due to the relationship itself and some is due to the particular people we have in our study. If we were to use the relationship obtained on this original group as the basis for estimating criterion scores for an entirely new sample of people (a *cross-validation* sample), the correlation of these estimated and obtained criterion scores would provide a validity index with the specific sample effects removed. Hence it would be lower and probably more accurate as an index of the validity relationship. This cross-validation procedure is the most common technique for estimating how much the original validity coefficient will shrink when the predictor is applied to other people. Recently, however, it has been shown that cross-validation often yields an excessive estimate of shrinkage (i.e., suggesting that there is less predictiveness in measures than in fact exists.) An alternative means of obtaining an unbiased validity coefficient is to apply a correction directly to the initial validation data. Several *shrinkage formulas*, as they are called, have been developed for this purpose.[14] The important point for purposes of the present discussion is that initial predictive validity estimates cannot be taken at face value; they must be corrected by either cross-validation or shrinkage formula procedures.

The processes involved in estimating the *concurrent* validity of a predictor are virtually identical to those just described for predictive validity. The only difference is that, as noted earlier, the predictor and criterion measures are obtained from job incumbents. This restriction means, of course, that the problem of preselection with its consequent restriction of predictor and criterion scores is always present.

Concurrent validity is often taken as an estimate of a predictor's ability to forecast success—i.e., it is looked upon as a substitute for predictive validity since both are criterion related. This can be a serious error. For one thing, job incumbents have already been selected and trained. They are not necessarily representative of the people waiting out in the employment office. Entirely different factors may determine how well these two groups perform. For example, an *applicant* may need at least a certain level of manual dexterity in order to succeed. Since all incumbents would exceed this level (or they would have long since departed), *their* success may depend on something entirely different (say, interpersonal skills). A second argument against regarding concurrent validity as a predictive estimate is that people who are trying to get a job and those who already have one may look upon the same predictor quite differently. Their scores may reflect differences in attitude as much as—or more than—whatever the predictor is supposed to measure. The point is, concurrent and predictive validity concepts do not have the same meaning even though they both involve predictor-criterion relationships. If it is necessary to take the concurrent estimate as a first approximation of predictive validity, we should recognize the potential pitfalls and work toward establishment of actual predictive values.

Correlation

In the foregoing discussion we have seen that both reliability and validity estimates depend upon the extent of agreement between sets of scores. We have also seen that the coefficient of correlation (r) is a commonly used index of this agreement. A brief digression into the nature of this statistic is in order.

Correlation refers to the extent to which sets of measures co-vary. The coefficient r is a statistic that summarizes the covariation between two sets of scores. Suppose, for example, we wish to determine how much correspondence exists between weight and speed in a squad of football players. We proceed to weigh each player and time him in the 40-yard dash. The results for the first 11 players are as follows:

Player	Weight (Pounds)	Time (Seconds)
1	175	4.3
2	190	4.2
3	187	4.4
4	255	5.2
5	240	4.5
6	180	4.3
7	195	4.7
8	225	4.9
9	220	5.1
10	250	4.9
11	160	4.1

We might show the extent of agreement graphically by plotting each pair of measures as a single point in a two-dimensional space defined by weight and time scales. A graphic representation of this sort, which is known as a *scatter plot,* is illustrated in Figure 7–3A for the 11 players.

It is apparent that heavier players tend to be slower because the points cluster around the diagonal: that is, low weights go with low times; high weights with longer times. Were the correspondence perfect, all points would lie exactly on a diagonal line, as illustrated in Figure 7–3B. Were there no correspondence at all, the scatter plot would be circular, as shown in Figure 7–3C.

The degree of correspondence or correlation between the two variables—the extent to which the scatter plot approaches a diagonal line or a circle—may be represented numerically by the correlation coefficient r. In essence, this statistic represents the proportion of variation in the scores on both variables that is *shared* variation.[15] Perfect correlation is represented by $r = 1$; no correlation at all by $r = 0$. If the two variables operate in the same direction, the value is positive; if they operate in different directions, the value is negative. Thus plotting weight against *time* yields $r = + .82$. Had we instead used an index of *speed,* our diagonal would have gone from upper-left to lower-right, and we would have arrived at $r = - .82$. In either case, the degree of correspondence would be the same.

Another way to think of correlation is in terms of what it contributes to prediction. Given that we know a person's score on one variable, how well can we predict his score on the other under the three conditions illustrated in Figure 7–3? If there is perfect correlation, as in B, we can make perfect predictions: A 230-pound lineman will run the 40 in 4.8 seconds. At the other extreme, the no-correspondence situation in C, it does us no

FIGURE 7–3   Illustration of Scatter Plots for Three Levels of Correlation (Range of Dash Time Predictions Illustrated in Each Case for a Weight of 230 Pounds on Hypothetical Data)

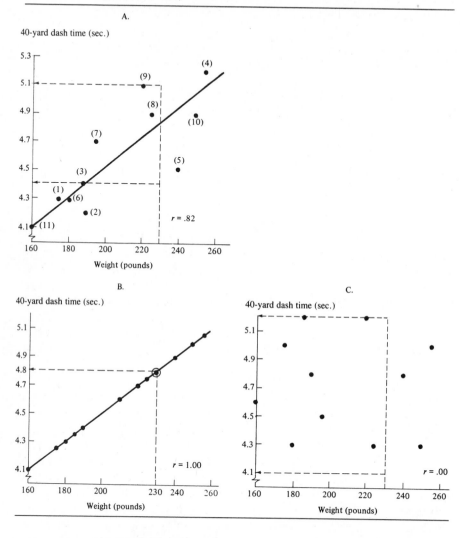

good to know the player's weight. Our prediction with this information is no better than without it. A 230-pound lineman, like any of the other players, will run the 40 in 4.1–5.3 seconds. Zero correlation means zero additional predictiveness.

Most cases, of course, fall somewhere between these extremes, as illustrated in our main example, A. There is some degree of correlation between the scores, hence some predictiveness, but some degree of error as well. Thus knowing that someone weighs 230 pounds reduces his range of probable times from the original 4.1–5.3 seconds to about 4.4–5.1 seconds. The size of this range gives an indication of the amount of error we can expect in our predictions. If we had to make a prediction where, within the range, a particular individual's time would fall, our best guess would be around the midpoint of the range (e.g., 4.8 seconds for the 230-pounder). If we plotted these midpoints for each of the weights and drew a line through them, we would have a best-guess function for the prediction of any football player's 40-yard dash time from his weight. Such a function is called a *regression line,* and it, too, can be expressed in numerical form. If we assume that this function is a straight line, it takes the form:

$$y = a + bx$$

where a is the intercept and b the slope constant. In our example, the regression equation is

$$y = 2.5 + 0.1x$$

As r approaches 1, the spread of scores around this regression line (the predictive error) shrinks to zero. As r approaches zero, the spread of scores increases until it approximates the full range of scores one is trying to predict. The regression line indicates the best prediction we can make of one variable, given a particular value of the other; the spread of scores around this line, which is indexed by r, indicates how accurate our prediction is likely to be.

Obviously there is much more to correlation and regression than what we have presented. Our purpose here has been merely to introduce the concepts. We should, however, point out two important qualifications to the concepts so far discussed. First, the r statistic is not the only index of correlation. It is an appropriate description only under certain conditions—most notably when only two variables are considered, when there is reason to believe that the "true" regression function is a straight line, and when the spread of scores around this line is comparable throughout much of its length. As conditions deviate from these, r becomes a progressively poorer estimate of correspondence. Other statistics have been developed to provide a better description under these and other special circumstances.

One, the *eta coefficient,* is more appropriate where the regression function is poorly represented by a straight line; another, the *point-biserial r,* where one variable is reduced artificially to a dichotomy (e.g., scores classified as pass-fail); a third, the *tetrachoric r,* where both are dichotomized; a fourth, the *phi coefficient,* where both variables are naturally dichotomous (e.g., men-women, blue-brown eye color); and a fifth, the *rho coefficient,* where the measures are rank orders rather than scores on a continuous scale.[16]

The most important exception of all for purposes of selection is the situation in which the regression function involves more than one predictor variable (e.g., a whole battery of test scores). In this case it often happens that, while the correlation of each separate test with the criterion may be substantial, only part of the predictiveness is *unique* to each test. This is because the tests or predictors themselves may be intercorrelated and therefore somewhat redundant in their combined ability to predict the criterion. Such overlapping predictiveness must be discounted if the composite predictor-criterion relationship is to be estimated properly. The statistical model that is most commonly used in combining predictor scores is the *multiple linear regression* model of the general form

$$Y' = a + b_1 X_1 + b_2 X_2 + \ldots + b_k X_k$$

where Y' is the predicted criterion score, X_k are the various predictor (test) scores, a is a constant that brings the scale of the predicted (Y') scores into correspondence with the actual (Y) criterion scores, and b_k are weights indicating how much importance is given to each predictor. In practice, the b weights are determined empirically (and referred to as *beta* weights) in a way that maximizes the correlation of Y' and Y. That is, the weight given to each test is proportional to its *unique* predictiveness for the criterion of interest. When the criterion scores predicted by this model (Y') are correlated with those actually measured (Y), the result is the *multiple correlation coefficient* (R), our last special index of correspondence.

The second qualification to our brief discussion of correlation and regression is that we always base our estimate on a *sample* of the people in whom we are interested, not the whole population. In our example, we included only 11 players, a very small sample of the population of football players in general. The accuracy of any computed value as a description of the true correlation that exists in the population, therefore, depends upon how well the sample represents the population. Other things being equal, larger samples provide better estimates than do smaller ones. The business of drawing inferences about populations from samples is a very complex topic, which lies beyond the scope of this book. It is important to recognize, however, that when we try to forecast the future performance of job applicants on the basis of predictor scores, our success will depend to a great extent upon the representativeness of the sample of people used to validate the predictor. We must keep in mind that the measures used to estimate the predictor's reliability and validity were obtained on a sample of people studied *in the past;* prediction involves *future behavior of a different sample of people.* The more assurance we have that these samples are comparable, the more faith we can put in our correlations (hence in our ability to predict).

With this brief overview of correlation in mind, it is perhaps easier to conceptualize what is involved in reliability and validity estimations. In the case of reliability, the two variables (axes on the scatter plot) represent two administrations of the same instrument (test or other predictor;

criterion). Each point indicates one person's standing on both sets of scores. A perfectly reliable test, for example, would produce a scatter plot with all points on the regression line ($r = 1$). In the case of criterion-related validity, one variable (usually the X axis) represents predictor scores, and the other, criterion scores. The higher the correlation the more accurately we should be able to predict the criterion on the basis of predictor scores. It is quite common for reliability coefficients (r_{11}) to run as high as 0.90. It is rare, however, to obtain validity coefficients (r_{12}) in excess of 0.5. It is mathematically impossible for a validity coefficient to exceed the square root of the average reliability[17] of the predictor and criterion, a fact that has some important practical consequences, which we shall explain in a later section.

Utility and Decision Making in Selection

The value of a selection procedure is not solely a matter of how well we can predict success. Two other important considerations are how many applicants we have to choose from and how many of these applicants are likely to succeed without selection. The former is usually expressed in terms of an index known as the *selection ratio* (SR): the ratio of *number of openings* to *number of applicants* for those positions. A *SR* of 1 : 1 is unfavorable for selection, in that everyone who applies must be hired. One of 1 : 10 would be much more favorable, in that we could try to select the best 10 percent of the applicants. In other words, selection procedures have greater potential utility under lower than higher selection ratios.

The other consideration, often called the *success rate,* or *base rate of success,* is indicated by the proportion of people who are hired without the benefit of the selection procedure and whose performance exceeds some fixed level (e.g., those rated superior). If a job is very easy, so that just about anyone could succeed at it, the success rate would be high, and the utility of a selection procedure would be low. A low success rate increases the potential value of selection.

From the standpoint of *efficiency* in selection, therefore, the utility of a selection procedure is a function of its *predictive validity,* the *selection ratio,* and the *success rate* for a particular job. How these factors interact to affect the efficiency of selection may be seen in the following example of what we will call the *traditional selection model.*

We wish to hire 12 new secretaries. Based on past experience, we can expect 100 applicants for these positions. To this point we have had no formal selection procedures, and about 40 percent of the secretaries hired have been rated satisfactory or better. We have developed a test battery that predicts success (satisfactory rating or better), with a validity of $r = 0.60$. Should we start using this test battery? The situation can be summarized graphically as in Figure 7–4. Without the test battery we would have to hire 30 people in order to get 12 who would be likely to

FIGURE 7–4 Illustration of the Traditional Selection Model (Cutoffs Set at Rating of 5.6 and Predictor Score of 82)

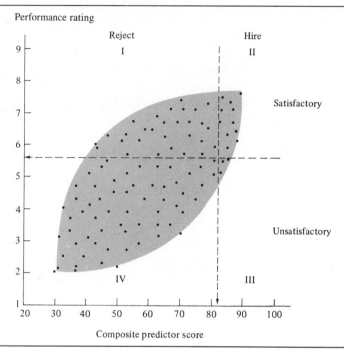

Performance rating

Composite predictor score

succeed since our success rate is 40 percent. With the battery, we can locate our cutoff score (composite test score, above which we hire and below which we reject) such that exactly 12 people will be likely to succeed (quadrant II in Figure 7–4). In the process, we will necessarily hire two or three who will probably fail (quadrant III). This, however, is considerably better than hiring 18 who will probably fail, as would be the case without the battery. In other words, the test battery would allow us to reduce our mistakes in the people hired by about 83 percent. If all we are interested in is reducing these mistakes, and indeed such is the case for the traditional model, then we should probably adopt the battery. In fact, it is possible to estimate the economic benefits to be gained through testing simply by calculating the average cost, in dollars, for each bad hiring decision. If the figure were $2,000, then the savings in this example would be: 18 (without testing) − 2.5 (with testing) × $2,000 (average cost) = $31,000 (total saved).

It is easy to visualize how the situation would change if the validity coefficient, the selection ratio, or the success rate were different. A higher validity would mean a reduced spread of scores around the regression line, hence a better ratio of successes to failures wherever we put the cutoff score. If the coefficient were high enough, we could locate our cutoff score such that we could hire 12 people for the 12 secretarial jobs and be just as confident they would all succeed: Our quadrant III error would reduce to zero. A reduced selection ratio would have much the same effect. If we only needed 6 rather than 12 secretaries (a selection ratio of 6 : 100), we could move the cutoff score upward (to the right in Figure 7–4) until there were only 6 cases in quadrant II. The number of quadrant III error cases would consequently also be reduced, in this case less than one. A change in the success rate (or alternatively, in the definition of success) would be indicated by a shift in the position of the horizontal line in Figure 7–4. A more stringent definition (say, to a rating of 6.5) would mean that we would have to relax our cutoff score in order to get the necessary 12 successes in quadrant II. If you visualize the horizontal line at 6.5, you can see that the vertical cutoff would have to be moved to about 70.

Fortunately, it is not necessary to draw scatter plots, cutoff lines, and so forth in order to implement decisions based on the traditional model. Rather, a set of tables is available that permits direct readout of the theoretical likelihood of success on the criterion for any combination of success rate, validity, and predictor score data. Known originally as the *Taylor-Russell tables,* they have been cast in several different forms by Lawshe and his associates to enable users to estimate *expectancy of success* for both *individual* and *institutional* prediction.[18] *Individual* expectancy tables tell us how likely it is (in chances out of 100) that an applicant with a score of x will succeed; *institutional* tables tell us what proportion of the applicants who exceed various cutoff scores on the predictor are likely to succeed.

Using the secretarial example to illustrate the *institutional* case, we would enter the 40 percent success rate table at the validity value of $r = 0.60$. Since our selection ratio is 12 : 100, we would be interested in the success expectancy for the top 12 percent of the applicants on the predictor. This can be read directly from the tabled values, as shown in Table 7–1. Since 12 percent lies between the .10 and .20 columns in the table, the expectation is that between 83 and 75 percent of our selected hirees will succeed (versus the 40 percent without selection). As we saw before, this means that we need hire only about 15 people rather than 30 in order to get our 12 "successes"; or, alternately, if we stick to our original 12 hirees, only 2.5 rather than 7 will fail.

In the *individual* case, we might want to decide whether to accept or reject *each applicant* at the time of the interview. To do this, we would enter the individual expectancy table as above (40 percent success rate; $r = 0.60$, as illustrated in Table 7–2) and read directly the chances in 100 of success, given the applicant's standing on the predictor. With a score in the top 20 percent on the predictor in this example, the applicant would have a 75 percent chance of success. We would make our decision on the basis of a preestablished *expectancy cutoff level.* By the logic of the traditional selection model, we would set this cutoff so as to ensure that

TABLE 7–1　Illustration from the Taylor-Russell Tables for Institutional Prediction: Proportion of Employees Considered Satisfactory (40 Percent Success Rate Only)

r	Selection Ratio										
	0.05	0.10	0.20	0.30	0.40	0.50	0.60	0.70	0.80	0.90	0.95
.00	.40	.40	.40	.40	.40	.40	.40	.40	.40	.40	.40
.05	.44	.43	.43	.42	.42	.42	.41	.41	.41	.40	.40
.10	.48	.47	.46	.45	.44	.43	.42	.42	.41	.41	.40
.15	.52	.50	.48	.47	.46	.45	.44	.43	.42	.41	.41
.20	.57	.54	.51	.49	.48	.46	.45	.44	.43	.41	.41
.25	.61	.58	.54	.51	.49	.48	.46	.45	.43	.42	.41
.30	.65	.61	.57	.54	.51	.49	.47	.46	.44	.42	.41
.35	.69	.65	.60	.56	.53	.51	.49	.47	.45	.42	.41
.40	.73	.69	.63	.59	.56	.53	.50	.48	.45	.43	.41
.45	.77	.72	.66	.61	.58	.54	.51	.49	.46	.43	.42
.50	.81	.76	.69	.64	.60	.56	.53	.49	.46	.43	.42
.55	.85	.79	.72	.67	.62	.58	.54	.50	.47	.44	.42
.60	.89	.83	.75	.69	.64	.60	.55	.51	.48	.44	.42
.65	.92	.87	.79	.72	.67	.62	.57	.52	.48	.44	.42
.70	.95	.90	.82	.76	.69	.64	.58	.53	.49	.44	.42
.75	.97	.93	.86	.79	.72	.66	.60	.54	.49	.44	.42
.80	.99	.96	.89	.82	.75	.68	.61	.55	.49	.44	.42
.85	1.00	.98	.93	.86	.79	.71	.63	.56	.50	.44	.42
.90	1.00	1.00	.97	.91	.82	.74	.65	.57	.50	.44	.42
.95	1.00	1.00	.99	.96	.87	.77	.66	.57	.50	.44	.42
1.00	1.00	1.00	1.00	1.00	1.00	.80	.67	.57	.50	.44	.42

SOURCE: Taylor, H. C. & Russell, J. T. (1939). From the relationship of validity coefficients to the practical effectiveness of tests in selection: Discussion and tables. *Journal of Applied Psychology, 23*, 565–578.

positions in this classification would be filled by applicants with the highest chance of succeeding. Given our selection ratio and expected rate of openings, we might find it possible to reject everyone whose chances of success were below 90 percent. Other models, however, might argue for either higher or lower values: The time and cost of interviewing might make it preferable to select the first 12 applicants whose chances of success were in excess of 70 percent.

While far from perfect, expectancy tables do encourage fairness in selection decisions by expressing cutoffs in terms of *success* probability rather than arbitrary *predictor scores*. We shall have more to say about fairness in a moment. Also, expectancy tables allow the employer to see clearly how much the success rate with the predictor (the tabled *expectancy*) exceeds the success rate without the predictor. To clarify the picture further, both individual and institutional expectancy data can be expressed in chart form for a specific predictor, as illustrated in Figure 7–5. Test publishers are coming to use expectancy charts more and more in the description of their standardized predictive instruments.

The traditional selection model that we have been discussing is concerned only with the minimization of errors in people actually selected. Returning to our Figure 7–4 illustration, these errors appear as quad-

TABLE 7–2   Illustration from the Lawshe Expectancy
Tables for Individual Prediction: Percent of
Employees Considered Satisfactory
(40 Percent Success Rate Only)

	Individual Predictor Categories				
			Middle		
r	Hi 1/5	Next 1/5	1/5	Next 1/5	Lo 1/5
.15	48	44	40	36	32
.20	51	45	40	35	30
.25	54	44	40	34	28
.30	57	46	40	33	24
.35	60	47	39	32	22
.40	63	48	39	31	19
.45	66	49	39	29	17
.50	69	50	39	28	14
.55	72	53	38	26	12
.60	75	53	38	24	10
.65	79	55	37	22	08
.70	82	58	36	19	06
.75	86	59	35	17	04
.80	89	61	34	14	02
.85	93	64	32	10	01
.90	97	69	29	06	00
.95	100	76	23	02	00

SOURCE: From Lawshe, C. H., & Auclair, G. (1958). Expectancy charts, III: Their theoretical development. *Personnel Psychology, II*, 545–599.

rant III. The idea is that people cost you something only if you hire them. Civil rights legislation, however, has forced organizations to consider other kinds of costs as well—notably the social costs associated with unfair exclusion of people from jobs. Looking at the rejection side of the graph in Figure 7–4 (the portion below the cutoff line), we see that the traditional approach results in a large number of errors of another kind. A lot of the people *rejected* would have made perfectly good secretaries (quadrant I). In fact, it is apparent that we have rejected far more good candidates than we have hired in this example.

The traditional model, then, has obvious limitations. One approach that has been used to deal with these limitations while preserving the essential logic of the model involves the application of *decision theory* to selection. It will be recalled from Chapter 2 that decision theory is concerned with the rational basis of choice. In its most prescriptive form, it proposes that any decision should be made according to the *expected utility* (EU) of the alternative outcomes: The EU of a decision outcome is defined as the product of its chances of occurrence and its utility (payoff or cost) for someone—usually the decision maker. Thus when faced with a choice among courses of action, say, which brand of toothpaste to buy, the rational decision maker should figure the anticipated costs (price,

FIGURE 7–5   Illustration of (A) an Individual Expectancy Chart and (B) an Institutional Expectancy Chart as a Function of Scores on the Purdue Mechanical Adaptability Test for the Same Sample of Job Incumbents

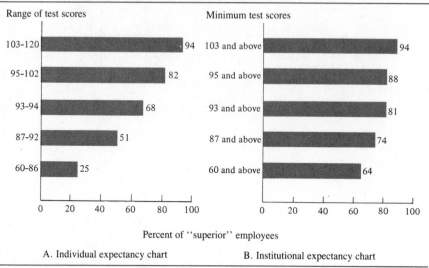

A. Individual expectancy chart

B. Institutional expectancy chart

SOURCE: McCormick, E. J. & Tiffin, J. (1974). *Industrial Psychology* (6th ed.), (p. 122). Englewood Cliffs, N.J.: Prentice-Hall. Copyright © 1974 by Prentice-Hall. Reprinted by permission.

abrasive risk, etc.) and payoffs (taste, reduced number of cavities, increased sex appeal, etc.) associated with each one, multiply every value by its chance of happening if that brand is chosen, and add up all these expected utilities. The brand with the highest positive (or lowest negative) aggregate value should be chosen.

Clearly, all the traditional selection model needs to qualify for this EU maximization strategy would be explicit costs and payoffs for the four possible decision outcomes illustrated in Figure 7–4. The ingredients for computing the expectancies associated with any predictor cutoff rule, as we have seen, are available in the validity, success rate, and selection ratio data. Since the main problem in selection is deciding where to draw the cutoffs, the decision maker would compute EU for different cutoff rules and choose the option that yielded the highest value. Ideally, one would like to consider *all* possible cutoff rules, and computer programs for this purpose have been available for more than 10 years.[19] The major practical difficulty in applying the EU model, of course, is that of generating the basic *utility* numbers. It is no easy matter to estimate the costs and benefits of all the possible outcomes of a particular hiring decision, even if they were known. Many of them, such as social or image considerations, are purely subjective.

The idea of using decision theory in the selection process goes back at least 20 years, but only in the last half decade has it been taken seriously.[20] Among the reasons for the renewed interest are the realization that businesspeople do not fully appreciate the value of anything that cannot be expressed in dollars and cents and the development of better procedures for estimating certain of the utility parameters. Schmidt, Hunter, and their colleagues,[21] for example, have estimated the potential productivity gains for our national economy in the use of one particular aptitude test for one particular occupation (computer programmer) to be in the *billions* of dollars! They have also used this approach to estimate the comparative economic merit of different classes of predictors (i.e., ability tests, biodata, interviews, experience) and even entire selection strategies, including affirmative action goals and quotas (see next section).[22] Cascio,[23] using a somewhat different estimation procedure, has illustrated the financial implications of a variety of personnel management strategies, including selection. Once again, the figures are of a magnitude that even the most hard-boiled businessperson would find difficult to ignore! In sum, the traditional model, augmented by techniques derived from decision theory, is an approach to selection that is easily justified from the employer's perspective in terms that he or she can understand.

It will be recalled that the recognition of considerations other than the employer's best interests is what distinguishes the traditional selection model from the more modern strategies. It is to these hard-to-measure other considerations that we must now turn. Our focus thus shifts from the fairly narrow objective of predicting success on the job to the more global one of achieving *fairness*. In decision theory terms, this is equivalent to considering multiple decision outcomes, each having a whole host of different utility values.

FAIRNESS IN SELECTION

Illustration and the Problem of Definition

Suppose that in our earlier example (Figure 7–4) 30 of the 100 secretarial applicants were black. Suppose further that 29 of the 30 were rejected because they scored below the cutoff on the test battery. One possible conclusion that might be drawn from this hypothetical outcome would be that blacks are unqualified for secretarial work. Much more likely, however, is the possibility that the test battery is biased against ethnic minorities. Although test publishers have for some years been attempting to rectify the situation, validity estimates for many standardized selection devices were established with validation samples comprised almost entirely of whites. Such devices may not have the same pattern of validity when applied to other ethnic groups. It could be, therefore, that of the 29 blacks who failed the tests, a large number might have succeeded if hired. In other words, the traditional selection approach may have resulted in a disproportionate number of blacks in quadrant I. If this is the case, then our selection device is serving as an instrument for perpetuation of what most would consider an unfair—and illegal—hiring practice, whether we intend it or not.

Consider, however, a second example. Suppose the job in question required lifting heavy boxes, and our selection battery included a strength test, which is known to be a valid predictor of tenure and performance on this job. Since it is well established that women, on the average, possess less upper body strength than men, our test will screen out a disproportionate number of female applicants. Is this also a case of unfair (and illegal) discrimination? Probably not, as it turns out, although the answer here, as in most other cases of *adverse impact* against protected groups, is not nearly as clear as one might like. The problem, as we discovered in Chapter 3 (equity theory), is that fairness is an inherently subjective concept. From the employer's standpoint, it may seem perfectly fair to hire only the people with the best credentials, even if the result is an all-white, male work force. To the black or female applicant, the same credentials may seem grossly unfair since past educational and employment practices may have put such credentials beyond their reach.

While there is no definitive answer to the question of what is fair, a person must reflect upon at least three kinds of considerations in order to make an informed judgment. Most of us rarely consider more than one. First, there are *technical* considerations derived from the very concepts that have occupied our attention thus far in the chapter: validity, success rates, selection ratios, utilities, etc. One can define fairly specific rules or models of fairness based upon such concepts. Unfortunately, however, which technical rule one prefers depends upon our second set of considerations, those of a *philosophical* (ethical, moral) nature. Here the question involves basic values such as the organization's responsibility to its stockholders, customers, present work force, community, and society at large. How important is it, for example, that an employer's payroll reflect the precise ethnic mix of its community and, if there be costs involved, who should bear that burden? Or, in a somewhat different vein, is a police department justified in prohibiting the employment of any individual convicted of a felony? If a person has "paid his or her debt to society" and seeks rehabilitation, is the public sector any less responsible than the private sector for providing this opportunity? Since philosophical considerations are even more debatable than technical ones, we are reduced to our last set of considerations, the *legal* ones. Increasingly, fairness has become a matter of statutory definition and judicial interpretation formulated, for the most part, in the interest of civil rights protection. But where do the legislators and judges turn for *their* guidance? To the *technical* considerations, of course. So, we have a catch-22 situation. A technical resolution is impossible without basic value assumptions; the basic values of our society are presumably reflected in our justice system; but our justice system tries desperately to find definitions of fairness in technical operations.

From a practical standpoint, it thus becomes imperative to understand the major technical concepts involved in the fairness controversy as well as the recent trends in legal opinion. We shall not discuss further the matter of *philosophical* considerations except to reemphasize that they are implicit in all legal decisions on fairness and are the necessary starting point for all technical models of fairness. If the court rules that an organization is in violation of the law because it pays lower salaries to women than to men for roughly comparable work, despite the fact that market conditions favor this strategy, it is making an important statement on the values held by society. If that statement is inconsistent with existing social values—as, for example, if society believed that organizations should pay only the minimum salary necessary to attract the requisite work force regardless of social impact—then we would expect that ruling and the statutes on which it is based eventually to be overturned. Similarly, if one accepts the traditional selection model as the best way to ensure fairness in hiring, one has already subscribed to the premise that the organization is entitled to minimize its costs regardless of social consequences. One must look elsewhere—possibly within oneself—for answers to these questions.

An excellent example of how changes in social climate can affect the philosophical concept of fairness—and eventually its legal interpretation—may be seen in the shift in American politics that has taken place between the early 1970s and the 1980s. At the beginning of this period, society's sensitivity to the need for protection against a variety of abuses by powerful institutions led to strong protective legislation, appointment of more "liberal" judges, and a host of rulings in favor of plaintiffs in civil rights cases (as well as environmental protection, occupational health and safety, and other cases involving individuals versus institutions). By the 1980s, the public's concern shifted to economic and national security issues; a "conservative" trend ensued, which has begun a widespread relaxation of the protective measures adopted earlier. Thus, a job applicant or employee who in 1972 was judged by the courts to have been treated unfairly because of race, sex, national origin, or religion— and awarded substantial compensation as a result—might today have the complaint ruled groundless by the same court and be sent packing without a dime!

Technical Considerations

Problems with the Traditional Model

The traditional selection model implies that fairness is chiefly a matter of the overall validity of predictors. Valid predictors enable the hiring organization to choose people on the basis of success probability rather than meaningless test scores or the whims and prejudices of managers. However, as we just saw in the hypothetical case of the black secretarial applicants, sheer validity data may not itself be sufficient to avert unfairness. The reason, you will recall, is that it is theoretically possible for a predictor to be highly valid for some people but not for others. Or, even worse, overall validity figures might obscure very different predictor-criterion relationships associated with different types of applicants. The first theoretical possibility is called *single-group validity* (since predictability is limited to one kind of applicant); the latter, which logically includes the first, is termed *differential validity*. The traditional model ignores both possibilities and considers only the costs to the organization associated with those people *hired*.

The Moderator Variable Model

Whether or not the differential validity hypothesis is plausible in any particular case is obviously an empirical question. The answer requires a validation strategy known as the *moderator variable model,* in which validation is carried out separately for whatever subgroups of applicants the researchers consider theoretically or practically important. The characteristic(s) that distinguish the subgroups are referred to as *moderator variables,* and the resulting validity estimates, as *moderated validities.*[24]

Some of the kinds of differential validity effects that might be found with the moderator variable strategy were described graphically by Bartlett and O'Leary in a very influential paper that appeared in 1969.[25] Three of the more noteworthy examples, as illustrated in Figure 7–6, represent potential differences between two hypothetical groups in validity, average predictor scores, and average criterion scores (or success rates). In panel A we see the case in which both groups have equal success prospects and moderated validity coefficients, but one (the hypothetical minority group) has lower average predictor scores. Our previous example of the black secretarial applicants could well fit this case. If our only concern were maximizing successful prediction, this situation would call for adoption of different cutoff scores on the predictor for the minority and majority groups. To the uninitiated this smacks of a double standard, something that all red-blooded Americans abhor. You, however, being more sophisticated, recognize that we are really looking at a single standard on the scale that counts—*success probability*. Were we to impose a single standard on the *predictor* scale, we would have a double standard on the success probability scale, and would thereby rule out practically all minority candidates. It is interesting to note that, had we used the traditional model rather than the moderator variable model for establishing validity in this case, the overall validity coefficient would have been close to zero. Thus what is actually a good predictor when moderated for race would have been rejected as worthless. Of course this, like the other illus-

FIGURE 7–6   Illustration of Scatter Plots for Three Hypothetical Selection Situations

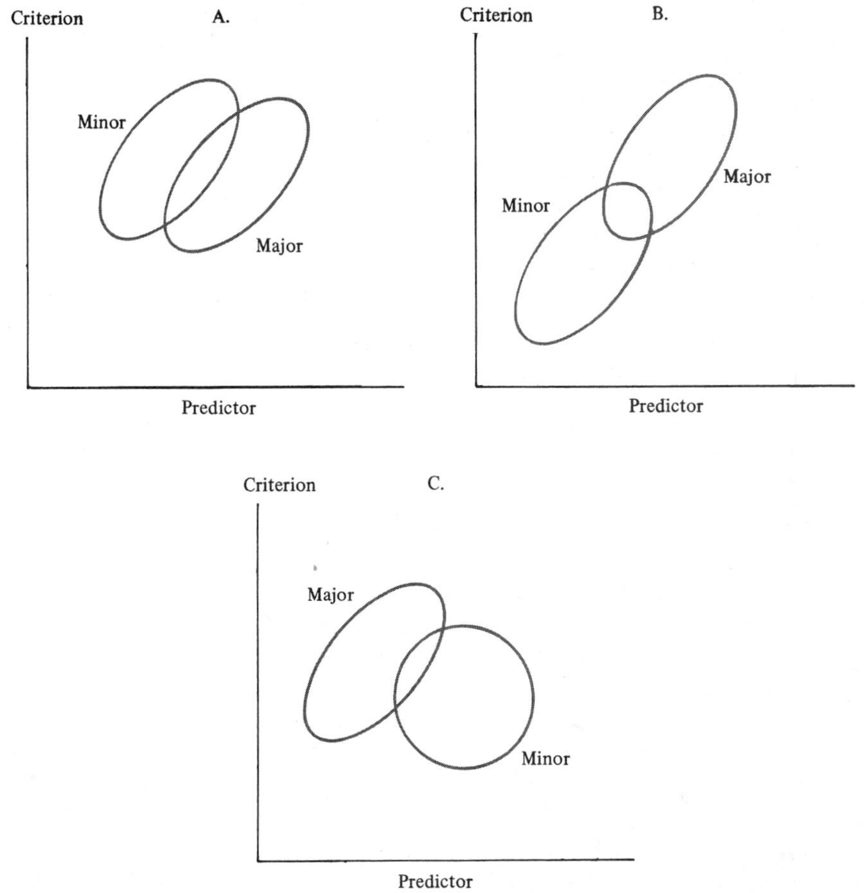

SOURCE: Adapted from Bartlett, C. J., & O'Leary, B. S. (1969). A differential prediction model to moderate the effects of heterogeneous groups in personnel selection and classification. *Personnel Psychology, 22,* 1–17, figures 1, 2, and 7.

trations, merely shows what form differential validity *could* take; it says nothing about how likely such a situation is to arise in practice.

Panel B illustrates a case that is identical to the first (similar moderated validity and lower minority predictor scores) except that the minority group also does more poorly on the criterion. This case is similar to our previous example of the men and women who lift boxes. Few women passed the strength test, but only those who did could handle the boxes. Regardless of race, creed, color, or IQ, the test predicts the criterion: Strength is the key variable in both. To maximize expected success in this instance, a single predictor cutoff would be in order, and few women would be hired. Were we to adopt a lower cutoff for women, as in case A,

---

FIGURE 7-7   A Model for Test Validation and Selection Research

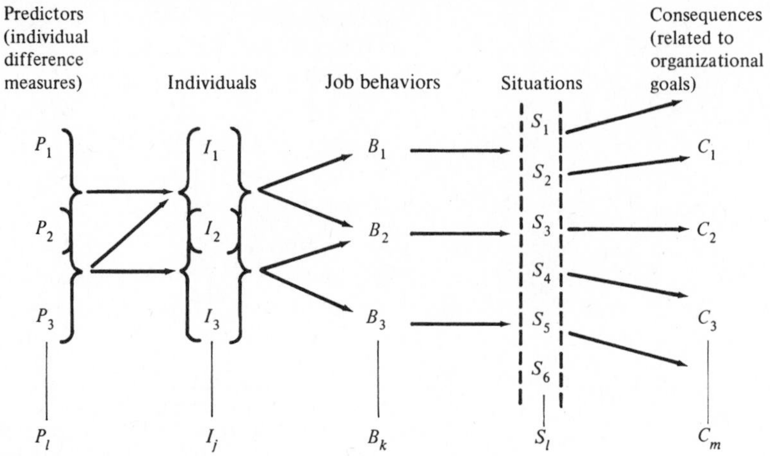

Predictors
(individual
difference
measures)   Individuals   Job behaviors   Situations

Consequences
(related to
organizational
goals)

P_1 I_1 B_1 S_1 C_1
                                  S_2
P_2 I_2 B_2 S_3 C_2
                                  S_4
P_3 I_3 B_3 S_5 C_3
                                  S_6

P_l I_j B_k S_l C_m

SOURCE: From Dunnette, M. D. (1966). *Personnel selection and placement*. Monterey, Calif.: Brooks/Cole Publishing.

we would wind up with a lot fewer boxes stacked and a lot more disabled females.

The third case (panel C), of course, is what we described earlier as *single-group validity*. Here, the predictor improves our prediction of success for one group only; it is of little help in selecting others. The obvious implication of this case would be to limit use of any predictor to those groups for which it is shown to be valid. Carried to the extreme, such logic would lead to a virtual customization of the selection process: Applicants would first be classified according to an appropriate set of moderators and then be administered a corresponding set of predictive instruments. A proposal of this sort was, in fact, suggested by Dunnette at one time, as illustrated in Figure 7-7. Returning to our illustration of the single-group case, however, it must be recognized that many other arrangements of the circle and ellipse (see Figure 7-6) are possible besides that shown. Suppose, for example, the majority ellipse were dropped below the minority circle on the criterion scale. Would it then be appropriate to ignore the differential success of the minority group on both predictor and criterion simply because there was no predictive relationship *within* the minority group itself?

The various illustrations developed by Bartlett and O'Leary by no means exhaust the list of potentially important moderator effects. For example, the slope and form of the regression function between predictors and criterion could differentiate groups and thereby contribute to predictive error if left undetected.[26] Furthermore, the variables used to distinguish groups need not be limited to such obvious categories as race and sex: The list of potential moderator variables is virtually infinite. It has even been suggested that an empirical index of the individual's *predictability* might be calculated and this score used as a basis for classification.[27]

Concern over fairness in selection has, of course, always been tied directly to civil rights issues. If the traditional selection model was flawed in the sense that it could result in disproportionate rejection of qualified minority and female applicants for seemingly just reasons, then the obvious solution seemed to be the moderator variable model with sex and race as the moderators. Fairness could then be defined in terms of true success probabilities for the various groups: People with equal chances of succeeding would have an equal chance of being hired.[28]

Fairness Models

As it turns out, moderated validity is not the whole answer either. The main reason is that merely identifying the ways in which groups might differ in predictor-criterion relationships says very little about how the discrepancies should be resolved. In fact, it suggests a whole array of strategies, each stressing a different combination of differentiating characteristics and methods for compensating for them. Thus the simple idea of looking into potential group differences has produced a dozen or so technical definitions of fairness.[29] We will not go into these models except to note that they run the gamut of philosophical emphasis from the *traditional (regression) model,* which recognizes the employer's right to maximize prediction as the only legitimate consideration, to the strict *quota model,* which disregards this entirely in favor of having all groups proportionately represented. Most, of course, fall somewhere between, with that attributed to Cleary (1968) seeming at present to have the greatest following.[30] In the Cleary model, predictor-criterion regression equations are computed for the subgroups of interest as well as for the combined (i.e., unmoderated) sample. If a subgroup's criterion scores are consistently above those predicted by the combined regression line (*overpredicted*) or consistently below them (*underpredicated*), the unmoderated version is considered biased or unfair. Fairness is then achieved by basing predictions on the moderated version. Of course, if neither under- nor overprediction is found, the predictor is proclaimed fair and the moderator variable is ignored. The underlying principle in the Cleary model is thus assuring that people are chosen on the basis of their chances of success with certain suspected biases controlled (see the discussion of case A in Figure 7–6).

While technical considerations give us options rather than a single definition of fairness, they are not without practical value. They enable us to see more clearly just how biases can operate and to appreciate the *real* issues that are involved in our choice of a selection strategy. They force us to ask what values we consider most important, and what classifications of people we wish to set up in our effort to identify unfairness. The reader must recognize by now that the whole technical approach to fairness assumes that we know what biases we want to prevent and what costs we want to minimize—for whom. So far, we have limited ourselves chiefly to characteristics with legal (and, we must assume, social) overtones: race, sex, age. The same logic, of course, could be applied to fat people, short people, bald people, ugly people, or people whose names begin with *P,* provided the classification is clearly defined. However, there are no technical means for defining or ensuring fairness in the abstract for *everyone.* The methods are inherently comparative.

Another virtue of the technical approach is that it casts fairness into a form that permits empirical confirmation. That is, once we have accepted a technical definition, we can conduct studies to discover whether suspected biases really exist, and if so, how serious a problem they pose. A considerable amount of literature has appeared over the last decade on the most frequently challenged class of predictors, common employment tests, and their presumed victims, minority applicants. The upshot of all this work is a growing realization that, for all its plausibility, the fear that such tests are more valid for whites than for minority groups is probably unjustified.[31] Hunter, Schmidt, and Hunter were able to find only about 7 percent of 866 reported white–black validity comparisons that resulted in significant discrepancies—a number that could easily have arisen by chance.[32] Subsequently, they have also shown that performance measures for blacks are predicted as well as or better than those for whites using standard employment tests, a finding that is certainly inconsistent with the differential validity hypothesis.[33] Thus it could well be that all the cases illustrated in the last few pages as well as the popular Cleary definition of fairness address a problem that never really existed!

Before we conclude that the whole moderated validity idea was a bad one, however, we should hasten to add that there have been some objections to the Hunter and Schmidt methodology.[34] And, more important, even if typical paper-and-pencil tests are proven equally valid for whites and blacks, this does not rule out the possibility that *some* tests might be differentially valid for *some* subgroups. Where there are good reasons to believe that such differences might exist, the moderator-variable approach affords a means of verifying or refuting that possibility.

Validity Generalization

The basic philosophy underlying moderated validity extends well beyond the idea of validating for specific subgroups. As illustrated in Figure 7–7, it includes the notion that validity applies rather narrowly to *settings* as well as *people.* A test that is a valid predictor for clerks at an insurance company in Columbus, Ohio, is not necessarily as good for selecting sales-persons in a Dallas department store, insurance clerks at another Colum-bus-based insurance company, or even clerks for the same insurance company in another city. The solution? Separate validation for one's own particular job classification in one's own locale—a *local validation* strat-egy. The assumption is that one cannot safely *generalize* or transport validities established in one context to another.

Customizing validation studies, however, has a serious drawback of its own—unreliable measurement. The more one subdivides a total valida-tion sample (by race, sex, age, geographical location, job title, etc.), the fewer cases there are in any subgroup, and the more idiosyncracies there are in the criteria by which any subgroup is evaluated. These and other artifacts tend to depress the obtained validity estimates, thereby increas-ing the chances that a "real" predictor-criterion relation would be missed. Thus local validation, particularly in conjunction with subgrouping for race and sex, substitutes one bias (underestimation of "true" validities) for another (the possibility of unrecognized differences in validity). Local studies are almost certain to depress validity coefficients even for the best predictors and particularly so for minority groups since sample sizes are generally much smaller for them than for white subgroups. According to Schmidt, Hunter, and their colleagues, this latter difference accounts for the occasional report of differential or single-group validity.[35] If a white subgroup is large enough to produce a significant validity coefficient, then the depressing effect of small sample size would be limited mainly to the minority group, thereby increasing the discrepancy between its coef-ficient and the white one. This discrepancy would appear to reflect differ-ential validity even though, in reality, it was just a result of the reduced reliability caused by the reduced sample size in the minority group.

An alternative to the philosophy of *customization* assumes that predic-tiveness *generalizes* very broadly from one group to another, or from one context to another. If this is so, the appropriate validation strategy would be to *pool* the results of local studies over entire job domains (e.g., all cler-ical jobs, all sales jobs, all managerial jobs) in all geographical regions for all kinds of people. This strategy, which is generally referred to as *valid-ity generalization,* regards the *aggregate* validity coefficient as the best estimate of a predictor's true worth because of the greater reliability af-forded by the larger (pooled) validation sample.

As noted in the last section, the Schmidt and Hunter group has mar-shalled considerable evidence in support of the generalizability of apti-tude test validities across subgroups. They have done the same for valid-ity generalization across job domains.[36] While not everyone would go so far as to declare, with Schmidt and Hunter[37], that "professionally devel-oped cognitive ability tests are valid predictors of performance and train-ing for all jobs in all settings; . . . for both minority and majority appli-cants," it is clear that many predictors are far more generalizable and useful than was once believed. It is also clear that, except perhaps for very large organizations with very large minority group representation, one is safer in relying on generalized validity estimates than on customized estimates—provided, of course, that the job requirements are at least roughly consistent with the predictor domain. One should not expect a physical abilities test to generalize to a clerical job domain; but one should expect a clerical aptitude test properly validated in other organizations to generalize to one's own clerical work force.

Legal Considerations

There are, of course, two main sources of definition in our system of legal justice: *statutes* (laws, executive orders, guidelines, and the like) and *precedents* established through court cases. The latter usually serve to elaborate upon or clarify the former. In the process, however, it often happens that the essential meanings—or at least the practical implications— of the statutes are changed. Such, many claim, has been the history of the main tenets of the Civil Rights Act of 1964.

Title VII of this act, as amended by the Equal Employment Opportunity Act of 1972 and several executive orders, made it illegal "to fail or refuse to hire or to discharge any individual, or otherwise to discriminate against any individual with respect to his compensation, terms, conditions, or privileges of employment because of such individual's race, color, religion, sex, or national origin."[38] It also established a federal agency, the Equal Employment Opportunity Commission (EEOC), to administer, promote, and enforce the law.

While the language of the law seems rather clear in the matter of fairness, subsequent events have proven it to be anything but. A whole succession of conflicting guidelines, EEOC rulings, and court cases has appeared, attempting to interpret, in explicit terms, what one must do to be in compliance with the law. The underlying philosophy, of course, was that people be hired on the basis of *expected performance* rather than by one of the designated irrelevant factors (race, sex, etc.). However, the law itself did not specify how one might establish such expectations; neither did it mandate that selection be fair except insofar as the protected groups were concerned. Thus it did not require that instruments (e.g., tests) used in selection be valid; only that if such instruments were used they not exclude disproportionate numbers of protected groups (i.e., have *adverse impact*).

What has happened in the ensuing confusion is that as the courts, state and local governments, and federal agencies have been forced to address such issues, the definition of fairness has taken on a succession of new dimensions. Testing, for example, was recognized from the beginning as a practice that could be used either to promote or subvert the intent of the law. Therefore, its proper and improper use had to be distinguished. Each court ruling and opinion seemed to contradict its predecessor in specifying the necessary conditions for the legal use of tests. Many employers, thoroughly confused, abandoned employment testing altogether rather than risk prosecution for improper usage. Only later would they discover that the alternatives to testing were often less efficient and even more vulnerable under the law than were the tests.[39] To illustrate the extent of the confusion as well as the general trend of legal opinion, let us describe briefly the implications of a few benchmark decisions. All save the first were rendered by the U.S. Supreme Court.

1.   *Myart* v. *Motorola* (1964).[40] The Illinois Fair Employment Practices Commission held that an ability test used by the Motorola Company in hiring was discriminatory since it tended to operate against disadvantaged and culturally deprived groups (a ruling that was later overturned). However, fearing the potential implications of such rulings, the U.S. Senate specified in an amendment to Title VII (the "Tower amendment") that ability tests could be used in selection as long as they were developed and validated by qualified professionals and their *intent* was not to discriminate unfairly against protected groups. The technical issue of what constitutes validity was thus, in effect, left up to "professional judgment."

2.   *Griggs* v. *Duke Power Company* (1971).[41] Here the intent principle was reversed with the ruling that the Civil Rights Act applies to the "consequences of employment practices, not simply the motivation." Further, the court removed the legality of a specific test procedure from the realm of professional judgment, making obligatory the *demonstration* of validity for the specific job context in which the predictor was to be used. It was in this case, considered by many the landmark decision, that the legal establishment began looking to psychology for a technical solution to the fairness question. Since psychologists had held for years that predictors should be validated empirically within the "local" setting, this became a legal standard under *Griggs*—provided, of course, there was evidence of adverse impact. (Remember, the law does not demand fairness; it merely prohibits unfair *discrimination*.)

3.   *Albermarle Paper Company* v. *Moody* (1975).[42] The emphasis in this decision was on job-relatedness and minimum adverse impact in testing. In this sense, it reinforced the *Griggs* decision and extended it by requiring that a procedure must not only be proven valid, it must be shown to have the *least adverse impact of any available* within the same degree of validity.

4.   *Washington* v. *Davis* (1976).[43] Once again, the technical quality of a testing procedure was at issue, the question being whether a verbal skills test that produced twice the rejection rate for blacks as whites was justifiable, given that it was a valid predictor of training scores. What was different about this decision was that it favored the defendant (the Washington, D.C., police department) and hence gave the first indication that a validated test could be defended despite clear adverse impact and a dubious criterion. However, there were other considerations in the case that may have influenced the decision, such as the defendant's past hiring record, so it could hardly be taken as a clear reversal of precedent.

5. *State of Connecticut* v. *Teal* (1982).[44] In this case, the issue was whether an employer whose *overall* selection procedure does not show adverse impact against protected groups is in violation if *some portion* of that procedure is discriminatory. The black plaintiffs claimed to have been unfairly excluded from eligibility for a permanent position by virtue of failing a screening test that was passed by 80 percent of the white applicants and only 54 percent of the black applicants. The state's contention was that of those who passed the test, a substantial number of blacks survived the remaining steps in the process; 22.9 percent, in fact, to only 13.5 percent of the whites who passed the test. The "bottom line" result was a process that produced no apparent adverse impact against blacks *as a group*. The court ruled for the plaintiffs, thereby establishing the principle that "bottom line" numbers are not enough. If *any part* of the process affects individuals unfairly, that part must be rectified irrespective of the impact on the group as a whole.

6. *Bakke* v. *Regents of the University of California* (1978).[45] Here the white plaintiff, Bakke, alleged "reverse discrimination," claiming unfair exclusion from medical school on the grounds that a certain number of positions were reserved for minority applicants. Since his qualifications for selection (including test scores) were admittedly higher than those for some of the successful minority candidates, his claim was exclusion by virtue of race. The court upheld Bakke's position in a very confusing argument defending the principle of "affirmative action" while denouncing that of "minority quotas." The decision thus seemed to shift the emphasis away from technical (predictive) concerns toward more philosophical ones, although it could scarcely be taken as a definitive statement on the proper weighting of values.

7. *Kaiser Aluminum and Chemical* v. *Weber* (1979).[46] In this reverse discrimination case, the court seemed to contradict the Bakke decision by ruling against Weber. However, in upholding an affirmative action program that favored black workers, it distinguished between two different kinds of preferential treatment: that aimed at *eliminating* an existing racial imbalance, which is legal; and that aimed at *maintaining* a balance, which is not.

If the reader can detect any coherent definition of fairness flowing from this stream of legal opinion, we offer our sincere congratulations. One legal aid that has helped to clarify the picture somewhat is the *Uni-*

form Guidelines, a document on selection that appeared in 1978.[47] The significance of this document, which represents many years of hard work on the part of a blue-ribbon panel of experts drawn from industry, government, and academe, is that for the first time everyone is playing more or less by the same set of official rules. The rules may not suit all concerned,[48] and they have certainly not eliminated all debate, but at least the argument can have a single point of focus. In the past, as we noted earlier, there were many official rulebooks, and fair employment practices depended upon the arm of government under which one's organization fell. Since it usually fell under several at once, the employer was in a no-win situation. Until Bakke, the only seemingly safe strategy was to maintain strict quotas, since in doing so adverse impact could not be demonstrated.[49]

Guidelines does not represent any drastic shift in the interpretation of the law. Basically, it calls for systematic recordkeeping on all relevant aspects of employment decisions (tabulation by group membership of who is and isn't hired, promoted, demoted, fired; compilation of all data on selection procedures used, including validity and minimum adverse impact studies), validation of all procedures used in these decisions, affirmative action, and careful description of jobs and job requirements. The main principle, once again, is that if adverse impact is alleged, it is incumbent upon the employer to prove that the procedures used—in aggregate and perhaps in isolation—are valid in all respects.

Several noteworthy points of clarification are included in *Guidelines.* *Unfairness* is defined as follows:

> When members of one race, sex, or ethnic group characteristically obtain lower scores on a selection procedure than members of another group, and the differences in scores are not reflected in differences in a measure of job performance, use of the selection procedure may unfairly deny opportunities to members of the group that obtains lower scores.[50]

"Adverse impact" is presumed to exist whenever the selection rate for a group falls below 80 percent of that for the group with the highest rate. For example, if 50 percent of all white male applicants were selected, at least 40 percent of all blacks, women, and so forth who applied would also have to be chosen in order to satisfy this definition.

The point developed in the *Albermarle* ruling is made explicit: where alternative procedures of roughly comparable validity exist, the employer must be able to show that he or she considered these alternatives and chose the one with the least adverse impact. This, of course, may prove to be an extremely difficult point to defend.

Much of the clarification offered by the guidelines involves the description of procedures for establishing validity—the technical considerations on which we have spent most of the present chapter. Criterion-related, content, and construct validation are all regarded as appropriate under the proper circumstances. Whereas previous guidelines tended to ignore practical difficulties faced by the smaller employer or the one with unusual labor market situations, the present rules provide sound practical advice on a variety of such validity issues. For example, where large, formal studies are impossible, *Guidelines* suggests that the emphasis be placed upon establishing job *relevance* (e.g., through the use of content-validated job-sample tests). Similarly, interim procedures are acceptable where considerable time is required to amass meaningful validation data. Of course, from a technical standpoint, *Guidelines* is not the best source of information on the proper use of tests. A much better document is the APA Division of I/O Psychology's *Principles for the Validation and Use of Personnel Selection Procedures.*[51]

And finally, the point is made that the concept of fairness and the techniques for validation are still in a state of evolution. Thus as newer, better ways of selecting people—and evaluating selection—are developed, employers are expected to use them. In other words, by one means or another, employers are expected to keep abreast of the technical aspects of selection.

PREDICTORS

To this point we have concentrated on the *processes* involved in selection: the concepts, models, and logic involved in fitting people and jobs. We have seen what factors contribute to effective and ineffective, fair and unfair, selection. We are now ready to look at the *predictors* themselves. What general kinds of predictive information can we get, and how useful is each in the overall selection picture?

There are three major categories of predictive information: *interview* data, *biographical* data, and *test* data. They are not totally independent with regard to content. We might learn, for example, that an applicant can type 50 words per minute by asking (interview), by looking at business school transcript or references (biographical data), or by giving a typing test. Furthermore, each data category encompasses a variety of specific techniques.

Interview Data

By far the most commonly used selection device is the employment interview. Rarely is anyone hired for anything without being interviewed by *someone*. Needless to say, the interview is also the least standardized, least quantitative approach. What information is sought, how it is gathered, and what is made of it are all highly individual matters.

As might be expected, a lot of research has been devoted to the interview in an effort both to describe what processes are involved and to determine how useful the resulting information is for predictive purposes.[52] The general consensus is that, however reliable and valid the approach might be, interviews as typically conducted are of limited predictive value.[53] They are subject to all sorts of biasing influences, and what information they do yield is either irrelevant or could probably be obtained more efficiently in other ways. On the other hand, the suspicion seems to be growing that the problem lies more in the way interviews are typically carried out than in the approach itself. There is at least scattered evidence that a properly conducted interview *might* yield some unique predictive information.[54] We are still a long way, however, from being able to specify what constitutes a proper interview, and what exactly this "unique information" is.[55]

Most employment interviews are conducted in a rather haphazard, unstructured fashion by untrained interviewers. Little or no planning proceeds them, and the result is some sort of overall suitability rating of the applicant (often a hire, no-hire decision). This kind of approach clearly does no good from a predictive standpoint and may do considerable harm. Interrater agreement is generally very low, and predictive validity is nil. Factors responsible for this total ineffectiveness are probably as many and varied as the people engaged in the interviewing process. We know from various studies that interviewers tend to talk more than the interviewees, to reach their decisions early in the interview, to be influenced by their own attitudes (preferring people who think as they do), to gather largely biographical information (which they could get from available records), and to weigh items of information in their own peculiar fashion. We also know that interviewers benefit very little from sheer day-to-day *experience*.

What, then, is likely to improve the situation? Some degree of structuring is apparently helpful. Both reliability and predictive validity tend to increase as a result of formulating the questions in advance, particularly if the same basic questions are applied to all applicants for the same job.[56] This assumes, of course, that the questions are relevant for that job. Naturally, a highly structured interview can reduce to little more than a verbal questionnaire. Whether anything is added as a result of the personal interaction is debatable.

Anything that would be likely to reduce interviewer and situational biases would probably improve the interview's value.[57] This would include interviewer training and provision of feedback to interviewers regarding the success of people whom they interviewed. One recent suggestion is that the information-gathering and evaluation functions of the interview be separated: One person conducts the interview (which is transcribed); another evaluates the interviewee based on the transcription.[58] This approach appears to have considerable promise. Another is based on the principles that (*a*) *multiple* interviews improve the reliability of whatever is measured and (*b*) use of job analysis can improve the interview's validity by focusing it on relevant requirements. In particular, use of interview *panels* or *boards* has been shown to yield at least modest predictiveness.[59]

Agreement is lacking as to what personal traits (if any) can be estimated reliably using the interview format. Some reviewers claim that general *intellectual* ability is about the only characteristic that can be judged with any degree of accuracy.[60] Others believe that *work motivation* and *interpersonal competence* can be evaluated with some reliability.[61] Again, however, one wonders whether even these traits could not be assessed more efficiently with some other procedure.

Whatever its shortcomings, the interview is probably here to stay. It is essential, therefore, that we continue the effort to understand the processes involved and that we seek to improve the technique. Theories of the interview process are sorely needed as are controlled studies to test those theories. For some strange reason, researchers who have studied the interview process have ignored the fact that it is an *interaction* between people—something social psychologists have been studying for years (see previous chapters on topics in Organizational Behavior). Recently, however, several investigators have begun to incorporate ideas from the person-perception and attribution-theory literatures into their models of the interview process. Dipboye, for example, sees the interview as a succession of exchanges between interviewer and interviewee, each of which is shaped in part by impressions formed during preceding stages. The interviewer's first impression of the interviewee is influenced by information available prior to the interview itself (i.e., resume, application blank, reference checks, job requirements). That impression, in turn, affects the way he or she begins the interview (which, of course, has an effect on the interviewee). The interviewee's impression and reaction then influence the interviewer, and the whole cycle repeats.[62]

This way of looking at the interview has several important implications. First, the prior information that conscientious interviewers rely on in preparing for an interview can actually *bias* the entire process. A negative impression will start the interview off on a downward spiral that will all but seal the candidate's doom; a positive one will escalate into an extremely favorable outcome. Second, the astute interviewee can do things to offset this bias since he or she is a part of the interaction. Knowing that the interviewer's first impression is likely to be negative, for example, the interviewee might behave in a manner intended to counter that impression at the very outset. Someone from a rural area without much formal education might pay particular attention to mode of dress and manner of speaking in interviewing for a position in a large, urban corporation. He could expect the interviewer to have stereotyped him as a probable "hick" and would want to present himself in marked contrast to that image. Third, of course, the interviewer, recognizing the interactive nature of the process and its potential for escalating bias, could take special pains to minimize his or her contribution to the self-fulfilling prophecy. Of course, at the present time, this whole conceptualization is very new. The basic propositions on which the theory is founded are just now beginning to be tested.

As our understanding of the process grows, we will undoubtedly discover better ways to conduct interviews. That, however, is a long-term goal. In the short term, it may be possible to increase the usefulness of most interviews simply by careful planning, structuring, and follow-up procedures.[63] One should decide in advance what information one hopes to get during the interview, structure the interview accordingly, and keep track of what happens to the applicant after the decision to hire is made. Of course, one should also be aware of the common biasing factors and try to resist being swayed by them during the interview or the decision-making process. And, in most instances, one would probably do well to keep one's mind open and mouth shut during more of the interview. It is important to realize that an interview is subject to the same evaluation considerations as any other kind of predictor. One is obliged to show that the behavior or traits it seeks to measure are job-related, representative, and predictive just as in the case of a test.[64]

Biographical Data

All major employers require applicants to furnish certain kinds of background information as part of the application process. Usually included are work history, education, and various personal items (marital status, birthdate). In most instances, relatively little use is made of this information. It is simply filed away for future reference.

It develops that there is a great deal of potential predictiveness in such biographical data. Numerous investigators have been able to demonstrate empirical relationships between certain biographical items and criteria such as tenure (how long the worker stays with the company) and performance in a variety of jobs. Age, marital status, education level, and previous occupations are among the most broadly predictive items.[65]

Findings such as these have prompted development of standardized inventories, known as biographical information blanks (BIB), and catalogs of items from which to compile one's own BIB.[66] The usual procedure for constructing and validating a BIB is similar to that discussed earlier in connection with actuarial predictions. Items are collected on a number of applicants and correlated with subsequent criterion measures. Those that predict, for whatever reasons, are kept; the rest are discarded or ignored. Frequently, the items are weighted according to how predictive they are, and the weights are summed to yield an overall score. Thus, for example, an applicant for a lathe operator position might score 5 points for having held a previous job for more than three years, 3 points for an age of over 30, 2 points for being married, 2 points for education beyond the high school level, and − 2 points for living outside the city limits. The total: 10 points.

There are clear advantages to the BIB approach. Bass and Barrett list seven, including low cost, high face validity, high construct and predictive validity, and a tendency to yield honest responses.[67] To the extent that they summarize one's life history, BIB scores should serve as a good index of a person's future behavior.

There are also, however, some serious drawbacks. For one thing, it has been shown that the validity of particular items can be rather unstable. What predicts this year may be totally irrelevant next year. Thus the validities must be constantly checked and the weights revalued as necessary. This, of course, is true of any strictly actuarial approach.

Another potential problem is that it might be difficult to justify the inclusion of some items even though they are highly correlated with success. Can we deny a woman employment simply because she is single— even if our married employees have been less likely to quit in the past? Where a person lives may be highly correlated with his race or color. Can we reject him on that basis—even if people from that locale have not done well in the past? Unless we can defend the job-relatedness of BIB items, they may well fail to satisfy legal guidelines for fairness in employment.[68] All these criticisms, of course, are predicated on the assumption that we are ignorant of the constructs that underlie whatever predictiveness the BIB has. In practice, that is usually true. Recently, however, several researchers have illustrated that a deeper understanding of BIB data can be achieved.[69] One can develop and test models of the characteristics represented by BIB items just as easily as with any other kind of predictive material.

A final thought on the BIB approach is that it makes explicit many of the questions that are usually put less directly to an applicant in an interview. Since these questions will be asked anyway, it is better to have them out in the open where their impact on the selection process is clearly visible than to have them hidden in the interview where their impact is known only to the interviewer.

Psychological Test Data

Nowhere has the influence of psychology on personnel selection been more apparent than in the area of testing. How valuable, on balance, standardized instruments have been in selecting and placing people is a hotly debated issue. Proponents claim that standardized tests offer greater potential for precise objective measurement than do most other techniques and that, properly constructed and used, they can greatly *increase* the fairness and efficiency of selection. Hunter and Hunter, for example, have recently calculated direct comparative estimates for the utility of alternative procedures and have shown all to be vastly inferior to ability tests.[70] Opponents argue that tests are rarely very powerful predictors of job performance but do tend to discriminate against certain groups. Therefore, what little difference testing might make in quality of selection is more than offset by its discriminatory consequences.[71]

Until a few years ago, we would have let the controversy rest there and refrained from stating a position. Today, however, the full weight of the consumerism movement has come down on the side of the opposition in a nationwide lobbying effort that has reached the halls of the U.S. Congress and virtually every statehouse in the union. At this writing, several states have passed legislation that will have far-reaching negative implications for the whole business of standardized testing. Cleverly but inaccurately billed as "truth in testing" (who, after all, could vote against *truth?*), the main thrust of this endeavor has been to make specific test results (i.e., correct answers on all items) available to all those tested. Test developers have always gone to great lengths to preserve the security of such information, since validity estimates, reference norms, and many of the other technical features that make the instruments useful are threatened by widespread exposure. The only alternative, developing all new items for every test administration, would be prohibitive in cost and could not possibly achieve the levels of reliability or validity that repeated use affords. One must either have an unlimited pool of items and an unlimited pocketbook for evaluating them, or one must live with tests that are considerably less useful than they could otherwise be—if one opts for full disclosure ("truth"). Should the present trend toward passage of such laws continue, we believe standardized tests will become either too expensive to use or too deficient to justify use at any cost. Since people will continue to be selected for schools and employment on *some* basis, whether testing continues or not, the reader would do well to consider the alternatives to testing that we have just reviewed. Can one really believe that people will be chosen more accurately or fairly on the basis of interviews or biographical data?

One other point in favor of standardized tests, properly used, is that a lot of evidence has appeared recently to dispel several of the major purported drawbacks of such instruments. As we saw earlier, the widely feared spectre of differential or single-group validity turned out to be a fairly rare occurrence. Moreover, the fear that typical employment tests are applicable to very narrowly defined task categories—that validities must therefore be established separately for specific jobs in specific organizations—has been seriously challenged. Validity appears to generalize over much wider domains than even the most cautious observer might have suspected. Standardized employment tests, it seems, are remarkably robust.[72]

Most would agree, however, that some tests are more useful and fair than others. We move now to a consideration of the various *kinds* of employment tests that are available. In our survey of this material, we shall consider only *standardized published* instruments. Many tests currently in use are of the homemade variety, constructed by an organization for its own use. The familiar academic course examinations are of this latter type. There is certainly nothing wrong with the homemade approach— indeed, such tests have the potential for being more predictive and job-related than standardized ones. Whether or not they realize this potential usually depends upon the amount of care and expertise that has gone into their development. Since we do not expect—and would not advise—the reader to undertake a program of test construction without expert help, we shall ignore the whole test construction phase.[73] Our earlier discussion of how one evaluates predictors should provide enough insight into the critical aspects of construction (reliability estimation, validation, sample adequacy, etc.) to permit initial judgment of the worth of standardized instruments.

Literally thousands of tests have been published for all sorts of purposes. A handy reference for information on those still in print is a book edited by Buros, which includes a description, technical data, and critiques of each available test.[74] More detailed information can usually be obtained from the test publisher. This is typically included, along with instructions for administration, scoring, and interpretation, in a manual supplied with test forms.

A test is nothing more than a standard set of tasks designed to measure individual differences on some trait or behavior. Various kinds of tasks may be included in a test: *paper-and-pencil* items; physical manipulation or *performance* items (e.g., putting pegs in holes); *verbal* items; *numerical* items; *job-sample* items; and so forth. Some tests are designed to be completed within a certain time interval (*timed* or *speed* tests), while others are not timed (*power* tests). Some items are presented in an *objective* format (true-false, multiple choice), while others require *subjective* responses (essay, short answer). All these task characteristics are used to define a particular test. Thus we might refer to a common arithmetic test as a *timed, objective, paper-and-pencil* test; to an essay in English as a *power, subjective, paper-and-pencil* test; and to a pilot's final check flight as a *power, objective, performance* test.

Even more important in the definition of a test are the kinds of behavior or traits that the tasks are designed to measure. Most tests used in personnel selection fall within one of four major content categories: (1) *achievement*, (2) *special aptitude* or *ability*, (3) *general intelligence*, and (4) *personality* (including motivation, temperament, and interest). As the reader might guess, these are listed in order of decreasing specificity as to what is measured. Thus *achievement* tests measure what a person knows as a result of a specific learning experience (e.g., an academic course), while *personality* tests try to measure abstract behavior tendencies.

It is a seldom-recognized but extremely important fact that, when used in selection, a test may no longer be described accurately according to the traits it purports to measure. If, for example, we take an inventory that was developed for purposes of clinical diagnosis and use it to select managerial employees, it becomes a *management selection test*. It must then be validated against criteria of managerial effectiveness. We cannot blithely assume that, since it measures traits in one population that we think are important in another, it is a valid selection device. It could conceivably measure none of the traits *in our population* for which it was originally designed and still be a good predictor of managerial success. This point is important because so many of the tests used in selection have been borrowed directly from other areas of psychology, where they were designed for purposes completely different from selection (for example, clinical diagnosis, counseling, predicting school success).

1. Achievement Tests

These tests are designed to measure degree of mastery of a specific content. Tests developed in conjunction with specific academic courses or industrial training programs would fall into this category. Since the content domain of courses and educational programs is rather idiosyncratic, achievement tests are typically homemade. There are, however, standardized versions for content areas that tend to be fairly uniform from school to school or company to company. The achievement portion of the College Entrance Examination Board examination (e.g., that devoted to specific subjects), typing and shorthand tests, and computer programming tests are familiar illustrations.

2. Aptitude Tests (Specific)

Whereas the focus of achievement tests is on a specified set of *material,* that of aptitude tests is on a specified set of personal *traits.* As the terms imply, aptitude tests are supposed to indicate something about an individual's *potential,* while achievement tests reflect actual *accomplishment.* A numerical aptitude test, for example, would presumably indicate the ease with which different people would be expected to learn and perform tasks involving use of numbers (bookkeeping, making change, checking). People scoring high on this test would be expected to show up well on measures of *achievement* in such tasks. However, a lot of other factors (motivation, amount of training, etc.) might also contribute to their achievement score.

In practice, few, if any, aptitude tests measure sheer *potential;* all aptitude test scores are influenced to a degree by past learning experiences, motivation, and a host of other achievement factors. Further, there may be little difference between the actual content of an achievement test and an aptitude test. The real distinction, as Guion notes, is one of use, not of construction.[75] It is important to keep this in mind whenever we are tempted to think of aptitude test scores as permanent indexes of capacity.

There are, of course, specific aptitude tests for almost every conceivable dimension of human behavior. Among the most prominent insofar as personnel selection is concerned are those designed to measure *specific intellectual abilities* (verbal skills, numerical skills, memory), *mechanical aptitudes* (ability to visualize spatial relationships, to assemble puzzles), *creativity and judgment* (problem solving, troubleshooting), *sensory and perceptual capabilities* (vision tests, hearing tests), and *psychomotor abilities* (eye-hand coordination, finger dexterity, vehicular control). The reader should consult the Buros yearbook, test catalogs, or a text such as Guion's for further details.

In many cases, test developers have assembled a number of aptitude tests into a *battery* or series of tests designed to predict performance on a particular type of job. For example, the General Clerical Test, published by the Psychological Corporation, consists of three subtests designed to measure clerical speed and accuracy, numerical ability, and verbal facility, respectively. These aptitudes tend to be important for success in a wide range of clerical jobs. Whether any or all of these subtests are valid *for a particular clerical job,* of course, should be established explicitly for the job in question by one or another validation procedure. At the very least, care should be taken to establish content validity or representativeness. Whether it is feasible to carry out one's own criterion-related study, however, depends on the size of the incumbent population (concurrent model) or the number of people hired over a reasonable period of time (predictive model). Where available samples are small (for convenience, let us say 30), it would probably be safer to rely upon the aggregate of published validity studies for similar jobs.[76] There are other methods for dealing with small-sample problems, notably a combination of content and criterion-related strategies known as *synthetic validation,* but these lie beyond the scope of the present book.[77]

3. General Intelligence Tests

If specific aptitude tests seek to measure a person's potential in rather narrowly defined areas (i.e., one or a few traits), intelligence tests try to measure it in the broadest possible terms. There is no universally accepted definition of intelligence. It should come as no surprise, therefore, that there is also not much agreement on how it should be measured. In fact, intelligence testing is a center of all sorts of controversy, particularly when used as a basis for personnel decisions.

Intelligence has long been conceptualized in two very different ways: (1) as a sort of *general aptitude* that governs performance on all kinds of intellectual tasks and (2) as a composite of the various *specific aptitudes* or dimensions of intellectual ability. The former is known as the *g-factor* theory; the most current version of the latter, as the *structure of intellect* model. Obviously, each of these views (as well as various hybrid models that include elements of both) suggests a somewhat different testing approach and a somewhat different interpretation of test data. If we believe in a *g*-factor, we would expect performance on almost any kind of item to reflect it to a degree. Those items having the least specificity, therefore, would be the best indicators of *g* and the best ones to include on an intelligence test. The *Ravens Progressive Matrices* test, for example, was designed with just this purpose in mind. If, on the other hand, we believe in *independent dimensions* of intellect, it becomes important to have all the specific abilities represented on our test. A battery known as the *Primary Mental Abilities Tests* (PMA) is a good illustration of this philosophy. In this view, it makes sense to look at intelligence analytically; people may differ from one another in the kind of intellectual skills that they possess as well as in their overall *amount* of proficiency.

As might be expected from this brief discussion, a lot of different tests have been devised to measure intelligence, each somewhat different from the others in item composition, theoretical underpinnings, and ultimate purpose. The most venerable of them all, now referred to as the *Stanford-Binet,* was originally developed by Alfred Binet for the purpose of predicting academic success among Paris school children. Believing that general intellectual prowess exhibits a normal rate of growth similar to that of physical development, Binet coined the term *mental age* (MA) and set about devising tasks appropriate for its measurement at each age level. He expressed performance on these tasks as a ratio of the child's MA score to CA (*chronological age*) and thereby saddled us with the widely misused (and dubious) concept of *intelligence quotient,* or *IQ.*

Other intelligence tests have been developed for such diverse purposes as classifying mental patients, placing military recruits, and predicting college success. Some have even been devised expressly for industrial selection, although the most popular of these (the *Otis* and the *Wonderlic*) are derivatives of an old military classification test. The point is, since the content of intelligence tests is far from uniform, we should try to match the specific mix of intellectual skills we are measuring with important task demands. We must remember that an *intelligence* test becomes a *performance prediction* test when we use it in selection. Its content must be appropriate for the job we are trying to fill; its predictive validity must be demonstrable.

Our emphasis on differences among tests of intelligence should not obscure the fact that there are also great similarities. Correlations among test scores tend to be high, suggesting that even though the items may be different, they do get at a lot of the same skills. Exactly what these skills are, whether they are chiefly a reflection of genetic, nutritional, or cultural influences, and how much they contribute to important social criteria such as school or job success, are all subjects of continuing controversy. The reader can easily guess the emotion generated by such issues, particularly in view of the fact that blacks and hispanics score consistently lower, on the average, than Caucasians on these tests. More-over, it has been charged that the test content is usually biased toward the kinds of skills that are developed or refined in school (thus theoreti-cally favoring the advantaged). The countercharge is that differences be-come even greater when this presumed academic bias is reduced. We are not about to see a resolution of this controversy any time soon. What *has* developed, however, is a new research perspective that may eventually reveal the key information-processing skills that underlie intelligence test scores. Drawing upon experimental research in human cognition, several investigators have been able to show consistent relationships be-tween intelligence measures and strategies used in various memory tasks.[78] "Intelligent" people, it seems, have more efficient ways of taking in and storing important information than do their less able counter-parts. While everyone recognizes that there is probably more to intelli-gence than this, it is heartening to know that the well-established corre-lations among these scores may reflect real, identifiable skill processes.

Assuming, then, that the intelligence construct (or constructs) has some validity, the practical question arises whether it is predictive of em-ployment criteria. Some years ago, Ghiselli and Brown surveyed the va-lidity data available at that time regarding the relationship between suc-cess on various types of jobs and intelligence test scores.[79] A summary of their findings is presented in Table 7–3. While these data are far from definitive in that they combine concurrent and predictive estimates, are not moderated for race or sex, and include both good and poor validity studies, they do provide some useful insights. For one thing, they show that intelligence tests are better predictors of how well people will do in a *training* program than how proficient they will be *on the job*. This is not surprising in view of the academic orientation of most such tests.

Overall, intelligence test scores do not seem to be as highly related to job success as one might like. One should not, however, jump to the con-clusion that they are therefore useless. First, as we saw earlier, failure to correct for a number of factors (such as small sample size and restriction of range) that tend to depress correlations may have produced an ex-tremely conservative estimate of the "true" validities. Second, just be-cause intelligence is not the *only* determinant of job performance does not mean that it is unimportant. Obviously, most work criteria reflect moti-vation, the ability to get along with one's peers, and a number of other nonintellectual qualities. And finally, in some specific areas—notably *managerial, general clerical, electrical,* and *inspection* occupations—the relationships are quite respectable despite these limitations. Certainly, we would not argue that general intelligence tests are *always* a justifi-able basis for hiring; nor would we contend that they should constitute the *only* basis for hiring even when their validity is demonstrable. Like any other class of predictors, their use should be dictated by the full range of considerations that we explored earlier in the chapter.

TABLE 7–3   Average Validities of General Intelligence Tests

Occupational Group	Average Validity Coefficient	
	Trainability	Proficiency
Machine tenders	—	.16
Assemblers	.02	.22
Inspectors	.19	.35
Packers and wrappers	.22	.13
Gross manual	− .03	.26
Average: All manipulative and observational	.10	.22
Mechanical repairmen	.38	.04
Electrical workers	.43	.47
Structural workers	.29	.09
Processing workers	.35	.24
Complex machine operators	.34	.28
Machining workers	.30	.08
Average: All trades and crafts	.35	.20
Protective occupations	.46	.26
Service occupations	.50	.07
Vehicle operators	.18	.14
Salesmen	—	.32
Salesclerks	—	− 10
General clerks	.41	.38
Recording clerks	.40	.25
Computing clerks	.23	.16
Average: All clerks	.35	.26
Managerial personnel	—	.37
Foremen	—	.27

SOURCE: From *Personnel testing* by R. M. Guion. New York: McGraw-Hill, 1965. Copyright 1965 by McGraw-Hill. Reprinted by permission.

4. Personality Tests and Related Devices

As we saw in Chapter 3, the term *personality* refers to a person's typical mode of behaving and thinking. In the broadest sense, therefore, we might include in this category any sort of instrument designed to measure *temperament, needs* or *motives, attitudes, emotional states,* or *interests.*[80] If intelligence tests try to define what a person is *capable* of doing, personality tests are more concerned with what the person *will* do—and, to an extent, with reasons why.

In most cases, the behavioral and cognitive tendencies that such tests proport to measure are expressed in terms of hypothesized *traits,* which are derived from someone's theory of personality. If there is little agreement on the composition of intelligence, there is even less in the case of personality. Instead of two main conceptualizations there are many; hence, each of the many available measuring devices seems to tap a different constellation of personality traits. Some traits do seem to show up rather consistently on the various tests in one form or another: *Sociability, masculinity, dominance, general activity,* and *anxiety* are among the most common. The validity of these and other personality constructs is open to question since it is typically established via factor analysis. It is well known that different factoring and interpretive procedures applied to the same test data can yield entirely different sets of constructs. Hence we cannot be sure how many personality traits there are, what they are, or whether a particular test does a good job of measuring them.

Theory and content aside, devices for measuring personality constructs can be distinguished on the basis of their general approach to measurement. The most straightforward technique is the *self-report inventory*. By this method, people are asked to judge how descriptive various statements, adjectives, or attributes are of themselves. Each answer contributes a certain amount to a score on one or more of the trait scales that the test claims to measure. For example, if a person were to indicate that he prefers arranging flowers or listening to classical music to playing golf or riding motorcycles, his answer would lower his general *activity* score and would push his standing on the *masculinity-femininity* scale toward the *feminine* side.

As this example suggests, the main problem with the inventory approach as applied to selection is that it is transparent: A person can see through the items and, if he wishes, distort his self-portrait to accommodate his ego or to meet the needs of the moment (for example, to assure selection for a desired position). Most such devices have built-in lie scales to indicate how likely it is that the person being tested (the subject) is faking responses. All this does, however, is tell us how much confidence we can place in the person's answers; it does nothing to rectify the faked data. Moreover, there is some question as to the proper interpretation of the lie scales themselves. On the other hand, the fact that people *can* distort their responses does not necessarily mean that they *do*. McCormick and Ilgen point out that the evidence on this question is sparse and mixed. Also, note that lie scales can themselves be predictive: Faking keys have been used with apparent success to predict performance of salespeople and naval officers.[81]

To combat the presumed problem of faking, a number of *disguised* techniques have been developed. Foremost among these are the *projective techniques* in which highly ambiguous or incomplete test items are presented to the subject for interpretation or completion. The idea is that since the items have little explicit meaning themselves, the subject must furnish her own in order to give a response: She must *project* her personality into the situation. According to projective test advocates, people's responses to such items reveal a great deal about their inner motives and cognitive states. For example, the *Thematic Apperception Test,* which we encountered in Chapter 3, was seen as the principal means of measuring *need for achievement* (nAch). An even more familiar example is the Rorschach ink blot test, which consists of a series of meaningless forms (literally ink blots) that the subject must interpret. Responses are scored according to how closely they resemble the norms provided by various reference groups (psychiatric patients; "normal" high school students; and so on). Interpretation of what the responses tell us about *personality* depends upon the theoretical preference of the examiner.

Projective tests undoubtedly reduce problems associated with transparency. It would be very difficult for a person to fake answers, since he or she has no way of knowing what various responses mean. The ambiguity may, however, be a two-edged sword. Opponents of the projective approach argue that *no one* knows what the responses mean. The examiner is as much in the dark as the subject.

The projective approach is only one of many ways personality test developers have tried to increase the objectivity of responses. Another procedure for disguising items is to require the subject to choose between self-descriptive alternatives that have been matched for social desirability (or undesirability); For example, would you prefer to be convicted of murder or rape? The subject would not know which is the "better" crime and would thus tend to respond on the basis of his "true" feelings. Once again, however, there is an interpretative problem. What can we infer about a person's personality traits from the fact that he prefers murder to rape? Of course, if we can show that people who choose the murder response make better salesmen or managers or widget assemblers, it doesn't matter so much that we are unable to unravel the personality dynamics involved.

As was the case for intelligence, most of the personality tests currently in use for selection were developed for some other purpose. The most popular self-report inventory (the *Minnesota Multiphasic Personality Inventory,* or *MMPI*), for example, was originally designed as a tool for the classification of psychiatric patients. Little wonder that its use in selecting "normal" job applicants has been questioned! The reader is reminded, however, that the true measure of a selection device is how well it *predicts* work criteria; not where it came from, what the items look alike, or how accurately it describes personality constructs. What, then, can be said about the *criterion-related validity* of such tests? Guion summarized the results of a large number of validation studies by test, job, and criterion index.[82] The most common finding was that personality and interest test scores were either unrelated or very weakly related to the various criteria of success. A more recent review covering selection of police officers was considerably more positive. In this case, the *California Personality Inventory (CPI)* was the instrument used, and validities were generally in the moderate range.[83]

Nowhere has employment testing been more roundly criticized than in the personality area. It has been charged that such tests have no validity, represent a serious invasion of personal privacy, encourages lying, and reinforce conformity. Unfortunately, all these charges are to an extent justified, with respect to the way personality tests have been *used.* In spite of all the effort on the part of professional organizations such as the American Psychological Association to formulate and enforce ethical standards, abuses continue to abound. The idea that it may be possible to screen out potential alcoholics, psychotics, thieves, or other troublemakers on the basis of a simple personality test is apparently too appealing for many organizations to resist. The idea that it takes a certain type to be a good salesperson or manager and that a personality test might be able to identify that type is deeply ingrained in the folklore of management (see Chapter 3). By now, the reader should realize that such lofty goals are well beyond the modest proven capabilities of existing personality tests. In deciding whether or not to include such tests in the selection process, one should weigh the potential increase in predictiveness against the ill-will that such tests generally create. If the decision favors their use, every effort should be made to restrict interpretation of the scores to areas in which validity has been proven and to maintain the confidentiality of any records.

Before leaving the topic of testing in general and personality testing in particular, it might be well to cite one notable success story to which we have alluded earlier (under the topic of *leadership*): the Exxon Company's Personnel Development Series (PDS) used in the identification of managerial talent. This battery, which includes personality scales, has been shown to predict clearly articulated criteria for Exxon managers with multiple Rs as high as .70![84] Success of this magnitude supports Hunter and Schmidt's contention that we have sorely underestimated the real potential of mental testing. The development and refinement of the PDS was done in a painstaking fashion over 30 years (and counting). It is extremely encouraging to see such a vivid illustration of what testing can accomplish when the job is done right.

Other Approaches to Selection

Recent years have seen an increase in the popularity of selection methods based on performance under actual or simulated job conditions. Rather than attempting to *abstract* the qualities required by the job, one simply uses the job itself as the basis for prediction. People are hired with a minimum of screening and placed in a training program or on the job itself with the understanding that continued employment is contingent upon level of performance during a specified *trial period*. Important considerations in any such approach, of course, are the validity of the trial period measures and the explicitness of the requirements for selection. What a person must do in order to "make the team" should be clearly spelled out and justified in terms of success-prediction data. As an example of how this approach can be misued, one of the authors recently testified in a discrimination case for a black plaintiff who was dismissed from the fire de-

partment of a west Texas city for alleged failure to survive the probationary period and its final examination. Despite the fact that this was 20
years after the passage of the Civil Rights Act, and the city had a black
population of over 8,000 people, the plaintiff was only the first or second
of his race ever to be admitted, even on provisional status, into this department! That apparently could not be avoided since his score on the validated screening test ranked fourth highest among those for 83 candidates. The probationary period, however, was another matter entirely.
Survival depended on one's attitude, initiative, appearance, and so forth
as judged by one's supervisor, and on the results of a final exam, which
had no explicit scoring system and had never been validated by *any*
method. Since the city had, however, performed a job analysis for the
firefighter position, the author was able retrospectively to estimate the
exam's content validity. It turned out that the exam dealt with only 4 of
the 104 tasks identified by the job analysis, and these were among the
items rated lowest in both frequency and importance for the job of firefighter! It is conceivable, of course, that the plaintiff did not perform well
during the trial period, as the defense claimed. However, it is hard to
imagine how he could *possibly* have survived this process were the department intent on excluding blacks as he claimed.

Another approach based in part on the job-sample philosophy is that of
assessment centers. Pioneered by the American Telephone & Telegraph
Company for the identification of potential managers, this method relies
heavily upon realistic individual and group exercises. Candidates spend
several days at the center performing a whole series of carefully designed
tasks under the watchful eye of trained evaluators. Although they are interviewed and tested for general intelligence and knowledge, candidates
spend the bulk of their time on an *in-basket* simulation consisting of representative real-life problems drawn from the in-baskets of actual managers. Each candidate's performance is evaluated independently and collectively by several staff members on a number of critical dimensions
(decision making, planning and organizing, leadership, etc.), and a thorough report is written. The reported success of this program in predicting
subsequent performance of managers is impressive.[85] Of course, the
AT&T program is but one of many assessment centers, each of which has
its own peculiar mix of content, measures, and strategies. As might be expected, results of these programs have been as mixed as their formats.
Moreover, one of the main arguments for the approach, its seemingly obvious conformance to both the letter and spirit of the requirements for
fair selection, has recently been questioned. The point is not that assessment centers are necessarily unfair to protected groups, just that one cannot simply *assume* that they are fair. Like any other technique, they
must be validated, and because we still know so little about them, validation is not always easy.[86]

SELECTION AND PLACEMENT AS SYSTEM FUNCTIONS

In view of the fact that most of this chapter, like the field itself, has been devoted to traditional selection and placement issues, it might be well to close as we began—with an attempt to put the whole process in perspective.

First, it should be reemphasized that selection of people by organizations is but one aspect of the larger picture of attraction-selection decisions. Second, the whole business of matching people and jobs is but one approach toward attainment of organizational and individual goals. It may often be the least effective, most costly, or most problem-ridden of the available alternatives. The manager should never lose sight of the complex system character of modern organizations, which we explored in Chapter 2. People may perform effectively or ineffectively in a particular organization or work role as a function of many interacting *individual, organizational,* and *situational* variables (skill variables, motivational variables, organizational climate variables, training variables, and so on). It makes little sense, therefore, to view selection—with its heavy emphasis on *individual* variables—in isolation. A high proportion of hirees may work out poorly because they lack certain skills, are not trained adequately, are ridiculed by their supervisors, are placed in unnecessarily complex jobs, or are not highly motivated. Even the obtained validity estimates can reflect broad organizational and social influences.[87] The solutions may well lie in changing something about the organizations rather than the characteristics of the people hired.

A third, and somewhat related point, is that organizations do not always have a free hand in selection and placement decisions even when they might use these functions to advantage. Labor unions very often determine the eligibility requirements of prospective candidates and even, in some cases, the actual choices of people for jobs. It is important to recognize, however, that unions are under the same obligation as management to justify their selection and placement procedures (the *Weber* case, for example, was filed concurrently against a union and an employer).

Finally, it should be noted that whereas much of the foregoing discussion has used blue-collar examples because they are simpler, selection and placement of *managers* is a topic of equally great significance. Of course, the basic concepts are the same in both cases; it is the specific predictors, constructs, and criteria that distinguish the two levels. One other possible difference is the typical attitude of organizations toward selection at the two levels: Organizations seem much more inclined to look upon the filling of management positions in the broad terms of mutual attraction-selection processes.

CONCLUSIONS

Few organizational decisions have as far-reaching implications as those involving the selection and placement of employees. If an organization is basically *people,* then recruitment, selection, and placement decisions go a long way toward defining what any particular organization will be like.

The logic of selection (and, in most respects, that of placement as well) involves four basic kinds of information: *predictors, traits, job characteristics,* and *criteria.* We attempt to use predictor information (interviews, biographical, and test data) to forecast how well people will do, if hired, on specific job criteria (performance measures, tenure, and the like) and to select accordingly.

Selection procedures are evaluated in a number of ways, most of which involve relationships among the four kinds of information outlined above. The first requirement is that predictor and criterion measures be *reliable,* a condition that is established by correlating two sets of measures obtained using essentially the same measuring instrument. Different procedures for estimating reliability yield coefficients of *stability, equivalence,* and *internal consistency.*

The second requirement is that the predictor be a *valid* indicant of whatever it purports to measure. This is established by showing that predictor measures are consistently related to hypothetical traits (*construct validity*) or criteria (*concurrent* and *predictive validity*); or that material included in the predictor is representative of job content (*content validity*). The correlation statistic is used directly in estimating concurrent and predictive validity. Less direct methods (often involving factor analysis) are necessary for demonstrating construct validity, while content validation is strictly a matter of logic and a good job analysis.

A third basis for evaluating selection procedures is *utility,* which depends on market conditions and job difficulty as well as the validity of predictors. In its broadest sense, the utility model offers a good way to view the total cost-benefit picture.

The final requirement is that the selection process be *fair,* although here we encounter problems because the concept is inherently subjective and value laden. Since the selection situation is often the focal point for *conflicting* values, fairness becomes a legal matter. Technical considerations have helped to define the conflict more precisely but not to resolve it. Legal actions, on the other hand, have resolved the conflict in many different ways, thereby producing multiple definitions and considerable confusion. A recent set of guidelines has been only partly successful in reducing the confusion.

Predictive data are generally gathered in one of three ways: via interview, biographical information blanks, or tests. The interview is by far the most common technique. As usually conducted, it is also the least reliable and valid. Although there is every reason to believe that careful planning and structuring can increase the value of the interview, it is debatable whether this approach yields any information that could not be obtained more efficiently by other means.

Biographical information blanks (BIB) provide much the same information as interviews and, if properly weighted, are often capable of good *short-term* predictions—especially of tenure, absenteeism, and tardiness criteria. The main problems are (1) the instability of predictive items and (2) the questionable legal and ethical status of some common—and possibly predictive—items.

Much of the debate over selection procedures has centered around the use of tests. The major attributes that tests seek to measure are *achievement, specific aptitudes, general intelligence,* and *personality traits.* How well the tests measure these attributes depends a great deal upon how clearly the attributes can be defined. In the case of achievement and specific aptitudes, there is little ambiguity in the nature of the traits, and precise measurement is at least possible. In the case of intelligence and personality, however, there is considerable disagreement on construct definition. Therefore, different tests, based on different theories of intelligence or personality, measure different things.

One final note on selection concerns the fact, introduced earlier, that it is but one approach to the problem of fitting people and jobs. Selection has been most successful in the case of clearly defined, generally low-level repetitive jobs. This is because it is clear what is involved in these jobs; hence, it is easier to devise good predictors for them and to evaluate performance on them. However, these jobs are also the ones for which it is easiest to devise training programs, for which errors in selection will prove least costly, and for which redesign of task procedures might be easily accomplished. In short, the conditions that make *selection* an effective strategy are often the very same ones that argue for alternative strategies. Even though techniques such as aptitude testing are probably a lot more effective than we had previously thought, organizations would do well to give careful consideration to the relative merits of *all* the options, not just the relative merits of different ways to select people. We move now to another of these options—*training.*

NOTES

1. Porter, L. W., Lawler, E. E., III, & Hackman, J. R. (1975). *Behavior in organizations.* New York: McGraw-Hill; Schneider, B. (1972). *Staffing organizations.* Pacific Palisades, Calif.: Goodyear; and Steers, R. M., & Porter, L. W. (1979). *Motivation and work behavior.* New York: McGraw-Hill.

2. Wanous, J. P. (1977). Organizational entry: Newcomers moving from outside to inside. *Psychological Bulletin, 84,* 601–618.

3. Wanous, J. P. (1976). Organizational entry: From naive expectations to realistic beliefs. *Journal of Applied Psychology, 61,* 22–29.

4. Wanous, J. P. (1973). Effects of realistic job preview on job acceptance job attitudes, and job survival. *Journal of Applied Psychology, 58,* 327–32.

5. Ilgen, D. W.,& Seely, W. (1974). Realistic expectations as an aid in reducing voluntary resignations. *Journal of Applied Psychology, 58,* 452–455.

6. Farr, J. L., O'Leary, B. S., & Bartlett, C. J. (1973). Effect of a work sample test upon self-selection and turnover of job applicants. *Journal of Applied Psychology, 58,* 283–285; Reilly, R. R., Tenopyr, M. L., & Sperling, S. M. (1979). Effects of job previews on job acceptance and survival of telephone operator candidates. *Journal of Applied Psychology, 64,* 218–220.

7. Schneider. *Staffing organizations.*

8. Jensen, A. R. (1980). *Bias in mental testing.* New York: Free Press.

9. Ghiselli, E. E., & Haire, M. (1960). The validation of selection tests in the light of the dynamic character of criteria. *Personnel Psychology, 13,* 225–231.

10. The procedure is actually a little more involved than this, as we shall see later. We are only interested in the *logic* of the approach here.

11. See, for example, Guion, R. M. (1976). Recruiting, selection, and job placement. In Dunnette (Ed.). *Handbook of industrial and organizational psychology.* Skokie, Ill.: Rand McNally.

12. Anastasi, A. (1976). *Psychological testing.* New York: Macmillan.

13. Guion. Recruiting, selection, and job placement.

14. Campbell, J. P. (1974). *A Monte Carlo approach to some problems inherent in multivariate prediction, with special reference to multiple regression.* Technical Report 2002, Personnel Training Research Program. Washington D.C.: Office of Naval Research; and Schmitt, N., Coyle, B. W., & Rauschenberger, J. (1977). A Monte Carlo evaluation of three formula estimates of cross-validated multiple correlation. *Psychological Bulletin, 84,* 751–758.

15. It is important to recognize, however, that r does not give this proportion directly—it cannot be read as a percentage. The computational formula is

$$r = \frac{N\Sigma XY - (\Sigma X)(\Sigma Y)}{\sqrt{[N\Sigma X^2 - (\Sigma X)^2][N\Sigma Y^2 - (\Sigma Y)^2]}}$$

where x represents the scores on one variable, y represents the scores on the other variable, and N is the number of scores.

16. See any basic statistics text for formulas and complete description (e.g., Guilford, J. B., & Fruchter, B. (1978). *Fundamental statistics in psychology and education.* New York: McGraw-Hill.

17. Geometric mean.

18. Lawshe, C. H., Bolda, R. A., Brune, R. L., & Auclair, G. (1958). Expectancy charts II: Their theoretical development. *Personnel Psychology, 11,* 545–60.

19. Sands, W. A. (1973). A method for evaluating alternative recruiting selection strategies: The CAPER model. *Journal of Applied Psychology, 57,* 222–227.

20. Application of decision models to the selection problem was originally suggested by Chronbach, L. J., Gleser, G. (1965). *Psychological tests and personnel decisions.* (2d ed.). Urbana: University of Illinois Press. The reader may note a similarity between EU and a central concept in VIE theory (Chapter 3). This is no accident; both have a common origin.

21. Schmidt, F. L., Hunter, J. E., McKenzie, R. C., & Muldrow, T. (1979). The impact of valid selection procedures on work force productivity. *Journal of Applied Psychology, 64,* 609–626.

22. Hunter, J.E., & Hunter, R.F. (1984). Alternative predictors of job performance. *Psychological Bulletin, 96,* 72-98.

23. Cascio, W. F. (1982). *Costing human resources: The financial impact of behavior in organizations.* Belmont, Calif.: Kent.

24. Guion, R. M. (1966). Employment tests and discriminatory hiring. *Industrial Relations, 5,* 20–37. In its strictest technical sense, a moderator variable should be uncorrelated with either the predictors or the criterion and should not add predictive variance of its own. This restriction, however, is rarely observed in practice (see, for example, Abrahams, N. M., & Alf, E., Jr. (1972). Moderator variables: Pitfalls in moderator research. *Journal of Applied Psychology, 56,* 245–251).

25. Bartlett, C. J., & O'Leary, B. S. (1969). A differential predictor model to moderate the effects of heterogeneous groups in personnel selection and classification. *Personnel Psychology, 22,* 1–17.

26. Einhorn, H. J., & Bass, H. R. (1971). Methodological considerations relevant to discrimination in employment testing. *Psychological Bulletin, 75,* 261–269.

27. Ghiselli, E. E. (1960). The prediction of predictability. *Educational and Psychological Measurement, 20,* 3–8.

28. Guion. Employment tests and discriminatory hiring, pp. 20–37.

29. Arvey, R. D. (1979). *Fairness in selecting employees.* Reading, Mass.: Addison-Wesley Publishing.

30. Cleary, T. A. (1968). Test bias: Prediction of grades of Negro and white students in integrated colleges. *Journal of Educational Measurement, 5,* 115–124.

31. Boehm, V. R. (1977). Differential prediction: A methodological artifact? *Journal of Applied Psychology, 62,* 146–154.

32. Hunter, J. E., Schmidt, F. L., & Hunter, R. (1979). Differential validity of employment tests by race: A comprehensive review and analysis. *Psychological Bulletin, 86,* 721–735.

33. Schmidt, F. L., & Hunter, J. E. (1980). The future of criterion-related validity. *Personnel Psychology, 33,* 41–60; and Schmidt, F. L., & Hunter, J. E. (1981). Employment testing: Old theories and new research findings. *American Psychologist, 36,* 1128–1137.

34. Katzell, R. A., & Dyer, F. J. (1977). Differential validity revived. *Journal of Applied Psychology, 62,* 137–145; and Callendar, J. C., & Osburn, H. G. (1980). Development and test of a new model for validity generalization. *Journal of Applied Psychology, 65,* 543–558.

35. Hunter, Schmidt, & Hunter. (1979). Differential validity of employment tests by race.

36. Schmidt, F. L., Hunter, J. E., & Pearlman, K. (1981). Task differences as moderators of aptitude test validity in selection: A red herring. *Journal of Applied Psychology, 66,* 166–85.

37. Schmidt & Hunter. Employment testing.

38. Committee on Labor and Public Welfare, U.S. Senate.

39. See, for example, Arvey, R. D. (1979). Unfair discrimination in the employment interview: Legal and psychological aspects. *Psychological Bulletin, 86,* 736–765.

40. *Myart* v. *Motorola,* 110 Congressional Record 5662–64 (1964).

41. *Griggs* v. *Duke Power Company,* 3 FEP 175 (1971).

42. *Albemarle Paper Company* v. *Moody,* 10 FEP 1181 (1975).

43. *Washington* v. *Davis,* 12 FEP 1415 (1976).

44. *Connecticut* v. *Teal,* 102 S. CT. 2525 (1982). See also Blumrosen, A. W. (1984). The "bottom line" after *Connecticut* v. *Teal* in R. S. Schuler & S. A. Youngblood (Eds.). *Readings in Personnel and Human Management* (2d ed.) (pp. 105–114). St. Paul, Minn.: West Publishing.

45. *Bakke* v. *Regents of the University of California,* 17 FEP 1000 (1978).

46. What the Weber ruling does. *Time,* July 4, 1979, pp. 48–49.

47. Uniform guidelines on employee selection procedures. *Federal Register* (Vol. 43), No. 166, August 25, 1978, 38296–38309.

48. Sparks, C. P. (February 1977). The not-so-uniform employee selection guidelines. *Personnel Administration,* pp. 36–40.

49. Seligman, D. (1975). How "equal opportunity" turned into employment quotas. In K. N. Wexley & G. A. Yukl (Eds.). *Organizational behavior and industrial psychology,* pp. 470–479). New York: Oxford.

50. Uniform guidelines, section 14B(8).

51. American Psychological Association, Division of Industrial-Organizational Psychology. (1980) *Principles for the validation and use of personnel selection procedures* (2d ed.). Berkeley: Author.

52. Ulrich, L., & Trumbo, D. (1965). The selection interview since 1949. *Psychological Bulletin, 63,* 100–116; and Wright, O. R., Jr. (1969). Summary of research on the selection interview since 1964. *Personnel Psychology, 22,* 391–413.

53. Carlson, R. E., Thayer, P. W., Mayfield, E. C., & Peterson, D. A. (1971). Improvements in the selection interview. *Personnel Journal, 50,* 268–75; and Mayfield, E. C. (1964). The selection interview: A reevaluation of published research. *Personnel Psychology, 17,* 239–260.

54. Grant, D. L., & Bray, D. W. (1969). Contributions of the interview to assessment of management potential. *Journal of Applied Psychology, 53,* 24–34; and Mayfield, E. C., Brown, S. H., & Hamstra, B. W. (1980). Selection interviewing in the life insurance industry: An update of research and practice. *Personnel Psychology, 33,* 725–739.

55. Arvey, R. D., & Campion, J. E. (1982). The employment interview: A summary and review of recent research. *Personnel Psychology, 35,* 281–322.

56. Carlson, R. E., Schwab, D. P., & Heneman, H. G. (1970). Agreement among styles of selection interviewing. *Journal of Industrial Psychology, 5,* 8–17.

57. Hakel, M. D., Ohnesorge, J. P., & Dunnette, M. D. (1970). Interviewer evaluations of job applicants' resumes as a function of the qualifications of immediately preceding applicants. *Journal of Applied Psychology, 54,* 27–30.

58. Grant & Bray. Contributions of the interview.

59. Arvey & Campion. The employment interview; Latham, G. P., Saari, L. M., Purcell, E. D., & Campion, M. A. (1980). The situational interview. *Journal of Applied Psychology, 65,* 422–427.

60. Mayfield. The selection interview.

61. Grant & Bray. Contributions of the interview.

62. Dipboye, R. L. (1982). Self-fulfilling prophecies in the selection-recruitment interview. *Academy of Management Review, 7,* 579–586.

63. Schmitt, N. (1976). Social and situational determinants of interview decisions: Implications for the employment interview. *Personnel Psychology, 29,* 79–101.

64. Arvey. Unfair discrimination.

65. England, G. W. (1961). *Development and use of weighted application blanks.* Dubuque, Ia.: Wm. C. Brown.

66. Owens, W. A., & Henry, E. R. (1966). *Biographical data in industrial psychology: A review and evaluation.* Creativity Research Institute, Richardson Foundation.

67. Bass, B. M., & Barrett, G. V. (1972). *Man, work, and organization.* Boston: Allyn & Bacon.

68. Arvey. Fairness in selecting employees.

69. Dunnette, M. D., & Borman, W. C. (1979). Personnel selection and classification systems. *Annual Review of Psychology,* pp. 477–525; and Schoenfeldt, L. F. (1974). Utilization of manpower: Development and evaluation of an assessment-classification model for matching individuals with jobs. *Journal of Applied Psychology, 59,* 583–595.

70. Hunter & Hunter. Alternative predictors of job performance.

71. See, for example, Testing and public policy. *American Psychologist,* 1965, *20* (Whole No. 11), special issue. The article reports on congressional hearings on testing.

72. Schmidt, Hunter, & Pearlman. Task differences as moderators of aptitude test validity in selection.

73. The interested reader should consult Guion, R. M. (1965). *Personnel testing.* New York: McGraw-Hill; or Chronbach, L. J. (1970). *Essentials of psychological testing* (3d ed.). New York: Harper & Row.

74. Buros, O. K. (Ed.) (1972). *The seventh mental measurements yearbook.* Highland Park, N.J.: Gryphon.

75. Guion. *Personnel testing.*

76. Schmidt, F. L., & Hunter, J. E. (1977). Development of a general solution to the problem of validity generalization. *Journal of Applied Psychology, 62,* 529–540.

77. Lawshe, C. H., & Balma, M. J. (1966). *Principles of personnel testing* (2d ed.). New York: McGraw-Hill; and Pimoff, E. S. (1975). *Job element methods (Vol. 3) The J-coefficient.* Washington, D.C.: Personnel Research and Development Center, Civil Service Commission.

78. Sternberg, R. J., & Detterman, D. K. (Eds.). (1979). *Human intelligence: Perspectives on its theory and measurement.* Norwood, N.J.: Ablex.

79. Ghiselli, E. E., & Brown, C. W. (1955). *Personnel and industrial psychology.* New York: McGraw-Hill.

80. Strictly speaking, personality tests seek to measure a number of these attributes. There are also instruments aimed specifically at *interests, temperament, attitudes,* and even particular *motives* (e.g., nAch).

81. McCormick & Ilgen. (1980). *Industrial psychology* (pp. 174–176). Englewood Cliffs, N.J.: Prentice-Hall.

82. Guion. *Personnel testing.*

83. Spielberger, C. D. S. (1979). *Police selection and evaluation.* New York: Praeger/Holt, Reinhart and Winston.

84. Sparks, C. P. Paper-and-pencil measures of potential. In G. F. Dreher & P. R. Sackett (Eds.). (1983). *Perspectives on employee staffing and selection* (pp. 349–368). Homewood, Ill.: Richard D. Irwin.

85. Campbell, R. J., & Bray, D. W. Assessment centers: An aid in management selection. *Personnel Administration,* March–April 1967, pp. 485–487; Howard, A. (1974). An assessment of assessment centers. *Academy of Management Review, 17,* 115–134.

86. Dreher & Sackett. *Perspectives on employee staffing and selection.*

87. Thayer, P. W. (1977). Somethings old, somethings new. *Personnel Psychology, 30,* 513–524.

8

Training and Development

As should be apparent by now, the research and theory in industrial and organizational psychology have spawned quite a large repertoire of techniques for changing organizations. Some of these techniques have been mentioned in the discussion of each of the preceding topics. If worker motivation is the problem, an organization can try job enlargement, goal setting, incentive systems, and a variety of other motivational strategies. If ineffective leadership is the problem, the organization might try training its managers to adopt leadership styles that fit the situation or it might try training them to change the situation to fit their styles. To improve group effectiveness, the organization might intervene with process consultation and problem-solving techniques. Instead of or in addition to changing the behavior of employees, the organization also can attempt to attract and select more competent and motivated employees.

Unfortunately, changes are easy to recommend but much harder to implement successfully. Even if an attempted change is firmly based on theory and research, there are a variety of reasons it might fail: It might pose a threat to employee job security, or it might not be adequately explained to those who must implement it, or it might not be endorsed enthusiastically by top management, or it might violate group norms, to name just a few. Perhaps the most common reason for failure, however, is that changes are too often implemented in a haphazard and piecemeal fashion without sufficient planning.

As an alternative to just letting things happen, the model of *planned change* has been presented as an ideal for organizations to follow in designing and implementing changes. Although several versions of the planned change model have appeared, all seem to contain three basic phases. The *assessment phase* consists of a careful determination of what

301

needs changing. The *implementation phase* consists of the evaluation and choice of change strategies and the actual implementation of the changes. Finally, the *evaluation phase* consists of a systematic appraisal of what happens as a result of the changes and a determination of whether to continue, modify, or terminate the intervention.

In this chapter, we will consider two general applications of the model of planned change. First, we'll discuss its applications to training, perhaps the common vehicle for change in organizations. Indeed, almost all interventions, whether they are implemented at the individual, group, or organizational levels, are accompanied by some type of training, even if it consists of little more than indoctrination. The second application of the planned change model that we'll consider is *organizational development* (OD), the most ambitious of intervention schemes. Its goal is to effect a major overhaul in large segments of the organization or, upon occasion, in the entire thing, using whatever techniques seem appropriate. These generally include some form of training, but they could also involve any of the interventions that we have discussed so far: structural reorganization, job redesign, selection, placement, or various motivational schemes. Above all, OD usually involves a comprehensive analysis of people, roles, and systems.

TRAINING

Training is defined by Hinrichs as "a systematic intentional process of altering behavior of organizational members in a direction which contributes to organizational effectiveness."[1] In the context of Hinrich's definition, behavior includes "any aspect of human activity, cognition, or feeling." Everyone who enters the world of work is exposed, at one time or another, to some form of training. It may consist of little more than a casual orientation to the policies of the organization and nature of the job, or it may involve the equivalent of a full-blown college degree program. However casual or formal, simple or elaborate it may be, all training is aimed at changing people in the interest of organizational goals.

Training is so commonplace that it tends to be taken for granted. Seldom does anyone question its adequacy. Because most of what passes for training lacks any systematic planning and makes an undetermined contribution to the organization, it doesn't really qualify as training under Hinrichs' definition. When training does occupy a defined role in the organization, which is seldom the case in any but the largest firms, the position is generally one of low prestige and power. Training groups and their directors are notoriously low in status. Nevertheless, training is an extremely important function that appears to be increasing in importance. Rapidly changing technologies have placed increasing pressure on organizations to retrain employees. Indeed, according to one estimate, employers in the future will have to retrain their office workers five to eight times during their careers.[2] One effect of these increasing demands on the training function may be to improve the position of training departments.

It is paradoxical that something that costs so much is valued so little. There are no reliable figures available on the annual training budget for the country as a whole, but everyone agrees that the amount is staggering. It has been estimated, for example, that about $400 million was spent by business organizations on outside programs in 1975 and another $1.6 billion was spent on in-house training.[3] Between fiscal years 1963 and 1974, the federal government spent $14.4 billion on categorical employment and training programs under the Manpower Training and Development Act.[4] Yet for all of this, maybe 1 program in 40 has received any systematic evaluation. It is a fairly safe bet that very few organizations are getting their money's worth out of their training programs.[5]

In its current state, then, personnel training is important, costly, and neglected. These, however, are but a few of its problems—by and large, problems attributable to organizational ignorance. Criticism can also be leveled against many of the programs themselves, the research and theory on which they are based, and the occasional attempts that have been made to evaluate them. Indeed, one cannot review the present status of the training field without a sense of deepening pessimism. To quote one reviewer, "By and large, the training and development literature is voluminous, nonempirical, nontheoretical, poorly written, and dull."[6] He goes on to note that it is also obsessed with techniques and subject to fads.

It is important to recognize the shortcomings in existing programs so that we know where to direct our efforts in attempting to rectify them in the future. We shall devote some attention to them in the following pages. Rather than dwell upon these deficiencies, however, we shall take a more positive stance and focus on what training could be if it were done properly. Of primary concern are (1) procedures for the design of a training program, (2) theories and principles of training, (3) specific training techniques, their strengths and weaknesses, and (4) training programs that have received attention in research by industrial and organizational psychologists.

Procedures for Program Development

Enough has been learned about the training process for us to present guidelines for developing programs. Although we have striven throughout this book to avoid the how-to-do-it form of exposition, it is perhaps appropriate here if only as a way of summarizing what is known. Our discussion will follow closely the general system model proposed by Goldstein, which is essentially a variation of the model of planned change that we discussed earlier.[7] In his flow diagram (Figure 8–1), one can see the three major phases of planned change that we introduced earlier: (1) an assessment or planning phase, (2) an actual implementation phase, and (3) an evaluation phase. All are essential for the success of any program. Let us consider each in turn.

The Assessment Phase

The essential first step in any program of planned change is the careful specification of objectives that one wishes to achieve with the change. Crucial to the success of any training program is advance knowledge of why a program is needed and what purposes it is supposed to serve. Training programs having specific goals are likely to be of more benefit to the organization than are programs that have vague or nonexistent goals.

This is the *assessment phase* of Goldstein's training and development model, and as commonsensical as it may sound, it is probably the weakest link in most training programs. Too many training consultants are willing to sell their wares, and too many organizations are willing to buy them without first determining the specific types of training needed or, indeed, whether any training is needed at all. Often, training programs are chosen because they are the current fad or because they happen to be the trainer's specialty. One unfortunate consequence of inadequate assessment of needs is that the material presented to participants in a training program is more appropriate for persons far above or far below the targeted audience. For example, first-line supervisors might be trained in how to make top-level policy decisions, or top-level executives might be trained in the basics of first-line supervision.

Three main steps are involved in a comprehensive assessment of needs.[8] First, an *organization analysis* is called for to determine the organizational objectives and the extent to which the organization is achieving these objectives. Organizational climate measures, which we will discuss later, are often quite useful for such analyses. If the organization is failing to perform in some areas, the question should be asked whether training can do anything to correct the problem. Of course, an organization analysis should not focus just on current problems but should also anticipate future problems that might be avoided through training.

Once we have located actual or potential problems in the achievement of organizational objectives and have determined that training can help achieve these objectives, the next step is to conduct an *operations analysis* to determine what form the training should take. An operations analysis is essentially a job analysis to determine the standards of performance for each task, how each task is to be performed to meet these standards, and the skills, knowledge, and attitudes required. A useful technique for conducting operations analyses is the critical incident method, which we discussed in several previous contexts. Folley made good use of this technique to design a training program for salespersons in a department store. Customers were asked to recall specific behaviors shown by successful and unsuccessful salespersons. From over 2,000 critical incidents, the specific behaviors related to customer satisfaction were determined and used as the focus of training.[9]

The final step in the needs assessment process is to determine the extent to which the present employees possess the skills, knowledge, and attitudes required to perform the job. The discrepancy between the requirements of the job and the extent to which the employees meet these requirements defines the needs for training. This *human analysis* should include a survey of what the population of potential trainees is like before training. What prior job training have they had? What is their capacity to learn? What sort of general education and background do they have? Knowing the limitations and handicaps of trainees (the starting point) and the desired human attributes (the endpoint of training), one has progressed a long way toward defining the kind of program that is needed.

A final step in the assessment phase is the description of specific *behavioral objectives* based on the organization, task, and human analyses. Naturally, both the design of the program and the criteria used to evaluate it depend to a large extent upon these objectives. According to Goldstein,

> Well-written, behavioral objectives specify what the trainee will be able to accomplish when he successfully completes the instructional program. Also, they indicate the conditions under which the performance must be maintained and the standards by which the trainee will be evaluated. Thus, objectives communicate the goals of the program both to the learner and training designer.[10]

Some training objectives focus on changes that can be demonstrated in the short term, such as retention of specific course information or behavioral techniques (e.g., how to handle a simulated problem in sales or supervision). Eventually, however, we expect the knowledge and behaviors acquired in the program to result in better on-the-job performance (e.g., higher supervisor ratings). Finally, the ultimate objective of most programs is improved organizational functioning (e.g., profitability or morale).

The Training and Development Phase

As shown in Figure 8–1, the main tasks in the implementation phase of a program are to select a set of methods or media and to construct a training environment using whatever learning or training principles that seem applicable. In this section, we will consider a few principles of learning and training that trainers should consider in designing and

FIGURE 8–1 An Instructional System

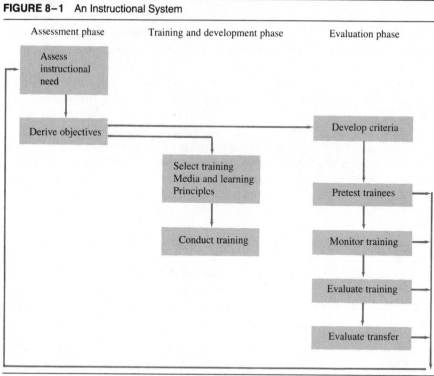

SOURCE: From *Training: Program development and Evaluation* by I. L. Goldstein. Monterey, Calif.: Brooks/Cole Publishing, 1974. Copyright 1974 by Wadsworth Publishing. Reprinted by permission.

implementing a program. Then we will discuss some of the more frequently used methods.

Principles of Learning. Psychologists usually define learning as a relatively permanent change in thought or action that results from practice or experience. Thus, training programs can be viewed as systematic procedures for helping people learn things that they can apply (or transfer) to their job situation.

Few aspects of behavior have been more strenuously researched than those involving learning and the transfer of what is learned. With all this basic knowledge at our disposal, one would think it would be a simple matter to design conditions for effective training. Unfortunately, such is not the case. Indeed, very little of what we have learned about learning has ever been applied directly to the training situation. For the most part, learning theory and training practice have followed separate paths. Reasons for this are probably many and varied: It is hard to translate learning theory concepts into training recommendations; there is lack of agreement among learning theorists themselves as to the key principles; and so on.

There is also debate over whether, in failing to make greater use of basic learning principles, training programs are any worse off. Some argue that we should try harder to apply what is known about learning.[11] Writers such as Bass and Vaughn and, more recently, Goldstein, have made heroic efforts to provide some translation of concepts. Others, however, feel that training requires an entirely different set of principles.[12] Speaking for the latter position, Gagne points out that where they have been put directly to the test, learning variables rarely have been shown to have much of an impact on the effectiveness of training. Be that as it may, we are in no position at this time to dismiss out of hand anything that might help. We shall consider the most promising learning principles now and, later, the (possibly) more relevant training principles suggested by Gagne.

Reinforcement and Instrumental Conditioning. The basic principles of learning are concerned mainly with the processes through which new habits are acquired and old ones are strengthened. Theorists argue about how many distinct processes there are, what conditions are necessary and sufficient for each to operate, and a host of other issues that we need not go into here. There is little doubt, however, that from the human training standpoint, the most salient principles, processes, and conditions revolve around the concept of *reinforcement*. The basic paradigm through which this concept is demonstrated is known as *instrumental conditioning*.

Instrumental conditioning involves the process whereby an organism learns to respond in certain ways in order to achieve certain consequences. The response is instrumental in the attainment of reward (*positive reinforcement*) or the avoidance of punishment (*negative reinforcement*). As animal trainers have known for centuries (and psychologists for at least a few decades), organisms tend to repeat responses that are followed consistently by desired consequences. Once the trainer has identified the kinds of things that are positively and negatively valued by the trainee, the trainer has a very powerful means of manipulating the trainee's behavior.

Things that have the power to influence behavior in this way are known as *reinforcers*; the process whereby they are presumed to operate, as *reinforcement*. In Chapter 3, we discussed a number of potential reinforcers associated with the work situation that can be used to motivate employees to higher levels of performance: pay, social interaction, achievement, and so on. To the extent that these are valued by the employee and the employee is required to perform in certain ways in order to get them, they also can serve to bring about learning of desired behaviors.

Much of our knowledge of instrumental conditioning phenomena derives from simple laboratory experiments, often involving *animal* subjects. Despite the fact that some reinforcement principles apply to "normal adult human beings" as well, one must be cautious in making this extrapolation. It is likely that many of the processes involved in human learning differ from the processes involved in nonhuman learning. In the case of nonhumans, the reinforcer is usually seen to act by "stamping in" or strengthening a prior response in some direct, involuntary way: If the rat pressed a lever and got a food pellet, it is more likely to do it again. Humans, however, have the advantage of *language capability,* which permits them to verbalize, interpret, and remember past events over long periods of time. When something they do is reinforced, they are very likely to know what happened and why they are inclined to repeat the instrumental act.

In the early stages of conditioning, it is desirable to reinforce every acceptable response. Once the response has become reasonably well mastered, however, its occurrence can be maintained at a high level by an occasional reinforcement. Several different *partial reinforcement schedules* have been defined, each of which produces a characteristic response pattern. If, for example, one only reinforces every second, third, fourth, or *n*th response *(fixed ratio schedule),* the organism will respond at a very high, steady rate. If, instead, one reinforces on a time basis such as the first response after each one-minute, two-minute, three-minute, or *n*th-minute interval *(fixed interval schedule),* the response rate will be high just before the reinforcement and very low right after it. Partial reinforcement schedules such as these seem to control *performance* to a greater extent than learning. When the response is conditioned using a partial schedule, it is established more permanently (it is more resistant to extinction) than under 100 percent reinforcement. The possible implication of these findings for the trainer is that, as training progresses and trainees acquire the desired responses, it is possible—and probably desirable—to cut down on the number of reinforcements.

Feedback and Goal Setting. We have devoted a fair amount of space in previous chapters to the topic of performance evaluation. We have also discussed the motivational importance of clearly defined relationships between performance and outcomes in the work situation. We now see that information regarding a person's performance is important for learning as well. Such information might influence learning in two ways: through its reinforcement of past behavior, as we just saw, and through its guidance of future behavior. *Feedback,* or *knowledge of results,* has been considered to have strong reinforcing properties—most people find rewarding the knowledge that they have done well and punishing the knowledge that they have done poorly. This, of course, should serve to promote learning of the behavior that was judged good and extinction (unlearning) of behavior that was judged poor.

Once persons have learned a behavior, reinforcement principles are useful for maintaining it and controlling its occurrence. As we have just shown, performance can be manipulated by variations in the schedules by which reinforcement is administered. If a pat on the back is an effective reinforcing agent for the performance of a high-quality piece of work, the supervisor can maintain quality performance by the judicious administration of this reinforcer. The supervisor might, for example, be careful to distribute such commendations so that no one received them frequently (*partial reinforcement*), everyone received them occasionally (*variable-interval schedule*), and they were awarded only for above-standard work (*continuous reward*).

The other contribution of feedback to learning is purely informational. If people are to learn to respond correctly, they must have some way of knowing what is and what isn't within the acceptable limits. Feedback gives them this knowledge. Provided that it is presented in clear, precise terms, knowledge of whether or not the person hit the mark allows him or her to adjust their future reponse in the desired direction.

There is substantial evidence that providing feedback to trainees regarding correct and incorrect responses facilitates learning. Komaki, Heinzmann, and Lawson, for instance, found that training employees in safe work practices was insufficient unless the training was followed with on-the-job feedback from supervisors.[13] Both training and feedback were needed to maintain high levels of safe behavior.

There is also some evidence that feedback combined with goal setting might be more effective than feedback alone. In one experiment, managers were trained in how to conduct performance appraisal sessions under one of two experimental conditions. In the feedback-without-goal-setting condition, the trainer gave them feedback concerning how well they did on 43 different behaviors in a series of role-playing exercises (simulated interviews). In the goal-setting conditions, each manager also set specific goals by choosing 12 out of the 43 behaviors on the list as targets of change. Those who both received feedback and set goals during the training exercises were able later to provide performance feedback more effectively than were those who only set goals or only received feedback.[14]

Shaping, Guiding, and Imitation (Modeling). If a response is to be conditioned through reinforcement, it must first occur. Many responses simply do not occur spontaneously in their desired form often enough to be reinforced. If animal trainers waited around for their bears to start riding bicycles or for their porpoises to start shooting baskets before administering reinforcement, there would be a lot fewer animal acts and a lot more unemployed animal trainers. Instead, several procedures can be used to help initiate the response. One is imitation or *modeling*. We can show trainees the proper response and have them try to imitate it. Another is *guiding*: We can place the person's limb in the proper position or take them through the desired motions. A third, and by far the most important procedure, is *shaping*: We can reinforce successive approximations to the desired response. Suppose we were trying to teach a person to serve a tennis ball. At first, we might model or demonstrate the proper way to serve the ball and ask the trainee to imitate this performance. Next, we might stand behind her, take hold of her arms, and physically guide her through the motions of serving the ball. Finally, we might, while observing her attempts to serve the ball, reinforce successive approximations to the ideal performance. We might reinforce a response of throwing the ball up in the air and coming close to it with the racquet. Later, we might require our student to make contact with the ball; still later, to get it over the net; still later, to get it into the serving court; and so on, until she had mastered what we considered a proper serve. At each step, we would reinforce only the level of proficiency that met or exceeded our criterion. In this way, we would shape her response pattern into the desired form. The principle of successive approximation is extremely important for training. It is not always easy to implement, however, for it may take a very keen and perceptive observer to decide what constitutes a reinforceable response. If one reinforces too remote an approximation, it could actually slow down the learning process. It is important, therefore, that trainers be well schooled in the art of shaping as well as knowledgeable about the job.

Material and Conditions of Practice.   In addition to reinforcement variables, human learning depends on various characteristics of the material to be learned as well as the manner in which it is structured for learning. For instance, meaningful material is more easily learned than meaningless material. Thus, it pays to organize whatever is to be learned such that it makes sense to the learner—that is, in such a manner that it conforms to prelearned rules, systems, or contexts. For example, a list of technical terms (say, the parts of an automobile engine) might be introduced in the context of a coherent presentation of their referent concepts (possibly a diagram showing how they function together). The learner would thus achieve a meaningful framework within which to fit each term, thereby increasing its meaning and ease of mastery. The alternative approach, presenting each term and its definition from rote memory, would be expected to result in much poorer learning.

There are several alternative ways material can be presented for practice to trainees. A trainer might either have trainees first master *parts* of it (subtasks) and then put it together or have them practice the *whole* task right from the outset. The part method is usually said to be better for complex materials; the whole method, for simple or highly integrated materials. Another distinction involves the spacing of practice trials: They might be *massed* (as in cramming for a test) or *distributed* over time. *Distributed* practice seems superior for lengthy or difficult material; *massed* for short, simple material. These are, however, only rules of thumb. The effectiveness of any particular approach is dependent on a lot of other factors as well.

Transfer of Training.   Even if training brings about a change in the trainee, it is of little value unless the change carries over to the actual job situation and in some way helps the trainee carry out his or her job duties. Unless the trainee performs better, is more satisfied, irritates others less, or is in some way a better employee, the program obviously has failed. The carry-over of what is learned in one situation to another is known as *transfer of training*. It can vary in both amount (how much the training influences job behavior) and kind (whether the change is for the better—*positive transfer*—or worse—*negative transfer*). High *positive transfer* is, of course, the aim of all training programs. If, however, the training is inappropriate, the results could be *zero transfer* or, even worse, *high negative transfer.*

Some theorists feel that the principal determinant of transfer is the correspondence of *stimulus* and *response elements* between the training and transfer situations. The more similar the response elements, the more likely it is that transfer will be positive; the more similar the *stimulus* elements, the more total transfer—positive or negative—is to be expected.

Other theorists emphasize the importance of general principles in transfer. In this view, positive transfer results from the mastery of principles that operate in the real situation even if many of the stimulus and response elements are different. Consistent with this view, learning the general principles by which internal combustion engines operate in the classroom is likely to show considerable positive transfer to the job of auto mechanic even though the tasks in the two situations are quite different. One highly general kind of transfer that has been found quite often in laboratory studies is *learning to learn* or *generalized transfer*. It appears that if subjects are required to perform a series of very different tasks, they are likely to do better on each successive one—presumably because they have mastered some very general strategies for learning.

It is not as easy to apply these transfer principles to the design of training programs as one might think. It is difficult, for example, to specify with any precision what constitutes "comparable stimulus and response elements" or critical "general principles" without resorting to the transfer measures themselves. Still, these are important concepts to keep in mind when designing a training program—even if they cannot actually be measured. Careful study of job analysis data should help us decide, on a logical basis, which features to build into the training situation.

In this brief overview, we have not exhausted the principles of learning and transfer. Neither have we discussed the theories or research on which they are based. Needless to say, few of the generalizations are without controversy, most are dependent upon a clearly defined set of conditions that can only be grossly approximated outside the laboratory. As a group they are probably best regarded as a source of ideas for training rather than as a set of commandments.

Principles of Training. As we noted earlier, Gagne has proposed an alternative set of principles that he considers more directly relevant for training.[15] These are not in opposition to the learning principles, just very different and, in Gagne's view, more important. One of the main differences is that they de-emphasize the initial learning of responses. Gagne contends that in most training situations the trainee already has in his or her response repertoire all the necessary *responses*. It is usually just a matter of putting them together in the right sequence in order to accomplish some task. Thus, a person learning to serve a tennis ball has the necessary component responses (i.e., throwing ball up, swinging the racket, hitting the ball) but must learn to connect these responses in a smooth and coordinated fashion. Learning principles, on the other hand, deal primarily with the *acquisition* of component responses. For this reason, Gagne's principles involve such things as *task analysis, intratask transfer, component task achievement,* and *sequencing.*

The essential notion behind Gagne's principles is that every task or job involves a set of distinct component activities, the learning of which can be enhanced by proper *sequencing.* The most efficient sequence is one in which *intratask transfer,* or the positive effect of learning one component on the learning of the next, is maximized. For example, suppose the task is driving a car. One must learn to operate the ignition switch, brake release, gear shift, accelerator pedal, steering wheel, foot brake, and so forth in the proper sequence under the proper conditions. Thus, there are several component tasks: (1) learning what and where a number of things are, (2) learning what each thing does in response to a control operation, and (3) learning in what sequence and under what circumstances to carry out the various control operations. Because 1 is subordinate to 2, and 2 to 3, one can probably maximize transfer—hence learning efficiency—by organizing a driver training program according to this sequence.

Task analysis, then, is the first principle or step in the design of a training program. It addresses the vital but all too frequently neglected issue of *what* is to be learned. One must break the task down into behavioral components and classify them.

The second principle is to determine the most efficient *sequence* for the learning of these components—which is chiefly a matter of determining what *transfers* best to what. Although this was done on a purely logical basis in our simple example, there is no reason why amount of intratask transfer couldn't be established empirically through controlled experiments. Finally, of course, one must decide how the actual learning of each component is to be carried out. Here the traditional learning principles might be invoked, especially those involving *reinforcement.*

According to Campbell, little practical use has been made of Gagne's ideas.[16] There are, however, scattered indications that the training field is becoming more concerned about the specificity and relevance of training content. Several investigators have used the *critical incident* approach to define, in behavioral terms, the relevant content of various jobs.[17] Other analytic procedures have also seen limited use. Far more commonly, however, training content is developed without any systematic analysis of the behavioral job requirements. It is altogether possible that the federal guidelines for personnel selection will eventually stimulate interest in the content relevance of training programs just as it must for selection programs. One can only hope so.

Methods of Training.   In addition to considering what principles of learning are applicable to the training situation, another component of the assessment phase is to select the techniques that will serve as the media of the training. Some alternative methods are presented in Figure 8–2. The reader will realize that, like predictors, training techniques cannot be evaluated properly outside the context in which they are used. That is, a particular method, say *programmed instruction* or *role playing,* is not necessarily good or poor in and of itself; it is good or poor for some particular purpose. Further, its effectiveness might depend upon characteristics of the *trainees,* the *material,* and the *situation* to which it is to be applied. Some techniques are more effective for *highly educated* than *poorly educated* people; some are good for *informing* but not *convincing* people; some are more useful for demonstrating *skilled movement* than *abstract concepts.* Many of these characteristic suitability patterns have been established rather conclusively through experimental research or controlled observation. Still, it is important to recognize that no amount of prior research can ensure that a particular instance of a technique will work in a particular situation. As indicated in Figure 8–2, programmed instruction, lectures, and the use of readings appear to be effective means of increasing knowledge. On the other hand, role playing, games, and group discussions may be a good procedure, in general, for changing attitudes. For a particular group of employees, however, and a particular discussion leader, these methods could turn out to be total failures. This is another reason why it is so important to have evaluation built into any program.

Training techniques fall roughly into two categories: on-the-job and off-the-job methods. The former, of course, consists of learning by doing at or near the actual job site, usually under the supervision of an experienced worker. The latter are typically carried out at a remote site designed exclusively for learning, often under the guidance of a training

FIGURE 8–2   Conceptual Grid of Learning Styles and Pedagogical Techniques

Applied	*Change in appreciation* Movies Applied lecture Dialogue Limited discussion Cases Problem exam Programmed instruction (skills)	*Change in skills and attitudes* Role plays Games Structured exercises Processing discussion T-groups Diaries Field projects
Degree of concreteness to students	II | III I | IV	
Theoretical	*Change in knowledge* Theory lecture Required readings Handouts Programmed instruction (concepts) Theory papers Content exam	*Change in understanding* Focused learning groups Argumentative discussion Experiments/Research Suggested readings Analysis papers

Reflective   Active

Nature of participation
and involvement of students

SOURCE: Randolph, W. A., & Posner, B. Z. (1979). Designing meaningful learning situations in management: A contingency, decision-tree approach. *Academy of Management Review, 4*, 463.

specialist. The real distinction is not merely a matter of training site; rather, it involves basic differences in training philosophy that show up in terms of where learning takes place. This should become clear as we discuss each category in turn.

On-the-Job Techniques.   It is customary to distinguish some half dozen specific training methods in connection with the on-site category.[18] *Coaching,* for example, refers to a relationship between the trainer and trainee in which the trainer provides feedback and guidance on the trainee's performance. *Job rotation* is a general strategy for acquiring breadth of experience, and an *internship* is an entire program of in-service training. Thus, a medical internship usually involves a fair amount of both job rotation and coaching. A more recent concept is *mentorship,* which typically refers to a more advanced, senior person taking under their wing a junior person and helping the junior advance in his or her professional or managerial career.[19] One study found that two thirds of prominent executives surveyed had mentors in the early period of their careers, and that those executives who had mentors were paid higher salaries than those who did not have mentors.[20] Because most higher-level executives are men who take on as their proteges other men, the informal mentoring that occurs in organizations often may serve as an impediment to women who aspire to managerial positions. To prevent this, some organizations are formalizing the mentoring process and assigning junior managers to mentors rather than leaving the process to the personal biases of senior managers.[21]

Whatever form it takes, the usual rationale for the on-the-job approach is that (1) the training situation is clearly relevant (one need not worry about transfer from the training to the job setting because they are one and the same) and (2) the cost of training is partially offset by the fact that the trainee is *producing* while learning (production and training goals are to an extent combined). These are apparently rather convincing arguments because on-the-job training has always been the most popular form of organizational instruction. Unquestionably, they can be very valid arguments in some cases. There are, however, potential drawbacks, both in the logic and the actual conduct of on-the-job programs.

1. Implementation problems. As usually carried out, on-the-job training is a very haphazard business. It ignores virtually all the systematic planning and evaluation considerations that we said characterize effective training. The trainee is simply turned over to a job incumbent or supervisor, told that the latter will demonstrate what to do, and then left pretty much to his or her own devices. The would-be trainer might or might not have any interest in the trainee's development; might, in fact, resent the added responsibility; or might regard the trainee as a potential threat. Very often, the incumbent chosen as a model is an excellent worker but has no particular understanding of—or skill in—*training*. If any systematic organization of the learning process takes place—if a favorable program of modeling, practice, and feedback emerges—it is largely by accident.

One of the authors can recall vividly an experience from his early working days in which he was to be trained as a packer for a large clothing firm. He was assigned to an elderly spinster who—he was later to learn—was noted primarily for (1) her incredible ability to select, make, and pack boxes rapidly, (2) her unwillingness to communicate with anyone, and (3) her total hatred toward males of any age and young people of either sex. One can easily guess the sort of learning environment this created. The "trainer" volunteered no information at all and answered questions only grudgingly. Feedback, when there was any, consisted of derogatory comments about the trainee's bumbling efforts, misshapen products, and questionable ancestry. The net result was a frustrated trainee, a reduced production level for a highly skilled worker, and a lot of boxes that probably disintegrated before they reached Oshkosh. We will never know whether this unfortunate situation cost the world a packing superstar; history will record only the demotion of one neophyte packer to the menial position of stockboy.

Although admittedly an extreme case, this kind of situation is all too typical of on-the-job training. Steps can, of course, be taken to avoid or minimize such problems. First, in *selecting* workers to serve as trainers, attention should be given to personal qualities—social skills, attitudes, patience, and the like—as well as to sheer technical competence. The best doers are not necessarily the best teachers. Second, the selected individuals should be given at least rudimentary *instruction* in principles of training: how to write behavioral objectives, how to use approval and feedback as reinforcers, how to shape desired responses, how to break down complex movement patterns into elements for learning, and so forth. Third, it should be made clear to prospective trainers, that the training function is an important part of their job. They should be assured that, while breaking in the new employee, they will not be expected to maintain their own level of productivity and will be evaluated at least partly in terms of their success as a trainer. Finally, performance as a trainer should be monitored, preferably by a training specialist, and feedback should be provided. In other words, on-the-job training can be made far more effective than it usually is simply by treating it as a legitimate and important organizational function rather than as a necessary nuisance for all concerned.

2. Logical questions.   Even if implemented properly, there is no assurance that on-the-job training is superior to other methods on either cost or transfer-of-training bases. Admittedly, there should be no transfer problem if one trains in the actual job situation. However, because the instruction is completely in the hands of a particular worker, and each worker tends to have their own way of doing things, it is at least possible that the trainee will learn some habits that detract from their performance on the job. If, instead, the trainee were schooled in the critical task elements through a carefully designed off-the-job program, he or she might develop more fully the essential skills and avoid the unnecessary ones.

Every neophyte would like to perform with the flair of a veteran. Hence, there is a great temptation to hurry the frills at the expense of the fundamentals, especially if one's model is a polished veteran. Joe DiMaggio, the great center fielder of yesteryear, adopted an unusually wide batting stance in an effort to correct a flaw in his swing—a tendency to overstride and therefore be fooled easily by curve balls. The wider stance (and shorter stride) overcame the problem but only at some cost in batting power. DiMaggio could afford this sacrifice because of his strength and quickness. However, many aspiring baseball players without these physical attributes copied the stance with predictable lack of success. For them, it was an inappropriate frill that they had to unlearn in order to master the essentials of batting—Willie Mays is a notable case in point. In batting and most other athletic skills, there are recognized fundamentals that one should learn at the outset if one hopes to become proficient. On-the-job training runs the risk of confusing the essentials with the frills, at least in the mind of the trainee.

The real cost of on-the-job training is not always obvious, either. To make a complete acounting, one must include the reduced output of the trainer-worker, the cost of mistakes on the part of the trainee, and the cost of tying up (and possibly damaging) operational equipment in the course of training. If, in fact, it also turns out that learning is less rapid or effective in a particular on-the-job situation, this cost too must be added in. Most of these costs can only be estimated. Still, they should be weighed againt the assumed advantages of production and transfer in deciding whether or not to adopt the on-the-job approach. Were it more commonplace for organizations to make such complete cost estimates, it is very likely that there would be some drastic shifts in training emphasis. Most organizations simply do not realize how costly on-the-job training can be. Although it certainly is not always true, attempting to combine training and production goals can result in efficient achievement of neither.

Off-the-Job Techniques. In contrast to on-site methods, which involve practice of the whole job, off-site techniques are usually directed toward specific aspects of the job or specific skills. One way of distinguishing among the different off-the-job techniques is in terms of the typology presented in Figure 8–2. Training techniques are distinguished on two dimensions: (1) the extent to which they require active participation of the trainee as opposed to more passive reflection and contemplation and (2) the extent to which the technique focuses on learning concrete applications as opposed to theory. We will not attempt to discuss all the techniques presented in this model but will focus instead on a few of the more controversial techniques that have stimulated research.

1. The lecture method. This is the standard classroom approach with which the reader undoubtedly has had ample experience. In recent years, it has become fashionable to attack the lecture method as a holdover from another, less enlightened era. Skinner, for example, bemoans the fact that "the typical classroom and techniques of teaching have hardly changed in a century."[22] He neglects to point out that some things survive because they are functional.

The shortcomings of the traditional approach have been widely publicized by advocates of the newer, innovative methods. First, it represents one-way communication from lecturer to student, a format that minimizes student participation and feedback opportunities. Second, because it proceeds at a single rate, the learner is forced to keep pace or fall by the wayside. There is no provision for *individual differences* in learning ability or interests. The more heterogeneous a class of learners, as the argument goes, the fewer served by any rate or style of presentation. Third, much of the actual nature of the presentation is left up to the particular lecturer: There are obviously wide differences in style and effectiveness. As opposed to some of the more method-dependent techniques, the effectiveness of the lecture depends primarily upon the effectiveness of the lecturer.

Rather surprisingly, there is really very little hard, cold evidence to substantiate either the general negative bias toward the lecture method or the seriousness of the specific drawbacks. In most studies involving this approach, it is cast in the role of brand X or the control against which other experimental methods are compared. Because the researchers are often interested in demonstrating the advantages of the newer methods, it is possible that the lecture is not always presented in its most favorable light. And, of course, there is always the threat of the transient Hawthorne effect, which would favor any new approach by virtue of sheer novelty. Even so, conventional instruction has often fared little or no worse than the innovative techniques. It has been reported, for example, that of 393 studies comparing conventional instruction with educational television, 21 percent favored TV, 14 percent favored conventional instruction, and 65 percent showed no reliable difference.[23] Similarly, more than half the comparisons of conventional instruction with programmed instruction were inconclusive.[24] Such inconclusive findings are often interpreted as failure of the innovative approach rather than as success of the conventional one.

The principal advantage of the lecture method is its *economy*: It permits the organized presentation of information to a number of learners at once, with at least some opportunity for personal interaction. Coupled as it usually is with some form of reading material (text), it can be a highly efficient procedure. Moreover, as Bugelski points out, it can create in the learner positive feelings toward the material—an emotional reaction that would tend to stimulate learning.[25] (Of course, a bad lecture can create negative feelings that would have just the opposite effect.) This motivational feature could very well be the unique contribution of the lecture per se, for it is virtually certain that people can absorb information more readily by reading it than by listening to a verbal presentation.

There are differences of opinion—and very little evidence, once again—concerning the educational objectives for which the lecture method is best suited. There is general agreement that it is not appropriate for learning "specific sensory-motor adjustments (such as heart surgery or knitting)"; but beyond that, the issue is unresolved.[26] The traditional view, depicted in Figure 8–2, is that lectures are better in imparting knowledge or an appreciation for the material than they are in changing *attitudes* or *opinions*.[27] Some evidence, however, suggests that even attitudes can be changed in this way. One would have to assume that Hitler, Churchill, Billy Graham, Martin Luther King, John Kennedy, Ronald Reagan, and other noted orators had some success in this regard.

It is doubtful that the lecture is effective enough to justify its almost total dominance of the educational field. Neither is it as devoid of merit as some of its detractors claim. Where there is reason to question its effectiveness, one might be well advised to seek ways of improving it before junking it entirely in favor of some unproven "wonder" technique. The key to effective use of this or any method proabaly lies in the appropriateness of its application. No method is ideal for everything.

2. Audiovisual techniques.   Movies, slides, and television (live or videotape) techniques have enjoyed wide popularity, occasionally as the sole learning vehicle but more often as an adjunct to lectures or other methods. It is difficult to make sweeping descriptive or evaluative comments about this approach because so much depends on the characteristics of the particular film or tape; some are highly effective, and some are useless. The one generalization that does seem to hold is that one cannot expect the *vehicle itself* to work any wonders. All the steps that go into making any one-way communication process effective—careful planning, selection, and organization of content; thoughtful composition and editing; thorough pretesting and evaluation—apply here as well. In fact, they are doubly important in the case of audiovisuals because the end product is a fixed—and often rather costly—program. Once produced, changes can be implemented only with great difficulty.

As we noted earlier, a considerable amount of research has failed to show any consistent advantage for these techniques over conventional methods. Neither have they proven consistently worse even when the content of both was an identical lecture. Some past research findings have shown that audiences learn neither more nor less from a filmed or videotaped lecture as from a live delivery of the same lecture.

There are, however, some practical advantages and disadvantages associated with particular applications of audiovisual techniques. On the plus side, these methods permit very dramatic illustration of certain kinds of information that could not be conveyed readily in any other way. Another positive feature is that film or tape can serve as a fairly inexpensive substitute for expert instruction when the latter is unavailable. In most instances, a carefully planned film featuring a competent and stimulating lecturer is vastly superior to a live presentation by a less knowledgeable, less exciting local instructor. Often the two can be combined effectively: a canned lecture followed by comments and discussion led by the local instructor. According to Randolph and Posner's model (Figure 8–2), movies (and presumably other audiovisuals) are particularly good at engendering an appreciation for the topic. On the minus side, audiovisual techniques amplify the problems inherent in one-way communication. Whereas the live lecturer does get some feedback from an audience and can alter the presentation to a degree, a film is totally unresponsive and inflexible. If it misses the mark, there is nothing to be done but replace it with another film.

3. Programmed, automated, and individualized methods. The most widely recognized break with tradition in educational methodology centers around the application of reinforcement principles to the learning situation. A host of different innovative techniques have appeared in the last 20 years, ranging from programmed textbooks to computerized tutorials, all based directly or indirectly on some combination of the following premises:

1. Educational objectives should be clearly specified in advance.
2. Material should be presented in easily mastered, logically organized chunks.
3. Learners should be required to become actively involved in the learning process—to *do* something in response to the materials for which they can be reinforced.
4. Feedback (or reinforcement) should be clearly related to that behavior.
5. The pace of instruction should be geared to the individual learner rather than to some group norm.

Clearly, the emphasis in these methods is on conditions for *learning* rather than *teaching*.

Most of the techniques of this kind are identified under the labels *programmed instruction (PI), personalized system of instruction (PSI),* and *computer-assisted instruction (CAI).* Obviously, these terms are not completely synonymous, although there is enough overlap in both the underlying philosophies and procedures to justify discussing them together.

The emphasis in PI is on the systematic presentation of very small units of information, each of which must be mastered before proceeding to the next. Proof of mastery, reinforcement, and feedback are all implemented through test questions that follow each unit. There are two types of PI. *Linear* programs are designed with such small steps that success on each unit is virtually assured: The learner simply moves on a *single* path through the material at his or her own pace. *Branching* programs permit the learner to skip steps or take accelerated routes based on past success: There are multiple routes to completion of the material. If learners fail a set of questions at any point, they take a remedial path; if they pass them, they forge ahead. This permits the material to be packaged in somewhat larger units because failure to master anything will be caught and remedied before moving on.

The PSI approach also stresses mastery and test of unitized material. However, the units are usually much larger—whole topic areas—and progress through the material is less rigidly controlled. For the most part, it amounts to a sophisticated version of PI or PSI in which the learner *interacts* with the computer to gain access to the stored information. A number of interactive modes have been developed, ranging from those that simply provide the learner intensive practice, with feedback, on material acquired elsewhere (*drill* and *practice mode*) to elaborate branching programs for the individualized acquisition and mastery of new material (*tutorial* mode).[28] One interactive mode (the *simulation mode*) allows the learner to test ideas, courses of action, or theoretical concepts on a simulation, or model, of some real-world situation.[29] The learner might, for example, see the impact of a decision to increase capital expenditures on the subsequent profit-and-loss statement of a simulated firm.

In contrast to PI and PSI, which appear to have reached a state of relative maturity in development, CAI is still very much in its formative stages. Although it has been around for over a decade, advances in both hardware and software technology keep extending its horizons of potential application.

Research aimed at evaluating PI, PSI, and CAI techniques has far exceeded that addressed to other methods. Generally speaking, such studies have involved direct comparisons with conventional teaching methods. Few of these studies, however, have included adequate controls against the influence of extraneous factors, and few have used suitable criteria as the basis for evaluation. Typically, the only criterion is a test given to both conventionally taught and experimental group students shortly after they have completed the program. What really matters in personnel training, of course, is long-term retention and transfer of the learned material. The importance of this point is illustrated in a study that compared PI against the lecture-discussion method for training telephone electricians in the basics of electricity. Better controlled than most, this study showed that a large *initial* superiority of PI declined markedly over a period of six months.[30] Actually, substantial forgetting occurred under *both* methods, in part at least, because much of the learned material was irrelevant for the jobs to which it was supposed to transfer. As an aside, it should be noted that such failures illustrate once again the importance of regarding training as a *system* function rather than as an isolated activity. Had adequate attention been given to the need assessment phase in the development of the program, the material would probably have been far more relevant.

With all due recognition of these research deficiencies, the evidence seems to be converging on at least one generalization: Material presented by the various programmed methods is learned *no better* than by conventional means but may be learned considerably *faster*.[31] Once again, it is altogether possible that such methods are better suited for certain kinds of *material* than for others and even for certain kinds of *people*. It would be difficult to say at this juncture precisely what the most suitable applications are.

Although programmed methods do seem to increase the *speed* with which material is learned, many of the premises on which programmed methods were originally founded, particularly those involving reinforcement principles, have recently come under fire. If programmed methods do have an advantage over the traditional methods, it is probably for reasons other than those originally advanced. The features that are now most commonly cited as responsible for any success that programmed (and related) methods may enjoy are (1) individualization, (2) participation, and (3) planning. As we mentioned, such methods almost force the program designers to give careful thought to organization of material. They can be designed to accommodate more or less of the learner's individual needs and capabilities, and they almost always demand active participation. To the extent that these features are emphasized, the approach can be expected to show promise. As McKeachie notes, the same might be said for *any* educational program. There is in these newer methods "no special magic that will solve our instructional problems."[32] All too often this nonexistent magic has attracted organizational management to these methods and promoted them to the level of a fad. The fad seems to have passed, but the memory—in the form of a lot of mediocre programs—lingers on.

4. Simulation. This approach uses *models of real-world situations* (problems, jobs, tasks, etc.) for purposes of instruction. The idea, very simply, is to train people on a replica of the operational task that is enough like the real thing to ensure positive transfer. Simulation training thus represents a compromise between actual on-the-job experience and off-the-job training in component skills. For example, rather than placing him right on the job or sending him through a program of classroom instruction in accounting, marketing, human relations, and other key subjects, we might require a management trainee to deal with a series of representative problems drawn from the in-basket of actual managers. The trainee would thus have the benefit of practice or authentic tasks but in a setting designed exclusively for learning.

The rationale for simulation is rather obvious. In theory, it affords a situation in which conditions for learning and transfer can be maximized without the necessity of tying up operational equipment and personnel and without the risk of some frightful accident or costly mistake. Consider the case of flight training for commercial airline pilots. An airborne jumbo jet is clearly not a very good place for the beginner to become acquainted with the essentials of flying or to learn the consequences of various control errors. Neither can such skills be taught entirely in the classroom. Consequently, airlines have invested heavily in very elaborate high-fidelity training simulators for each type of aircraft flown. Not only do these simulations permit development of the essential skills required to fly the aircraft, but they enable the trainee to experience emergency situations—and practice appropriate responses—that everyone hopes will never be faced. He can see firsthand the results of grossly inappropriate action and can be coached without danger to himself or anyone else.

Naturally, simulation training is carried on in connection with all sorts of tasks, from simple machine operation to the running of an entire corporation. *Business games,* in which teams of players compete against each other or some optimal model in the operation of a simulated business, have become a popular method for training executives. Usually they require the trainee to deal with a large number of contrived problems under realistic assumptions about the operation of the business and its relationships to the outside world. Each participant receives feedback on the results of his or her decisions (such as in terms of a profit-and-loss statement) as well as critical analyses of his or her behavior.

Our discussion to this point has skirted the most critical and nagging issue of all in simulation: What characteristics of the real-life situation should be modeled? We have spoken blithely of essential features as though it was clear to everyone what they were. This is by no means the case. It is just as difficult to establish the validity of a simulation as it is the validity of a test or anything else. In fact, the problems are identical, although in simulation jargon the term *fidelity* is usually substituted for *validity*. A model can possess high or low *physical fidelity* to the extent that it bears more or less physical resemblance to the operational situation (much as in *face* or *content validity*). It can have high or low *psychological fidelity* to the extent that the behavioral requirements are similar.[33] The only way to prove psychological fidelity, however, is to demonstrate that what is learned on the simulator actually transfers to the operational task. Evaluating a simulator for psychological fidelity is directly analogous to evaluating a test's *predictive validity*. Essential task features are *hypothesized* on logical grounds and are *verified* through their demonstrated effect on criterion measures. The criteria of interest are *terminal performance* on the simulator, which indicates what was learned; *retention* measures, which indicate how well it held up over time; and *transfer* measures, which indicate its relevance for the operational task.

Edwards, Hahn, and Fleishman provided an example of just how the psychological fidelity of automobile driving simulators might be examined.[34] Surreptitiously, the researchers observed the on-the-street driving behavior of 304 taxi drivers. Later, the same drivers were put through two different driving simulations. Very little correlation was found between performance on the street and performance in the simulators, a finding that casts some doubt on the fidelity of these widely used simulators. As it turns out, in very few training simulators currently in use has any attention at all been given to *psychological* fidelity measurement. Rather than testing psychological fidelity, as did Edwards, Hahn, and Fleishman, designers usually have been satisfied to concentrate exclusively on physical fidelity (or face validity), assuming that if it looks right it will serve the purpose. When behavior measures are taken at all, they are generally limited to the terminal training performance criterion—clearly the least important of the three. The net result is that many existing simulators are far more complex and costly than they need to be. Because no one has determined how much physical fidelity is needed, the tendency has been to go overboard on appearance. This is nowhere more apparent than in the flight simulators and business games mentioned earlier.

Closely related to the fidelity problem is the general matter of evaluation. Deficiencies in criterion measurement that make it impossible to specify an appropriate level of fidelity also make it impossible to state how effective or ineffective simulator training has been. It is simply not enough to show that practice on a flight simulator, for example, results in improvement in performance on that *same simulator*. Despite the costliness of such elaborate devices, this is exactly how evaluation is usually done. Moreover, the terminal performance criteria themselves leave much to be desired.[35] The situation is little better in the case of business games or other simulations. Indeed, in a recent review of research testing the effects of business games, the conclusion was reached that "the many benefits claimed for business games are not supported by any but anecdotal evidence."[36] In short, most of today's simulation training operates on a combination of face validity and faith.

We should point out, however, that simulation is still conceptually a very sound notion. With proper attention given to validation and evaluation procedures in the design of such techniques, they could well prove invaluable. The problem is not with the concept but, as so often happens in the training field, with the way it is implemented.

5. The conference method.   Many of the shortcomings of the lecture method result, as we just discussed, from its basic reliance on one-way communication. The conference method is designated specifically to encourage two-way communication between instructor and trainee and to actively involve the trainee in the learning process. Variations of the conference method, found in Figure 8–2, include processing discussions, focused learning groups, and argumentative discussions.

The typical format consists of a relatively small group of trainees (5 to 10 in number) and an instructor, all of whom address themselves to a common set of problems or other content that forms the basis for discussion. Often the group will have listened to the same lecture, seen the same film, or read the same list of readings prior to the conference. The role of the instructor or discussion leader is to arrange conditions so that the learners can *discover* correct answers, draw conclusions, or achieve insights themselves (individually and collectively) rather than merely *absorbing* what the instructor has to say. Instead of lecturing, the instructor organizes materials, stimulates discussion, poses questions, summarizes key points that the learners have made, steers the discussion into productive channels, and generally orchestrates the discovery process. The instructor tries not to dominate the discussion.

It is usually claimed that the conference method is a more effective learning procedure than the lecture method, particularly for changing opinions and attitudes and facilitating understanding (see Figure 8–2). The validity of this widely held position, however, is questionable. As Bugelski explains, it is virtually impossible to compare the methods in any scientifically controlled fashion, and the comparisons that have been made have generally proven inconclusive.[37]

Whether or not it promotes either attitude change or understanding, the conference format does seem to be a good way to generate ideas and stimulate active participation on the part of the trainees. In its most democratic form, it can be a painfully *slow* process that produces both positive and negative interactions among its participants. If the purpose of the discussion is to arrive at solutions or generate ideas, this approach may yield more good ones than other methods. It might also ruffle a few feathers along the way.

6. The case method. As tends to be true with other training techniques, there are believers who staunchly defend the case method as the preferable approach to instruction. Indeed, in some business schools, notably Harvard, the *case method* is used in virtually all courses.

In the case method, the trainee is presented with situations that are designed to illustrate real-world problem types. It is the trainee's task to identify what kinds of problems they are, what their parameters are, and what some alternative solutions are, based on the information provided. Usually, after the individuals have prepared their individual analyses, the instructor leads a group discussion, soliciting different views and encouraging students to defend their individual opinions. Instructors may use this approach to give trainees practice in problem solving and decision making, as well as to illustrate general principles. The different points of view that are invariably elicited in the discussion also emphasize the point that there are usually several alternative ways to approach any organizational problem. All these features of the case method provide important lessons for managerial and supervisory trainees who must learn to cope with the ambiguity inherent in managerial and supervisory roles.

As one might judge from this brief description, there is a lot of latitude in how cases are used and how the method is actually carried out. Some instructors simply lecture on the case and provide their own insights and solutions; others see themselves as discussion facilitators or devil's advocates; still others use a Socratic approach, confronting students with questions that draw out the important lessons to be learned. Because of this diversity in implementation, it is difficult to evaluate the overall effectiveness of the case method. Nevertheless, there are a few obvious limitations in how it is typically used. As in any technique in which group discussion plays an important role, not all trainees participate to the same degree. In case discussions, there are often a few talkative persons who dominate the discussion and prevent other trainees from benefiting as much as they could from the case analysis. Another problem is that there is often little opportunity for providing detailed feedback to discussants regarding their individual analyses. Although case discussions can be quite stimulating, and even fun, frequently neither student nor instructor can articulate what actually has been learned from the session (although both might argue strenuously that it is something important). In this respect, the method resembles simulation training; how much positive transfer one can expect is indeterminate. On the basis of his observations of case discussions in several executive development programs, Argyris further criticized the case method for encouraging conformity, the hiding of errors, face saving, and risk minimizing.[38] Of course, supporters of the case method have countered each of these criticisms with arguments in behalf of the case method.[39]

One of the strongest points in favor of using cases is that they provide an inexpensive way to afford trainees the opportunity to apply abstract notions to concrete problems. According to Randolph and Posner, cases are better at engendering an appreciation of the material than they are at increasing knowledge, skills, understanding, or changing attitudes. One approach that seems to have particular merit in certain contexts is to have trainees discuss cases that have been taken from their own experiences. White, Dittrich, and Lang, for instance, had groups of nursing supervisors describe the problems they had most frequently encountered in the course of their work.[40] Later, in a workshop setting, each group generated solutions to the three most common problems. The supervisors then attempted to implement the solutions and, in follow-up sessions, discussed these attempts. On the basis of self-reports of the trainees, this application of the case method appeared to have been quite successful in solving some real-world problems.

In general, then, it seems that the case method can be a useful training technique, but its success, like that of the lecture method, rests heavily upon the skill of the instructor; like that of the conference method, depends heavily upon the nature of the group dynamics; and like that of the simulation method, relies upon the unproven assumption that something transfers positively from the classroom to the job situation. As Harvard's president recently implied, that might be too many *ifs* to support an entire curriculum.

7. Role playing. When the focus of training is on the interpersonal skills of the trainee, it is difficult to design an effective program around a content-oriented technique. We can lecture on the right and wrong ways to give performance feedback, for instance, but we do not know how the trainee will actually use the knowledge when it comes to sitting down with a subordinate in a feedback session. Training sessions often include role playing as a way for participants to try out what they have learned before applying it on the job. For example, the trainee might be given the role of a supervisor and be asked to conduct an appraisal interview with another trainee who assumes the role of a problem employee. After playing the role, the trainee receives feedback from the trainer, and possibly other trainees, on the good and bad points of the performance. Role playing might be viodeotaped and played back to the trainee and trainer for a critique. In one version of role playing, the participants reverse roles. For example, the person playing the supervisor's role might switch and play the subordinate role to gain some insight into how it feels to be on the receiving end of an appraisal.

Despite its popularity, there are problems with role playing that limit its usefulness. The technique is time consuming. Some participants invariably feel uncomfortable and resist role playing, whereas others go too far in the other direction and overact. It is often difficult to provide immediate feedback on correct behavior in role-playing situations, and, in fact, incorrect behaviors might be reinforced by fellow trainees. Unfortunately, there is little research on the effectiveness of role playing in changing behavior or improving performance. The research that has been done suggests that role playing is most effective as a means of changing trainee attitudes (Figure 8–2), although the changes induced appear to be short lived.[41]

8. Behavioral modeling. An approach that seems to qualify as a current fad in training is behavioral modeling. The technique is loosely based on Albert Bandura's social learning theory. According to this theory, persons do not have to experience the consequences of their behavior directly in order to learn, but they can do so by observing another person enact some behavior.[42] Several cognitive components are involved in vicarious learning. At the very least, the observer must *notice* the model and *remember* the model's actions. Then, to the extent that he is capable of reproducing the modeled behavior and appreciates the potential payoff to be gained from it, he is likely to attempt the act himself.

Goldstein and Sorcher provide some suggestions for applying social learning theory to the training of supervisors in human relations skills. First, the specific behaviors that the trainees are to acquire are presented *verbally,* followed by a *filmed* model displaying these behaviors. Next, the trainees role play the behaviors displayed in the film and are *reinforced* for correct role performances. In the final part of the training, each trainee *plans* how to *transfer* the skills back to the job situation. Goldstein and Sorcher report numerous training programs at General Electric Corporation that have used behavioral modeling successfully to improve supervisory skills in orienting new employees, teaching employees job duties, motivating poor performers, correcting inadequate work quality and quantity, conducting performance reviews, and handling racial discrimination complaints.[43]

At first glance, the evidence seems to support the effectiveness of modeling, but much of this research is so poorly designed that no clear-cut conclusions can be drawn regarding its effectiveness.[44] Recently, a much better controlled study by Latham and Saari provided more substantial support for this method.[45] Twenty supervisors were assigned to an experimental group that received behavioral modeling training in nine different skill areas (e.g., disciplining workers), and another 20 were assigned to a no-training control. The training appeared to be effective on several different criteria. From a subjective standpoint, supervisors performed better than the control group both on paper-and-paper tests in the skill areas and in role-playing situations. Also, the trained supervisors received more favorable performance evaluations from their superintendents than did the untrained ones. And finally, when the control group was trained at a later time, all these differences between the groups were eliminated.

Although Latham and Saari's study is in many respects an excellent example of evaluation research, enough methodological questions remain to prevent an unequivocal interpretation. Did the subordinates actually transfer the behaviors learned in the training sessions to the job, or did they simply learn how to role play? Was the superintendent biased in his ratings of the supervisors' performances by his knowledge of which supervisors were in the control group and which were in the experimental group? And, even if one accepts the conclusion that behavioral modeling was more effective, could the same results have been accomplished with other, less expensive forms of training?

These and other questions remain to be answered, but the early returns on behavioral modeling appear promising, particularly if evidence is added from research in nonwork settings.[46] For example, behavioral modeling has been used quite effectively in clinical practice to eliminate phobic reactions. Still, we must reserve judgment on this approach as a general training technique, recognizing that it is still very much in its experimental stages.

Which Technique Should Be Used?

As we have seen, there are many techniques from which to choose when designing a training program. We cannot conclude that one technique is the best; all of them can be effective, given that they are used in the right situations. But what are the right situations? Randolph and Posner recently presented a decision tree (see Figure 8–3), patterned after Vroom and Yetton's leadership model, to assist trainers in choosing among the training methods depicted in Figure 8–2.[47] They state that the technique chosen should depend on the goal of the course (specifically, whether it is intended to develop conceptualization skills or behavioral skills), the *abstractness* of the material, the *motivation of the students*, the *skills of the students*, the *resources available* to the instructor, the *amount of time allowed*, and *the skills and values of the instructor*. If the goal of the course is to develop specific behavioral skills (e.g., how to give perfor-

IGURE 8–3   Decision-Tree Framework for Designing Learning Situations

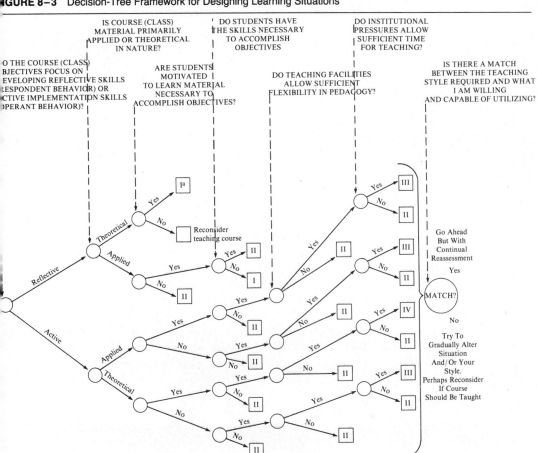

SOURCE: Randolph, W. A., & Posner, B. Z. (1979). Designing meaningful learning situations in management: A contingency, decision-tree approach. *Academy of Management Review, 4,* 465.

mance feedback to subordinates), the material is concrete and applied, students are motivated and have sufficient ability to master the material, teaching facilities are good, there is sufficient time, and the instructor's own values and skills are congruent with the methods, then Randolph and Posner recommend the use of more experiential techniques such as role playing and simulation. On the other hand, if the goal is to develop applied skills but the students are not motivated and are at a low initial skill level, these researchers suggest using more content-oriented or mixed methods such as lectures, movies, cases, and programmed instruction. Although such prescriptions are based almost entirely on speculation, the model has some intuitive appeal and at least provides a logical basis for choosing from among alternative techniques of training.

Another important variable to consider in choosing among training methods is the personality and aptitude profile of the trainee. Kolb developed a nine-item self-report inventory to measure differences among people in their learning styles and claimed that it can be used to predict how trainees react to different training methods.[48] Four basic types are distinguished with this scale. *Convergers* prefer to take an abstract idea and apply it to a practical problem that has a correct answer. *Divergers* enjoy taking some concrete experience and viewing this experience from several different perspectives. *Assimilators* like to take abstract ideas and integrate them or take disparate observations and "mold them into an integrated explanation." Finally, *accommodators* are doers and like to carry out plans and experiments. Ideally, one should be able to design a training program so that it contains the amount of content and experience that matches the learning style of the trainees. Unfortunately, Kolb's test does not appear to possess sufficient reliability or validity (with respect to the learning style construct) to justify its use for this purpose.[49] Nevertheless, the concept is an interesting one that deserves further attention.

In general, ideas seem plentiful regarding factors presumed to control the success of experiential versus content-oriented techniques, but there is little hard evidence on which to base practical guidelines. At this time, about the best we can do is suggest that the trainer consider—logically, if necessary—the pros and cons of the various approaches for the intended purpose and, if possible, incorporate several into the program.

Implementation

From our discussion so far, one could get the false ideas that effective training was only a matter of putting together the right set of techniques and that most training programs are impersonal machines that, once set in motion, run themselves. Rather, most must be implemented by human hands, and their success or failure depends on just how they are implemented. There are a variety of factors to consider in implementing a program.

One such factor is the trainer's expectations for the performance of the trainees. Research has established that trainer expectations can be self-fulfilling. Eden and Ravid demonstrated this in a recent experiment conducted in a military training program.[50] Instructors were falsely led to believe that some of their trainees had high success potential. Even though the trainers' perceptions were unrelated to the actual competence of these trainees, those who were described as having high success potential actually performed better than the other trainees. The higher performance of these trainees appeared to have resulted from the better treatment they received from the trainers. These findings suggest that using the right technique may not be enough; the trainer also may have to possess at least some confidence that the training will succeed and must communicate this confidence to trainees.

Another factor to consider in implementing a training technique is whether to instruct the trainees individually or as a group. For some techniques of training, such as the conference and case discussion, group participation is intrinsic to the technique. For several other methods, however, an option exists as to whether to implement it on an individual basis or on a group basis. There are at least two advantages of training groups as opposed to individuals. First, it is usually less costly to train several persons at a time than one at a time. Second, a fair amount of research suggests that individuals do a better job of remembering material when they learn it as a group than when they learn it as individuals. Persons who are trained in a group also may learn faster than those trained as individuals. In a recent demonstration of this, Dossett and Hulvershorn compared soldiers who had been trained with computer-assisted instruction (CAI) with those who had been trained in pairs with the same CAI materials.[51] Those trained in pairs learned the material 25 percent faster than did those trained individually. In a second study, it was found that peer training worked best when one of the pair was highly competent.

Evaluation Phase

We have placed so much emphasis upon the evaluation process in our previous discussion that we are a bit reluctant to belabor the point again. Nevertheless we feel obliged to mention several comments specific to training. Returning to Figure 8–1, we see that several steps are required for a program to be evaluated properly. First, criteria must be specified against which we can evaluate the effects of training. These criteria should be based at least in part on the objects that were established in the assessment phase. If at all possible, four criteria should be used to evaluate the success of training programs.[52]

1. Trainee reactions: How well do the trainees like a particular program?

2. Learning: What principles, facts, and techniques were understood and absorbed by the trainees?

3. Behavior: Does the training program result in changes in trainee behavior that transfer to the actual job situation?

4. Results: To what extent does the training program result in long-term improvements in job performance as reflected in reduction of costs, turnover, absenteeism, and grievances, or in improved quantity and quality of performance?

A second step is to pretest the trainees on these criteria in order to establish a baseline against which to measure the effects of training.

Third, the training program should be *monitored* at frequent intervals while in progress to ensure that everything is going according to plan. There are, of course, as many ways to monitor progress as there are training methods. Film or videotape can be useful. So, also, can interim performance evaluations (tests) and feedback from the trainers and trainees themselves. Such information is useful for the planning of future programs as well as for the control of ongoing ones. A step-by-step analysis of filmed records, for example, allows the trainer to isolate sources of wasted time, confusion, or other areas of ineffectiveness in the procedure.

Finally, the overall program must be evaluated by gathering post-training test scores on each trainee for each criterion of interest. Several evaluation design procedures differ chiefly in terms of their ability to show the effects of training uncontaminated by extraneous factors. McKinney has distinguished three levels of design in somewhat the following terms:[53]

1. Posttest Only. Here one simply decides whether the posttest seems to indicate that the trainees are adequately prepared for the job. If they are, the program is judged successful. Obviously, this is a totally inadequate evaluation of the training program. Trainees could do well or poorly on the posttest because of their prior experience, because they were highly or poorly motivated, because they felt someone cared about them (or didn't), or for any number of reasons other than training. Obvious though this might seem, the *posttest-only* design is still the most widely used.

2. Before-After Comparison. In this design, one compares pre- and posttraining criterion scores. This is, of course, a distinct improvement over the previous method in that it reduces the possibility that final performance is a function of conditions that existed before the training began. There is still the possibility, however, that the change that occurred during the training period is not entirely the result of training. A complete discussion of the factors confounding this type of research design can be found elsewhere. We present just a sample here.

One is essentially a novelty effect. Since the time of the famous Hawthorne studies (see Chapter 1), it has been recognized that any sort of change in a work routine can have a transient positive influence on performance or morale irrespective of whatever true effect that manipulation might have—positive or negative. In fact, this phenomenon has so often had a confounding influence on studies designed to measure other things that it has been dignified with a label: the *Hawthorne effect*.

Another source of confounding is extraneous events. In a simple before-and-after design, many things can happen during the training period that are totally unrelated to the program but show up as a change in the criteria. For instance, personnel layoffs occurring in the midst of the program might constitute one such external event. In this case, an improvement in *after* scores compared to *before* scores could just as easily be attributed to trainees working hard to avoid layoff as to the effects of training per se.

A third problem in the before-and-after design is that the act of measuring the criterion before the training program might cause subsequent changes in the criterion measures. This *pretest sensitization* is more apt to occur with obtrusive measures, such as questionnaires or tests, than with unobtrusive ones, such as performance records. If trainees were pretested on their knowledge of how to operate a machine, for example, the test might spark their curiosity enough so that they familiarized themselves with the machine on their own. Consequently, gains in knowledge occurring over the course of training will have less to do with the training than with the pretest.

A fourth question that remains when improvements are shown in performance with a simple before-and-after design is whether performance is due to the training program or to improvements that would have *occurred naturally* without formal training. For instance, larger increases in performance can be expected when an employee is new to a job and has a lot to learn than when the employee is an old hand. If we find improvements in the performance of new employees following training, the simple before-and-after evaluation design does not allow us to eliminate the alternative explanation that employee performance improved simply as a result of job experience.

3. Experimental Design.   In order to avoid the confoundings inherent in the other designs and to be sure that criterion changes are in fact due to the training program, we need to use an *experimental design* in our evaluation of the program. There are two essential characteristics of a true experimental design. First, as noted in Chapter 1, a *control group* is needed that is treated just like the experimental group except for training. They might be taken off the job and allowed to relax, read, or engage in some other activity unrelated to the specific training program. Or, if the object of the research is to evaluate a new program, they might be trained using the old methods. If the experimental trainees are aware that they are participating in an experiment, the control trainees also will be given this information. With a control group, one can legitimately make claims regarding the effectiveness of the training program on the basis of differences in terminal performance.

The second characteristic of an experimental design is *random assignment* of employees to the experimental and the control conditions. *Random* means that persons in a population have an equal chance of being assigned to the experimental or the control conditions. If people are assigned nonrandomly, one cannot ensure that differences on the criteria between the experimental and control conditions actually are due to training. For instance, if participants are selected for a program by asking for volunteers and those who do not volunteer are used as the control, any differences found between the experimental and control sessions might reflect differences between personal characteristics of volunteers and nonvolunteers. Given that training is associated with higher performance, an obvious confounding factor might be that those who volunteer are more motivated or more competent than those who do not volunteer.

A design that is far superior to a simple before-and-after design, then, is a before-and-after *design* with a *control* group and *random assignment* of persons to each group. This is only one of many available experimental designs—actually, the simplest possible arrangement.[54] There are other potentially troublesome extraneous factors and other designs appropriate to control for them. The point is, however, that a really meaningful evaluation requires experimental control of at least the major confounding influences.

The information from the evaluation phase—particularly that involving transfer to actual job performance—should serve as input to the planning phase for subsequent revision of the program. This "feedback loop" allows us to conceptualize the entire instructional model as a "closed-loop system," a type of system in which compensatory adjustments are made on the basis of output data in order to achieve a desired state. In the present case, this means that we should compare the ultimate results of training with the original objectives and see whether we have moved closer to or farther from these stated goals. We then consider how things might be changed—objectives, procedures, or evaluation—in order to bring results and objects into closer accord.

Specific Areas of Training

So far we have discussed general principles of designing, implementing, and evaluating training programs without going into specific types of training programs. The problems confronted in successfully implementing and evaluating a program, however, depend in part on what one is attempting to modify. The research and theory in each of the topics we have discussed have led to specific training interventions. It is illuminating to consider some of the successes and failures of training in each of these topical areas.

Motivation Training

Typically, psychologists have suggested that to increase the motivation of workers to work hard, we need to change the situation (e.g., provide rewards, set goals, enrich jobs) or hire people who already are motivated. Another alternative that seldom has been attempted by psychologists is to increase employee motivation through training. Perhaps psychologists tend to avoid such an approach because it smacks of success seminars in which a charismatic speaker uses God, mother, and country to inspire participants to strive for success, money, and fame. One of the few psychologists who have attempted to compete with Dale Carnegie and the Reverend Ike is McClelland, who designed achievement training programs based on his need achievement theory (see Chapter 3).[55]

In McClelland's courses, participants are taught to "think, talk, and act like a person with a high nAch" through training aimed specifically at skill in thematic apperception story-telling; that is, trainees learn to make up answers that would be scored high on nAch. Also, participants plan realistic goals for themselves and, in follow-up sessions, review their progress in achieving their plans. Finally, an attempt is made to develop a group esprit de corps, with members providing support for each other as they seek to accomplish their plans.

In an ambitious application of this program, McClelland trained 52 businessmen from a small city in India. Before the course, 18 percent of the participants had shown "unusual enterprise." In the 18 months after the course, this increased to 50 percent. According to McClelland, "something clearly happened in Kilkinada: the owner of a small radio shop started a chemical plant; a banker was so successful in making commercial loans in an enterprising way that he was promoted to a much larger branch of his bank in Calcutta."[56] Unfortunately, neither this study nor the subsequent studies evaluating nAch training have been true experiments.[57] The findings provide, at best, very tenuous support for its effectiveness in improving job performance. There are also some serious ethical questions related to nAch training.[58] Presumably, the participants in the Kilkinada study served voluntarily. We must again caution, however, against the ethical implications of using organizational pressures to *force* this kind of change on employees, no matter how good for them we may believe it to be.

Leadership Training

One of the most common types of training in industry is leadership training. The particular leadership style advocated in these programs depends on the theoretical framework on which the training is based (see Chapter 5). Human relationists have always argued that managers should be trained to adopt a highly considerate, participative, and people-oriented style. On the other hand, contingency theorists have advocated training designed either to help managers diagnose the situation so as to adopt their style to fit it or to help them change the situation so as to bring it into line with their style. Despite the millions of dollars spent each year on leadership training, such programs rarely have been shown to be effective, regardless of the theoretical framework on which they have been based.

Based on his VDL model, Graen and his colleagues provided LMX (leader member exchange) training in which managers were instructed in what seems very similar to good old-fashioned human relations skills.[59] Managers were taught the model underlying the training and then instructed in how to interact effectively with their subordinates. Compared to control managers who did not go through the training, the subordinates of trained managers showed a 19 percent improvement in productivity that resulted in an estimated annual cost savings of over $5 million. We cannot state conclusively why human relations succeeded in this study and failed in so many others. Two possible reasons are that it (1) emphasized specific communication skills rather than general styles of leadership and management and (2) was consistent with the organizational climate.

The importance of higher management's support for human relations training was demonstrated in a classic study conducted by Fleishman and his colleagues at International Harvester.[60] Training was conducted to increase the consideration behavior of first-line supervisors. Two years after the program, only those supervisors with bosses who were highly considerate and thus supportive of the goals of the training still showed higher consideration. Trained supervisors whose bosses were low in consideration were even less considerate two years after the training than untrained supervisors. It appears that for the effects of leadership training to transfer back to the job, the nature and role of training in any organization should be consistent with the general philosophy of that organization. If, for example, a firm subscribes generally to the classical (bureaucratic) model of management, it should not expect good results from a program designed to make supervisors more sensitive to the needs of their subordinates. This type of program would place the supervisors in a difficult position. If, in fact, it were effective and the supervisors came to adopt a more considerate, people-oriented style, they would run the risk of being judged weak and permissive by their superiors—a distinct minus in the eyes of bureaucratic management. On the other hand, if the training failed to take, it would have been money wasted.

The lack of success of many of the other human relations training programs has led Fiedler to suggest that it is futile to attempt to change leadership style. As an alternative, he proposes that leaders should be trained to *modify the situation* to fit their styles. Recently, he and his associates have designated a training package, *Leader Match,* which does just that.[61] The Leader Match program consists of a self-paced programmed manual in which the trainee first completes Fiedler's leadership scale, the least preferred co-worker (LPC) scale, and learns how to interpret the score. The trainee then learns to diagnose the situation in terms of leader-member relations, task structure, and position power. The remainder of the program focuses on how the trainee can modify the situation to fit his or her style of leadership. This is accomplished through a series of vignettes in which the trainee diagnoses the situation and then